THE MAGNIFICENT MAYS

Benjamin Elijah Mays. Courtesy of the Moorland-Spingarn
Research Center, Howard University.

❋ THE MAGNIFICENT MAYS ❋

A Biography of
Benjamin Elijah Mays

John Herbert Roper, Sr.

The University of South Carolina Press

© 2012 University of South Carolina

Published by the University of South Carolina Press
Columbia, South Carolina 29208

www.sc.edu/uscpress

Manufactured in the United States of America

21 20 19 18 17 16 15 14 13 12   10 9 8 7 6 5 4 3 2 1

Library of Congress Cataloging-in-Publication Data

Roper, John Herbert.
  The magnificent Mays : a biography of Benjamin Elijah Mays / John Herbert
Roper, Sr.
    p. cm.
  Includes bibliographical references and index.
  ISBN 978-1-61117-077-1 (cloth : alk. paper)
    1. Mays, Benjamin E. (Benjamin Elijah), 1894–1984. 2. Morehouse College
(Atlanta, Ga.)—Presidents—Biography. 3. African American
educators—Biography. 4. African Americans—Civil rights. I. Title.
  LC2851.M72R67 2012
  378.0092—DC23
  [B]   2012003647

This book was printed on a recycled paper with 30 percent
postconsumer waste content.

For John and Kyle

CONTENTS

ILLUSTRATIONS

Word about Words

This book is a biography of a good man who made a difference in what is often called the "long civil rights movement." He never called it by that name himself, but he certainly understood that the movement started for him when night riders attempted to kill him in 1898, and he certainly considered that it was uncompleted when he faced his final days in 1984. An accomplished mathematician and statistician, he could count, and as a thoughtful theologian, he knew what counted. He knew that the movement started before him and would continue after him, and he knew that he was only one in a procession of dedicated servants of the movement.

The title *Magnificent Mays* is not a celebratory judgment, however much deserved. Instead my title represents the thesis, or at least the organizing theme, of this biography: Benjamin Elijah Mays self-consciously and methodically measured himself by a classical standard of conduct and performance that he learned as an undergraduate student of ancient Greek language and culture at Bates College. He then refined it over the decades. The idea is a combination of concepts he drew from Aristotle's *Nicomachean Ethics* and the Roman Stoicism of Marcus Aurelius, but the reader need not be versed in classical ethics to follow this study of his life. I do believe that the best way to understand Mays's actions, especially the courageous ones, is to understand his version of the Greek *megalosukos* or the Latin *magnanimatatum* (both of which may be translated as "high-minded soul") as he built it and as he employed it over his long years. I have tried to show faithfully the building and the employing without trying to judge how accurately he understood Aristotle or Marcus Aurelius. By his own lights, he successfully followed his model, and I judge that he was useful and good in his dangerous and challenging time because he faithfully used that model—always in his way since he was also "still a Baptist," as he put it.

The title of this book is thus not a judgment or an effort to be artistic. It is my attempt to understand a particular man according to his own ethical standards of personal and professional conduct. Related to that attempt are other decisions about language. As much as possible, I have let Bennie Mays speak in his own voice and have tried to keep my own voice out of his way. Thus I quote him saying "Negro," which most serious students considered the proper term in the period 1894–1968. It was always his preferred term, although he did begin to use "black" in print after 1970. Also I have quoted his relatively exclusive or exclusionary language about gender, not because I agree with his usage, but because I do not want to distort his voice, view, or record. This point about gender and language is especially important in his last collection of essays, *Disturbed about Man,* but it is also vital to my considered understanding of the "double portion" of prophetic power that he intended to leave—not to all people of both genders—but to his metaphorical "sons" at Howard University, at Morehouse College, and in the student body of the Atlanta public schools.

The one exception to my practices with regard to language concerns his term "tribe"—generally used in a biblical sense of believing communities of extended families marked not only by color and physical characteristics but often by "blood relationships." Although he uses the term "tribe" often, I have generally avoided it, except where essential to catch his meaning, and then I have put it into quotation marks. It is essential to note the epiphanic moment when he decided to discontinue use of the term or the thinking involving the term because he realized that all men (if not women) were equal in standing before the "Real Lord."

By and large Bennie Mays did the right things, thought the highest thoughts, took the bravest and best actions—at least in my view. The reader will not have to agree with my judgment, however, to get something out of this study. I am not interested in defending or prosecuting every action he took—especially not from the viewpoint of a white humanist in another era. Instead I have focused on showing clearly what was going on around him and his second wife, Sadie Gray Mays—between their marriage in 1926 and her death in 1969—and to what extent the couple (or sometimes he acting alone) transformed given people in particular places at specific times, especially Howard University from 1936 to 1940, Morehouse from 1941 to 1967, and Atlanta's black schoolchildren from 1969 to 1981. I have tried to capture what he intended to do when and where "he lived, moved, and had his being," as he liked to quote from Epimanides and as I recite in my high-church Episcopal lectionary.

With apologies to Shakespeare's orator, I have not so much endeavored to praise Mays as to *unbury* him—unbury him from the considerable shadow of his student Martin Luther King, Jr., and from the shadows of his legions of students and colleagues and allies. To be sure he was "mentor" to the prophetic King, and he was "schoolmaster" to the long civil rights movement. Yet he needs to be understood as more than these things. He needs to be recognized for contributions he made beyond, above, and outside those two roles, important and interesting as they are. I consider that he was a prophet in classic Hebrew sense (discerning in his opinion the right path to justice and peace revealed to him by God and then showing that path to others). I judge that he did indeed leave a "double portion" of such prophetic power to the men he taught—not only at Howard and at Morehouse and not only those involved in the Atlanta public schools in a later season. For reason of that belief, I dedicate this biography to my own biological sons but also to spiritual children of Bennie Mays's movement—in which I include myself.

Acknowledgments

As in all projects that take more than ten years, there is no way to acknowledge adequately the many people who have helped me along this path. Some who have helped me, however, must go in this space.

For teaching me about race relations and other things southern: Joel Williamson; George Tindall; Joseph A. Herzenberg, Jr.; Frank Ryan; Edward Beardsley; Tom Terrill; Robert Weir; Jacquelyn Dowd Hall; C. Vann Woodward; Paul Green; Glenn W. Rainey; Ronald McInnis; and the martyred Reverend William McNeill.

For teaching me about things theological and about the lives of ministers: the Reverend James W. Dawsey, the Reverend Craig Wylie, Bishop Neff Powell, Bishop Heath Light, Bishop Peter Lee, the Reverend Hopkins Weston, the Reverend Tom Carson, the Reverend James Rogers, the Reverend John Miller, the Reverend Alex Barron, and the Reverend Tommy Tipton.

For persuading me to take on this project and for encouraging me along the long way: Malcolm Call and Nancy Grayson.

For resuming the project, rethinking and redirecting it, and riding it through to its end: Alexander Moore and Karen Rood. For preparing the index: Kyle Roper.

For help from their research work in related fields: Orville Vernon Burton, John T. Morgan, Charles W. Joyner, Dennis Dickerson, Charles W. Eagles, Ralph Luker, and the two anonymous referees who reviewed the manuscript for the University of South Carolina Press.

For opening up the treasure trove of Mays's papers and those of other leaders: the wonderful staff of the Moorland-Spingarn Research Center of the Founders Library of Howard University, especially Dr. Joellen El-Bashir, archivist extraordinaire.

For reading the many versions of this biography and helping me with concepts, facts, and stylistic questions: Ava Yates Gilmer, Mary Elizabeth Marshall, Ashley Haines, and John H. Roper, Jr.

For preparing the typescript and settling many questions of style and presentation: Joyce Wentz.

For helping me with collecting data and finding sources: Jane Caldwell and Patty Greany, reference librarians without whom I am quite helpless; Lorraine

Abraham, Jody Hanshew, Robert Vejnar, Whitney Mullins, Dick Shrader, John White, Tim West, Rachel Canada, Harry McKown, and Janet Kirby.

For finding grant money and for encouraging me: Emory & Henry College, especially Deans James Dawsey and Chris Qualls and Social Science Division chair John T. Morgan.

And most important, for bringing me into the civil rights movement and for reminding me always about truth and reality: my wife, Rita Bowers Roper.

THE MAGNIFICENT MAYS

INTRODUCTION

Getting Dr. Payne

Benjamin Elijah Mays. His given names were chosen with care, chosen for their magnificence. They are names of biblical characters chosen to lead.

Mays was magnificent even in his youth, especially in 1917, when he was a college student recently matriculated at prestigious Bates College in New England after study in his native South Carolina. Tall, with an absolutely vertical posture that only God could lay out with a master's plumb line, Mays was always dignified, able to smile broadly without playing the clown and able to cry without being maudlin. The physical embodiment of God's priest for the city of heaven, he was in 1917 living in the city of people, and that city employed him not as a priest but as a Pullman porter.

In the summer days when Bates College was not in session, Bennie Mays earned money on the passenger train running out of Boston, the hub of his adoptive Yankee region. It was good money for a kid, and this kid looked right for the job. The carriage, the visage, the body, the voice, and the manners were all perfect for a porter on a Pullman car in 1917.

Perfectly understandable too was the emotion he recorded to describe how he felt for "several summers." That is, the emotion was understandable if you remembered that the inhabitants of the city of people were created a little less than angels. He was waiting anxiously to see Dr. Wallace Payne, a physician from Epworth in the student-porter's native Greenwood County, South Carolina. When Mays was a child, he had called this place "Rambo" instead of "Epworth," and many African Americans still called the crossroads community Rambo. As the train moved southward, Mays watched eagerly. Surely one of these days, on one of these runs, Dr. Payne from Epworth would board Mays's car.

When Dr. Payne did climb aboard, Mays the magnificent intended to avenge himself. In 1916 the doctor had struck Mays in the Epworth post office, and the youth had never forgotten. Now the aggrieved youth was a porter on a train, and he was trusted to be alone and unsupervised with white passengers. There was a lot of time, and there were surely a lot of places where a white passenger would be alone with Mays, without witnesses and without defenses. In the city of people, the passenger train was a good place for the sin contemplated by the magnificent one. He was going to arrange for the good physician to heal himself after a terrible beating. He later said with modesty and understatement:

> I intended to get him. . . .
>
> I guess he should be glad . . . because if I had ever met him in a place where the odds were not all against me I certainly meant to repay him in kind and more. . . . I was not as nonviolent then as I am now.[1]

Dr. Payne never boarded a train on which Mays was porter, and the moment, but not the thought, passed from Mays's life.

The thought was later brought back to Mays, however, in exactly the way that every southern white man fears. In 1950 Dr. Payne's wife came forward to declare her admiration for the mature Mays. By then Dr. and Mrs. Payne had moved to the bright and hopeful "civil yet progressive" North Carolina, a half-day's drive but really a full epoch away from Rambo. Here was Mays the magnificent speaking to liberal women at a Methodist meeting in Cleveland, Ohio. At session's end a clutch of liberal women insistently revealed themselves to be from the leader's home place. Most prominent was Mrs. Wallace Payne, who wanted to be introduced to Dr. Benjamin Mays. Even in the civil rights movement, even in attempting a rebellion of the most radical sort by treating an African American man as a social equal and as an intellectual mentor, Mrs. Payne was yet "down home" and still a Sandlapper. She was determined to establish the hometown connection, to share names of people commonly known in their old home place.

Evidently she and her physician-husband had never talked about how he beat young Mays in 1916. But the magnificent Mays was still that youth, and the sore was still festering there. Whether the larger hurt was guilt over his continuing desire to flail Dr. Payne or regret that he had never done so, the memoir writer did not say. But he did say that it was uncomfortable standing there being polite to Mrs. Payne while she went on and on about his importance to the movement. He suggested that she sounded, and probably was, absolutely sincere. Thus he maintained deportment, retained dignity, and was polite, perhaps appearing interested in what she had to say.

He was not Jesus, nor even Gandhi; and he used his memoir, *Born to Rebel,* to settle the debt: "She was not the guilty party; and it may have been that being married to and living with such a person as Wallace Payne was unpleasant enough."[2] In a life lived out amid great changes—and many of those changes coming with violence, if not always because of that violence—Mays the magnificent was almost fated to do the right thing in public, even if he occasionally intended in private to do the wrong thing. That sense of connectedness across the decades, plus practiced experiences painfully won, served him well in these two incidents that link him with the Paynes between 1916 and 1950. The poetic roundness and the prophetic nature of these two incidents involving the same white family reveal many things, not least that the South Carolina countryside was not about to relinquish claim on its son. To lead rebellion Mays had to live out a career all but overwhelmed by the darkest regional history and by the brightest personal destiny. Only by constantly reminding himself, and the rest of us, that he was so chosen could he get through the challenge of it all.

1

SEED OF JAMES, BRANCH OF
PROPHETS AND JUDGES

1894–1898

He was the son of slaves. His mother, Louvenia Carter Mays, was born into slavery in Virginia, and his father, Hezekiah Mays, was born into slavery in South Carolina. His mother, called Vinia, did not really remember slavery, but his father Hezekiah did, as Benjamin Mays reported in *Born to Rebel.* His parents' stories of the valley of the Saluda are frustratingly vague at crucial points, but this much can be recovered: Hezekiah and Vinia Mays—and the patriarch James Mays before them—saw and felt the worst of slavery, including the peculiar institution's violent intrusion into family life. More focused memories of his parents show a married life marked by great turmoil between Vinia and Hezekiah inside the home, but they also show a home even more violently intruded on by white people.

The Mayses lived in a beautiful valley; they loved the land and often marked the "rainbow 'round their shoulder." They also marked the "blood on the Carolina moon."[1]

The Hebrew chronicler of Judges in the Bible wrote admiringly and longingly of a promised land "washed by nether springs"; and the black song master inspired by such Hebrew images sang of a "goodly land." Surely the verses describe the valley of the Saluda, a goodly land washed by springs in Greenwood, which was part of Edgefield District in the Piedmont of South Carolina in 1894, when Benjamin Elijah Mays was born. Men of color had come, and they had settled this land generations earlier, perhaps as long ago as when Jesus Christ walked the earth. These bronze men were called "Cherokee" by the European settlers who found them, and European scholars have called the forefathers of these Cherokees "Mississippians." The land was rich with topsoil that was thin but fertile. The soil was bright red, the color of blood, and it made its mark on people. Some of their clothing was always red, no matter how long they soaked things in boiling water: red soil and bronze people, themselves often dyed red.

Then white men had come from England and had displaced these men of color. They were new folk with new techniques, new beliefs, and new systems; it was an old red land with new white people. Following the patterns established in the lowcountry of South Carolina, themselves patterns established in Barbados in the Caribbean, these Englishmen pushed northwesterly into the Piedmont frontier, cleared the land, and began to raise cash crops. The most important of the crops became cotton: King Cotton, short-staple cotton. This short-staple cotton had bolls with thickened fibers enmeshing many seeds, and only Eli Whitney's cotton gin could pull the seeds out quickly enough to make it a cash crop fit for the world markets. Once ginned, however, this short-staple cotton was sold by the boatload to the lords of the mills in Old England and in New England. Still following the patterns they had learned in Barbados, the Englishmen imported black folk from Africa, who were bought and brought forward to work the cotton fields in that land. The enterprise made the Englishmen at once lords of the land and lords of the labor, and these fellows who were lords of this red land and lords of this black labor became rich indeed. Yet they spared little of their silver and none of their gold for the black people who were the slaves plowing, sowing, weeding, hoeing, and picking the cotton, and then bringing the jute bags stuffed with it to the cotton gin.[2]

Black men and women found themselves "strangers in a strange land," as the psalmist wrote. They found themselves obliged to sing songs for their overlords in the strange land. They sang their songs; they worked their work; and at least a portion of their songs they sang for themselves, and at least a portion of the work they did for themselves. The young child Benjamin Elijah Mays learned about the seed of James, his own black people, from his grandmother Julia, wife of James, and from her daughter and his mother, Vinia Mays. He learned too that this same red soil had produced men who became judges, even over the white folk, and—more important—prophets who reminded people of all colors—black, red, and white—about the right way to live.

Julia and Vinia Mays both told him to be proud of being black, and both told him to be cautious around all white people, but especially the lords of the land and the lords of the labor. From his father, Hezekiah Mays, son of James, Bennie Mays learned a few facts and many emotions. When Hezekiah Mays was in his liquor, he cursed the absent white lords and then cursed and struck at his current wife, Vinia, and his present children. In his drunken anger he recalled the cruelties he had suffered from his master in the days of slavery. In his sober moments he recalled the kindnesses bestowed on him by the master's son. In other sober moments Hezekiah Mays marked the kindness of William

H. Mays, the man who rented land to the children and grandchildren of James after freedom came but before the prize was reached. Bennie Mays saw with his own eyes and heard with his own ears the kindnesses of William H. Mays.

Bennie Mays did not write it, but the record seems clear: The cruel master was Henry Hazel Mays, the kind son was William H. Mays. After the cruel master was forced by soldiers in blue to free his slaves, it was the kind son who rented out the same goodly land to his old playmate Hezekiah Mays. The unnamed kind son of the unnamed cruel master and the named kind lord of the land were one and the same: William H. Mays.

In the eyes of Benjamin Mays, believer and preacher, such an abomination as slavery could have been permitted by the Lord God only for some purpose of testing, refining, and toughening a people whom he loved. Hezekiah Mays's father, James, was a man of dark skin who was born to a family of slaves who lived and worked in the Saluda Regiment of the old Edgefield District, in the portion that later became part of Greenwood County. Following custom, James's family had no last name. James was born in a place called Rambo, a Finnish name suggesting that the white "tribes" who settled the area were not exclusively from England and Scotland as was generally claimed. There were two Rambos, A. J. and Joseph Rambo, and these Rambo families owned fifty-four slaves in the area. In keeping with the custom in antebellum days, the Rambo surname became the name of the neighborhood in this tiny corner of the huge and sprawling Edgefield District.[3]

A family larger and more spread out than the Rambos was the Mays family. Had they arrived earlier, the same area might have been named Maysville instead of Rambo. There were at least seven white lords of the land and the labor who were named Mays, and these people were all related to each other. William, Henry, Henry Hazel, S. W., John, B. F., and George R. Mays formed an extended family, which controlled a total of 137 slaves in the final decade before the Civil War, when it seemed that every slave-owning family in Edgefield District was busy trying to buy more slaves. The most likely owner of James was Henry Hazel Mays. This Mays is not recorded by name in the memoir prepared by Benjamin Mays, but he does seem the most likely owner. Henry Hazel Mays had land in the area, and he had 14 slaves. In the course of enumerating slaves in the slave lists, the census takers did not even list the first name of the enslaved people, but they did list by age and complexion (black or mulatto), and they did group by families. One of Henry Mays's slaves was exactly the right age, twenty-five, to be James and was listed as "black," not "mulatto"; next to this man was listed a woman, age unknown, who was "mulatto," and next to these two was listed a boy slave, then three years old, who was also called black, not mulatto. James and his son Hezekiah were famously black, and Julia, of undetermined age, was famously light skinned. Julia said that she had four children, all girls, before Hezekiah, and one son after she bore Hezekiah. The four sisters, who were Francie, Roenia, Janette, and Polly, should have been old enough by the time of the 1860 census to be out on their own, perhaps even coupled with male slaves to begin producing their own children. No female slaves are listed next to this unnamed couple, but there are four other female slaves listed as the possessions of Henry Hazel Mays. The youngest man child, Isaiah, should have been barely one year old when the census taker came round, and there is a one-year-old black male child listed with this couple. These are coincidences, but the coincidences do not line up in the same way with the other six Mays lords of land and lords of labor whose slaves are enumerated.[4]

Better proof that Henry Hazel Mays was the owner of James and Julia and of Hezekiah is seen in the white family. Henry Hazel Mays had a child, William H. Mays, who was the same age as the unnamed black child who was the son of the unnamed twenty-five-year old slave. In Benjamin Mays's memoir Hezekiah is said to have recalled great cruelty visited on him by the master but great kindness from the master's son. Among other things it is written that the unnamed master forced his slaves to eat from a trough on the ground, much as he fed his livestock. Yet the unnamed son of the master began to teach Hezekiah to read and write as soon as the son himself began to learn these skills. In the days of slavery no more than one in twenty slaves could read and write, and here was Hezekiah learning to do so under instruction from the master's own son. This instruction was done in secret, for the law of the white lords said that a slave could not be so taught. Indeed across the Savannah, a white man had been hanged because he was found to be teaching black children to read and write. So frightening was the prospect of punishment for slave student and free teacher in such cases and so much did the matured Hezekiah distrust and despise white people, that decades after the fact of freedom Hezekiah continued to tell census takers that he could not read and write even though family testimony makes it clear that he certainly could.[5]

Hezekiah could tell this story of the master's kind son, but Hezekiah could tell other stories too. On balance, whether Hezekiah was drunk or sober, the stories told of cruelty and not kindness. The much more talkative Julia and Vinia much more consistently told stories of cruelty and even terror. While his father, Hezekiah, might have kind words for William H. Mays, Bennie Mays the child and the young man heard tales aplenty to convict all southern white people, and likely all white people, as usurpers of the goodly land and as dastardly masters of the good black people; but he also early took hope that the unjust rule was not divinely sanctioned and thus was not fated to last forever. The call and response of the song master from the psalm "How long, O Lord?"

elicited the fervent and deeply believed response "not long, not long," whether the call and response were sung by people of color in their pews, by work crews chopping cotton in the field, or rhetorically by their ministers of color standing tall in the pulpit at a Sunday service or a Wednesday evening prayer meet and sing.[6] Even, and especially, in his mature years as distinguished academic, Benjamin Mays tasted the bitter draft of sorrows when he referred to the self-proclaimed "lords" among the white people, but he spoke with sincerity about the real Lord.

It is recorded in the memories of the white lords and the memories of their slaves that James worshipped the real Lord as did all his seed. At some time during seven fat years in the 1850s, James was given Julia, and she became his wife as recognized by the Mayses' slaves and by the real Lord—but the white lord of this land did not call their marriage a union, insisting instead that he had given Julia to James in the same way that he had taken Julia from another "common husband" from another "custom marriage" in Virginia. No one has named the husband from the custom marriage back in Virginia.

This Julia was lighter skinned than James, enough so that dark people in Rambo often asked if she might have a white parent or at least one white ancestor. Julia had high cheekbones, which led the same dark folk to ask if she might have an Indian parent or an Indian ancestor. People outside Rambo sometimes said that Julia had a white parent, and sometimes such people said that Julia had an Indian parent, but of course they did not know. Among James's people, to whom Julia came, it was declared that she was neither from the white world nor from the Indian world, and they took her as one of them. They told their children to quit asking about her forebears. Recalling their teaching in his own later years, Benjamin Mays wrote, "I do not recall ever hearing her or my parents make any reference to any white ancestry."[7]

Julia did not tell James or his people much at all about her days in Virginia. She told him that there were three daughters and three sons in her family there; her brothers were Abner, Harper, and John, and her sisters were Sarah and Susi. No one among James's people remembered her telling the names of her parents in Virginia, and none of James's line ever met these parents of Julia, Sarah, Susi, Abner, Harper, and John. There was more not known than there was known about Julia.

What was known—from Julia—is that she came from somewhere in Virginia, that she had had a common husband there in a custom marriage, and that they had two children. Her girl child had died young, perhaps in infancy. Her boy child had been killed in the fields where he worked, working as a man, slain as a man, but still a child. A white man had killed him. What she could tell James about her late Virginia family is what he could tell her about any Carolina family: the babies never had enough to eat or the right clothes to wear, and when they became children, they were set to work and they worked hard "from day clean to first dark."[8] And James could tell her that her white lord in Carolina, who had bought her from her white lord in Virginia, was just as likely to slay one of their offspring in these red fields.

But there was still the real Lord, who would not let the travail last for all time. Another day would come. Their day would come, a day of "Jubilo," and they could see the prize up there, and they had to keep their eyes on the real Lord's prize.

So James took Julia to him and begat their six children, who were born into this travail, and these six lived to see freedom but not the prize. Julia and James's Hezekiah, born next to last in 1856, took Vinia for his wife. Hezekiah could remember what James and Julia had told him, and he had seen and felt the lash and the knout of slavery, for he was working as a man in the fields before slavery at last ended.

In taking Vinia to his side, Hezekiah was following James and his tribe. Vinia too came from somewhere in Virginia and from a past in which more was not known than was known. She was born in 1862, during the Civil War, and she remembered almost nothing of the time of slavery, for she was only three years old when it ended. She also remembered little, or in any case told almost nothing, about her own family. Hezekiah and all James's people did not know the names of her parents. She, like Julia before her, became a part of James's family and took that family's story as hers. There were some differences in the story, however. Above all Vinia was not given to Hezekiah by some white lord, and they were not common husband and common wife in a custom marriage. Indeed the marriage of Louvenia and Hezekiah Mays was written down in books and accepted by people of all colors, even the white ones, in Carolina.[9]

Hezekiah took the surname "Mays" because he wanted it. He did not want it because he had happy memories of white lord William H. Mays, although he did like Bill Mays, and Bill Mays did like him, just as Bill's wife, Nola Barmore, liked Hezekiah's wife, Vinia. Hezekiah took the name "Mays" because it named all those 137 people of color in that fine land where "he lived and moved and had his being." Nor did he take Vinia from anyone but herself, and when they married, they recorded it not only before the real Lord but in the same book now open to black people as well as white people.[10]

Those white lords had lost their war, and they had lost it thoroughly, but they had not lost their land. Hezekiah and other young newly freed men recognized this Canaan for what it was, a land of such richness that a man ached to look at it. Perhaps someday the land would be Hezekiah's and would belong to the seed of James, but for now the seed of James had to share this land with other peoples, including the once and future white lords of the land, who had lost the war and lost their slaves, lost so much—but not their land.[11]

Hezekiah could leave, as Joseph in the Bible had once left to find favor with a pharaoh in rich land with better weather in a dry season. Perhaps across the Savannah River there was some such postbellum pharaoh. But a stranger in a strange land would be no less a servant across the Savannah, and pharaoh's favor in a strange land was no better than the favor of a "cotton snob" in the red clay of the land Hezekiah knew. So Hezekiah stayed, and he worked land that was not yet his, but he was not slave now. When the cotton crop came in, Hezekiah gave part of the harvest to the lord of the land, but he kept a portion too. In that way he was like a sharecropper. Most of James's seed were share-croppers, but some of their neighbors—one in ten among black people—owned their own land; and now even some of the children of the old white lords were themselves sharecroppers. Hezekiah was not a sharecropper and was above the run of croppers of both races because he rented the land from Bill Mays instead of going into debt on a share of the crop. Hezekiah was also above the run of renters of both races because he owned his own mules—two of them and some-times three—no small treasure in such a land in such a day.[12]

Benjamin Mays wrote in *Born to Rebel* that his father was probably not a habitual drunk but rather one unaccustomed to liquor and unable to "hold much." On his rare, but frightening, drinking occasions, Hezekiah Mays raised his voice to utter harsh words and laid rough hands on his family. In 1907 Louvenia Mays compelled Bennie to vow to her that he would never drink, and the mature man kept that adolescent's promise. The son's path was surely influenced by Hezekiah Mays's awfulness when full of wine.[13] But Hezekiah was also a man who raised crops successfully when many failed, a man who fed and clothed his family even during the seven lean years that started in 1873 and the seven lean years that started in 1893. Moreover Hezekiah was a man who made sure that his children learned to read and to write, and above all Hezekiah saved Bennie's life in 1898, the worst year in the second set of seven lean years.

Through most of Bennie Mays's childhood, the patriarch James was not there to tell him in person about their family, and James's Hezekiah did not always wish to tell the children much. But James's Julia was there, and while she was secretive and even silent about her Virginia days, for long years she talked and talked about the people of color in old Edgefield District and in Greenwood and elsewhere in South Carolina. Hezekiah's Vinia was still there too, through ten decades, and she talked and talked, again not about her own Virginians but about people of color in the same area. There were prophets and judges among the dark people, and Julia and Vinia told of them.

They told about Booker Taliaferro Washington, who had built a college for African Americans in a place far across the Savannah River; there black people learned not only to read and write and figure, as Hezekiah could do, but also to do scientific research in modern laboratories, something Hezekiah barely dreamed of. They told about Thomas Ezekiel Miller, who had built such a school for African Americans on their side of the Savannah, over in Orangeburg. They told about Frederick Douglass, who had written books about his blackness and who had been to the White House to argue with Mr. Lincoln about letting black troops fight for their own freedom. They told how Douglass had won that argument, and how scores of thousands of men "with sable arm" had fought in Federal blue to earn their people's own freedom. They told how there was a poet, Paul Laurence Dunbar, who sang a song that was dark and comely. They told how in their own red land there was Thomas Williamson, a "free man of color" who had owned a lot of land even before the war and who had helped to write the new state constitution after the war. Vinia told Bennie often, what Bennie believed at once and repeated often, especially to himself: "You are as good as anybody!"[14]

Young black boys in this red land could see such black leaders with their own eyes and hear them with their own ears. Among their teachers and preachers in Abbeville, Edgefield, and Greenwood was William Henry Heard, who had studied at the University of South Carolina, where he was taught by Harvard-educated African American Richard Theodore Greener. In Greenwood there was the Reverend James F. Marshall, a minister written about respectfully in the white newspapers and a man who came to preach and teach in Rambo as well as in his fine church building in the railroad and textile-mill town of Greenwood. The South Carolina General Assembly seated African American assemblymen, especially William Henry Heard and the lawyer Samuel J. Lee, who with other black men had represented their part of the Piedmont in the capital in Columbia. Jonathan Jasper Wright, from the dark lands of the lowcountry, sat as associate justice on the state's Supreme Court. And even the South Carolina delegation in Washington, D.C., included the African Americans Robert Smalls, Thomas Ezekiel Miller, Robert C. DeLarge, and George Washington Murray in the United States House of Representatives.[15]

Yet in this red land still held by the white lords, African Americans—and two out of three people in the county and in the state in those days were black—were not without power and influence. At the ballot box, at the train depot, in their own churches, and in their own schools, James's descendants really were "as good as anybody else" in the first years of Bennie's life, 1894–98.

Vinia Mays never did learn to read and write, but she loved to hear her favored son Bennie read to her, especially from the family Bible. The Bible told stories of slavery, exile, natural disasters, incest and intrigue, and betrayal, but there were also miracles, visions, and prophecies. There were twists and turns in the densely layered plots, and the themes of the stories were sometimes elusive. The Lord God they worshipped had permitted much hurt of his chosen people, and he had endured much resistance to his plans. But always he had stayed by them, and always he displayed that prize in the sky and gave them eyes to see it and arms to reach for it.

In reading the Bible, Bennie could see that the names in his family, not least his own name, all had meaning. James the patriarch was named for a son of the fisherman Zebedee and was one of the first disciples chosen by Jesus Christ for the years of fervent teaching; James was also one of those who stumbled unreliably through the time of the Passion, but then he witnessed the Resurrection and Ascension and thereafter preached the Gospel of the risen Lord no matter the dangers. Hezekiah, son of James and father of Bennie, was named for the Hebrew king of Judah who resisted Sennacherib's invasion. Hezekiah was one of the small group among the southern Hebrews marked by loyalty, steadfastness, and dependability during a "time of troubles" after the kingdom was sundered by willful disobedience of the law and the prophets. Among a series of faithless kings, Hezekiah heard and heeded the word of God from his prophet Isaiah.

The name Benjamin Elijah was a glorious combination: Benjamin was patriarch of one of the original twelve tribes that had helped Joshua capture the Promised Land of Canaan. But the men and women of Benjamin's tribe spun out no simple story of themselves—they built a famous shrine at Gilgal, but for long decades they had to share the Promised Land and the city of peace, Jerusalem, with those who did not believe. And the tribe of Benjamin had once stolen women from another tribe and brought them forcefully into their place and raped them in order to perpetuate their own line. Not only were Benjamin and his descendants former slaves rescued from Pharaoh by Moses, but they were also men who had captured and raped and enslaved women from another tribe. Jacob on his deathbed had proclaimed the tribe of Benjamin to be a "ravening wolf," and that proclamation seemed to suggest a warring group; the characterization had been accurate enough—and there had certainly been a season for such men. In the ripe time, in the New Israel, the prophet Obadiah prophesied, "The tribe of Benjamin will occupy Gilead," the Promised Land, a better land than that claimed by the white lords of the land of the valley of the Saluda. There were thus indeed twists and turns in their long history, but they were among the chosen, and they had had their moments, including that of their leader Sheba, whose bold cry—"to your tents, Israel!"—still echoed down through the years to young Bennie, who later proclaimed himself "born to rebel." In so proclaiming he was speaking from the depths—and the heights—of the name "Benjamin."

Equally tangled was the identity of the Benjaminite Saul of Tarsus, the Pharisee who once persecuted Christians but became the disciple Paul, who built the church in the ancient world—the man who gave all Christians the image of the prize in the sky and the man whose epistles developed the formula for writing sermons that Bennie and the other civil rights leaders later preached.

Finally there was the second part of Bennie Mays's name, "Elijah." This man had been a prophet of such overwhelming strength that he could command Elisha to leave his father's field to follow prophecy without even the chance to kiss his father goodbye. Elijah called on the seed of Israel, the seed of Jacob and Isaac and Abraham, to return to the right way. And of course Bennie read to his mother that Elijah had never died but rather had ascended straight way to the side of the Lord God. Elisha had seen Elijah go up into the sky, and so it was written as Elisha himself had witnessed and testified.

The Bible made it clear also who was the real Lord and who among temporal lords were just permitted to hold sway for the nonce, serving thereby in some complex fashion a larger and providential purpose. The Bible also made it abundantly clear that all things come about in their own time, that there was a time for every season.

This biblical wisdom of the preacher included the season of 1898, a time in the red land of Old Edgefield that closed off once-bright promise for James's family. And not a time for a modern-day Sheba. Not yet.

2

THE RAVENING WOLF

1898

As Bennie Mays read it in the Bible, Joseph did not come to realize at once that his brothers' ill treatment of him could follow a providential design, that they meant him evil but that the Lord meant him good by their actions. That understanding came for Joseph in his final season, nor would such a season of understanding come easily in Bennie's life. Instead, when he was four years old, he saw only why Benjaminites were a ravening wolf. It was because the Benjaminites were hunted by those who were even more ravening.

In his memoir Mays wrote of an encounter with armed white men on November 8, 1898:

> I remember a crowd of white men who rode up on horseback with rifles on their shoulders. I was with my father when they rode up, and I remember I started to cry. They cursed my father, drew their guns and made him salute, made him take off his hat and bow down to them several times. Then they rode away. I was not yet five years old, but I have never forgotten them.
>
> I know now that they were one of the mobs associated with the infamous Phoenix Riot, which began in Greenwood County, South Carolina, on November 8, 1898, and spread terror throughout the countryside for many days thereafter. My oldest sister, Susie, tells me and the newspaper reports of that period reveal that several Negroes were lynched on the ninth and others on subsequent days.
>
> That mob is my earliest memory.[1]

That memory came out of local history at the time of Bennie Mays's first years, the last years of the nineteenth century. That memory comes from what George Brown Tindall calls the "context of violence" in which that historian's native

South Carolina must be understood in that day.² The Phoenix Riot crystallizes the violence that gives the context for the prelude and first chapter of Mays's life. He saw the ravening wolf of racism and the violence that comes with it, and that image never left him.

The years 1895–98 were a period of change for the postage stamp of territory stuck between the sandhill midlands and red-hill upcountry of South Carolina, and between the Old South that was gone but still remembered with love and hate and the New South still unidentified and even unidentifiable, without bona fides because it was still being born. In fact these years formed a period of change everywhere in the Carolinas and Georgia, for all regions of the former Confederacy were then going through broad and deep changes.

The larger and longer story was the economic change in which Benjamin Mays's community was pulled by fits and starts into an industrialism marked by an interconnected world economy. These changes gradually displaced the old white elite who relied for their wealth and power and authority on African American slaves and tenants. In the New South the new white elite—sometimes comprising the same people as the old but with new ideas and sometimes comprising entirely new people—came to rely for power and authority and wealth on the white working class, some still on the farm and others coming from farms to the mill villages, but always a white group whose labor provided the fuel for the growing industrial economy and whose votes could put you in office—or put you out of it. What that meant for Hezekiah Mays's family and for other African Americans is that their labor was valued far less than before, and their votes for some politicians were regarded as a liability rather than an asset. It entailed a host of proposals on the state agenda to limit black suffrage and office holding and to segregate public facilities.

That change transpired so slowly that contemporaries could barely sense it. What they could perceive was economic dislocation, shown by a terrible worldwide depression set off in 1893, great racial violence everywhere in the region, and nothing less than a political revolution in the Palmetto State. In 1895 South Carolina got a new state constitution and soon thereafter a new set of state leaders vastly different in tone, manners, and even dress from their predecessors but above all different in substance. Benjamin Ryan Tillman from Trenton in Old Edgefield had risen to power. He was important to the poorest white people and useful to some of the new elite among the textile industrialists. He built farm-to-market roads, regulated railroads, and established Clemson Agricultural and Mechanical College to educate rural middling farmers and the slowly rising middle class in the cities and towns. For black folk, however, and especially the Mays family, this Tillman was a terror, "a ravening wolf."³

This Tillman was called admiringly "Pitchfork Ben" by the white masses, but the Mays family always remembered Pitchfork with fear and trembling—

Senator Benjamin "Pitchfork Ben" Tillman, who for Mays always represented white southern violence toward African Americans. Courtesy of the Library of Congress.

and a resentment that made them something of ravening Benjaminites. Governor Tillman pushed for measures to help white mill hands and white farmers, but he also favored measures to hurt black farmers—and he spoke ominously of killing black men, perhaps even with his own hands. More to the point, Tillman displaced the conservative Wade Hampton, a Civil War cavalry leader and Old South planter who until then had functioned almost as a living memorial to another era, even though in his practices he was deeply involved in building railroads and banks and textile mills and the other elements of the faster paced and much more self-consciously capitalist industrializing economy. This displacement was no mean feat, and its impact was profound. Above all it brought with it a dramatic increase in racist violence during the 1890s.

In fact General Hampton had once used antiblack violence with his Red Shirt troops—led by Martin Witherspoon Gary, also of Edgefield—to gain the governorship in 1876 and thus "redeem" South Carolina from Republican rule; but the general had always been able to distance himself from the violence—and even from the complex "honeyfugling" political horse trading that gave him the governorship while giving the presidential electoral votes to the Republican Rutherford B. Hayes. However, Hampton had convinced many African American political leaders that he was the only safe port in these storms, and he had largely kept his promise to protect the rights of African Americans to vote, to hold office, and to exercise the other aspects of citizenship set forth by the Thirteenth, Fourteenth, and Fifteenth Amendments, enacted in the aftermath of the bloody war that Hampton had fought in and lost.

In 1879 Hampton ascended to the U.S. Senate, but he continued to send instructions back home for the running of his state. He influenced state appointments for selected Democratic African Americans of his acquaintance, and he cooperated with—that is, never got in the way of—federal authorities, who made minor federal level appointments for selected Republican African Americans. As for laws about access to public facilities and segregation, practices were probably already changing, but the laws as written stayed on the books in accordance with the recorded laws of South Carolina, congruent with the three constitutional amendments that vouchsafed black freedom, citizenship, and voting rights. In particular the trains—so vital for moving people in the era before inexpensive and mass-distributed automobiles—remained available to African Americans, and the train depot remained an integrated public station.

Hampton had retained the style of the courtly patriarch who loved his troops, his slaves, his tenants, his mill workers, and his investors because they were underneath him. His style of orotund rhetoric and close-to-the-vest counsel—all brought off with an almost arrogant shambling and rambling—suited the old elite well and for a time served the managers of the new industrialism busily establishing a New South creed that rationalized new economics with symbols and gestures from the Old South. With his whiskers, his high and wide brow, his horses, his broadcloth, and the unfathomable meanings in his always ceremonial pronouncements, Hampton was the perfect "front man" for the new order of railroad builders, mill builders, investors, and developers— except that he was not only the man sitting out front but also the man doing all those things behind the scenes, a front man or a figurehead for his own operations. In many ways he represented South Carolina as its prime symbol for these years of change after the Civil War, and he was so accepted even by northerners. It was not, however, a long rule, for he was shoved aside by the gathering forces of Pitchfork Ben's revolt in 1890.

African Americans in Bennie Mays's community were hardly in love with any white people, but there was an acceptance of Hampton as compared with the alternatives. Indeed the African American journalist Robert "Preacher" Carroll had interviewed Benjamin Tillman to confirm the Trenton planter's intent in the constitutional revisions; and the white-owned (and usually non-political) *Edgefield Advertiser* had printed the long account even though the correspondent was a black man. Preacher Carroll quoted Tillman about the constitutional proposals: "I intended to do it from the jump because I wanted to save the State and the white people." Those blacks who could read absorbed Pitchfork's message that he intended to diminish, if not completely do away with, black suffrage, and they passed along the information to those who could not read. It made Wade Hampton look a lot better by contrast.[4]

A prominent Republican leader among African American politicos in the Greenwood area was even named for the old general by a conservative father who hoped that Hampton's top-down style of leadership and management would protect African Americans from newly prominent politicians such as Tillman. This black leader was Wade Hampton McKenney, but he soon abandoned the Democratic Party of the Tillman day and joined the Republicans, as did quite a group in Greenwood, Edgefield, and Abbeville in South Carolina's Third Congressional District.[5]

The Democratic Party of Wade Hampton, racist and paternalistic with its half-a-loaf for the black man, was gone by 1895. It was replaced by the Democratic Party of Pitchfork Ben Tillman, who promised poor-white farmers and poor-white mill hands a full loaf—and his promises to them may have been truly made. Tillman saw that Clemson was built to educate white countrymen in scientific farming, and he saw that railroad rates and insurance rates were regulated. But this Tillman also threatened black farmers with something just short of political death—and sometimes he seemed to urge literal death for black men, "the black beast rapist." Tillman ran for governor in 1890, and he won.[6]

He then gathered his forces in the General Assembly, for that body selected U.S. senators in those days before direct elections. He told them to vote for John Laurens Manning Irby instead of the sitting senator, Wade Hampton. The old general was too proud to campaign personally on the floor of the assembly, and he stayed distant from the fray, "available" for reappointment. Perhaps Hampton stayed away because he was too proud to come home and campaign—and still lose. Hampton thereby stood for office while Irby ran. Tillman's hard work behind the scenes and Hampton's uninspired efforts combined to give Irby the Senate seat. Thus the Tillmanites tasted a second victory, and four years later a third when they lifted the Trenton planter to the state's other Senate seat alongside his handpicked "senior" colleague Irby.[7]

For Hezekiah Mays and other African Americans, Hampton was retreating and Tillman was advancing. The alternative was the Republicans, led locally by the Tolbert family. They were planters—and indeed Confederate veterans—led by the patriarch John R. Tolbert. As with the Democratic white leaders Hampton and Tillman, the Republican Tolberts were also from the same dark and bloody lands bounded by the Savannah River and washed by the Saluda River. Black people in the Rambo area, like white people in the same land, could look close to home for those who would lead the whole state.

In 1896 the Third Congressional District was represented by conservative white Democrat Asbury C. Latimer, but the Tolbert family proclaimed that the black majority could regain power despite confusing ballot procedures and antiblack violence of the well-armed and tightly organized white tribes. John R. Tolbert looked the part of a biblical leader with his bushy hair and his gray beard, and he lived the part of a patriarch who had no intention of folding his tent and taking his leave. In 1868 this Confederate colonel and large landholder had set off a riot by voting Republican in the public polling place. He had lived through that crisis, had seen the coming to power of a dominant black Republican Party in the 1870s, and then had seen the rise to power of Wade Hampton in 1877. Now there was Pitchfork Ben Tillman. With Hamptonites, Tolbert could get along, but with the Tillmanites he could not even coexist, for they spoke openly of killing Republicans.

Yet John Tolbert still stood erect. He remained collector of the port of Charleston, a handsome federal appointment worth a small fortune in any day. He intended that his sons, especially R. R. "Red" Tolbert, carry on the family politics in company with the black people who rented and shared crops on the family's several thousand acres of cotton land. Son Joseph Tolbert was a candidate for postmaster of Phoenix, a minor federal job but, in these seven lean years, a much-coveted prize. Red Tolbert, John's chosen son, was chairman of the state Republican Party and candidate for Congress from the

Third District. The patriarch had plans for his sons and for his allies, the black farmers.

The Tolberts encouraged the black majority to arm themselves and to gather together for safety on Tolbert lands whether they worked for the family or not. Such plans were made with good cause, for a black politician could be killed if he walked alone, as Orangeburg assemblyman Benjamin Randolph had been killed by the state's Ku Klux Klan while campaigning in this district in 1868. In fact the Ku Klux Klan and other organized antiblack groups were always severe here. The awful Hamburg Massacre of black Republicans on July 8, 1876, had taken place in this district, only a little south and east along the Savannah River in Aiken County. White newspaper reports counted eight African American men lynched in the counties of the district during the weeks immediately preceding the Phoenix Riot of 1898. Nor did Democratic violence confine itself to black people. Tillmanite editor W. W. Thompson had established the *Greenwood Advocate,* and in May 1898 he had shot and killed P. E. Rowell, the anti-Tillmanite editor of the *Greenwood Leader* newspaper.[8] There was thus good reason to arm oneself and to band together with other men for protection in any kind of public contest. The Tolberts tried to organize themselves and their supporters in light of the violent realities of the day.

The second part of the Tolbert plan involved a protest against practices that either confused black voters or prevented them from casting their ballots at all—and against violence and fraud. The Tolberts intended nothing less than voting despite the South Carolina laws because they regarded the 1895 state constitution as inferior to the U.S. Constitution—and it was clearly inferior to the "higher law" of the one Bennie Mays always called the real Lord God. Red Tolbert arranged for Republican candidates to compete in every congressional district, including the First District, where black man and onetime congressman George Washington Murray made bold to run against the incumbent William Elliott. The First District was the heavily black coastal area, but it was also claimed secure by the white Democrats. Red Tolbert ran hard in his own district against Latimer, another incumbent elected by successful use of Tillman's strategies. Tolbert wanted every African American man to try to vote at the polling places. If denied—or rather, when denied—by polling officials, a black man could then sign an affidavit that he had attempted to vote. Republicans were planning to collect these affidavits and turn them over to Republican congressmen as proof that Republican voting was denied in the South by reason of race in defiance of the Fifteenth Amendment—and also contrary to the Compromise of 1877, which General Hampton's men had enforced until the advent of the Tillmanites. Red Tolbert understood that the national Republican Party had little interest in the rights of black South Carolinians, but he thought that a collection of thousands of affidavits showing proof of damage to the Republican Party might appeal to their self-interest in the actual survival of their party.[9]

Election Day on November 8, 1898, found quite a scene at the polling place, which was Johnson Sales Watson's country store. It was a familiar place. On normal working days, black folk went there to pick up sacks of fertilizer or blankets or shoes and to sign—or sometimes make their mark on—Watson's ledger of debits. On such days black men did not tarry, for their work was long and hard, and they needed to get back to it in Rambo; neither did they go in with eyes lowered and feet shuffling, for they were valued customers and valued workers. All the same the store was always more of a gathering place for the white farmers and the few white professionals of Phoenix than for the black farmers and the even fewer black professionals of Rambo. White fellows often lingered by the store's stove drinking coffee and chatting on the chilly mornings and brisk evenings of the late harvest season. Black fellows, no matter how valued their work, did not expect to linger by the stove to drink coffee or chat, even if they had finished all their chores and even if they knew and liked the white fellows standing at the stove.

Every farmer of any color likely owed money to John Watson, and in hard times such as these with a pound of newly picked middling-grade cotton fetching only a nickel, all farmers owed him a lot. Watson was generally honest and fair, and in any case there was almost nowhere else to go, unless a farmer rode his mule for three hours into the town of Greenwood to try to convince a banker there that a poor farmer deserved a loan secured by nickel cotton.[10]

On this Election Day, Watson's was packed. A gaggle of white farmers was gathered inside sipping coffee—and a few occasionally slipped outside to sip strong spirits. The polling boxes were set up on the countertops among Watson's dry goods. The ledger book was packed away, for today's business was about settling other accounts. The voter-registration ledgers replaced the credit-and-debit ledger, and today's ledger recorded the intricacies of the voting rules. The gaggle of farmers watched closely to see how their neighbors voted. Some of these men were Ku Klux Klan members. They knew exactly who each black farmer was, and they took careful notice that he tried to vote. And each black man knew that Ku Kluxers were watching him but did not know for certain which of the watchers were Klansmen. He knew only that they had your identity pegged.

On the store's veranda, or piazza as John Watson liked to call it, there was a gaggle of black farmers. On this day they held their heads as high as did the white farmers who were downstairs. They too watched closely as farmers of both races came and went in and out of the store to try to vote. Red Tolbert had set up a box that looked much like the box downstairs and inside. It was for collecting affidavits, and his brother Thomas Paine Tolbert was in charge of this task. The affidavits were displayed on the table in front of the box. These affidavits looked like ballots, but they said that the signer had attempted to vote and had been denied.

On this day twenty-two of the men who had come to vote had been turned down. Two of this number were white men, and they left quickly and quietly after briefly visiting the Tolberts and the black men on the piazza. But twenty were black, and eighteen of these men marched up to the piazza, took an affidavit from Thomas Tolbert, signed it, deposited it in the box, and spoke with Red Tolbert and with the group of black farmers. These eighteen said that they would vote one way or another.

The white group downstairs knew all about this process on the piazza. There was an increasing murmur among them, and then Bose Ethridge left the white men, came up to the piazza, and approached Thomas P. Tolbert and the black men. Ethridge said that he "knew Negro psychology," and he said that the Tolbert affidavits made the black men think that they were actually getting to vote when the Tolberts knew perfectly well that they were denied the vote by the real authorities inside. Ethridge was mad, and Tom Tolbert got mad. He and Bose Ethridge began to shout at one another. The gaggle on the piazza and the gaggle inside the store began to face each other on the steps and in the doorway. Men in both groups looked hard at each other and edged their hands toward their weapons. It was hunting season, and many men carried guns then; it was also a day when trouble was brewing. It seemed that every man was carrying a gun.

Red Tolbert said later that Ethridge kicked over the box of affidavits, and most of the white Democrats remember what happened that way too. Tolbert said that a piece of wood popped off the box, bounced up, and struck Ethridge hard in the head. Ethridge's friends insisted that Tom Tolbert took an iron rod and hit Bose in the head hard enough to kill him. As to what happened after Ethridge was struck in the head, the only general agreement is that dozens of men drew their guns and began shooting. In the smoke and the sulfur, Tom Tolbert fell to the floor mortally wounded, and Bose Ethridge fell in the same place bleeding profusely. Red Tolbert and the black gaggle gathered up Tom, who was able to limp but died by the next morning, and the Republicans left Watson's quickly, pushing their way down the stairs. They went to Rehoboth Church nearby, where they knew other black Republicans would be gathered. At Watson's store some men put Bose Ethridge on a wagon and carried him to W. H. Stallworth's plantation nearby.

Ethridge died there. Likely he was beyond saving from the moment he fell. Others in the white gaggle used John Watson's telephone, the only one for miles around, to notify Sheriff Robert F. McCaslin in Greenwood town and

Governor William H. Ellerbe in Columbia that there was a race riot in Phoenix. In their messages, they said that black men were gathering at Rehoboth Church to kill white men and that they needed as many white men with guns as soon as they could get them to Phoenix.

The sun sank on November 8 with everyone uneasy. It was not a normal chilly night but a downright cold one. No one could understand how only two men had been shot in the hailstorm of bullets. More important, no one could understand how more men could escape shooting on the morning to come as the ravening bands faced each other.

On the cool and drizzly gray morning of November 9, heat and color prevailed. Black men at the Rehoboth Church talked about where to take their stand. Red Tolbert insisted later that these men confined their talk to defensive tactics in case of attack, but at least some black Republicans went out on an offensive sortie, catching three white Democrats in an ambush on a country road. No one knew which African American men set the ambush, and Red Tolbert and his party leaders said that the unknown men acted on their own and alone, and not as Republicans. Everyone knew who the three white Democrats were. They were a young merchant, a prominent young farmer, and a young farmer recently returned from the Spanish-American War. M. J. Younger, the merchant, was shot in one foot; Creswell Fleming, the farmer, suffered multiple wounds; the young veteran, Stuart Miller, never recovered from the wounds he suffered that day.

Before the ambush, hundreds of white Democrats from the towns of Greenwood and Edgefield and from the nearby countryside, gathered at Watson's. Many of these young men waved their rifles and shouted, "Go after the Negroes and dispense them." All knew that the armed band was at Rehoboth Church. In the morning and early afternoon, however, Watson and State Senator J. M. Gaines, supported by "cooler heads" of "high repute and known grit," were able to dissuade the would-be vigilance group from setting off in pursuit of black Republicans.[11]

By early evening, there was a general knowledge about the ambush, for doctors G. P. Neil and B. W. Cobb were tending the three victims at A. C. Stockman's farm. Incredibly Republican Elias Tolbert, who was also wounded on that same day, was recuperating at Stockman's as well. Stockman hid Elias in a separate part of his house. When Democrats came to visit the wounded men, several asked Stockman directly if he knew anything about Elias and where he was, but the planter lied convincingly.

Councils of peace failed, for many of the Democrats demanded vengeance for the ambush on Younger, Fleming, and Miller. A large Democratic vigilance group formed and marched in quick time to Rehoboth Church. Before dark the white gunmen and the black gunmen faced each other in the churchyard. The much larger group of Democrats prevailed, capturing four black Republicans while wounding at least two others. The two wounded men, plus at least five others, were able to escape the churchyard and the avengers. The four captured men were tied up, each with a hangman's noose around his neck, and they were given the chance to confess to the ambush. White Democratic testimony was that two men confessed, but many Republicans disputed the claim that any confession was ever made. Democratic and Republican witnesses agreed that at least two men refused to confess.

The vigilantes then shot all four men, and they fell dead in the shadow of their church, whose name, Rehoboth, means the "wide spaces" in the language of Abraham. The Rehoboth of Bennie Mays's Bible was a place much fought over, but Isaac had succeeded in digging a well there and thus had established that particular wide space as a place of refuge and refreshment. Despite the optimism of the African Americans who had so named their church, there was no chance that it would serve as a place of refuge and refreshment this November. Indeed a small group of Democrats stayed in order to shoot "volley after volley" into the dead bodies. The Republicans killed on November 9 in Rehoboth Church were Wade Hampton McKenney, Jesse Williams, Columbus Jackson, and Drayton Watts.[12]

Some of the mob had taken Frank Latimer and were trying to fasten a noose around his neck, but E. C. Rice, brother of the newspaperman James Henry Rice, Jr., interposed himself and persuaded the mob that Latimer was "a good Negro whom he knew to be innocent." This pattern—capturing a black man, tying him up, putting a noose around his neck, seeking his confession, and asking white men for testimony prior to executing or freeing the captive—was followed consistently during the Phoenix Riot. In this case the mob readily believed Rice, and Latimer was released.[13] Men in the small group that remained talked among themselves and decided that they had recognized Essex Harrison and Ben Collins as the two black men who had been wounded in the first shooting at Rehoboth Church. They agreed that they must find those two the following day. Harrison and Collins succeeded in reaching the Stockman farm, where they could hide, bleeding and untended in the rain and cold that long night.

The ninth day of November, the second day of the riot, thus ended with this driving rainfall. Communication with the outside world was now impossible because some Democrats had cut the telephone wire to Watson's store. However, the young reporter for the *State* in Columbia, James Allen "Jim" Hoyt, was able to obtain full details from the men who had tied up suspects and shot them. He took notes, and then all the men sat in Watson's store, drinking coffee and listening to the rain on the roof. They knew that this rain was washing away the blood of Bose Ethridge and Tom Tolbert. Although they did not yet know the details, they knew that the blood of other Republicans and Democrats was being washed away in many places in the county. Watson arranged to restring his telephone wire. All awaited the dawning of November 10.

Daybreak brought no real sunrise, but it did bring a gray light and less rain. It brought as well August Kohn of the *Charleston Courier*. Kohn was publisher James Hemphill's lynching writer, and he traveled the South to report on lynchings and riots. His coverage was thorough, but his signature gave him license to editorialize, and he always closed his accurate and balanced accounts with two messages. The first message was that white people must stop the killing, but the second message was that black people must forget about equality and accept Jim Crow. Kohn had gone to Wilmington, North Carolina, that same week to cover the large and terrifying—and fully expected—race riot there after tumultuous elections and Wade Hampton–style Red Shirts had restored white Democrats to full power in that port city. Now, however, this special reporter was pulled from his Wilmington assignment and sent to this little place where no story had been expected.[14] The *Courier* people knew from fragmentary reports that this South Carolina riot was a big story, deserving their biggest reporter—and they also knew that the rival *State* paper was there first, albeit with the "cub reporter" Jim Hoyt.

Despite his youth Hoyt was by now something of a veteran of lynching stories, for he had already seen the bodies of four men who were executed, and he had listened with a dread fascination as the killers told in full detail how they had done their work. Hoyt had even ridden in the buckboard with Sheriff McCaslin, and in so doing he had been in charge of the lawman's bloodhounds. Hoyt greeted his much older and much more experienced colleague and rival Kohn and caught him up on the events. Both reporters from now on traveled with the vigilance squadrons with Kohn even stopping activities from time to time in order to verify someone's name or occupation. The squadron went first to the Stockmans' place, having learned that Collins and Harrison were "holed up there." Vigilance men insisted that Collins had not only fired a pistol during Election Day at Watson's store, but had attempted to secure another weapon when he ran out of ammunition. Finding the two, the vigilance men shot Collins dead at once, and then they took Harrison prisoner. Collins's body was left on display at the Stockman place. It was important to these men that Republicans of both races see his body, and see that there was no safety at the Stockmans'.

There was less certainty about Harrison's role, so he was marched back over to Rehoboth Church. He was given the chance to confess, which he did not do. Kohn interrupted the interrogation to talk with Harrison to make sure of the spelling of his name and to take a statement from him. Harrison was tied up and placed in the middle of the four corpses, "now putrid . . . and some of them in a posture of sitting against trees." He never confessed, as Kohn's notes made clear, but the vigilance men determined among themselves that he was guilty, and they began to shoot him. Hoyt reported that Harrison "was shot at from so many directions that the executioners endangered each other. He dropped dead, across the corpse of one of those killed the day before, and he was left." White vigilance groups continued to search for suspected black activists. There were many Democrats who insisted that the African Americans Will White and Joe Circuit had been on the piazza and had fired their guns there on Election Day. Platoons went through the counties of the Carolina and Georgia Piedmont looking for White and Circuit, intending to bring them back to Watson's store.[15]

Meanwhile an unidentified vigilance man raised the cry that the Tolberts must be captured and punished. This fellow, although never named in any of the many newspaper accounts, was certainly memorable to look at. He was a burly man with a huge and tangled beard, and he rode a large gray horse. Most memorable was the patch he wore over one eye, lending an extra intensity to his uncovered good eye. "The Tolberts!" he cried, and other Democrats took up the slogan and followed the unknown horseman on searches through the several Tolbert plantations.

In fact most of the Tolbert family members had already escaped before the unknown leader led his hunting party. Red Tolbert had somehow gotten to Columbia and from there had ridden a train incognito to Washington, D.C., where he revealed his identity and met with some officers of the Republican Party and some assistants to President William McKinley. Red still harbored the notion that McKinley would take action, if not to protest voting fraud, then at least to send federal marshals and perhaps troops to protect Republicans of both races in Greenwood. Other Tolberts fled to other places, apparently near South Carolina's only towns of size: Greenville, Columbia, and Charleston. Exceptions were the gravely wounded Elias Tolbert and a fifteen-year-old named Kim Tolbert. Elias, who was too hurt to move, remained safely hidden at Stockman's. Although vigilance men were frustrated that they could not find Elias, the missing man was gaining sympathy. Neighbors pointed out that he was never involved in politics and that his wife spoke out loudly and loyally at Democrat meetings even though women did not usually attend and certainly did not speak at such meetings since they could not vote. As for Kim, he was so young and so badly wounded that most mob members felt sorry for him.

In some way, however, the growing sympathy for Elias and Kim—the most helpless members of the Tolbert tribe—increased anger against John and Red. Frustrated in their efforts to find these three, the vigilance groups seized the

Tolbert lands. Democrats then issued a remarkable statement saying "we are not capitalists"—by which they evidently meant to say that they were not speculators who would take economic advantage of the events. The Democrats announced that the Tolbert farms would be worked as normal, that the November cotton harvest continued, and that payments and collections of and for all workers of both races would be handled fairly. Most extraordinarily, the Democrats announced that they would hold any profits in trust and would return lands and any accumulated profits to the heirs and assigns of the Tolberts as soon as surviving family members agreed to quit politics in the area and return to farming. The statement thus made it clear that John and Red Tolbert were going to be killed, but that no Democrats would seek any economic gain from the promised political executions; and other Tolberts were invited to return to the circle of the community by disavowing politics.

Besides this revolutionary appropriation of land for political reasons, many Democrats in less organized fashion yelled for the execution of more black Republicans. Many in the vigilance groups insisted that a dozen identified African Americans who had shot guns at Watson's remained at large. The eleventh day of November thus ended with the seizure of Tolbert lands and with small—and less well-organized—vigilance bands searching in the wet and the dark for Tolberts and for their alleged allies among the black farmers.

The twelfth of November featured a "mass meeting of the citizens of Phoenix," though of course "citizens" described only white people. Hezekiah Mays and other African Americans stayed away. Indeed a young white woman wrote to her boyfriend, "The majority of the Negroes are still afraid to come back to their homes and work."[16] The site for the mass meeting was Watson's store. Although Hoyt estimated that perhaps two hundred or more white farmers attended, he also noted that members of the self-elected Committee of Safety did all the talking. The chairman of the ten-man committee was W. H. Stallworth, the landowner on whose plantation Bose Ethridge had died; the secretary was large landowner J. W. Bowers. The committee had definitely met the evening before in order to draft the Watson Store Resolutions—also called the Phoenix Resolutions—and the "excellent English" of the document suggested that it had been drafted and then revised and then refined by some well-educated people. The crowd, while reportedly agitated, listened attentively and then adopted resolutions blaming Tom Tolbert and "certain Negroes" for starting the hostilities and asserting that "the first shot fired was the one that killed Ethridge and [it] was fired by a Negro." They also claimed that "deluded Negroes" had been misled by "'the evil influence exerted by John R. Tolbert, R. Red Tolbert, Joseph W. Tolbert, Thomas P. Tolbert and Robert L. Henderson" and expressed the belief that "their further residence in Greenwood County or its vicinity will tend to imperil the lives and property of both the white and colored people."

After the people at the mass meeting shouted their loud support for these resolutions, the document was forwarded to newly elected State Senator C. A. C. Waller of Greenwood, who officially "approved" them. On November 15 a special session of county court was called. There the resolutions were again approved, and the special session heard assurances by Sheriff McCaslin that the property of the Tolberts would be protected for their heirs and assigns; significantly the sheriff did not attempt to guarantee the safety of any Tolberts who returned to the county. On the same day, a grand jury was convened to hear evidence concerning the killing and wounding of white Democrats. The grand jury officially declared that blame lay with "the incendiary speeches made to the colored voters at midnight meetings by the Tolberts, thus inciting the Negroes to violence and lawlessness."

Then and decades later Hoyt was struck by the fact that the grand jury made absolutely no inquiry at all into the reasons for the deaths of the African Americans. Hoyt knew exactly who the "lynchers" were, and he contended: "No attempt had at any time been made to conceal their identity. What they did was done openly and boldly, with uncovered faces and in the sight of all men." Their names could have been easily secured, although Hoyt did not write down those names on the scene or in his 1935 recollections.

With the grand jury findings, the Greenwood and Edgefield newspapers declared that the troubles were ended. The *Greenwood Index* printed a statement by Elias Tolbert when the severely wounded man was finally discovered at the Stockman farm: "I find that in many things I have made mistakes. That the two races cannot act together in the formation of a Government and that the county should have white supremacy, that the Anglo-Saxon race should predominate, and hereafter I intend to stand shoulder to shoulder with the white people to [*sic*] all in my power to have a government that will protect every one alike, but let it be made by the white people."

Thus joining the Democratic Party of his wife, Elias Tolbert, who had never been active among the Republicans, was welcomed back into the circle of the white people. The *Index* reported under the heading "Closing Chapter" that the much-maligned Robert L. Henderson and Red Tolbert and J. W. Tolbert were "waited upon" in Washington, D.C., by a "committee of citizens" who told them that their return to Greenwood County would bring their deaths. President McKinley also met with Henderson and the two Tolberts, and informed them of his concern that they not return to Greenwood.[17]

By December, Henderson had issued a statement to the white people of his hometown: "[I] have always when the occasion offered itself tried to impress the Negro with his insignificance & inferiority as compared to white people. I am full blood Anglo-Saxon & have as good pedigree as any Caucasian. As you can testify & you know too that I was always active in keeping the nigger [*sic*] in submission to the whites."[18]

Given his close work with African Americans in the campaign of 1898, Henderson's statement was shocking, and its immediate effect was to convince people of both colors that he was not to be trusted at all.[19] While no white people forgave Henderson that year, he was eventually able to return as part of the community. About ten years later, long after African American voting and the Republican Party were only memories in Greenwood, all the fugitive Tolberts returned, apologized to the members of the community for their actions and thoughts, and reclaimed their farms and their accumulated money held in trusteeship. On the other hand, many black families left and never returned. Two men, Will White and Joe Circuit, fled forever because they were marked for execution; yet the much-discussed "Negro exodus" obviously included much larger numbers of black folk who had never been on the infamous piazza and who left in search of a safer place to live and work. As the 1898 Christmas season came on, the *Index* reported that fully 104 African Americans had left in a group for the Mississippi Delta, a region then advertising itself as being safer for black people than Greenwood. August Kohn reported such a "large exodus" of black farmers that there could be a "labor shortage" in Greenwood County, and indeed the census records for 1900 show a decline of 4,526 in the population of Edgefield, Greenwood, and Abbeville since the previous census, that is 7 percent in a region where black population had been increasing at the rate of nearly 11 percent per decade.[20]

The white Democrats lost Bose Ethridge, and white Democrat Stuart Miller never made a full recovery from his wounds. There was also a white Democrat named Kennedy McCaslin, who was in a labor dispute and killed by people of color; and the white people always said that he was killed as part of the riots. The people of color did not all agree, but many acknowledged that McCaslin's death was because he was white and because it was the time of the Phoenix Riot.

The white Republicans lost Tom Tolbert and James M. Collins, Republican candidate for postmaster of Abbeville, a relative of the Tolberts and one who often "presided over Negro meetings."[21] The patriarch John R. Tolbert was wounded, along with his grandson Kim and Elias Tolbert, the man who publicly recanted his Republican identity. Most white and black people, however, counted Elias as a white Republican victim of the Phoenix Riot.

The Republicans of color who died were Wade Hampton McKenney, Columbus Jackson, Essex Harrison, Drayton Watts, Ben Collins, George Logan, and Jesse Williams. There was also Eliza Goode, a woman of color who was shot and died in her house during the riots. The white Democrats said that she was not killed because she was black, but they did admit that she was killed by some of the mob that had got out of control. The people of color counted her among those killed because of her color, and the white people did not count her. One man of color, Charley Hall, was beaten but was saved from lynching by Sheriff McCaslin; and an unidentified man of color was shot dead by John Fell in the nearby Smithville district of neighboring Abbeville. Still another unidentified "young Negro boy," who was driving a wagon for landowner Stan Marshall, was "pistol-whipped" by white vigilance men in Phoenix—an incident reported by Ella Dargan in her correspondence with her fiancé Harry LeGare Watson, who was the son of Johnson Sales Watson.[22] The people of color counted Hall as a wounded victim of the riot, and they counted the two unidentified men as fatalities of the riot, but the white people did not count Hall or the two unidentified men.

People of both colors said they were disturbed that Governor William H. Ellerbe "took no cognizance of the situation at all," as young Hoyt reported. The governor's papers show that he received quite a lot of correspondence, especially telegrams, from people who called the riot "the War." Ellerbe's outgoing mail and his statements indicate that he was "cognizant" of the situation, encouraging sheriffs in the counties of Greenwood, Edgefield, Abbeville, and Saluda to find and arrest anyone who committed violence and paying for additional sheriffs' patrols out of state funds. He also offered rewards in the "hard cash" so seldom seen by farm workers of either color. Yet it is certainly the case that neither black people nor white people believed Governor Ellerbe had done all he ought to bring peace and justice to Greenwood. He was subject to particularly heavy criticism from antilynching editor Narciso Gonzalez of the *State,* but Tillman's white-supremacy Democrats were equally scathing.[23]

Thus there were at least twenty men and women who were killed or badly wounded during the days of the Phoenix Riot when Bennie Mays was four years old. His first memories included fighting, rioting, death, and flight. He remembered too that Hezekiah had saved their lives by playing the Sambo for the night riders; and he remembered that Hezekiah was taking a risk in staying on Rambo land, which was located on the road favored by Democratic night riders, when other black people were actively fleeing the scene of the Phoenix Riot.

A RAMBO BOY AFTER THE RIOT

1898–1911

As 1898 ended and as the new year of 1899 came on, the *Charleston Courier* proclaimed that the "War" was over and that the killing had stopped, declarations repeated more loudly by the local newspapers, especially the *Greenwood Index,* in which the Mays family read the editorials by publisher S. H. McGhee and the byline stories by Kohn. Most of the white people repeated over and over that the killing was finally done with and "War" was over.[1]

Yet the killing did not end, for young Bennie still saw white mobs searching for members of his and other black families—sometimes right on Mr. Bill Mays's lands that Hezekiah Mays rented—and he still saw other black people hiding out in the woods near the cotton fields where he worked. The farm that Hezekiah Mays rented from Bill Mays lay alongside a country thoroughfare traveled by many, including Klansmen in full regalia. From that early age, Bennie learned not to talk to the groups looking for African Americans nor to the African Americans who were in hiding. Among the white folk, schoolteacher Ella Dargan wrote of one landowner that "out of the thousand Negroes he has on his place only one talked as though he would stay with him another year." She noted that it was unusual to see black children at play near white people, and in general "the Negroes around here are scared."[2]

Such white recollections confirm what the mature Mays remembered from his early days in Rambo: "It certainly 'put the rabbit' in many Negroes. . . . Few dared to stand up to a white man. When one did, he got the worst of it. It was not unusual to hear that a certain Negro had been run out of town, or fearing he would be, had left the county before 'they' could get him. Most Negroes grinned, cringed, and kowtowed in the presence of white people."[3]

There was yet good land and good weather for the rest of the harvest. Late November and early December of 1898 featured cold nights and short days, but there was no killing frost, and the fluffy cotton bolls sat there in the fields, waiting to be picked. In the Bible, Jesus says to "lift up your eyes, and look on the fields; for they are white already to harvest."⁴ But who would pick the cotton?

Cotton prices were low, "nickel cotton" folks said, although you might get six or seven cents a pound. In addition to the 104 black people who had left right after the killings, hundreds more black folk—and even a great number of white folk—left, pulled away by the hope of better cotton prices or real wages somewhere else. So many black people left in that season that the tiny short-haul Savannah Valley Railroad filled its Jim Crow cars full with African Americans going west. The Jim Crow passenger cars were a new practice, just enforced that year under Governor Ellerbe, as was the careful segregation of the railroad stations. Even local white people were surprised by the effects of the new laws, and they noticed how seldom they "passed" black people. Looking back years later, Benjamin Mays could scarcely remember seeing white people when he was young. After 1898 Greenwood County became an extremely segregated little world, with the races much more separated than in the decades before the Phoenix Riots.⁵

The people of Hezekiah Mays's extended family, and people of other black families, called it "the exodus," and the white lords of the land called it the same thing; but black people used the term to signal deliverance while Bill Mays and other white landowners used the term to signify disaster as their cotton crops sat there untended. So many black folk left so often in such a short time that Bill Mays and other white landowners grew uneasy. They talked to railroad agents, the sheriff, and finally the governor. Governor Ellerbe even wrote to a judge in Memphis with a governor's requisition order to return African Americans "stolen" from Greenwood. Police in Memphis actually detained a white agent and his recruits on their way to the Mississippi Delta because of the governor's requisition order, but a judge in that city released the agent and all the workers so that they could continue their journey to a better and safer land. The judge sent word to the Governor Ellerbe, telling him that there was no proof of "theft" because a free man could go anywhere he wanted to go and work for anybody he wanted to; and these black workers certainly did not want to work any longer in South Carolina. So the white lords of the land were left to gnash their teeth over the "exodus."⁶

These white lords insisted that the killing was done with, that the rout of the Tolberts, segregation of the trains, and voting disfranchisement had set everything right and that now there would be peace. They said that black folk could stay and make real money, paid in cash, to get in the harvest. Only a few black people took the white men up on their offer. Indeed within a few years there was no more Rambo of black folk and after that no Phoenix of white folk. After some years the community vanished, with only Epworth nearby to offer postal service, feed, seed, and dry goods. But Hezekiah and Louvenia Mays and their relatives chose to stay in diminished Rambo for this season and the next several seasons. Julia, who could remember such days of blood from long before the Phoenix Riot, could help with her faithful prayers. She could tell them that the white people always acted so and that one must trust the real Lord through yet another "time of troubles" as the Bible said. It was hard for the good people to sing the Lord's song in a strange land "by the rivers of Babylon," but Julia reminded her people that they had done it before and could do it again. Her words gave strength and comfort. There were the seven children, "growing strong and gaining favor in the eyes of God and man," and they could help Hezekiah and Louvenia on the farm.

Hezekiah had saved Bennie by bowing before the white horsemen, and now he saved all of them by bending to the first ingathering of the season. He paid Bill Mays what he owed for rent on the land, and he paid what he owed at the dry-goods store, likely Johnson Sales Watson's place with the infamous piazza. After paying his debts and making sure he could feed his mules and still buy fertilizer and seed for the next season, there was still enough left over to buy things that he and Louvenia and Julia and the seven children could not make for themselves: a few tools and a few warm clothes. As before and after, Hezekiah did not have to share the crop. He was a renter not a sharecropper, and he owned his own tools and two strong mules. He had bowed to save his Bennie's life; he had bent to pick the cotton bolls out; but that bowing and bending was to protect and to provide for his family. He had not bowed or bent other places, and he could walk tall and straight in Rambo among black people. He could even walk so in the white people's Greenwood on Saturday business days when farmers came into the old trading center and self-consciously New South town to buy equipment and clothes of better quality than those available at Watson's.

Julia and Louvenia reminded him that he owed his God. The Reverend James F. Marshall reminded Hezekiah that God had protected them from the killing by the white forces. The Reverend Marshall reminded Hezekiah, Louvenia, and Julia that the Mays children must learn their Bible lessons. They certainly did so, and by the time he was nine years old, Bennie could recite passages for the assembled adults in the congregation at their country church, Mt. Zion in Rambo.

The Reverend Marshall still had his fine church, the Morris Baptist Chapel in Greenwood, a church nice enough that black preachers from all over South Carolina had come there in the quiet days before the Phoenix killings. Even the white newspapers had taken notice of the grand gathering there. White reporters wrote about how polite and upright were the "colored preachers" who gathered at the Reverend Marshall's church to talk about the right way to

Benjamin Mays's eldest sister, Susie Mays Glenn, and her husband,
Samuel Glenn, revisiting the so-called Brick House School, where
the Mays children received their early education. Courtesy of the
Moorland-Spingarn Research Center, Howard University.

worship one God. That was before the Phoenix killings. After the killings the
same reporters and editors, especially S. H. McGhee of the *Greenwood Index,*
still talked about how the Reverend Marshall was a "good colored man" and
how the people at his church were good people and were not a problem. When
Marshall visited Mt. Zion Church in Rambo, the white folk there said the same
things about this preacher and his congregation.[7]

This good preacher was also a teacher. In fact he organized and inspired the
Brick House School, which the black children attended in Rambo. (Though
the school building itself was wooden, it stood close to a prominent brick structure and thus took the name "Brick House School.") This school was as important to the black folk of Rambo as Mt. Zion Church. The Reverend Marshall
likely saw little difference between preaching and teaching. After all he could
tell them that Jesus Christ was the great teacher, the master teacher. In his own
later years, Bennie Mays could see a difference between the Reverend Marshall's
preaching and his teaching, and Mays came to regret that small difference. In
the classroom Marshall stood erect and fretted over the posture of the students
in his charge. He wanted them to "declaim" correctly in the fashion of the

southern old-school education that once belonged exclusively to the children of planters, who were educated gentlemen and ladies taught to stand straight, speak correctly, and be dignified, "as good as anybody!" Since he himself possessed only a grammar school education, Preacher Marshall ensured that the college-educated teacher, Miss Ellen Waller, directed the children. A graduate of Benedict College in the state capital, Ellen Waller was the daughter of Tom Waller, a light-skinned man who owned hundreds of acres and who actually hired croppers and renters to work his cotton lands. Bennie Mays knew of only three other African Americans in Greenwood County who held college degrees in those early days of the twentieth century. The African American people in the county called the Wallers "the quality," and the Reverend Marshall was pleased that Ellen Waller set a high tone for the Brick House School.

Yet in the Mt. Zion Church, the Reverend Marshall left off his own Brick House rules, for he preached to the unlettered, who were after all the larger portion of his flock. In so preaching, he "whooped and hollered." In the fashion of country ministers, he "whooped the benches," moving through the congregation waving his arms and yelling until the worshippers too were on their feet and shouting with emotion. It is not known for certain what young Bennie Mays thought of such preaching, but the mature man did not kindly recollect "whooping the benches." He regretted this aspect of the Reverend Marshall's preaching, insisting instead on careful study of the Bible in Hebrew, Greek, and Latin. The word, the logos, Mays decided in his mature years, was indeed inspired, but its meaning could be found and followed only by diligent, painstaking, thoughtful study and discussion, not by the country preacher's whooping and hollering.[8]

But these were the self-consciously analytical judgments of a theologian looking back a long way. When he was a child, what Bennie heard was that Preacher Marshall possessed "special powers." Louvenia had gone to him early, and she had him baptize each of her children by full immersion when they were old enough to "declare intent." She pushed them to ask for baptism, but they did have to ask—and not when they were too young. Louvenia agreed with her minister that the Colored Methodist Episcopalians were committing nothing less than an "abomination of desolation" in baptizing infants who were too young to declare intent. Although the Reverend Marshall roomed and boarded with a friendly C.M.E. clergyman while staying overnight in Rambo, he cordially consigned all the infant baptizers to a flaming hell that he vividly described for his own Baptist parishioners.

This hell was also the spoken destination for the adults who avoided baptism, and for some years—long years indeed for the steadfast Louvenia and Jesse—Hezekiah was such a one who declined immersion. Hezekiah seldom even visited the Mt. Zion church. Preacher Marshall talked in his sermons about those in Rambo who did not join the church, and he promised to preach them "smack into Heaven" or "smack into Hell" according to their own choices of accepting Christ or rejecting him. Louvenia and Jesse knew that the minister was speaking of their Hezekiah; they told him so often. Then in 1886 an earthquake struck Greenwood County, something unheard of in South Carolina and indeed something still spoken of with "fear and trembling." When the ground quit moving, many of the black farming men came forward for full confession and declaration of intention. Among that large number was a much-humbled Hezekiah Mays.

Bennie Mays had not been born yet to see his father's transformation experience and conversion, but he did witness firsthand what happened to people who "make a pretense of repentance." As he wrote in his memoir:

> I was present at a Church Conference when a young couple appeared who had been sexually intimate; the young woman was pregnant. They admitted what they had done. Marshall advised the young man to marry the girl. With his right hand lifted toward heaven, Marshall told the young man that if he didn't marry the young woman and live with her, fulfilling the duties of a husband, something unspeakably bad would happen to him. The young man married the girl on the spot, but then went on his way, never assuming any responsibility for his wife or child. Not long afterward, he was killed one midnight, so viciously beaten to death with a club that his brains were spattered all over the ground. In the summer of 1968, my sister [Susie] told me Negroes believed that a certain white man had killed this young man because he was hanging around a Negro woman with whom the white man was having relations. Neither whites nor Negroes did anything to apprehend the murderer. This apparent fulfillment of Marshall's prophecy in the case skyrocketed his prestige in the community. Thereafter nobody wanted Preacher Marshall to "put bad mouth" on them.[9]

For his part, the Reverend Marshall saw at once that Bennie Mays was a special student, one who could become an educator and minister, and the teaching preacher took special pains to help him. If a student at Marshall's school missed a day for any reason, he was "sent to the foot," or the rear, of the class on his return. Far from frustrating Bennie, this system engaged him fully. Good performance moved the returning student progressively, seat by seat, toward the "head," or front of the class. When Bennie had to miss class, he recalled, "I was always glad to go to the foot," because he knew "I would soon be right back at the head." Marshall and all his teachers noted Bennie's fine qualities, and Miss Waller in particular took special pains with the star student. Young Bennie was delighted that this "pretty woman" who was "quality" considered him a scholar and bound for a life as teaching preacher like the best of the biblical nation of Benjamin. Her warm support helped him to forget the other heritage of the Benjaminites, the ravening wolves. She encouraged him to work with the Lord to overcome the white power structure by force of Benjaminite knowledge instead of by force of Benjaminite arms.[10]

So enthusiastic were Miss Waller and the Reverend Marshall about young Bennie's prospects that the other children in Hezekiah Mays's family began to share this dream that the youngest of the seven remaining would go to college and become a man of books, especially a man of the Book. Louvenia and Julia spoke long and often about this goal; and they who could not read pushed Bennie to read more and more, to declaim with a straight back and a strong will, and to write as well as any of the white children who were over at the large and new white school. They did not talk about Harry LeGare Watson, who graduated from the University of North Carolina and became an important newspaperman in Greenwood town. They did not talk about Senator Tillman, who still had his lands in nearby Trenton and who had started Clemson College. Nor did they talk about the professors in Columbia at the University of South Carolina. No, they did not tell Bennie about these white fellows. Instead Louvenia and Julia talked about Preacher Carroll over in Edgefield, who wrote so well that the white people read what he wrote. Even Senator Tillman had sat and talked with Preacher Carroll for a newspaper interview. They talked about President Thomas E. Miller, who ran the South Carolina State College in Orangeburg. They talked about Paul Laurence Dunbar, the black Orpheus, who sang for the gods—and for the black folks. They did not tell Bennie about these black heroes because they considered themselves inferior to the white heroes or because they wanted the boy to stay safely "in his place." They told him because Paul Laurence Dunbar or Preacher Carroll or President Miller was "as good as anybody!" And they intended that Bennie be as good as anybody.

Hezekiah Mays certainly believed that he and all his family were as good as anybody. All around him black people and white people were falling deeper into debt, drowning in the sharecropping system. But he cleared his debts each harvest season, and he rented carefully, sixty acres if he had three good mules, forty acres if he had only two. He never had fewer than two mules. He never let a debt stay on the country store's ledger book after the harvest season. He was not Tom Waller, and he was not Preacher Carroll. He was not of that quality. But neither was he Wade Hampton McKenney, who was gone to dust for defying the white forces, nor was he Will White, always on the run, often far across the Savannah River, with white sheriffs in three states watching for him. The McKenney family and the White family were poor, for a man was no good for feeding his family if he was dead in the clay or running out of the Saluda valley. Hezekiah was not going to see the Mays family suffer so.

Hezekiah was proud that his boys could do arithmetic for themselves and could tell at once if a white landowner or a white gin operator was trying to cheat them. Bill Mays spoke straight with Hezekiah Mays and his boys, and he dealt with them true—Bill Mays said it was because he loved them "in their place." Hezekiah Mays said it was because Mr. Bill Mays needed their work when the fields were "white already to harvest," as the real Lord, Jesus, had said. And Hezekiah said that Mr. Mays paid the boys square because they could read and count and see for themselves that they were treated right.

All over the countryside, all the other renters and certainly all the share-croppers of white and black families insisted that they were routinely cheated, even by Bill Mays; but these others could not read and write a contract and could not calculate what they were owed, and so they could not prove anything. The Bible says that a laborer deserves his wages; but Mr. Mays's book or Mr. Watson's book said only that the laborer owed his debts. Bennie was well aware that Hezekiah Mays had helped his entire family in their dealings, and that they were protecting themselves in their dealings while neighbor black farmers could only suffer without protection.

For these reasons Hezekiah Mays kept his seven children in Preacher Marshall's Brick House School until they could do the fifth grade work of arithmetic and English. That alone put them ahead of half of the people of color and a third of the white people in Greenwood County. He even let his son Hezekiah—called "H.H." by the Mayses—complete the high school degree, something that set H.H. apart from folk of any color in the valley of the Saluda River. Hezekiah was proud and thankful that H.H. could so use his mind to protect himself when he put his hands to work in the cotton. And Hezekiah was no less proud of the way that his other children could so use their minds to protect themselves.

But Hezekiah was not happy with all his children and everything that they wanted. In country talk, sometimes they wanted to "cut a hog" in the wrong season, that is to "show off" and "play the fool." And such cutting a hog fed no children, secured no family, and in fact could push a family toward the share-cropper's trap. Will White had cut a hog, and Wade Hampton McKenney had cut a hog when they challenged the white forces. But there were other ways to cut a hog, like spending your credit on fancy clothes or fancy wagons to take girls to dances and parties. When he was sober, which was most of the time, Hezekiah cast a clear eye on his children and told them steady and plain to cut no hog and play no fool. But on those awful days when he was drunk, Hezekiah rolled a rheumy eye toward them and gnashed his teeth and blew his breath of strong spirits into their faces and beat them with his strong hands. His sons would cut no hogs. His sons would play no fools. They were as good as anybody, but they were not better than their father.

Brother John was often the object of Hezekiah's wrath. John, a hard and effective worker, was the "sport" of the family, and he carefully set aside a portion of his wages to use for his sport. Where most farmers drove the same rickety wagon on the farm and to market and to church, John bought himself a sturdy new wagon with hard-rubber wheels—the tires were gleaming white. And he bought a fine mule, which he named Kate, and he and Kate drove the wagon to church meetings and to social gatherings with pretty girls who sat proud beside him on the solid new buckboard. Sober, Hezekiah warned John that white people hated sporty blacks. Drunk, Hezekiah leaned close and yelled that the "white bastards" would kill the "fool nigger." Drunk or sober, Hezekiah likely spoke the plain truth on this issue, but John somehow survived to cut the hog and still meet the rent. Eventually he borrowed a sum of money to work his own farm separate from Hezekiah. Later John moved to Cleveland, becoming completely independent of Hezekiah—but not before he made sure of his younger brother Bennie's education.

By contrast James Mays was no sport at all, and he received fewer admonitions, suffering only when Hezekiah's drunken rages swept in all the Mayses. Yet James unwittingly probed the rules of jealousy among the poor farmers. Working hard and saving his money, James married to start a proper family on his own rented farm. Never boasting, never cutting the hog, James and his bride learned happily that they would inherit a piece of good land from her father. It was much like the wonderful story of Achsah and Othniel in the Bible, where the worthy bride asks her father, Caleb, for land, and he gives her not only land but "the upper and nether springs" to water that land. But in much knowledge is much grief, as Bennie also read in the Bible,[11] for James's wife died. Although he waited a decent time to marry again, the anguished brother of James's first wife could not abide "two strangers" on his father's land and slew James.

Whether it was Hezekiah drunk or a jealous in-law with a weapon or white men yelling "run, nigger, run," there was much violence and grief in Rambo, and Bennie Mays was often asked to read aloud from Psalm 37 to his sorrowing mother, Louvenia:

> Fret not thyself because of evildoers, neither be thou envious against the workers of iniquity.
>
> For they shall soon be cut down like the grass, and wither as the green herbs.

Trust in the Lord. . . .

. . . and wait patiently for him: fret not thyself because of him who pros-
pereth in his way, because of the man who bringeth wicked devices to pass.
Cease from anger, and forsake wrath; fret not thyself in any wise to do evil.

For evildoers shall be cut off; but those that wait upon the Lord, they
shall inherit the earth.

For yet a little while, and the wicked shall not be; yea, thou shalt dili-
gently consider his place, and it shall not be.

But the meek shall inherit the earth; and shall delight themselves in the
abundance of peace.[12]

The Reverend Marshall arranged for Bennie to declaim before the Mt. Zion
congregation at some of the special Saturday conference sessions. At such times
Bennie reached for something far beyond the approval of the good country
people on those hard benches. On such occasions, from the first time when
he was fourteen, he stood his tallest and sent his voice the farthest on behalf
of magnificence. He reached for what Aristotle called "greatsouledness" and
"highmindedness."[13] Bennie would never sin by arrogance—that is, by claiming great honors and responsibilities beyond what he was warranted. But it was
equally a sin to be falsely humble, to claim less than "your powers and your
desserts" and thus hide from the battles by hiding your "light under a basket."
The magnificent man of profound courage must make his claim "exactly adequate to [his] capacities and desserts, provided they and it are on a grand scale."
As Paul said in his epistle to the Philippians, "let your magnanimity be manifest to all." And so the teenager reached for what the medieval schoolmen call
magnanimatatum—the virtue of the courage to serve the highest purpose. Bennie Mays knew that some boys and some parents would be jealous of his
moment, but he spoke beyond them and their jealousies, deliberately indifferent to the petty resentments of the crowd. He put into practice *magnanimatatum,* and he longed to leave Rambo and study with scholars even more learned
than his beloved Miss Waller.

4

THE STUDENT

1911–1917

It cost money to go to school. The people of the extended Mays family received a portion of South Carolina's revenues for public schools, but that portion was only the lesser part. There were twenty dollars for each white student in a public school, but only two dollars for each dark student in a public school. As for Greenwood County, the local monies were also marked by disparity. The largest group of children, the six of ten in Greenwood who were black, received the smallest portion, a little more than twenty cents of each dollar spent on schools. Greenwood's white boys and girls, who were only four of ten, received more than eighty cents of each dollar spent on schools.[1] The Bible says that in the fullness of time the last shall be first, but in Bennie Mays's teenage years, the black majority was assuredly the very last.

To have a "teacher of quality" such as Miss Waller, to buy books to read and slates to write on and benches to sit on, the people of the Mays family and their dark neighbors turned to Preacher Marshall, who passed the hat at Saturday conferences to keep the Brick House School going. Back in Greenwood, Preacher Marshall was even trusted to "live in" with a white Methodist minister: The public role of "living in" manservant gave him a protection among white people, especially during the riots in this long season of death talking and dream slaying. While Preacher Marshall told the black folk that no Methodist was going into glory, he was grateful to at least one white man who professed the Gospel in the style of John Wesley and Francis Asbury and sang hymns in the style of Charles Wesley. For his part Preacher Marshall was careful to avoid liquor and fornication and any other sort of cutting a hog—and of course after 1898 cutting a hog included any effort to integrate anything, so Preacher Marshall also accepted the new Jim Crow laws of South Carolina.

H.H. and Bennie played and talked and worked together, but they also strove together, and there was a friendly but intense rivalry between the brothers. They competed in picking cotton, and both did well, so well that they had hard cash to put in their pockets even when nickel cotton was the rule. In 1911 the price fell just beneath a nickel. If one of them picked 300 pounds of cotton in a day, he could make $1.25, as much as some grown men might make in a week; and if he kept at that pace, he could make more in a week than most adult farm laborers.[2] One memorable day H.H. and Bennie pushed each other along, and each picked more than 420 pounds of cotton—each earning more than $1.80. But the brothers were dog tired by dusk. Much as H.H. and Bennie loved the physical tests of the body and the feel of the soil and the smell of the air, each boy ached for some kind of job where a man would make $10 a week, every week, without superhuman exertion.

H.H. found his own answer, the same way that older brothers John and James had discovered theirs, leaving their father's farm and starting their own. Eventually H.H. went to New York City, and John to Cleveland, but James went to glory when he was murdered by his jealous in-law. Before each brother left, he encouraged the favored young Bennie to earn a high school degree—and to leave Rambo and the valley of the Saluda River.

Actually Bennie wanted much more than a high school diploma like H.H.'s. Bennie wanted a college baccalaureate degree like Miss Waller's, and he wanted it from a school such as South Carolina State College in Orangeburg or Benedict College in Columbia or even Virginia Union University in Richmond, where Baptists "of great quality" studied. But in 1911 he dared not approach his father about college, since his father grew angry and roared even at the mention of high school.

Instead Bennie talked with the elder Mays women, and he talked with H.H. and John, and only then did they talk with Hezekiah, who at least agreed to let Bennie continue his studies for a high school diploma. Then Bennie pushed harder, asking to attend the good high school in McCormick, a town also in the valley of the Saluda but much closer to the river and some twenty-odd miles from Rambo—and indeed a train ride away that cost at least a half-day's earnings on nickel cotton. Just to catch the train to McCormick, a boy had to make a trip of seven miles to the Ninety Six depot. Once in McCormick, he would need to room and board there so as to avoid the expense of daily train travel; he could work there to pay for his schooling and living expenses, but that money would not make up what Hezekiah stood to lose if Bennie were not working for money at home. Already Hezekiah had lost good hands as John, James, and H.H. took their leave from the white Mr. Mays's farmland. Even with Preacher Marshall pleading Bennie's case, it was a hard argument, but Hezekiah at last relented, albeit with smoldering resentment, and allowed his son to study at the big, new school in McCormick. It was on the train trip to McCormick that Bennie learned how a boy could earn decent summer wages by working as a porter on the passenger cars that served the rich white people.[3] He stored up this knowledge, for the wages from such a job could someday pay matriculation and perhaps even room and board at college. At the school in McCormick, Bennie certainly did benefit, but the greater challenges and rewards there only stirred in him the desire to learn still more by studying at an even better high school.

By the fall harvest of 1911, Bennie had saved enough to pay for room and board at the short-term high school operated on the campus of the South Carolina State College. The train ride completely out of the valley of the Saluda River cost the earnings from the famed 420-pound day of cotton picking, and matriculation cost six dollars per month, a sum that would exhaust the boy's savings altogether. To cover other expenses, Bennie had to work, cleaning the latrines in the school's outhouses. Even then he would need Hezekiah's blessings to go to Orangeburg.

And that blessing was far to seek. One day Mrs. Nola Mays, the white matriarch of the land—and a lady who professed warm affection for Julia and Louvenia—scolded Bennie roundly because he had come to her front door on an errand when "niggers" should approach only to the rear door assigned them. She made it clear to him that he must serve by coming promptly to her home when summoned, but only to the back door and never the front door that opened to white people. It was no minor matter, for Nola Mays realized exactly what was happening, that Bennie was rebelling against his ascribed place in a society built on the careful calibration of role and duty according to station. It was not only Hezekiah who was threatened by the ambitions of the boy who could declaim like an angel at the Saturday conference; now the white lords of the land themselves were threatened, and some of Hezekiah's stiff-necked obstinance can be traced to his knack for surviving by not cutting the hog.

Other white people learned of Bennie's dreams and determined to kill the dreams if not the dreamer; they wanted to push the boy back down into the station where they wanted him. There was the day when Dr. Wallace Payne struck him in the post office in white Epworth, and the next day Bennie was instructed by a white store owner that "niggers" had to walk lightly and humbly. Finally Mr. Bill Mays took Bennie aside and told him plainly that "niggers" did not need to study at any high school, especially not at Orangeburg, something that Bill Mays said also to Hezekiah with equal plainness. Hezekiah roared at his son about his rebellion, and he reminded Bennie that these were the kind white people, the nice ones, and not night riders or vigilance posse members, or drunken white croppers of low quality. Bennie heard all this all right, and later he recorded that, as a teenager, he simply hated all white South Carolinians in the valley of the Saluda River. He recorded also his determination to carry himself with dignity and self-respect and to be a man of magnificence and "greatsouledness." In that day he saw no contradiction in being magnificent with great soul and hating the white people in the valley.

When the fall harvest was done, Bennie was riding the train to Orangeburg for the 1911 short session that ended in February 1912. His father threw a ten-dollar bill at him, a fair sum in that day, but he also uttered an oath; and so Bennie went to high school with no blessing from his father. In fact the boy went with his father's curse. Even so, as he rode the train, he was figuring a way to start attending the long sessions, or full terms, so as to prepare himself more quickly for college—and also so as to escape sooner Hezekiah's work on Bill and Nola Mays's farm. By attending the short terms of 90 days, Bennie would have to study for at least six years to gain his high school diploma; the long terms of 180 days could cut that time in half, and Bennie intended to arrange for those long terms in spite of Hezekiah and the white lords Dr. Wallace Payne, Mr. Bill Mays, and Mrs. Nola Mays.

Arriving in Orangeburg, he was duly impressed by the South Carolina State College, built by Thomas E. Miller, once a powerful politician in South Carolina before the strong arm of the Red Shirts and then the infringements of voting rights silenced the voices of black people, who made up the majority of the state. Miller, called "Canary Bird" because of his light or "high yellow" skin color, remained strong enough to build a college to train the people of color in scientific farming and "normal instruction" for teaching in secondary schools such as the Brick House School or the school in McCormick. The Canary Bird had studied at South Carolina University when it admitted African Americans in 1873, and he saw how that university had done well to set up a college preparatory high school of its own on campus so that entering university freshmen were well prepared for serious college work. Then in 1877 Governor Wade Hampton had closed the doors of the integrated South Carolina University, rechristened the institution the University of South Carolina, and thereafter turned away African American applicants. Finally in 1896 the South Carolina State College, where African Americans could study, had opened in Orangeburg. The Canary Bird, with his own student-day recollections, had immediately set up his own residential high school on that campus so that his college professors could prepare black boys for college challenges.[4]

By 1911 President Miller was long gone, and Bennie Mays was not entirely sorry for him to be gone. For the Mays family members were dark people, and sometimes the "high yellows"—certainly including Miller—set themselves apart from people with darker skin color. State College's president was now Robert Shaw Wilkinson, a man of quality who was too dark to set himself apart from boys and men who were darker. Wilkinson held a degree from the private, predominantly white, Oberlin College in faraway Ohio, and his wife, Marian Birnie Wilkinson, was a woman who insisted that black was beautiful. Marian Wilkinson carried herself proudly. Even the white merchants in Orangeburg called her Mrs. Wilkinson. All faculty members were African American, and all held degrees from good schools: Fisk University, the national center for humanities and the arts in Nashville; Benedict in Columbia; Biddle (later Johnson C. Smith), the Presbyterian school in Charlotte; and Lincoln University in Pennsylvania. Of course to study with these demanding professors in college, Bennie first had to earn his high school diploma.

First he had to be tested to see at what grade level he should commence his studies. These tests were conducted by Julie Mae Williams, another "woman of quality" who held herself proud and erect. She impressed Bennie, and he bent himself to the task of answering her questions. He did well, and especially in the mathematics that so bedeviled most college students. He did so well that Mrs. Williams praised him and then hurried to find Mr. N. C. Nix to tell him that a boy had arrived from the Greenwood countryside and that this boy could do higher mathematics with the best of them.

Mr. Nix could do more than differentiate an equation, for he also knew the way to the soul of an ambitious boy. When students paused long over some problem and protested its difficulty, Mr. Nix loudly told them "the boys at U.S.C. can do this problem!" These words stung, for each boy knew that once black boys had sat in those university halls and worked mathematics problems for college professors who had been trained at the University of Pennsylvania and at Yale University. None of those black students had cried out, and none had been given anything, and now only white students sat in those halls and performed the mathematics exercises.[5] A few students at State College came to believe that God had made them less than white boys at the University of South Carolina. But for the ninety and nine, Mr. Nix's words produced hard work and success, and Bennie swore to be in front of that ninety and nine and never to be among those who cried out and fell behind or even ceased their labors. He swore to do no less than the hated white boys at their university.

For two years Bennie followed only the path permitted by his father: four months (120 days) of school at State College and eight months (240 days) of farm work. Hezekiah resented the four months; Bennie resented the eight months. At school he at once drew attention from several instructors, not only those in the preparatory department but also those involved with the college curriculum. They urged him to attend the high school full-time, finish his degree in three years, and then enter State College. Mr. Nix offered several times to make his own personal appeal to Hezekiah, and it pleased Bennie to be so respected. But he knew that the professor did not understand Hezekiah at all.

At any rate Bennie Mays flourished in Orangeburg with respect for him growing among members of the high school staff. Oftentimes Mr. Nix even had Bennie teach mathematics class, and on occasion the teacher left the room so that the student could teach on his own. Not all boys at the college high school were serious students. Indeed a group called themselves "don't care boys" and called Bennie and the other serious students "odd bookworms." Then Bennie and the other serious students began to use the same terms themselves. Each side stiffened in its dislike of the other, especially when the teaching staff was not around them. One day when Mr. Nix left the classroom to Bennie's charge, some don't care boys acted. One of them pulled a knife on Bennie and said he would cut him. Another don't care boy came forward to hold Bennie in place for the cutting. Bennie broke through the don't care crowd and found Mr. Nix to talk to him about what to do. Professor Nix said it was time to move Bennie to the highest level of high school and for him to attend high school eight months a year in serious preparation for baccalaureate studies at the college. Professor Nix moved Bennie away from the don't care boys, gave him the heavy assignments of the odd bookworms, and told him to prepare for the demanding eight-month curriculum. The nightmare of one afternoon had brought about the dream of a new and better day.

While home, Bennie talked with his father and told him what Professor Nix had said. Hezekiah swore and roared and said he would beat his son. In his grief Bennie realized that he could study for a college degree only by breaking with his father. Could his father kill the dream? Could any mortal kill a dream? From Kings in the Bible, Bennie could read "And Solomon awoke, and behold, it was a dream. Then he came before the ark of the covenant of the Lord, and offered up burnt offerings and peace offerings and made a feast for all his servants."[6]

So resolved, in his third spring planting season after entering the State College high school, Bennie at last had it out with his father, as had his brothers before him. Professor Nix did indeed write a note, but the message only made Hezekiah angry. And his anger involved more than words or even beatings. Hezekiah roared that he would send the sheriff of Greenwood to Orangeburg to pick up the prodigal son. Sheriffs routinely picked up and returned laborers, especially when the laborer was underage and the complainant was a white landowner. If Hezekiah Mays had sought the help of Bill Mays, then it was likely that Bennie would be taken up in Orangeburg and returned to Rambo beaten and bound. The threat was a terrifying one, but Bennie determined to go to Orangeburg anyway, praying that the Lord would soften Hezekiah's heart. Finally the father let his son depart in peace. No matter how mad Hezekiah was with that son, Bennie was bone of his bone and blood of his blood, and he could not bear to see another black man brought home in bindings.

Over the decades the rift between Hezekiah and Bennie finally healed, and the father came to take great pride in his son the rebel, as the son came to take great pride in his father; the man who had saved his life from the vigilance posse, the man who had fed, nurtured, and educated him in the ways and the wiles of southern cotton-farm renting—and the man who had shown him simple decency in the commonsense maxim, "never cut a hog like a fool." All these legacies—life itself, a strong supporting family with a hard-working and self-reliant father, and the common sense not to cut a hog over the trivial and thereby lose the prize—all these things Bennie accepted and used and eventually acknowledged as pearls of great price dearly bought but freely given. In 1913, however, he knew only that an incredibly stubborn father wedded to the ways of the cotton farm refused a kiss of blessing for Bennie's high school and college studies. In those years what this son appreciated was his mother, Louvenia, and his grandmother Julia and his sister Susie, all of whom told him, "you are as good as anybody." And he appreciated how his brother John blessed him and gave him money and showed him that life apart from Hezekiah was not only possible; it was the only way.

There was the matter of financing studies now that Hezekiah had resolved never again to throw a ten-dollar bill Bennie's way. Brother John provided three dollars a month, which paid half Bennie's expenses, but the remaining portion he earned the hard way, standing in the filth and breathing the stench of human waste in the college's outdoor latrines to earn another three dollars monthly. Bennie held those dollars only briefly before handing them over to the college bursar, and still the expenses came. For the years 1914, 1915, and 1916, he had to replace the ten dollars from Hezekiah in another day.

He knew the answer. Those young black men who conducted passengers in the shining Pullman cars made a real salary in the summertime, enough to pay living expenses beyond room and board at the State College high school. They even made enough to set savings aside. Staff members whom he respected as the "fine ladies" at State College assured Bennie that he could serve as well, that his tall and erect frame made him eligible to become a Pullman porter. There was money to be earned in the summer.

But Piedmont blues singers sang that it takes some to get some! First he had to pay seventeen dollars to buy his own porter's uniform: close-cut jacket, styled trousers, and snappy cap. There was no country-store credit arrangement, and he could not pay "on time" or through service. He had to produce seventeen dollars in cash to buy the uniform to wear even for an interview. For a country boy cut off from his father and scrubbing latrines, seventeen dollars sounded like a rich man's purse.

In that same blues song, the desperate singer goes begging from friend to family member but finds that none has money. And so that blues song ends where it begins: "I'm busted!" But Bennie Mays was not fully a blues man, for the blues are not fully a part of the church, and the church brothers and sisters even regarded the Piedmont blues singers as worshippers of a false god. Bennie remained faithful to his true God, and he prayed with his eyes fixed on the prize. When the words of the blues singer grew especially loud, Bennie raised his prayer voice, and then when things were truly desperate, his ears were opened to hear Professor Bollie Levister, who said he would lend the boy the seventeen dollars for the Pullman porter's uniform—and that he could be re-paid over time.

Thus staked, Bennie made himself ready for his interview, attended in his preparations by the fine ladies. They were proved right, for he did well in the interview, and he was thus assured enough money for his high school diploma and college degree, plus travel to places such as Richmond, Washington, or Boston—and this for a fellow whose only railroad travel experience was from Greenwood to Orangeburg, a fellow once overwhelmed by a trip from Green-wood to McCormick.

Among the odd bookworms, Bennie Mays was a little different because he had had to work so hard to get his chance to differentiate equations and read the best literature. He did not forget. He studied hard, inspired by a love of learning and love of family and friends and teachers—but by hate too. White folk would always say that a "colored boy" at a "colored school" was there be-cause he could never compete with the white boys at the white schools. Of course Bennie and all in the State College student body knew men who as boys had once competed quite well in Columbia until the university doors were shut against the people of color. The words of Mr. Nix reminded Bennie that those privileged white boys sat in mathematics chairs denied to him. Those same boys—sons of the powerful, offspring of the four among the ten who owned the land and all good things—also sat in chairs denied to Bennie for literature, the classics, and modern languages. When the love was not enough, the hatred of those boys drove this odd bookworm on into more and more studies. Paul's motivating injunction to "let your magnanimity be manifest to all" was for the angry young Bennie Mays one portion love of family and one portion hatred of white folk.

One thing some don't care boys enjoyed was the favor of female students styled "pretty girls" in Orangeburg. Bennie and the other odd bookworms looked on these girls and were smitten, but sometimes they could do nothing. At times Bennie despaired. Why did these pretty girls hitch their stars to boys who would never be more than sharecroppers—and even to boys who seemed bound for the county chain gang? The "fine ladies" at State College who tutored Bennie surely must have been "pretty girls" themselves when young, and these fine ladies now said that Bennie was their "Exhibit A" for good looks. But the pretty girls looked at Bennie and the other odd bookworms and laughed if they looked at all. Bennie was unhappy about this state of things, but he did not bow his head. He kept his eyes on the prize, even if it led him to no pretty girls.

Yet, as he walked toward the prize, in time he did find his own pretty girl. Ellen Harvin was from Clarendon and Sumter Counties, where the soil was black and not red, and where the river was the Santee and not the Saluda. Her life had not been easy. She rose above difficulties and overcame obstacles— some visible and some invisible but all of them real. It is not recorded why, but her biological mother, Sallie Conley, in the country village of Pinewood in Sumter County, was not the major parent in Ellen's life. For much of her youth, there was also no male parent much involved in her upbringing. Apparently Ellen was raised primarily by Theodosia Richardson, a dark "lady of quality" in Manning, a larger town and the county seat of Clarendon County. Theodosia Richardson raised her children largely by herself. There is no record of a Mr. Richardson helping her or even living with her in the early 1900s. However, Theodosia Richardson did well in bringing up her adopted daughter, Ellen, and her biological son, Rufus Richardson, who was four years younger than Ellen. Ellen and Rufus both studied hard and dreamed large dreams.[7]

Rumors drifted around Ellen, and much is unknown. The Harvin families and their color seem to be key components of the rumors and mysteries. In the valley of the Santee, the Harvins—like the Mayses in the valley of the Saluda— comprised a black family and a white family. The white Harvins owned much land, had owned many slaves, and had fathered some of the black Harvins. Talk persisted that Ellen's father could be a white Harvin and not one of the black Harvins, especially because Ellen was very light skinned, and therefore, folks said, she "must have a lot of white blood." In any case Sallie Conley kept the name "Conley" and did not marry a Harvin of any color. Eventually she married Gilbert DuBose, who sometimes seemed a parent to Ellen and sometimes did not. Sallie never took the name "DuBose," and Ellen kept the name "Harvin." For long years in her adolescence she was part of Theodosia Richardson's somewhat mysterious family of outliers.[8]

The minister to the Richardsons was the Reverend J. P. Garrick, pastor of a church in nearby Sumter. This minister wanted his congregation to be educated, including the girls of the dark families. In Sumter there was a college for people of color, Morris College, and its college professors and administrators, men and women from the black families in that valley, were examples for Ellen and Rufus. Morris College was a small school, and its staff was small, but its professors and administrators stood out in a valley whose black and white people sweated over the hard, hot, harsh work of picking cotton. Encouraged by Theodosia Richardson and by the Reverend Garrick, Ellen and Rufus intended to be more in life than small-time farmers.

By the time she met Bennie Mays, Ellen Harvin had already taught some, and she would teach more, becoming a Jeanes teacher in Clarendon County. These teachers were paid by the one-million-dollar Rural School Fund set up in 1907 by Anne T. Jeanes, a white woman from Philadelphia who wanted black children to learn and knew that white southerners would never pay for quality teachers of color. To become a Jeanes teacher, a young woman had to be smart, to work hard, and to show that she was of high character. The Jeanes Fund Teachers taught other teachers, and the head Jeanes teacher had to supervise the other teachers of color in a given county, leading by example and by giving orders and disciplining where necessary. Ellen became the head Jeanes teacher because she possessed all the requisite qualities. She was not going to lie down with the don't care boys and bear children for sharecroppers. She hitched her star to Bennie Mays, and she told him to go to the "fine colored school" in Richmond and someday perhaps even to a quality New England school founded for the children of the white lords of the North.

Bennie and Ellen became engaged to marry, apparently in 1916.[9] Yet they were careful not to marry too soon. Ellen returned to the Clarendon County schools to teach teachers, to supervise teachers, to serve, to save money, and to wait while her odd bookworm completed his studies. She said that she would wait until he held the baccalaureate degree, even if the wait was until 1920. If "pretty girls" in Clarendon teased Ellen and asked, "where did your Beloved go, o loveliest of women?" she could look them level in the eye,[10] and say "I am my Beloved's, and my Beloved is mine. He pastures his flock among the lilies."[11]

Moved by love as well as by hate, Bennie Mays passed the years quickly in Orangeburg, attaining his high school diploma in 1916. Besides his prowess at mathematics, Bennie also became a devotee of three literary figures, William Shakespeare, Alfred Tennyson, and Henry Wadsworth Longfellow. It was their poetry rather than their plots or themes that moved the young man, and he worked to develop the rolling cadences of their verse for his speeches. At declamation time Bennie's teachers reminded him that an educated man talked differently from a country boy. And so he worked to replace the speech of the valley of the Saluda with the high-toned eloquence of Victorian England. It took effort of course, and sometimes no matter how hard he tried, the echoes of that red hill country still could be heard in his casual speech. But generally the elder scholar of 1978 and the schoolboy of 1916 spoke as a gentleman-scholar with the cadences of Shakespeare, Tennyson, and Longfellow deepening the long narratives of Jesus's parables, the prophets' prophecies, and the Hebrew histories.[12]

Bennie Mays won at least two awards for speeches at the Orangeburg school, and he delivered the 1916 valedictory address, called "Watch the Leaks!" Nothing seems to remain from that speech except its intriguing title, although the elder Mays was careful to preserve other speeches from his youth. In fact Bennie Mays was not proud of that or other speeches he delivered between 1914 and 1916. He always focused more on his audience than on his subject, and thus he aimed speeches of those days at some target in between don't care boys and odd bookworms. His speeches and other work in 1916 were preparation, only marking time before he could enter greater contests in another place. He made himself be patient.

Professor Nix had convinced young Mays to reach high, to seek a graduate degree from the University of Chicago, where the professor himself had studied one glorious summer that he never forgot. To gain entry there, Bennie had to leave his native state altogether to strive and win among the best students in the land, preferably the best students in the North. Thus he set his cap for a fine preparatory school, Holderness School in Portsmouth, New Hampshire. Graduates of this school went on to Harvard and Yale and Chicago. Bennie wrote a letter inquiring about the admissions process, and in late July 1916 the school's president, the Reverend Lorin Webster, wrote back praising Bennie for "your laudable desire to get an education" and professing his desire to help. Nevertheless the Reverend Webster told young Mays that "if I should admit a boy of your race to Holderness School I should lose several students. So I am obliged to decline to receive you." The letter was honest, and Bennie Mays ever preferred the straightforward statement, especially where race was concerned, to the mumbled dissembling favored by some others. It was also definitive, and the response came too late for Bennie to seek entry elsewhere.[13]

There was another possibility, which was suggested by several of the fine ladies and some of the State College professors. African Americans of quality studied at the Baptist Virginia Union University in Richmond. This school could prepare him for a successful entry into a graduate program such as the one at the University of Chicago, even though it could not let him compete at once and directly with the hated and envied white boys. Indeed Virginia Union offered not only opportunities but also perils, which Bennie had to understand. From Nix and from the ladies of quality, Bennie came to understand that being at the top in the South Carolina backcountry would impress no one in the large and sophisticated capital of Virginia. Indeed to reveal much of his backcountry background would "cut a hog" in front of those high-toned folks. Everyone warned him that the white folk of quality in Richmond were much more

powerful than the white folk of the valley of the Saluda River. The white folk
of his home state could beat you and cut you and shoot you and leave you for
dead in a churchyard as a sign to other country black men; but the white folk
of Richmond could cut black people with a smile and a nod and a knowing
glance. These white Virginians could make a black man feel so bad that he
might prefer to be murdered in a backcountry race riot rather than to be humil-
iated in uptown Richmond. But Professor Nix and several of the fine ladies of
the State College campus persuaded Bennie Mays to make his effort among
African Americans of quality in order to go on to greater things and to compete someday with the white students in the northern schools.

Bennie Mays went to Richmond with admiration and awe for the black city
folk there. Those people were really no longer "colored people" as in the country but instead a new people of power and influence who served the high officials. He went to Richmond with no less apprehension about—and in fact
resentment of—the white people there, those people of sophistication and wit
who laughed down long Episcopalian and Presbyterian noses at the white people of the backcountry, such as Mr. Bill Mays. No country doctor in Richmond
struck a black child for entering the front door of a business establishment
there. Indeed no white person needed to use violence for such causes; the fine
stores of that capital city were entered by the front door only by the highest
quality of white people, and all other people—white country folk too—walked
the streets quickly, eyes averted from the gaze of the powerful townsmen. There
was no special Saturday time for settling bills and buying necessaries at the fine
stores; instead the people of color shopped for what they needed on the "nigger side" of the proud city. The Bible says that Yahweh once stretched a plumb
line to mark things in his chosen city, and certainly the city fathers of Richmond had stretched a plumb line down their broad and busy streets.[14] Above
all, Bennie Mays learned never ever to look directly into the eyes of a wife or a
daughter of one of the white Richmond townsmen.

   The love of learning burned deep for the matriculating Virginia Union student, and that flame was matched by the burning hate of the white lords who
had come to town and ruled from mahogany and brass boardrooms instead of
plantation-house drawing rooms. Even these rich and proud must learn of his
magnificence but only in the fullness of the Lord's time. Bennie again made
himself be patient.

His train rides as a Pullman porter allowed the bright-eyed young man to see
Washington, New York, and Boston. The cars served passengers who included
the rich and the powerful, the New York men who held the notes that Mr. Bill
Mays—or even Senator Tillman—owed, and these affluent men made Carolina

backcountry white farmers look like lesser figures, even like rubes and hicks. And the cities made Richmond look quaint, for there was national power in Washington, money power in New York, and historical rectitude and righteousness in Boston. Yet much as he thrilled to these sensations, Bennie Mays was shocked and frustrated to see that New York and Boston and Washington were fully segregated. Damnable Jim Crow, though not spoken of much, existed in the cities of the North. During his train trips he found black men to admire and to copy, and he saw real hope for people of his family and his neighbors and for other black people in the rich and growing urban centers. But those same train trips showed him how much to be feared, and yes hated, were the finely appointed white men who ran the North and who could and did exact tribute from the men who ran the South.

The firemen on the train stoked the engine with mountain coal to move the leviathan of a train north and south; so too did the firemen of damnable Jim Crow stoke the engines of racism to move that leviathan on its travels north and south. Young Bennie Mays straightened his back and learned to let his smile serve him in the face of racism and segregation. He banked his own hot fires, for he understood that this was not the time to make the crooked way straight or to make the high places low.[15] Now was the time for learning and preparation, and Virginia Union was the place to make him ready for much greater fights to come.

Virginia Union University was another Richmond story, one quite different from that told by the humble black folk on the other side of the plumb line in the capital. The university was a good one, and Bennie was surprised to find white men serving on the faculty. It was his first proof that some white men could help a black fellow to learn. Two men in particular helped: mathematics professor Roland A. Wingfield, who saw at once that Mays was a good student of calculus, and chemistry professor Charles A. Hadley, director of the local Young Men's Christian Association (YMCA) facility "for colored" and Bennie's academic adviser. Wingfield and Hadley had both earned their baccalaureate degrees from Bates College in Maine, and each man told the student often that a New England school offered a greater challenge and a better education than those available in the South. Each man encouraged Bennie to attend their alma mater in the rural hills of Maine, far from cotton, tobacco, lynch mobs, and Jim Crow. Each man wrote to Bates College president George Colby Chase urging that the college find a full scholarship for a deserving young man of color from the Carolina backcountry. This talk and these challenges made Bennie light-headed, but he did not forget Mr. Nix's descriptions of the University of Chicago. In the summers of 1916 and 1917, Bennie traveled to Chicago as Pullman porter. With some free time on his hands, he went to see the school built by a portion of John D. Rockefeller's lordly fortunes. The university was immense, and the buildings made the proud capital in Richmond look humble. The student knew from his history how the Medicis built monuments to themselves in Florence, and this monument built by Rockefeller was surely the equal of what they had built. Chicago itself was a city marked by the same damnable Jim Crow as other parts of the mighty nation, but the university was opened to students of any race or ethnicity if they had the money and if they were smart enough. Money and academic achievement: those were the two great challenges. Bennie saw the magnificent school of divinity, and he heard of the rare books in Greek and Latin and the even rarer parchments and scrolls in Hebrew. This was the place for the truly serious, the top-drawer odd bookworms. To study in a graduate seminar here, Bennie would have to show even more than what could be found on a résumé prepared by the people of quality in Richmond. To go to this place, he must do even better at Virginia Union, must then go to Bates and do best of all there. He saw the prize. Chicago was not the prize, but it was the most important step toward it.

Back in Richmond, Bennie strove to show the Virginia Union professors just how good he was. He attacked English, mathematics, German. and Latin. Professor Wingfield, like Mr. Nix before him and like Miss Waller before Mr. Nix, saw a mathematician of the highest quality. Not only that, but Bennie Mays could explain mathematics to boys who found it a terrifying puzzle. There were almost no don't care boys at Virginia Union, but there were students who panicked when faced with symbolic notation and simple substitutions. Bennie was told that half the young men at Virginia Union were failing mathematics, and he was paid a small sum to help them. He enjoyed the work. Although many still failed, Professor Wingfield noted with approval what a fine job Bennie did in tutoring the struggling scholars. News of the backcountry boy's skill and intelligence reached all the way up to George Rice Hovey, the president of the university. President Hovey was pleasantly surprised by this news, but he was unhappy to hear that Bennie was striving for scholarship money to go to a New England school. Hovey called Bennie in, encouraged him in his fine work and his plans for graduate school at Chicago. Hovey was blunt in telling Bennie that New England was not the place for him. Bennie was polite, but he did not change his plans. He redoubled his efforts to be the best student at Virginia Union, for that would move him toward the prize.

Besides his studies, there was life on the streets of Richmond, at least on the colored side of town. There were movie theaters with fascinating images on the screen and with words of dialogue displayed. There was music to accompany the action, what Bennie had learned to call the *melos,* which Aristotle said should be present to complete drama. Sometimes the music was on a piano roll manipulated by a fellow who sat pumping a player piano in the "well" or "pit" recessed beneath the screen and in front of the theater seats. But often there was a real pianist at a good upright set in the pit, and sometimes even a small group with stringed instruments and horns. Then truly there was *melos* to join the drama and make a perfect poetic art, as Aristotle would have it. This then was cinema, and Bennie could appreciate, again because of his Aristotelian studies, that the word came from *kine,* the Greek for action. The word even sounded exciting, and such entertainment was hard to find back in Rambo or even in Orangeburg.

Yet Jim Crow made even his cinema attendance into a problem. White people sat in the banked seats on the theater's sloping floor. Those white folk who chose could sit right by the pit and look in and see the musicians, and they could look up and practically be in the action on the screen in front of them. Others could sit farther back, so to gain a better view of the action while still hearing the music. But no dark-skinned audience member could sit anywhere on the main floor. Instead students from Virginia Union and others who were dark made their way into the theater by climbing an outside metal stairway that was also a fire escape. Nearing the top platform, they could look out over the fine stores and shops of the white folks' city; and then they could enter to find seats in the balcony. The sign for Bennie and his people said "Colored Entrance."

The white people strode across carpet in a decorated hallway and handed their tickets to young men dressed almost as well as Pullman porters. The white people's shoes made soft sounds on that carpet, even if there was a crowd down there, and their voices were soft too, relaxed and sure in the confidence that they were lords of this city. The "colored" people's shoes rang sharp on the fire escape steps, no matter how quietly they tried to walk. Sometimes colored boys talked and laughed louder than they had to, and sometimes the young fellows deliberately shuffled and scraped their shoes on the balcony floor, for that might annoy the white people below. But generally the black theatergoers settled quietly into their seats and watched the images with fascination and awe.

As a serious bookworm, Bennie could look at a film and see the things Aristotle told him to see in the best poetic art. Other people, simple ones who could not even read all the dialogue, could hear the music and see the action, and they seemed to enjoy themselves and have just as much fun as the learned theatergoers. It seemed to be part of what Aristotle called "the good life," this higher form of entertainment in which education and pure joy commingled. As the psalmist said, "Righteousness and peace have kissed."[16]

Or perhaps not. Some of the students back in the dormitories at Virginia Union talked about the Jim Crow balcony and the Jim Crow entrance. Some of them declared that they would not pay to see cinema if they had to use a "colored" entrance and sit in a Jim Crow balcony. Others said they deserved cinema in order to live the good life fully in the Aristotelian sense. Bennie thought, and he declared that he wanted cinema badly, but he wanted it the right way. He wanted to view the action and hear the music while sitting in a seat that he chose. He agreed with the young men who said that they would not attend cinema at all if it had to be Jim Crow cinema. He gave up a personal pleasure because of the people's pain. He resolved to stay away from the cinematic performances he loved. And he never again went into the Richmond theaters with their wonderful *melos* and *kine* because of the damnable Jim Crow balcony and the damnable Jim Crow entrance.

It was time to move on again. Virginia Union had prepared him well, but his best and most challenging teachers and advisers there assured him that Bates College in Lewiston, Maine, could provide him a greater challenge. There was much going on in the world in 1917, not least the terrible war that people called simply the Great War. Rumor persisted that the United States was going to enter the fighting even though President Woodrow Wilson and his Democrats in the 1916 campaign had reminded everyone that "we didn't go to war" when provoked beforehand. On April 2, 1917, the president asked that the United States enter the war, and on April 6 the United States Senate so declared.

Soon thereafter, former president William Howard Taft spoke in Richmond before a crowd that included African Americans, but of course the black folk were separated from the white peoples by another of the white lords' plumb lines. Taft was a huge man and impressive as a judge, which he was; and he was a professor at Yale University. The huge man was said by some to be racist, and certainly the party of Lincoln held few friends now for Bennie's people; although the Democrats were and always had been strictly an "abomination of desolation" as the Hebrew people had put it in describing doers of evil. At the moment all Bennie knew was that most white people hated black people, and his real reason for being there was to find out from this man if this country really was going to get into this cataclysm. For Bennie entry of the United States into the war probably meant being drafted into a Jim Crow company of infantry "grunts," who would be sent across the ocean to fight in Flanders on behalf of freedoms that none of his people had in Richmond. Taft was impressive, and his speech confirmed Bennie's gravest fears: the war was on. We were in, and all hands would be needed.

In August, Ellen's foster brother, Rufus Richardson, was called to Camp Stuart, Virginia, where he was enlisted in the 371st Infantry, an entire regiment made up of drafted black Carolinians and volunteer black National Guardsmen from eight states to train for trench warfare in France. Some 440,000 men of color eventually entered the armed forces, but almost nine in ten of them served as cooks and hospital orderlies and other noncombatant workers. By contrast Rufus Richardson had joined a fighting unit, Company H of the 371st. All the young black men in his company were shouldering guns and wearing the combat gear otherwise reserved for the white men whose guns and laws so terrorized the dark peoples of the valley of the Saluda. Indeed many a white lord of the land and many a scratch-ankle white farmer or textile-mill worker was distressed by the idea of black men armed and trained to use arms. Still more distress came later, when Rufus and his fellow Carolinians of the 371st marched shoulder to shoulder with white French soldiers in the Red Hand division under General Mariano Goybet. The French soldiers accepted the black infantrymen as brothers in arms; the general praised them; French civilians thanked them; and French women welcomed them as friends and sometimes as lovers. Rufus and his fellow black troops were doing their part to upset the upholders of Jim Crow, and surely theirs was good work, to show the hated and stupid white men of the South that anyone could shoot a gun and wear a gas mask—and kiss a white girl in France.[17]

Bennie Mays registered properly for the military draft. Yet he did not want to march in this Great War. The prize in his eye was still justice and peace achieved by an academic, and he was not an eighteen-year-old youngster like Rufus Richardson. Bennie was actually old enough to have finished college, and here he was in 1918 still scheming and straining to arrange things so that he could attend a New England college alongside brilliant if resented white men. Thus, on the forms Bennie marked that he was a candidate for the ministry and would be seeking entrance to a divinity school. This was close to "cutting a hog" with the white draft board people, who seldom showed much interest in "deferring" inductions for African Americans. At the same time, with help from professors Wingfield and Hadley, Bennie filled out forms to attend Bates College. Apparently there was at least one more conference with President Hovey of Virginia Union, who again tried to discourage him. Even while he awaited the ruling of the draft board, Bennie received word from President George Colby Chase that he would be admitted to Bates and would receive full financial aid.

All that summer, as Bennie worked the Pullman cars, he dreamed and schemed. His fellow porters all told him that Maine was too cold for a black man in the wintertime, and they reminded Bennie that he had seen Boston only in the summertime. He remembered the words of President Hovey, who seemed to be saying that Bates College was too challenging for a black man. And he had to remember that the draft board could well decide that a "colored boy" was more useful in the trenches than in preparation for seminary; he would not have their decision before it was time to matriculate. But mostly he remembered the prize, and where it was. It was not in Maine, but the path guided by the prize led through Lewiston. He traveled to Boston as a porter all summer, and at summer's end he traveled to Boston as a passenger, catching another train to Lewiston. He would meet President Chase and the professors who taught professors Wingfield and Hadley. He would meet other professors and smart students—"and not as a stranger."[18]

WISDOM IN NORTHERN LIGHT

1918–1919

It was not only that he ran away from the tyranny of the lords of the South. It was not only that Bennie Mays was drawn to the morality, the right conduct, and the good hearts of the men in the North. There was more. Bennie was a stirring man, a man who strove. He was ready to set himself against the best, against brilliant Yankees. He had ached to compete with the white boys at the University of South Carolina, but he thought them to be "intellectually inferior" to the boys of New England. He was going to Bates College to do what the white boys back in Greenwood and Orangeburg were afraid to do. He was going to Bates College to compete with Yankees in a Yankee school.

It was the hate and the love that stirred inside him: "How could I know that I was not inferior to the white man having never had the chance to compete with him?" Now he would take that chance. Nor could he turn back without dishonor: "Yankee superiority was the gauntlet thrown down. I had to pick it up."[1]

Yet the love was there too, and cooperation as well as competition. He found it so on the train ride north. A young white northerner introduced himself as a Bates College student, and Bennie and his new schoolmate talked as the train made its way into the northern woods. The boy was filled with the wisdom that comes from several years study at a small college, and he freely shared it. In particular he told Bennie about places to live and things to do. He was friendly and warm, and he loved his school. He hoped that Bennie would love it too. He seemed to regard Bates College as a kind of family.

Mays did not record the name of the friendly welcomer. He did record that on the same trip he met a black youth named Julian Coleman. This Bates student was not from a southern family though his father's people may have been. Julian was from Pawtucket, Rhode Island, and he also told Bennie that Bates College was a family, a good place for a young man to learn and grow.

Young Benjamin Mays.
Courtesy of the Moorland-
Spingarn Research Center,
Howard University.

Julian helped Bennie find a home in Lewiston, Maine. It is not recorded if black people owned the home where he lived. It is recorded that Bennie soon came to agree with Julian and the unnamed white boy that Bates was a family, even though it was bigger even than any extended family Bennie had known.

Like siblings in a family, the college students sometimes picked on each other. But even the teasing at Bates was different in kind and degree from what Bennie had seen before. Back in Orangeburg don't care boys had teased the scholar and even pulled a knife on Bennie. Now at Bates there was a family member who teased, Paul Tilden. He had no knife, but his cuts went deep, deeper than any threatened cut from a don't care boy. Paul Tilden cared much, and he could do much, and his teasing cut sharp and deep. He was a smart white boy, a brilliant Yankee who spoke the proper New England way as he recited his Greek lessons in the classroom with Bennie and the other scholars of Greek. As Bennie recited, Paul Tilden laughed and laughed at his Piedmont dialect because, even when Bennie got the emphasis right and got the classical rhythm right, he sounded wrong, what with the rolling cadences of his black Piedmont speech. He sounded like a Carolina farm boy practicing words in church, and Paul laughed and laughed at the sound. Paul laughed at all the black fellows who attempted Greek, not that there were many, and he laughed at all the black folk he encountered, and there were some numbers of black folk in the largest cities in New England. Bennie was not the only dark man who had abandoned his own community to seek a better way in the far North, not the only dark man who had run away from the white lords in the southern valleys of the slow moving rivers. Bennie's mathematical mind told him that Paul must spend much time and energy laughing at black people he met in New England. It was not Bennie alone that Paul Tilden trifled with; it was all the dark people who were leaving southern white oppressors in order to make a life in the North.[2]

Bennie's anger smoldered under the teasing, and he attacked the problem with work. He lit his lamp and parsed and transliterated—and above all he practiced pronunciation. The work was hard and long. He studied Greek until midnight, slept fitfully, and then arose at 4:00 A.M. or even earlier. Still he erred, and still Paul Tilden laughed and teased, and Bennie was tired and uncomfortable in this family. Professor George Millett Chase even scolded Paul for teasing in Chase's classroom, but still Bennie foundered and still Paul could look at him with eyes that laughed and mocked, even and especially as the stern professor kept everyone's voices stilled.

At last Bennie went to Professor Chase's home and begged for help with Greek. Professor Chase showed him some techniques for study and some simple drills for practice. Now Bennie put in the same hours, but with the mentor's own system of study skills. Results came quickly, and Bennie began to pass his tests. Then he began to earn an *A*. When he declaimed, eyes no longer laughed. In fact Paul came forward to ask for help in Greek, and the two became study partners and even friends.

Bennie would not be set beneath the planters. Their children had attended the University of South Carolina and had learned Greek and Latin, and they had used these ancient languages as signs and symbols of their status as superior folk. Bennie had run away from those white lords and their children, but he intended to show that he was better than they were.[3] Nor would he be set beneath the brilliant Yankee students. He learned to write μεγαλόψυκσς.

Bennie sounded the word out as *meg-a-loh-soo-cose* and he wrote it out as *megalosukos,* although he also liked to write it and other Greek terms in the Greek alphabet. The word meant many things, but to Aristotle it meant a high-spirited soul who did what was right without worrying about the opinions of those who could not tell right from wrong. It was wrong to claim to be more than you were, for that was arrogance. Yet it was also wrong to claim to be less than you were, for that was false modesty, and the falsely modest man hung back and failed to help the assembled group, the polis, when it really mattered. No, a man could not hang back because of cowardice, laziness or false modesty.

A man must find and then do what Bennie sounded out as *meg-a-loh-soo-kee-uh,* and wrote out as *megalosukia,* the condition of living the "good life" of the high-spirited soul. It too was a state of being magnificent. Achieving that condition by practice, a man was then a *megalosukos.*[4]

Again following Aristotle, Bennie could do what was right without worrying about contrary opinions from those who could not do what was right. In the doing, he would *become,* as Aristotle taught. Bennie would be magnificent by doing magnificent things. Of the English words that might catch the full spirit of *megalosukos,* "magnificence" seemed to be the right word. The magnificent Mays. It was a goal. Bennie would know when he got there. Others would know when he got there too. It was most important that Bennie himself know when he got there, and most important that Bennie stay there by right actions. The magnificent Mays. Paul Tilden recognized it. Now Paul Tilden knew so. The rest of the Bates family came to know so too.

To catch the eye of the entire Bates family and thus fill the full role dictated by *megalosukia,* Bennie Mays needed to give a public speech and win a medal for the effort. There was a contest attended by most of the bookworms at Bates and by the faculty, and Bennie signed up to participate. He chose as his oration, "The Supposed Speech of John Adams," a eulogy delivered by Massachusetts senator Daniel Webster at Faneuil Hall on August 2, 1826, to memorialize the Revolutionary leaders Thomas Jefferson and John Adams, both of whom had passed away on July fourth of that year. To mark the occasion, Webster delivered words supposedly spoken by Adams in the second year of the Revolution. The speech celebrates Adams's moment of revolutionary zeal, when he sought support for Jefferson's Declaration of Independence. Neither Adams nor Jefferson was a great speaker, but Webster was, and he served these dead heroes well by speaking for them when they could not, much as Aaron had done for the stuttering Moses.

Webster's discussion of justice and honor and duty was a good one, a fit one for the man who was *megalosukos,* and Bennie leaned into his task with vigor. He could hear Aristotle in the words, which called for a conscious practice of seeking independence, the *doing* of independence in order to *become* free: "Read this Declaration at the head of the army; every sword will be drawn from its scabbard, and the solemn vow uttered, to maintain it, or to perish on the bed of honor. Publish it from the pulpit; religion will approve it, resolved to stand with it, or fall with it. Send it to the public halls; proclaim it there; let them hear it who heard the first roar of the enemy's cannon; let them see it who saw their brothers and their sons fall on the field of Bunker Hill, and in the streets of Lexington and Concord, and the very walls will cry out in its support."[5]

Above all Bennie could hear rebellion, and already he pronounced himself "born to rebel." Twice in that speech Webster quoted Adams and Jefferson to say that slavery was wrong, that countries and the men in them must be free. To Bennie slavery was not only the slavery that his grandfather James endured, but also the Jim Crow that the sons and grandsons of James still endured. Slavery was not dead yet. It must go.

Webster also quoted St. Augustine, already a hero to the bookworm: "Through the thick of the gloom of the present, I see the brightness of the future as the sun in heaven. . . . [English] pride will be less wounded by submitting to that course of things which now predestinates our independence, than by yielding the points in controversy to her rebellious subjects. . . . All that I have, and all that I am, and all that I hope in this life, I am now ready to stake upon it; and I leave off as I began, that, live or die, survive or perish, I am for the Declaration."[6] These words were right for a great speech, and it established him properly as a man of magnificence in the college community. Back in the valley of the Santee, the Jeanes schoolteacher Ellen Harvin knew about this mission and this Webster speech. She traveled from one rural schoolhouse to another to listen to black teachers and correct their speech—though not laughingly and never in front of their students. Her supervising white agent reported up the line to his white agent superintendent in Clarendon County: "She is worth her salary in just seeing that the teachers are on the job." Ellen knew of Bennie's struggles, for she saw the same struggles in the teachers she assisted, and she knew these struggles in her own efforts to speak correctly. She knew of his struggles, but she could do nothing to help him in person. She could not travel to help him in the North. But she could pray for him, and she did. She prayed for him, and she hoped fervently with him as he prepared himself for the contests.[7]

Yet there was still his heritage. He sounded still like a young man from the valley of the Saluda, and to sound so was to make a Yankee audience suspect ignorance. Bennie would not be guilty of false modesty, he would not be a man of *mikrosukia;* that is, one who would hide his talents and thus shirk his duty to the polis.[8] To earn his just rewards and to serve the polis, Bennie had to strive against his Rambo dialect and learn to speak in the Yankee way.

Mrs. Fred Pomeroy, wife of the Bates biology professor, learned of Bennie's mission. She worked with the striving young man at length, correcting him firmly. He did not resent her corrections but in fact welcomed them, and she coached him into an effective diction and pronunciation—and above all a faster pacing than his heritage had taught him. She worked to eliminate the elisions and the sibilants, and she worked to sharpen his accent as it occurred on the correct syllable, and she pushed him to speak with precision. It was difficult work, but he improved, and he made the speech his own. On the evening when his turn came, he stood his tallest, which was very tall, and he spoke with forceful projection, and he tried hard to employ his newly learned Yankee patterns of speech. It was good, and the audience responded with enthusiasm. The panel of judges awarded him first prize, and people gathered around to congratulate him, especially Julian Coleman, his friend from the original northward train ride. Now it was not only Paul Tilden who knew Bennie Mays was a man of magnificence. Now the entire faculty and most of the student body knew it. Now it was family knowledge.[9]

He left the place of his triumph and went to his room, where A. Craig Baird, professor of English and speech, visited him. The distinguished professor, already author of a textbook on speech and rhetoric, was himself bound for places greater than Bates. But on this night he was the Bates man, and he stood at Bennie's threshold to ask the winner to enroll in a speech class and join the debate team. Even on a night of such a triumph, Baird's offer was a little much and the student politely demurred. He learned, however, that the speech professor could not be denied. Professor Baird returned "three or four nights" insisting that Bennie join his team, and finally the student agreed.[10]

Bennie enjoyed the class with Professor Baird, for it gave him great confidence as he developed techniques for argument and as he worked on his pronunciation so to make a way of speaking that was acceptable to the people of the North. The professor caused him to watch other people talking and to think about the art of making speeches. Bennie watched and listened, and there were many chances to see and hear at the little college, for Bates provided a good series of speakers and lecturers.

Dr. Baird taught about the power of rhetoric, and he taught about the need to criticize it. Such criticism, Dr. Baird said, "sets up standards of excellence." Quoting Cicero on Brutus, Dr. Baird stated, "I will not hesitate to affirm, that whether it [eloquence] is acquired by art or practice, or the mere powers of nature, it is the most difficult of all attainments; for each of the five branches of which it is said to consist is of itself a very important art; from whence it may easily be conjectured how great and arduous must be the profession which unites and comprehends all." Moreover Dr. Baird defined rhetorical criticism as a "comparative study in which standards of judgment deriving from the social interaction of a speech situation are applied to public addresses to determine the immediate or delayed effect of the speeches upon special audiences, and ultimately, upon society." This duty, this moral charge to judge the good and the bad in speech, Bennie took to heart, especially Aristotle's note that "the instrument of proof is the moral character, when the delivery of speech is such as to produce an impression of the speaker's credibility." After all, back in the valley of the Saluda, there were great speech makers such as Benjamin Ryan

Tillman of the white people and William Henry Heard of the black people. Much as he might hate and fear the racist Tillman and much as Bennie might admire William Henry Heard, Bennie Mays's duty as rhetorician was to appreciate the good qualities in their presentations and to note the effects on their audiences, and then to judge how to stop the evil effects—no light charge where the brilliant Tillman and those who came after him were concerned.[11]

With others Mays observed Williams Jennings Bryan, once "the boy orator of the plains" and now a restive elder who was exiled from the Woodrow Wilson administration because of his opposition to American entry into World War I. Bryan had visited Greenwood, South Carolina, in 1898, when he was young, and several thousand farmers, including black farmers concerned about falling prices, had come out to hear him speak about silver and gold and money.[12] Bennie had been about four when the Nebraskan spoke in his native county, and so he did not remember hearing the plainsman delivering his "thunderbolts." Now in Lewiston, Maine, Bennie took his place in the Bates audience to study this man who stirred such excitement. In Aristotle's phrase Bennie could examine Bryan's life as he examined his own life, and he could do so without apologizing to white leaders and without fear of white roughnecks and without any trouble from the black don't care boys.

Bennie was properly impressed with Bryan the orator: "He said, 'You have to believe in what you say.' When Cicero spoke, people said, 'Didn't he speak fine?' and that was the end of it. But when Demosthenes spoke, they said, 'let's go against those. Let's do something about what this man is saying.'"[13] It was good that Bryan spoke of Demosthenes, for here was another orator who could not lead effectively until he corrected his speech patterns. Yet once he corrected his stutter, the people followed him! Bennie had no stutter and no mumble, but only a county boy's drawl and a country boy's eccentric use of words and phrases and grammar. He could make his speech acceptable and sing his song in a strange land on Professor Baird's debate team.

Bennie's enjoyment of the debate and speech course was not the same as his participation on the debate team. In fact that semester of his sophomore year he did not get to debate in a match, and he was not even carried with the traveling squad for matches away from Lewiston. The same was true of his junior year, and he became frustrated, wondering if racism would be a problem here too. His grades were good; fellow students admired his speaking skills; and he was a finalist in the junior oratorical contests as voted on by his classmates. Yet he could not travel with teammates to compete at Cornell or at Harvard. After much thought, he wrote long years later, he decided it must be racism that kept him off the "real" debate team that actually made the trips to represent Bates.

Finally in his senior year he "made" the traveling squad and became a bona fide member of the Bates debate team. He did well; the team did well; and the experience confirmed him in his opinion that it was racism that had worked against him in previous seasons. Perhaps his successful performances in his last year could help in the fight against racism. Some of the responsibility for these strange results might be laid at the feet of Professor Baird, but Bennie kept such thoughts close to his heart and kept himself on the best of terms with this fine scholar, not only in 1918 and 1919 but deep into the decades after a second world war.[14]

Racism appeared one more time, and in a way that there could be no mistaking the identity of the real thing. Lewiston, unlike Richmond, featured a cinema hall that was completely integrated. Bennie had foresworn the pleasure of cinema in his native South because he rebelled against the Jim Crow entrance ramp and the Jim Crow balcony imposed in Richmond. In Lewiston, however, he and his friends of all hues walked together through the snow drifts to sit together and enjoy the shows. For a bookworm it was almost Bennie's only nonacademic pastime—except for playing football. Football was one activity where traveling with the team was permitted for the big country boy even during his sophomore year, and it was permitted exactly because he was a big fellow from the countryside.

Bennie loved the moving pictures—"movies" they began to call them—and it was a marvelous thing to sit with friends and be entertained. But there came a movie of a terrible talent with a terrible message. This was *The Birth of a Nation,* produced in 1915 by D. W. Griffith, and it was the first great American-made film. For audiences, it never grew old, and it was shown and reshown for years. Bennie saw it in either 1918 or 1919. It was marked by brilliant technological innovations in camera work and editing, and it changed the way that pictures were made and shown in this country. it was also choreographed dramatically for the pianist-accompanist in the pit of the cinema hall, for there were Wagnerian operatic flourishes to catch the mood of hard-driving cavalry charges and other horse-ridden chases flickering on the screen. It was in so many ways a thing of rare beauty and accomplished art, and Bennie had to admire Griffith's skills. Yet it was awful. It served the Ku Klux Klan, and it glorified the murdering and marauding that the Mays family and other black people had suffered for hundreds of years. Indeed this kind of mounted band was exactly like the white men seeking to kill black people that Bennie remembered from his experiences as a four-year-old at a crossroads in Greenwood County. The white people "in black face" on the screen portrayed beastlike beings— now comic, now pure evil, generally apelike, and always pure *appetitive,* to use the neo-Aristotelian term that Bennie applied to the excessive pursuit of bodily pleasures. The movie could make a white woman terrified of a black man, and it seemed designed to make a white man try to kill a black man.

Of greater concern was the response of the cinema crowd. Usually Bennie sat comfortably among friends and shared the happy and the sad and the excited emotions generated on the screen; and he shared those emotions not only with the actors and with his closest friends sitting by him but also with the larger crowd of halfway familiar townspeople and college students. On this day, however, only the little knot of friends sitting right by his side shared his emotions of outrage, pity, and fear. Indeed most of the audience stamped their feet and hooted and yelled as the Klan, tricked out in outfits like medieval knights at a tournament, killed the bestial images that resembled the Mays family and of those complected like them. How the audience loved it all! The movie was set in Carolina, and this Lewiston crowd was acting as if they were white folk from Carolina.

Bennie left the building hurt, wounded by *The Birth of a Nation* but also by the Lewiston celebration of Griffith's evil masterwork. It was known that President Woodrow Wilson deeply admired the film, as he had deeply admired the novels of his former graduate-school classmate Thomas Dixon that inspired and informed Griffith.[15] The Lewiston crowd, including some Bates students, was telling Bennie that they agreed with Dixon, Griffith, and President Wilson: this nation was united by whiteness, and there were times when white forces must kill black people to maintain the unity.

The racism in *The Birth of a Nation* was real, but the fighting in it was all staged for the cinema. There was real fighting, completely unstaged, in the world during the autumn of 1918, and Bennie learned from Ellen Harvin that Rufus Richardson was in the thick of it. That fall American troops led the way as the French and British charged with a final push against the long entrenched German and Austrians of the Central Powers. It was a bloody charge against a wall of bullets and against terrifying nerve gas. The bullets could kill with dispatch, but the nerve gas could make a soldier long for death as his body imploded with pain and devastation. The lead troops in the charge, the "shock troops" who were first up and out of the trenches and over the top into the no-man's-land of bullets and gases were American troops. They were brave to charge, but they were not selected to charge because of bravery. Plainly, they were selected to charge first because they were new, "green," untried, and— frankly—expendable. The veteran troops came forward after the first wave of these shock troopers had absorbed the damages, and these veterans exploited the advantages won by the Americans. First among the shock troops in the charge northwest of Verdun were the black draftees from South Carolina and the black National Guardsmen from New York and Mississippi and Ohio who were once the old 371st Infantry and were now part of the Red Hand division commanded by General Goybet.

For nine days without rest, black American troops and the French troops ran against the Central Powers entrenchments, breaking the line in late autumn, the harvest season if anyone could farm on those blood fields. One hundred and thirteen African Americans from the old 371st died on the field, and 859 black Americans Negroes were wounded. Grateful for their sacrifices, General Goybet spoke words fit for Demosthenes in an oration for another war in another place: "Never will the 157th Division forget the indomitable dash, the heroic rush of the American regiment (Negro) up the observatory ridge and into the plains of Monthois. . . . These crack regiments overcame every obstacle with a most complete contempt for danger. Through their steady devotion, the 'Red Hand Division' for nine whole days of severe struggle was constantly leading the way for the victorious advances of the Fourth Army.[16]

Back home, at Carnegie Hall in New York, former president Theodore Roosevelt said:

> Well, thank Heaven we went in, and our men on the other side, our sons and brothers on the other side, white men and black, white soldiers and colored soldiers, have been so active that every American now can walk with his head up and look the citizen of any other country in the world straight in the eyes, and we have the satisfaction of knowing that we have played the decisive part.
>
> And now friends I want as an American to thank you, and as your fellow American to congratulate you upon the honor won and the service rendered by the colored troops on the other side.[17]

Ellen Harvin and Theodosia Richardson and Bennie Mays could read about these events with pride and with gratitude. Yet their happiness was mixed with sadness, for one of the 859 men who suffered wounds was the newly promoted Corporal Rufus Richardson. As the Armistice of November 11, 1918, was rung out, Corporal Richardson was prepared for transshipment, back across the ocean to a debarkation hospital in New York City, where he could be treated. Corporal Richardson had sacrificed much, as had all his fellow black men from South Carolina, giving, as Abraham Lincoln had put it in 1863, "the last full measure of their devotion" to the cause of freedom and equality. Bennie Mays and other black men stateside had to stand in pride and gratitude before these fellow black men who had given their quarts of blood and pounds of flesh and even bones and sinews in another measure.[18]

Besides that awful time when moviegoers celebrated Carolina's night riders, Bates College and Lewiston offered up little in the way of overt racism. Nor was the covert racism worth Bennie Mays's fretting over, for it could be met and defeated by the dignity of personal *megalosukia* and by demonstrating extreme competence. Bennie thought himself very much a part of things. By his senior year the debate squad had elected him captain, and he was called on often to speak in public at events sponsored by the YMCA and at leadership conferences for the college set.

He turned his mathematical and analytical mind to examine the college and the town, and he could see some things clearly enough. These were the vaunted Yankees of the big time, and they were smarter than the white folk back in the valley of the Saluda. They were suspicious of black folk and dubious about black intelligence and willpower, but they would give an individual a chance; and if a young black man took that chance, as had Bennie, then they would acknowledge his accomplishments. Especially if he practiced *megalosukia,* and remembered that Yankees did not like a lot of close contact and did not favor the country style of drawn-out storytelling and gushing good humor. These white people could be trusted to do the right thing, if they could be shown the right thing.

Certainly they recognized hard work. Once Bennie had been shoveling snow from the porch and driveway of President George Colby Chase (apparently no close relation to his Greek professor, George Millett Chase). It was a bitterly cold day, and the snow was several feet deep. Bennie got soaked through with his own sweat and with the snow and the ice that slipped inside his boots and through his gloves. Still he shoveled away, and still the snow covered most things, but finally the daughter of the president commanded that he come into the house and be warmed by the family fire in the sitting room. This was his first trip through the front door and foyer of a white family, and such a thing was barely conceivable to the boy who had been struck violently for crossing the threshold of a white man's store on the wrong day—as it was barely conceivable for the boy who had been cursed as a fool by the white lady because he had set a foot onto the front stoop of her house. He was warmed in front of the fire at the president's hearth, and it was found that he had suffered permanent damage to some of his fingers and toes. Decades later he would still "feel the miseries" deep in his fingers and toes on cold days even in mild Georgia winters. But the frostbite was only one memory of that day, and it was a small one. What he really remembered was being treated like a child of God in the presence of a man of God. It was a feeling that set in, deep in his bones, and he came to expect to be so treated at Bates College. Thereafter he went through many front doors and many foyers of the homes and office buildings of Yankee leaders; and from that bitterly cold day of the frostbite and the warm hearth, he went through those doors with confidence and the full measure of an earned *megalosukia.*

There was still more about Bates College. The word "network" was not so used in 1918 or 1919, but Bates had long ago established exactly that, a network of alumni who watched out for each other and who built contacts and connections in their places of work to help each other in their careers. Bennie loved the imagery of St. Augustine, and he could see a city of man with its own structures all planned and operating to help the Bates man in the broader world beyond the Lewiston campus.[19] He could not be certain that the Bates city of man was a good reflection of the City of God, but he could be sure that the Bates city of man would help him in his own strivings—as he could be sure that no such thing existed on such a scale back home or even among the quality folk of Richmond's Virginia Union College.

In fact he spoke thus about his Lewiston days, and how the little college's challenges and competitions compelled a personal development of *megalosukos:*

> One of my dreams came true. . . . Through competitive experience I had finally dismissed from my mind for all time the myth of the inherent inferiority of all Negroes and the inherent superiority of all whites—articles of faith to so many in my previous environment. I had done better in academic performance, in public speaking, and in argumentation and debate than the vast majority of my classmates. I concede academic superiority to no more than four in my class.
>
> I had displayed more initiative as a student leader than the majority of my classmates. Bates College did not "emancipate" me; it did the far greater service of making it possible for me to emancipate myself, to accept with dignity my own worth as a free man.[20]

He did not win admittance to the honorary society Phi Beta Kappa, despite the academic record he compiled and despite the hard work of Greek professor George Millett Chase. Chase believed that his prized student was denied admission because of race, but Bennie himself saw a more indirect racist reason: his year of straight *A* grades at Virginia Union College was largely discounted by the national organization, which tended, as Bennie had put it before, "to put it on the South," in terms of African American academic performance. Three years of superb grades at Bates College were not enough to overcome the deep discount assigned an academic record at a "Negro school" in the South. Yet this was a national rather than a Bates College ruling, and Bennie could be nothing but grateful for his treatment at the little college with the warm heart in the cold woods.

As graduation season came on, Bennie learned from his fiancée that Rufus Richardson had died. Like twenty-four other black soldiers from the old 371st

Infantry, the corporal did not survive his battlefield wounds, and he perished in the army debarkation hospital in New York City. Theodosia Richardson arranged to have the body of her son brought home, and she built him a fitting memorial, a tall gravestone set in the Richardson family plot in the "Colored" section of the stately memorial cemetery in Manning. The gravestone was as tall as the young soldier had been when he was still living, and its marble side was inscribed with his rank and years of service for the old 371st. Now Rufus Richardson too was among those who had given "the last full measure of devotion." The family plot was lovely, hard by the woods at the edge of the cemetery. It was shaded by well-tended trees, and the whole plot was closed off by a small concrete wall and set on well-tended grass, as befitted a combat hero from the Great War. Yet, like the other "Colored" plots, it was set carefully aside from the plots of the white soldiers and civilians of Manning. Ellen Harvin, the Jeanes teacher, and her adoptive mother Theodosia Richardson, and still later Bennie Mays, could each in their turn visit the site to pay their respects and to remember, but above all they had to remember that Jim Crow ruled that valley of the Santee in death as well as in life.

In any case, it was time for Bennie Mays to move on beyond his kind friends and mentors at Bates College, and what he wanted above all was his chance to lead. In 1919 he had attained a license to preach, and he was already better educated than ninety and nine of the dark ministers back home. But he wanted still more. He confided to his pretty girl Ellen Harvin, at work in the valley of the Santee, that he wanted to lead a congregation the right way, as a thoughtful student and teacher who would bring his people into their own *megalosukia* by showing them plans founded on reason and reason grounded in faith. To do that he needed to attend a northern divinity school and learn from—and show to—the Yankees with the highest attainments that he deserved their respect. He needed to show them as well that he deserved their comradely assistance in the task of saving the dark people still captive, not in Babylon, but in their own promised Canaan. With the support and encouragement of his Greek professor, George Millett Chase, and the full support of President George Colby Chase and debate coach A. Craig Baird, Bennie made his application to two excellent schools, the divinity school at the University of Chicago and the Newton Theological Seminary at Newton Centre, Massachusetts (now Andover Newton Theological School). Given his newfound acceptance among the New Englanders in Lewiston, he was especially interested in Newton—and especially hurt and angered when he was denied admission because he was an African American.[21]

So too were his Bates College mentors, especially his Professor George Millett Chase, shocked and dismayed at still more evidence of severe racism among the northern academics. Yet the Bates men were all convinced that Bennie Mays should complete his application to the University of Chicago, and each was also convinced that, if admitted, he should go. Each Bates man was sure that the University of Chicago was actually the better school and hoped that the racial liberalism already displayed there would be in evidence again. In fact Bennie was accepted there, much as his old mentor Professor Nix had willed it and much as the Bates men had prayed for it. Bennie Mays was determined to attend. He would go to the University of Chicago as a Bates man and become a Chicago man, and he would lead his people along "the paths God hath prepared for them to walk in"—even in the valley of the shadow of death and even in his own native valley. On taking his baccalaureate in 1920 he became a Bates man in full standing, and he can no longer be called Bennie in these chronicles, but rather Mays. Nor was Ellen Harvin, the Jeanes scholar, any longer merely a pretty girl, but now a good woman and his wife, and she too must be called Mays in these chronicles. They married in Newport News, Virginia, in August 1920. This couple was determined to be duly recorded in the chronicles as the Reverend Doctor and Mrs. Benjamin Mays.

There were still some days more to pass and there were still some tasks to do before they could go to Chicago. Mrs. Ellen Mays returned to the valley of the Santee to earn more money as a teacher until Christmas season. Mr. Bennie Mays returned to work as a Pullman porter on New York and Boston runs, hoping to live cheaply and to save more money. He found odd jobs, among other things painting floats on the docks of New England harbors.

For all the sweat of his brow, he did not earn many coins. His goal was to have fifty dollars in his purse by registration day on January 3, 1921, for the convocation of winter studies at the University of Chicago. Another goal was to have Ellen Mays join him in Chicago, perhaps by convocation of fall studies in September 1922. In the meantime he could earn board money by washing dishes in Chicago, and he could room in the divinity school at no charge while meeting tuition expenses from a scholarship fund plus the savings from Ellen Mays's teaching and jobs he worked from August through December 1920. As usual the financial plans were tightly drawn, with little room for error and no margin for luxury. So he prepared himself for matriculation in the "City of the Big Shoulders" during the 1920s, the decade when Chicago enjoyed its greatest prosperity as a major industrial center.

6

FOR EVERY TIME
THERE IS A SEASON

1920–1924

The autumn season of 1920 began a time of troubles for the new couple with bright dreams. Bennie Mays labored in many places but with Boston as his hub. Ellen Mays labored in the valley of the Santee. Though they sowed much, their harvest was spare. Bennie and Ellen Mays loved one another, and they loved their callings, he to preach and she to teach. If they missed their drink and their meat one day, yet the lovers were filled with bread from heaven to eat.[1]

Bennie Mays worked for money and for a cause. Enemy of the bosses, he was no more respectful of the lords of industry and labor "at the North" than of the lords of land and labor "at the South." Pullman porters became his brothers in still another branch on the large dark tree, and he fought for their cause. He stayed with porters, rooming with them in boardinghouses for African Americans near train stations. He continued to practice his speech, his declamation. Sometimes he was in front of church groups, sometimes in front of labor-union organizers, and other times before self-help and charitable groups. Always he worked to do the magnificent preaching and speaking fitting a man of true *megalosukos*. His magnificence now included the knowledge that some white people of the North could be trusted to practice the right habits of "the good."[2]

He must have worried about his wife, Ellen Harvin Mays, supervising her own people in her valley of the Santee, where still other white lords ruled that flat land with no more justice or righteousness than such people exercised in his native Piedmont. The Mayses needed to get her out of South Carolina. They needed to be together, but first they needed to serve out this hard season in order to enjoy the fruits of the next season promised them in Chicago.

There was just no money. Ellen Mays earned her Jeanes Fund income by working with Sumter County and Clarendon County schoolteachers, teaching the teachers, all women, to teach the children most desperately in need of teaching. She did not live with Theodosia Richardson in Manning, but rather with Sallie Conley and Gilbert DuBose in Pinewood. This arrangement is a little hard to make sense of, given Richardson's kindness and her pain and emptiness after losing her son, Rufus Richardson. Nor was anything written to show that Gilbert DuBose and Sallie Conley assisted or in any way encouraged Ellen Mays in her chosen career or in her marriage. The living arrangement in some way had to do with the mystery that was Ellen Mays, the "very fair skinned" and "pretty girl." As noted earlier, Bennie Mays had met her in Orangeburg at some point not recorded anywhere, then became engaged to marry her at some secret point in his Bates College days, and thereafter spent long seasons apart from her, apparently losing or destroying all correspondence with her during their time apart. And they were apart more than they were together. In *Born to Rebel* Mays wrote that she helped persuade him to become a theologian rather than a professor of mathematics and that they talked long and feelingly about racism and white people. It is obvious that this man, who could stir emotions in others and who could tightly control his own emotions, fully intended to keep entirely unto himself most of what he alone knew about Ellen Mays.[3]

Christmas season drew near, and Bennie and Ellen Mays told each other that during the new year of 1921 they must remain apart yet a little longer, at least until summer. Bennie Mays counted his savings and found that he had forty-five dollars to take with him to Chicago, where his university matriculation was set for the first Monday of 1921. He had gone to Bates College in the town of Lewiston with ninety dollars, and now he was going to an expensive city with half that sum. His mother had always told him that God will provide, and he kept these words in his bosom. He prepared himself to study among the brilliant Yankees at what Dr. Nix had assured him was the world's greatest university.

Then came the news that he was no longer a Pullman porter. In *Born to Rebel* Mays stated tersely that he got into a dispute about assignments and duties, was found to be wrong, and was promptly dismissed. It is recorded among the Brotherhood of Sleeping Car Porters labor records, however, that Mays lost his job for a bolder and nobler reason. In 1920 there was no labor organization to protect the rights of the porters, almost all of whom were black. Mays was one of the first men to attempt to organize the porters into a collective unit.[4]

The records show that he had organized openly, directly, and aboveboard. Above all, he had worked without any help from experienced labor activists, who understood collective bargaining among workers. He did not choose to campaign alone because of arrogance or even innocence. He simply could get no help. The rapidly growing American Federation of Labor (AFL) in 1920 and for more than a decade thereafter actively discouraged organizing among black laborers. The AFL apparently had a general policy of racial exclusion, but the policy was quite specific concerning the Pullman porters. A young countryman with no real experience organizing labor in an urban setting must have been quite a sight. For his clumsy efforts Mays attracted the attention of the Pullman Company managers. He was promptly fired—so promptly that the manager forgot to collect Mays's treasured porter's keys, the main identification that allowed a porter to be hired for a train run.[5]

Yet the Brotherhood of Sleeping Car Porters historians, following the lead of the labor organizer and civil rights leader, Asa Philip Randolph, record an appreciation for Mays's failed efforts: "It had thus become common wisdom among the porters that the only way they could organize and sustain a union was to do so in secret and to secure a leader who was beyond the reach of [owner George Mortimer] Pullman. They found that organizer in 1925 . . . [in] A. Philip Randolph."[6] In other words Mays in a bold failure had taught all organizers, especially Randolph, important lessons. Mays was thus years ahead of an eventually successful labor movement. Those who did one day organize a labor union that could protect the largest single block of black workers in the United States remembered Mays favorably. In particular Randolph always remembered both the negative lesson about practice—do not go aboveboard too soon—and the positive lesson about Bennie Mays the brave and forthright man, whom he arranged to meet and with whom he worked from the 1930s onward in labor activism and civil rights.[7]

In 1920, however, the pioneer faced a pressing personal difficulty. His plan to "work" his way west to Chicago and thus save the railroad fare was undone. Counting his money, he realized that he would need more than 10 percent of his savings just to go from Boston to Chicago. Undone too was his plan to "work" his way south to see Ellen Mays and then work his way west and north to start his schooling. Their time apart stretched not from last August to this December, but from last August to the next June.

Christmas season thus passed in a sad blur as Ellen Mays worked on her programs for African American schools in the valley of the Santee and as Bennie Mays worked in Boston harbor—"slaved" was the word that could be attached—at odd jobs to pile up a little more money for the rapidly approaching new year. There was a friend named Bryant among the Pullman porters, and this Bryant schemed to help his old workmate. He told Mays to meet him in Springfield, Massachusetts, so to arrange passage westward to Cleveland and thence somehow on to Chicago. Having no other hopes, Mays laid down several more dollars of his diminished savings and rode on a passenger car to

Springfield. There Bryant slipped him aboard a westbound Pullman car and stowed him away in a linen closet. A day's bouncing ride in the dark and cramped closet put him at the station on the shore of Lake Erie, and there he and Bryant were able to find a railroad official who knew nothing of Bennie Mays's New England Pullman history and who knew only that he needed a good man to make the run. Since Mays still held his Pullman porter's keys, the official hired him at once for this late-December Chicago run, and so the Bates alumnus arrived at the divinity school in the year 1921 to begin his studies.

Safely arrived in Chicago, Mays matriculated at Dr. Nelson C. Nix's wonderful alma mater. Laid out with Yahweh's own plumb line on the north side of town, the University of Chicago was even more than Nix had said, for the school was the beneficiary of John D. Rockefeller's money, and that lord of oil had built his spectacular campus near Lake Michigan. The University of South Carolina—once a center for sons of the white lords and then for a season a center for sons of the black slave force and now again strictly the province of the sons of the white lords—could fit easily inside one wing of the huge physical plant of Rockefeller's University of Chicago. The University of South Carolina in the year 1921 had fallen on hard times, with buildings faded and decaying and its faculty no longer top drawer. By contrast the University of Chicago boasted a faculty to compare with the best in the world. And that after all was the reason for Mays's tortuous and seriocomic route to divinity school. He knew that he could compete with the best of the North, and he knew too that the northern students, while not without their own racism, would accept a dark man of the South if he was obviously excellent—as long as such a man remembered not to stand too close and as long as he remembered his carefully constructed Yankee way of speaking—sharp and fast and precise.[8]

He moved into a handsome dormitory with the name Goodspeed. Though only a man's name, Goodspeed was yet propitious and portentous, a sign of good things to come. Indeed, Ernest Johnson Goodspeed had written books that Mays soon read in his seminars and that he would cite in his graduate thesis. Goodspeed had taken newly found scrolls and other matter and translated the Gospels anew, with simple and forthright language that Mays admired and used in his own studies—although as a preacher he continued then and later to use the familiar rolling cadences of the King James translations. Goodspeed had also produced a "harmony," or concordance, of the three synoptic gospels of Matthew, Mark, and Luke for study of context and content, and Mays used these books almost at once. Above all, Goodspeed had served the University of Chicago divinity scholars by clearly marking the way in which newly found scrolls and newly unearthed archaeological matter explained the early Roman Empire and the Jews and the Jewish Christians in that empire.[9]

The name Goodspeed also foretold good things coming quickly. Mays by now had taken the full measure of the divine words spoken to the prophet Isaiah: "A little one shall become a thousand, and a small one a strong nation: I the Lord will hasten it in his time."[10] The lesson of those words was going down hard, but it was going down. Justice would come with stunning quickness and with no advance warning, but when it came, the events would be hastened by the real Lord, and all on his own timetable. His time was not Mays's time, but neither was it the time of the white lords of the land back in the valley of the Saluda. The timing of God's unfolding plan was not for humans to know.

In this spell before God's time was revealed, the righteous man was still required to examine his life, to live it fully and fairly, to serve, and to prepare himself. There was, Mays realized, a little leeway permitted, a providential dispensation for the black folk to do a few things on their own behalf without pretending to know the exact due time of the coming of the Lord's justice. Looking around the place where he now lived, Mays came to understand that black students in the divinity school roomed exclusively in Goodspeed and not in the white neighborhood then surrounding the university. This was not like the Bates College community, where a black man could live anywhere in Lewiston. Here the black men who were divinity students stayed in Goodspeed, and the black people of the city of Chicago—many from the valley of the Saluda or the "black bottom" of the Congaree, but many more from the Mississippi Delta—rented rooms way across town on the South Side, with some newly arriving and desperately poor black folk beginning to fill up tenement rows on the West Side.[11]

Besides rooming, there was also the issue of boarding, the simplest taking of a meal. In Mays's own lifetime back in the valley of the Saluda, the breaking of bread and the taking of drink had been fully Jim Crowed once the railroad station dining room was declared by constitutional law to be "for whites only." And where once the white lord Wade Hampton, governor and senator, had sat at table with black preachers and teachers, now the new South Carolina leaders still railed against the late Theodore Roosevelt, who while U.S. president twenty years ago had sat at the White House table with Booker T. Washington. Indeed, one of South Carolina's own, President Woodrow Wilson of the white Thornwell family, had between 1916 and 1920 joined with his white cabinet members to Jim Crow every federal building in the people's capital. Now black officeholders and clerical workers had to take meals in places removed from the federal buildings.[12] Surely Professor Nix's wonderful school would not submit itself and its students of color to such rules.

But the otherwise magnificent University of Chicago reflected the segregation of the era. Habit born of many personal choices fully segregated the tables in the dining room of the commons, a handsome place—and with its shining floors and expensive wood—virtually a palace to a country fellow from the valley of the Saluda. It was expected, though never stated, that the black divinity students were to sit at table with each other. At once Mays began to test these expectations, as did many of his fellows. For instance a black student would take his seat next to a white professor or students at table in the commons. Sometimes the white man would stay, though usually not talking, for by now Mays understood that the northern white folk were not a chatty lot, especially when approached by dark people from the rural South. Other times the man might get up and move to another table. Then Mays or another black student would move to that table to sit by him. With more than one emotion, Mays recorded that he saw one black student follow a white man to three different tables in succession. Finally the man left the commons and did not eat a meal at all at that hour on that day. By and large Mays and the handful of other black divinity students changed the segregation of the commons, the sort of action that Mays had read of in Aristotle's *Nicomachean Ethics*. Mays found that this Aristotelian principle applied as well to integrating a dining table as it had to better speech giving. The right practice, the right habit, the doing of the good thing, and the doing of it well, finally produced the good. A man of color could sit at table with his elbow near a white man, though he could not, as Jesus had done, dip his hand into the same bowl. Nor could they, as Jesus had done, talk casually at table like a guest or a friend of the publican or the tax collector.[13]

On the campus grounds outside the commons and outside the class halls—in the elaborate walkways and the more informal student-created pathways—there were yet more expectations, and against these expectations Mays also rebelled, as if born to rebel. He was, after all, a labor organizer who knew how to mobilize. He saw that the white professors, brilliant men, sometimes spoke and sometimes did not speak to the white students whom they passed on the paths. Some professors, as elsewhere, were so fully inside their own world of thoughts that mere humans of any hue never registered in their vision. But not all professors were so preoccupied, and these noticed humans and thus spoke in passing, sometimes warmly and familiarly. There was a color difference, and Mays marked it: a white student could expect to be ignored by some professors, but he could also expect to be hailed by others. In contradistinction a man who was black could expect to be ignored uniformly, both by the preoccupied scholars and by other professors who passed by the unacknowledged black students while acknowledging, even celebrating, the presence of white students.

African American students rebelled, and while Mays did not start the rebellion, he entered into it fully. They set about their rebellion with subtlety and craft. They edged close to the middle of the walkways, and they looked with wide-open eyes at the professors passing by. They smiled broadly, and they said with enthusiasm, "Hello, sir!" They took off their caps. Two professors—names not recorded but their cases enumerated in *Born to Rebel*—looked through them and hurried by, sliding to the far side of the pathways. No professor could now pretend that black students did not exist. Not a few began to speak back in acknowledgment, and some—not many, but actually some—began even to offer a smile.

Mays was at the University of Chicago to earn a degree, to convince yet another set of brilliant Yankees that he could do their work. Surely he had to protest inequities, but above all he needed to study in order earn his Ph.D. He had been licensed to preach since 1919, and 1921 he was ordained among his Baptists as well; he was qualified to do the Lord's work among people of color. He took these official licenses and recognitions as important signs, but he was in Chicago to convince great white scholars that he could win their imprimatur, if not their fellowship. A good Aristotelian insisted on proper recognition of his qualities from proper authorities. As he wanted it to be, the divinity professors at Chicago gave nothing away, lightened no loads, and loosened no tethers. They were masters of what they had studied, lords of what they chose to survey, and Mays took their demands and their established regime as a chance to prove his mettle, as much to himself as to them.

And challenge anew they surely did. His basic command of classical Greek, his passion for the classical thinkers Aristotle, Thomas Aquinas, and Augustine, these endowments could help him and indeed were necessary, but they were not sufficient at the divinity school. These professors assumed their students knew the classics of old, but they were quite bored with tradition, and they brooked no claims to authority, not even from the Bible—at least not from any currently published translation of the Bible. Dr. Goodspeed's New Testament translation was available to them in typescript form, and the scholars read it with respect. Yet even their colleague's good work in one part of the Bible could not escape their rule of procedure: all texts must be interpreted. By and large they were believers who sought Truth "unto its deepest parts" by discerning sacred meaning, but only by using the tools of analysis—which were contextual historical research into the evolving meanings of words, logic, and social-science explanatory models—and using those tools on more than one available text preserved from the ancient of days. Unlike his preachers back home, who took literally the Word of the King James translation of the Bible, these divines took nothing literally, nothing at face value, but rather interpreted God's revealed and inspired Word as it unfolded imperfectly and unclearly among man's many words. They were liberal theologians, and Mays accepted that label— liberal theologians—for them and for himself. He had always had an analytical and mathematical mind, and interpretation of sources appealed to that large part of his mentality.

So focused were these Chicago divines of 1921 on what they called sociohistorical methodology that scholars named their approach the "Chicago School" and attached that name to any scholar practicing their methods regardless of where such a professor actually taught. Like the Baptist founders of the University of Chicago before John D. Rockefeller bestowed much of his fortune on it, the divinity school faculty was pietistic, insisting on a close and personal and immediate relationship with God; and it was evangelical, that is responding to a deeply felt need to spread the Gospel—or as they preferred to say, the "good news"—to nonbelievers and even more so to those believers whose belief had grown cold or flabby. Unlike the founders of the university, these 1921 divines were not fundamentalists and never took the Bible in a literal sense. Indeed, Shailer Mathews, dean of the divinity school, preached that Christians must provide ethical grounding and ethical direction for the people in a modern democracy. If the Bible were interpreted aright, the interpreting ministers in their evangelizing could inspire civilization to become more humane.[14]

In this early season of his study at Shailer Mathews's school, Mays was most touched by Shirley Jackson Case, master of the sociohistorical research that informed the Chicago style. This man Case was not unknown to Mays before he arrived in Chicago because Case was known to Herbert R. Purinton, who had taught Mays back in Lewiston. Case had earned a doctorate from Yale University, but along his way to Chicago he had taught in the 1907–8 sessions alongside Purinton at Bates's Cobb Divinity School. The professors formed a friendship, and they kept in touch thereafter. In later years, when Case wrote important studies of the New Testament, Purinton made sure that Bates students and alumni knew of these works.[15]

Taking up his Bible—that is, searching the library of translations of texts—Case declared that the Lord's will was indeed revealed therein, much as might be said back in the valley of the Saluda by the Reverend Marshall and other pietists. In broadest patterns, Case said, the Lord revealed what he wanted from believers: love and loyalty, with sincere actions dedicated to service because of that love and loyalty. The fundamental message could not be missed, and its specific charges could not be ignored. God said to love one another as I have loved you; and do all such good works as I have prepared for you to walk in. Such good works included service and sacrifice and did not exclude suffering and scorn. And this God in the person of Jesus Christ had "lived and moved and had his being" among us, had suffered with us and for us. In so many words then, Professor Case believed exactly what the Reverend Marshall believed: that

God was personally known to us and personally involved in our lives, providing in deliberate revelations his divine plan in outline.

On the other hand, Case did not believe and did not preach what so often went with pietism: a literal reading of all words inspired by that foundational Word. What Case did not agree about with the Reverend Marshall's literal reading was that the Lord's will was revealed in full and specific detail. Indeed Case worried a great deal about the ears and the hands of those who wrote down what the Lord revealed of his divine will. The professor said that those who heard God's Word were men who lived in a specific time and in a particular place, in fact a rather cramped and compact Hebrew corner of the far-flung and mighty Roman Empire. Moreover Dr. Case liked to remind his students and his readers that the New Testament Gospels and Acts and Epistles were not written down for long decades—thirty to sixty years—after Jesus ascended. Thus the earliest church builders functioned without any written New Testament scriptures, and some of their non-Hebrew, gentile, and in fact completely pagan words inevitably found their way into an otherwise faithful recording of God's Word. These problems of remembering and recording and transcribing did not negate miracles, for miracles there surely were as Case read it and believed it and taught it: Jesus on the cross for us, Jesus rising from the dead, Jesus preaching love and loyalty and then ascending, a revealing God once again breaking into human history. Such miracles were denied once by self-professed deists, and now were denied by self-professed modernists, but not by all liberal theologians and never by Mays.[16]

The inspired Hebrew- and the Greek-speaking gentiles who told those miracles were led to yet another miracle: a church of thousands and tens of thousands that was finally accepted by nothing less than the Roman Empire itself; and through that odd—and somewhat problematic—agency spread God's Word to the far corners of its vast imperial borders. As a matter of fact, to Case it was the spreading of Christian belief among the many different peoples of the Roman Empire that was especially miraculous, given the starting point of popular opposition to Christianity in most of those peoples. Case and his students at Chicago spent some time demonstrating that popular hatred of Christianity predated Roman persecutions—and in fact it was that popular hatred that produced the official persecution and not the other way around. Case noted that the non-Hebrew peoples of the empire had "deep" and "vital" and "complex" emotional needs, which were deepened and sharpened by various financial, climatic, and political crises that produced "times of stress"—and that Christianity rather suddenly in the third and fourth centuries became an "emotionally" and "psychologically" satisfying answer and solution to these dreads. Church historians, Case insisted, must be attuned to the economic, geographic, political, and other environments in which a religion is taught.[17]

Unlike the Reverend Marshall back home, Dr. Case was more dubious about other miracles, especially because so many of them were written down by and for people in the extended Roman Empire long after Jesus actually walked and talked on the earth. To Case the particular features of many of those miracles were not especially connected to the Lord's main teaching, seeming rather to be connected to old folktales and oral traditions passed along by non-Hebrews long before—and quite independent of—Jesus Christ and his teaching. Separating out those pagan supernatural—and in some cases purely superstitious—parts of the New Testament from the Word of God was a most important task for the believing scholar.[18]

Case was thus going places to which the Reverend Marshall certainly never went back in his Baptist sanctuary in Greenwood. Yet Mays had never cottoned to "whooping the benches" and had long been suspicious of his down-home preachers, some of whom could barely read and write English, much less master and use the classical languages of the educated men who were passing along the inspired Word of God. Mays was not only willing to go along with Dr. Case on his intellectual journey, but Mays was in fact eager to run as fast and as far as his mentor. So inspired by Case's sociohistorical lectures, Mays determined to write a master's thesis discussing the pagan folklore that made its way into Christianity, especially those parts that had shown up in the New Testament.

Shirley Case above all else caused Bennie Mays to articulate previously undigested concepts and ideas. Case was such an imposing authority for Mays that, in one part of his thesis, he cited his mentor in a footnote as "Dr. Case," although the University of Chicago style manual, rapidly becoming the style authority for all persons writing theses, plainly states that authors should be cited first by their full names and thereafter by their surname alone (unless there might be more than one author with the same surname). Academic titles were never to be used, but Bennie Mays used the title as an appeal to authority, and the authority, Case himself, missed the stylistic infraction when looking through the thesis.[19]

There were also influences beyond Case, but Case fully accepted and sometimes even celebrated those influences. Above all there was the spirit of Walter Rauschenbusch, progenitor of the social-gospel movement in the United States before World War I and a figure whose memory was hallowed at the University of Chicago. Rauschenbusch's personal traits were still discussed among admiring professors, administrators, and city reformists who knew him before his death in 1918. They knew Rauschenbusch from prewar conferences on race relations and settlement-house work—and after his death there survived his many writings, by which still others could come to know him. Rauschenbusch said that the hungry had to be fed, the sick treated, the wounded bandaged, the downtrodden liberated, and the poor lifted up in order to fulfill the true teaching of Jesus. His was the most liberal of translations of God's Word, but many of this season's scholars were struck by the many, many literal examples one could find of Jesus as a savior of the poor, the sick, and the outcast. Although Rauschenbusch focused his personal labors in New York, he preached so effectively that he was partly responsible for the way that the social-gospel people in Chicago turned their eyes to the plight of the African American in their city—and Rauschenbusch's writings were directly responsible for the way that at least one educated black man turned his own eye to the social gospel as a movement that could help his community and other people of color.[20]

Mays was thrilled to absorb the lesson in social justice taught by a white man who said that lynching—and of course Mays was nearly lynched himself as a child at the time of the Phoenix Riot—was an offense against God and against what was right, and that it must be stopped—and stopped by churches. Even more was Mays thrilled to read the lesson from this same white man that economic discriminations and injustices—and Mays was a man who had picked cotton for fourteen cents a day—must be countered by a "Kingdom of the Brotherhood" of all races and all classes: "I believe in gentleness and meekness, but not in servility. I have no faith in force methods, and even believe in non-resistance, but not in a non-resistance of cowardice and silence. There was nothing cringing in Jesus. He did not strike back, but neither did he flinch. He was 'the terrible meek.' I am thinking of the Negro race in saying this."[21]

The Rauschenbusch message thus moved Mays and set him to planning. He too would be a scholar-activist in the mold of the Chicago scholar-activists he met that season. He would be liberal in theology but radical in political economics; that is, he would interpret the Bible liberally according to the socio-historical context in which he considered it to be recorded; but in economics, he wanted complete change from the bottom up, with good land for the outcasts. Like the departed Rauschenbusch, Mays the student in 1921 still believed that wealth was in land, that therefore inequity was the most marked in unequal landownership and landholding, that only a single tax on land itself could bring equity—and that finally the churches must unite with the land reformists and the surviving disciples of Henry George in order to give the blacks a chance in the valley of the Saluda, the valley of the Santee, and even and especially alongside the Chicago River. The detested lords of the land were not only arrogant and racist but were also delaying industrial progress, and their power must be broken.[22] Mathematical analysis of land value and fair-tax levies must be joined with biblical exegesis, and these two academic exercises must be joined with an activist socialist program so that "righteousness and peace" could indeed kiss, even as Mays had envisioned it while reading his Bible as a boy.

With his head and his heart so happily stuffed with unfamiliar facts and figures and with plans both grand and specific, the divinity student learned through the mails that his "pretty girl" Ellen Mays had moved upward in the valley of the Santee, joining the faculty at Morris College, the Baptist-supported Sumter institution for people of color that she had long admired. Still training and supervising teachers, Ellen Mays now enjoyed considerable prestige in the eyes of the local black community, especially among her fellow churchgoers, who attended the Baptist church in Sumter served by the Reverend J. P. Garrick. Of course, in the eyes of the white lords of the land and in the eyes of the ninety and nine white peasants and mill workers there was not prestige, but rather scorn of the "nigger college." Regardless of white scorn or black pride, her new position at Morris College did not bring her any closer to her husband the divinity student. But she had come to her new status honorably and fairly, she could serve her people better than before, and Mays was rightly pleased with his hardworking wife.[23]

In his busy first semester at the university, Mays was surprised to encounter in the library a legend among the people of color, Dr. John Hope. Hope, president of Morehouse College in Atlanta, was a graduate of an Ivy League school, and he had been hard at work since 1898 trying to make his Atlanta Baptist school something of great service to the people of color throughout the South and nation. Indeed Hope had increased the school's physical size from six to sixty acres, had brought in good teachers, had toughened academic standards, and had changed the name of the school from Atlanta Baptist College to Morehouse College in honor of Henry L. Morehouse, corresponding secretary of the Atlanta Baptist Home Mission Society. In later years Mays described this meeting in the library as "fortuitous," but he believed that God produced few accidents and John Hope fewer still. The world of the scholar of color was a tiny one at the University of Chicago and far tinier in the valley of the Savannah, on whose western banks John Hope had been born in 1868.[24]

Extremely light in color, John Hope was a son of James Hope, a Scotland-born white landowner who lived openly with his black lover, Mary Frances or Fanny, who was mother of John. The boy was raised in their large and opulent house near Augusta, and the mixed-race couple was often visited by white farmers and merchants who were friends of James and Fanny Hope and who seemed to accept the two as a couple. But in 1876 James Hope died suddenly, and when white lawyers came to settle affairs, the boy John Hope learned that he was in his own shamed words "only another colored boy" whose mother could not successfully lay claim to James Hope's fortune despite the Civil Rights Act of 1873 or the Fourteenth Amendment to the U.S. Constitution.

Moving to New England, the suddenly penurious John Hope could easily have "passed" into the white world and so become an "ex-colored man," but he chose instead to proclaim his color among northerners. Distinguishing himself in public schools, he won a scholarship to Brown University, where he earned the admiration of his brilliant Yankee classmates and teachers and became a successful journalist and educator, determining finally to live among the people of color in his native South despite their many troubles and despite his own successes and proffered opportunities in Providence. A founder of the National Association for the Advancement of Colored People (NAACP), Hope boldly stood up for the rights of people of color in Atlanta after the terrible riots of 1906. This was no man likely to mince words about what he wanted—or about what one owed to his people.

President Hope was also deeply involved in helping the other Atlanta colleges for people of color: Atlanta University, Spelman College for Women, Morris Brown College, Clark College, and several seminaries where Protestant ministers were trained. He worked for cooperation between and among these different schools, trying to make their few coins go as far as they could by avoiding needless duplication and by sharing resources. The Atlanta schools for people of color grouped themselves around Atlanta University Park, an arrangement eventually formalized into the Atlanta University system, of which Hope took overall charge in 1931. This handsome and shaded park, with its young and struggling African American colleges, was a source of pride and optimism for the people of color in the Georgia capital. And the man who did the most for all the schools was the one fittingly named Hope. This leader now approached the student Mays with an assignment.

The Morehouse president explained that Georgia provided no public high schools for the black boys and girls in Atlanta, even in this capital city with a population of 270,366 people and the 318,587 people in surrounding Fulton County. Because of this Jim Crow denial of opportunity, the black colleges provided preparatory training for young people of color, much as South Carolina State College had on the other side of the Savannah River. Indeed in 1921 Morehouse, Spelman, Morris Brown, and Clark matriculated a total of 527 college students and 1,139 preparatory, or high school, students. All this was done with money from African Americans and some white friends at the North— and none of it with tax money from the State of Georgia.[25]

Hope was a man who understood *megalosukia,* a man who disdained bragging but who also disdained false modesty, and he did not parse phrases with delicate regard for the feelings of the overawed student Mays. Hope had indeed graduated from Brown University, and he was proud of his accomplishments among the brilliant northerners there, as he was politic with those Brown alumni, who included, after all, John D. Rockefeller, benefactor of several schools in addition to the University of Chicago. For all that, Hope said of himself and other black products of the Ivy League that he "graduated" from Brown University but was "educated" at Morehouse College. He was also candid that black colleges in the South could not easily hire Ph.D. faculty members, there being few schools where an African American could be admitted into candidacy for the doctorate. Instead, even Fisk and Morehouse and Howard, had to find and hold onto the best-trained men from the best northern universities, sometimes in cases when such people had not yet attained master's degrees. Bates College was a superb northern institution, and it trained its baccalaureate graduates well. That reference of course struck home with Mays, for he was just then completing his first full year of graduate studies.[26]

Hope struck quickly, as he also liked to say, not like a thunderbolt but instead "like first lightning that burns up the poison and purifies the atmosphere." His first lightning came at Mays, who was told also that the business of Morehouse College was to train leaders: "Whether with the spelling book or a course in chemistry, whether in a prayer meeting or in the abandon of a football game, the purpose is the making of leaders, and the leaders must be Christian."[27]

The lightning did not spare Mays, and he had to leave the University of Chicago now, delaying not only his doctorate but even his master's, for Hope took his measure and saw at once what kind of man Mays was. Hope liked to say, "Some men get a thrill and other men get the blues out of the same experience. . . . Some are constructed for carrying a pack and whenever it is not on their back they are looking around to find out what they have lost."[28]

Plenty of black people were singing the blues in Chicago, but not Mays, and Hope knew that for a fact. Hope knew that Mays needed money and that he needed an immediate challenge. This was a man filled with too much energy and optimism to worry about the weight of a pack. Hope told Mays that he would pay him $1,200 per year to teach mathematics, and that instructors could live in a plain but clean and ample dormitory appointed for them and could board inexpensively on campus. He also told Mays he would be teaching the first college-level course in calculus offered to black students south of Howard University in the nation's capital. This was excellent bait, but Hope was too sure a fisher of men to spoil the catch by reeling in the line too quickly. He told Mays to take his time, to think it over, and to get in touch before the dog days of summer.[29]

From Atlanta to Pinewood, where Ellen Mays lived with Gilbert DuBose and Sallie Conley, was a working day's trip in an automobile—if one could beg or borrow one of the still-new contraptions; and it was a ride of some hours requiring some changes if one took a Jim Crow train ride. But Atlanta to Pinewood, or Pinewood to Atlanta, was a doable trip for a long weekend for husband and wife. Mays stated that he intended to go twice per month to be with Ellen in Pinewood. By contrast the trip from Chicago to Pinewood was a long, long journey, and one that Mays had not been able to afford to make. Much as he longed for a doctorate, even considering the bypass of the master's degree on his way, Mays was drawn to the idea of teaching calculus to Morehouse men, and he was drawn to the idea of a professor's pay—about one-third the pay for a white professor at the University of South Carolina but about ten times the pay for a black schoolteacher in the valley of the Santee. With a professor's salary, there could be some savings set aside, and from those savings there could be funds for completing his graduate studies. And he and his Ellen Mays, who had made sacrifices on behalf of becoming professionals in careers, could see one another on regular occasions for at least a few seasons.[30]

There remained challenges of finance and travel, even to get to Atlanta to take this opportunity. He had no savings and no income. Yet he needed money. The penurious student had not had the money to buy a proper engagement ring for Ellen Mays, but in Chicago he had at last found one that cost thirty-nine dollars. He needed another thirty or so dollars to buy a train ticket, and too much time had passed for him to play the role of a porter and "work his way" down South. Although he still had his set of porter's keys, the Pullman Company's spy network had been able to inform every regional center that Mays was a troublemaking labor organizer.[31] Finally he needed ten or eleven dollars for food and drink until he could draw a salary at Morehouse this summer. Even with this careful calculating and nickel pinching, Mays could not do everything he needed to do for less than eighty dollars—and he had nothing.

Plainly Mays needed to borrow that amount against his first paycheck, live out the second month on a shoestring, and then begin saving in a serious way by the arrival of his third paycheck. Such arrangements were quite typical at small black colleges of the era and indeed not unheard of at white colleges, for the presidents of such institutions, white or black, took a benefactor's role with their low-paid faculty. A note to President Hope would get everything arranged promptly; but such a note would not be in good order for a man beset with his station and with *megalosukia*. Mays was not willing to start life at Morehouse as a man already beholden to the college president for personal favors, loans or otherwise. He would make it or fail to make it at Morehouse on his academic doings alone. He cast about for someone in Chicago to lend him money, finding that banking institutions regarded him universally as a terrible risk. At last he found a Mr. Williams, apparently the attorney L. K. Williams from South Carolina, who practiced law in Chicago on behalf of the large and constantly increasing African American populace who arrived daily from that state.[32] Williams proffered the eighty dollars and said he could wait until fall quarter to be repaid, at a nominal interest rate. Williams wished Mays well, for not all black people could possibly make a living in Chicago, and thus some of them had to stay in the South, if not on the farms of the still-fertile valleys then in the cities of the hill country with their factories.

With his ring, less than he wanted for his "pretty girl" and yet still the biblical "pearl of great price" for the indebted scholar, Mays took a train, taking his first long Jim Crow ride without the privileges permitted a working Pullman porter. Below St. Louis he had to ride in the Jim Crow car, which had no berth for sleeping and which marked no distinctions among first, second, and third class. All people of color—preacher, teacher, bonds trader, factory worker, farmhand, or unemployed—sat bolt upright on hard seats, babies at the breasts of mothers, who sat next to loud drunkards passing around bottles of cheap liquor, while the train clicked and clacked more than five hundred miles. Sometimes a clever, courageous, and fortunate black professional, such as John Brown Watson of the Arkansas Agricultural, Mechanical and Normal College, could bribe an agent and hide out in a sleeping berth or in a deadhead car (an empty car with no reserved seats on a particular leg and one where the Pullman porters slept, played cards, and sometimes secreted black friend travelers).[33] But no man of *megalosukia* was about to pay a bribe, and Mays recognized no porters on this southern journey who might have worked with him three years ago on New England and New York routes.

The experience of this trip stayed long with him, and he vowed that in another season, when the time was right and not long from now, he would challenge the Jim Crow laws designed to embarrass God's black peoples. Blues singers could sing cleverly about Jim Crow in a way that mocked the hapless black preacher and the mighty white oppressors, but the magnificent Mays faced this miserable long ride knowing his Bible and especially his thirty-first psalm:

> To every one of my oppressors
> I am contemptible loathsome to my neighbors
> to my friends a thing of fear
> . . .
> But I put my trust in you, Yahweh.
> I say, You are my God.
> My days are in your hands, rescue me
> from the hands of enemies and persecutors;
> Save me in your love
> . . .
> Be strong; let your heart be bold
> all you who hope in Yahweh.[34]

Arriving in Atlanta with this doubled understanding of time, Mays found that Morehouse College had a doubled understanding of status and duty. To a graduate of Bates College, with its Ivy League professors and its venerable oak and stone and brick and walnut, Morehouse was new to the point of rawness and plain to the point of spartan. To a student from the University of Chicago, Morehouse was simply tiny and cramped, much as its home city Atlanta was modest in size and activity compared to Chicago. But to a country preacher from the valley of the Saluda, Morehouse with its solid buildings and efficient heating system was handsome to the point of sumptuousness; and its professors, if not Ph.D.s, were well-trained—not a few by the Ivy League—and its oak and pine trees shaded things well, just as Atlanta, while no great shakes next to Chicago, overwhelmed Greenville or Columbia or even Richmond. Of course Mays in 1921 saw Atlanta and President John Hope's institution from all these angles, for Mays was a dark licensed minister from the valley of the Saluda as well as a graduate of Bates College and a matriculate at the University of Chicago.

One perspective was clear: the Morehouse man was a leader in any community among African Americans. In this modern world, leading entailed higher mathematics as well as higher criticism. Mays was distressed to see some spotty teaching in both mathematics and theology at this important school. For his part he lay into his teaching tasks much as he approached his studies. The fishes and loaves could feed the thousands, but only if disciples believed and acted on their belief. Where Mays marched away from many black ministers was on this issue of belief and action. Hard work had to be grounded in firm belief—but there did have to be hard work done and not just "whooping the benches" about the faith. Always there was that much of Thomas Aquinas, that schoolman's insistence that the scholar employing reason might well find true belief and thus the good in life.[35]

Yet another perspective about Morehouse was also unambiguous. It was the viewpoint of white people. Many of them called it a "nigger school," and they did their best to make the black professor, much more than the black student, understand how far down the tall totem pole he stood. Some have said that cities by their nature integrate and miscegenate and liberate; but Atlanta segregated as it grew, and Jim Crow was terribly important to the white city leaders, who, as an Italian sociologist might put it, used their wealth to gain political power and used their political power, once gained, to expand their already large wealth and who inflamed the racist passions of powerless white people in order to keep in motion the whirligig of power and wealth.[36]

The black scholar E. Franklin Frazier, a sociologist who became Mays's colleague and a man whom Mays quoted, summed up what he saw happening in the South:

When agrarian unrest among the "poor whites" of the South joined forces with the Populist movement, which represented the general unrest among American farmers, the question of race was used to defeat the co-operation of "poor whites" and Negroes. It was then that the demagogues assumed leadership of the "poor whites" and provided a solution of the class conflict among whites that offered no challenge to the political power and economic privileges of the industrialists and the planter class. The program, which made the Negro the scapegoat, contained the following provisions: (1) the Negro was completely disfranchised by all sorts of legal subterfuges, with the threat of force in the background; (2) the funds which were appropriated on a per capita basis for Negro school children were diverted to white schools; and (3) a legal system of segregation in all phases of public life was instituted. In order to justify this program, the demagogues, who were supported by the white propertied classes, engaged for twenty-five years in a campaign to prove that the Negro was subhuman, morally degenerate, and intellectually incapable of being educated.[37]

The sociologist's explanation worked for Mays, who also refused to blame the "poor whites" who supposedly created and ran the Ku Klux Klan: "All the things that were going on in Atlanta to degrade Negroes when I 'discovered' the city in 1921 cannot be attributed to the Ku Klux Klan. The foundation upon which the Klan stood had been laid in laws and custom decades before the second birth of the Klan in 1915."[38]

Mays noticed many instances of Jim Crow as he moved about Atlanta, but one especially angered him: "Shortly after I came to Atlanta in 1921, a Negro who was working for a white woman fell from a ladder and broke a leg. The woman, not knowing that in the South pain is segregated, called a white undertaking establishment to send an ambulance to take the man to the hospital. When the white ambulance driver arrived and saw the suffering man was a Negro, he drove away leaving the Negro lying in his own blood and pain."[39]

Mays came onto the Atlanta educational stage as part of a wave that amounted to a third generation of black educators. During this phase of institution building, few African Americans made as significant an impression as John Hope, and Mays's close association with the great Atlanta educator made an appropriately deep imprint on the young calculus instructor. After all Hope was by his own description "the first lightning that burns up the poison and purifies the atmosphere." Among other things, the image that Hope had chosen for himself reminded Mays to take the longest view; and that perspective of a widening horizon suggested a future day when other forces beyond the "first lightning" must be set in motion. That is, Mays also had to think so long term that he could image a Morehouse College after John Hope. Mays did not agree with everything that Hope said and did, and he marked both his admiration and his reservations.

For instance Hope really loved football and other sports, and he was convinced that men learned to be leaders and followers in such games at the same time that the institution gained notice in the press. Practicing maneuvers and moves, studying play formations, cooperating with teammates when one was tired or hurt, especially in front of hostile spectators—all these aspects of team sports appealed to Hope's philosophy that the Morehouse man must grow through all experiences, only some of which were academic. To Hope, sports were cocurricular and not at all extracurricular. Successful sports teams were always mentioned in newspapers and magazines, firing the hearts of students, alumni, and potential donors (those potential "friends" Hope looked for among the northern whites). Occasionally even the racist members of the "raging white tribes" in the area spoke favorably and said, "Our nigger team is better than your nigger team." Other fine educators, all of whom Mays admired, agreed; and these included John Brown Watson and Samuel Howard Archer. In fact only a few seasons before 1921, Morehouse football practices routinely featured Hope, Watson, and Archer jogging alongside the players at the end of the day's workout.[40]

By contrast Mays was doubtful about all team sports and most skeptical where football was concerned. Many a young man willing to work hard at football was unable or unwilling to work hard at his studies, and there was always pressure from fans, not excluding fans among the faculty and administrators, to help the man who was a strong athlete but weak scholar, the man who was fast afield but slow in his studies. Such pressures were especially keen in the field of mathematics, including calculus. Now was no time to ease expectations in the mathematics classroom; indeed now was the time to raise expectations. After all Bennie Mays was teaching the first advanced calculus course ever offered at "the House." To survive academically weaker and slower students probably needed to reduce time spent on extracurricular activities, especially football with its heavy demands. Mays rejected John Hope's concept of sports as cocurricular instead of extracurricular and was always clear in his assessment that sports interfered with studies.

Mays was notably plainspoken about football. Players and fans often referred to him as a professor who stood as an enemy to their sport, while he pronounced himself a classicist who wanted balance, order, and harmony in a world where sports were decidedly unbalancing the budget of time, money, talent, and even emotions. During the first months of his appointment, Mays largely kept his own counsel on college sports and did not say anything contrary to President Hope. Occasionally football players and other athletes complained that Mays was opposed to sports, but he always insisted that he treated all students the same, a policy fully supported by Hope, who wanted no special treatment for athletes in the classroom, no matter how much he appreciated their prowess and accomplishments on the field.

On the other hand, a disagreement that could not be so diplomatically handled had to do with Mays's tests. In addition to calculus, Hope persuaded Mays to teach psychology and to coach debate. Coaching debate seemed natural enough, especially given Mays's own undergraduate efforts at Bates and given the long decades that white men trained at the University of South Carolina had arrogated to themselves classical rhetoric as an entitlement of white people and then laughed at black efforts. Morehouse men had to be able to debate, and Mays knew well how to coach that skill. Psychology was something else again, and Mays had to struggle to get it across to the students, for it was not his research specialty. Still and all, it was hard to comprehend the racist forces raging in Atlanta those days without a grounding in psychology, and there was a solid mathematical and statistical foundation for most of the serious psychological studies. Mays thus had pedagogical, moral, and methodological reason for teaching the subject. How galling then to have President Hope interfere with his testing!

In preparing his final examination for that first academic quarter of psychology at Morehouse, Mays had written out his questions on a paper and then given it to a secretary to type and duplicate sixty times on the mimeograph machine for the students enrolled in the class. Administering his test, he was mindful that some fifteen of the sixty students had failed the midterm test, and he was curious to see that many of those fifteen had finished their tests in good order and confident spirits. His suspicions aroused, he next learned from a fellow teacher that she had seen a baker's dozen of young men examining a paper, which they tore up and threw away when she came toward them. Retrieving torn pages from the ash can, she recognized Mays's handwriting and could piece together enough of the scraps to identify the document as Mays's test. By the time she reached him, the test had already been administered. To Mays—with his classical sense of right and wrong—the entire examination was compromised beyond usefulness or goodness, and the only valid thing to do was to give a second test, awkward as that was with the academic quarter coming to an end. He sent word to his sixty scholars to prepare for a second examination, one that would be monitored closely throughout its production phases. He also sent word that he was not going to grade the first examination, but that he would keep all copies as evidence in any investigation of wrongdoing that he intended to conduct.

Students complained, and some went to see President Hope, who called Mays in and told him he was being unfair to the innocent, which by Mays's own count must number close to forty-five of the sixty in class. Hope ordered

Mays to cancel the second examination and to grade the first examination forthwith. Mays declined, arguing both on the statistical principle of the invalidity of a compromised test and on the moral principle that no professor's academical prerogative over testing should be tampered with by administrators unless there were questions of incompetence or malfeasance. Mays was the debating coach, and Dr. Hope's rationale is available to a later generation only through Mays's own memories of the dispute. The compromised evidence certainly weighs heavily on the side of the young instructor's logic. Yet Hope was president, and a powerful figure on campus and beyond, and he had spoken. It was a resignation issue for the president, and principle clashed with practicality. Mays reluctantly conceded the presidential authority as a matter of fact if not an element of morality. He graded the tests and notified the students that the second test was canceled. Thereby he gave passing grades to an indeterminate number of students who probably cheated on his test.

Hope rehired Mays for the 1921–22 academic year. Although he did not cite them at the time, Mays was fully aware of two ironclad dicta of Thomas Aquinas, someone whom he quoted often and always with a sense of gravamen in the citing: never go to war if there is no chance of your winning, and prudence is a primary virtue that distills all other good qualities of personhood. As he generally did, Mays retained his magnificence, that Thomistic word, through a difficult situation by the way he fought the fight and by the way in which he moved onward after losing the fight. Recognizing and respecting the magnificence, President Hope named Mays dean of faculty.[41]

Sometime in summer or fall of 1922, Ellen Mays became pregnant. The pregnancy, whenever conception came, is not mentioned in Bennie Mays's memoir, and neither is there correspondence about it, at least not in the records carefully preserved and turned over to Howard University by Bennie Mays in his final season. A man, especially a countryman in the valley of the Saluda, would be proud to father a child; and a woman, especially a countrywoman in the valley of the Santee, would be proud to bear a child. For a country couple, such a pregnancy was proof of God's blessing and a reassurance that there would be another hand to turn the plow and to hoe and to chop. But Bennie Mays was no longer that kind of countryman, and Ellen Harvin Mays was no longer that kind of countrywoman. Instead Bennie Mays was an urban professional, not only the licensed preacher who was pastor of a church in Atlanta but also a dean of a college faculty and a research scholar seeking full and propitious certification from the University of Chicago. As for Ellen Harvin Mays, she was already a certified professional, earning a stipend to train teachers and was herself aspiring—reaching to the stars themselves—for her own career as an academic, and not at Morris College. Both Mayses were reaching beyond their little country villages. Yet now Ellen Mays was back with Gilbert DuBose and Sallie Conley in Pinewood, and neighbors and relatives saw only another country girl who was beginning to show that she was in a family way. There was really no role permitted a pregnant Jeanes Fund teacher in that time and that place, and Ellen Mays's time as a professional seemed to be rapidly concluding its brief season. As for Bennie Mays, the stipend he would earn at the University of Chicago, around $110 in the academic year of 1924–25, was nowhere near enough to pay for room and board for a wife and child and himself. In fact, even his salary as dean at Morehouse, around $1,200 with a place in the dormitory, was nowhere near enough to pay for room and board for a wife and child and himself. No man of *megalosukia* could fail to support his wife and child, and really, no man of *megalosukia* could study at the University of Chicago while his wife raised their child on Gilbert DuBose's small farm. There was more wrong than right for this couple, who surely did not plan this pregnancy.

But the worst part was still to come. The pregnancy went badly. Bennie Mays gnashed his teeth at the poor health care afforded African Americans in the valley of the Santee. Anxiously he searched Atlanta for a well-trained doctor who was willing to assist a black woman in a difficult childbirth. Although he never said that pregnancy and difficulties in delivery were the grave problem, Mays did write that he found a physician—never identified and at a facility also not identified—in Atlanta who could and did perform "an operation." He wrote that the operation failed, and Ellen Mays died shortly thereafter.[42]

In fact Ellen Mays lost the baby during delivery at the Atlanta facility and then returned to her people in Pinewood. She was severely stricken, even hemorrhaging, but Bennie Mays did not leave Atlanta and go to Pinewood with her. He had noted that he was able to visit her twice a month by train, but he never went to Pinewood between her failed operation on February 20, 1923, and her death on March 30. Perhaps he did not know the severity of her condition after the failed delivery. Perhaps he could not be spared from Morehouse even for a few days, not even to sit by his wife's death bed.

According to the brief and almost illegible notes of the attending physician, Ellen Mays seems to have suffered placenta previa, a condition in which the placenta, instead of "interlocking" with the uterus, covers some part of the uterus and cannot be easily separated from it. Around the seventh month of pregnancy, a slight hemorrhaging is the main symptom, and coming along with this slight bleeding is anemia, pallor, weak pulse, air hunger, and low blood pressure. This bleeding recurs and becomes more severe over the final term of the pregnancy, but is not painful to the mother. The treatment is to conserve the blood supply before and during delivery, prevent postpartum hemorrhage, and combat anemia before and after labor. Particularly dangerous is sepsis, or the introduction of poisonous microorganisms into the blood and the organs, a condition that often appears with placenta previa. A warning note to caregivers is that much of the condition is "potential"; that is, "it is not evidenced by signs and symptoms" and thus must be prevented rather than treated once bleeding becomes severe and after the pulse rate has dropped and anemia is obvious. If too much blood is lost, or if sepsis ensues, the unborn fetus and the mother each could be lost in a stillborn delivery to "sudden exitus," as the doctors phrased it, meaning to say a sudden leave taking from life itself.[43]

Dismissed from the Atlanta hospital in the third week of February, Ellen Mays went to Gilbert DuBose's farm in Pinewood. Her condition declined rapidly, and on March 23, DuBose called a local physician, apparently Dr. Charles J. Tenhover. The physician found Ellen Mays in a bad way, victim of an embolism, a condition in which a "mass of undissolved matter [which may] consist of . . . clumps of bacteria"—could form a thrombosis, or blockage of a blood vessel, possibly her pulmonary artery. Mortal dangers of this development could include, perhaps at the same time, lack of blood to the brain, heart stoppage, severe lung damage, as well as poisoning by "purulent" matter from the bacteria. Nursing care prescribed by medical handbooks suggested raising the head of the victim, giving additional oxygen, and giving mechanical ventilation as well as administering some anticoagulant drugs likely not available then in a rural, southern setting. Dr. Tenhover did take her to a hospital in nearby Sumter, where he and other caregivers attempted an operation on March 26. This may have been an effort to put a tube into her trachea, which could let in oxygen but prevent purulent matter from getting into her bronchi. Whatever was attempted on March 26, it did not succeed, and Dr. Tenhover allowed Gilbert DuBose and Sallie Conley to take Ellen Mays to their home, where she could be made comfortable.[44]

At dusk on March 30, Gilbert DuBose called Dr. Tenhover again, and the physician came to the farm to confirm her death, marking her passing at 7:00 P.M. True to South Carolina traditions regarding African Americans, Dr. Tenhover did not perform an autopsy but simply wrote from his notes and memory and filed a death certificate for Sumter County showing placenta previa as primary cause of death, embolism as secondary causal condition, and both conditions resulting from a failed operation on March 23 to repair damage from the failed February operation after the placenta failed to separate from the fetus in the stillborn delivery in Atlanta. DuBose called mortician George H. Hurst of Sumter, a man who may have been Jewish. Hurst handled African American bodies for burial preparation, something avoided by other white morticians; in fact Hurst appears in the records almost exclusively as the caring mortician for "Colored and Negro" clientele in Sumter County that year.[45]

Theodosia Richardson arranged for a handsome gravestone to be set along-side Rufus Richardon's marked grave and alongside her own dedicated space inside the Richardson family plot in the black section of the Manning cemetery. Like the grave marker of the soldier Rufus Richardson, this stone rose in tribute to the Jeanes teacher. It was as high as the markers for the white lords and ladies memorialized at the other end of the cemetery. She erected this second memorial now knowing that she would leave no progeny behind on her own appointed day, not even progeny adopted and sponsored informally as Ellen Harvin Mays had been. She must have talked with Bennie Mays, and surely he approved the words she arranged to have inscribed:

> As a wife devoted
> As a woman virtuous
> As a friend ever kind and true

And, on the eastern facing, Richardson had inscribed:

> Mrs. Ellen E. Harvin
> Wife of
> B. E. Mays
> Jan. 26, 1895
> Mar. 30, 1923
> MAYS[46]

It galled Bennie Mays to lay his wife's body in a Jim Crow cemetery, no matter how well-made the marker or how well-kept the family plot. And there was bitterness in the sacrifices memorialized there in one spot: the infantryman killed with honor in France and dishonored in Manning, the educator honored in New York and Chicago and dishonored in Sumter and Manning. Yet there was more gall and wormwood to be forced down the black man's throat, even if no arrogant white lord had ever showed disrespect for Bennie Mays and his people. This even more bitter draught was that a husband and a wife had sacrificed time together for a future that would now be spent apart. The hardness of life in the South was upon Bennie Mays. His "pretty girl" had lived away from him as many days as she had lived alongside him, and that sacrifice was by his own design for what John Brown Watson and John Hope called the long run, the lengthy journey toward the prize out there on the most distant horizon. She had even suffered and traveled and died apart from him. The pain of the South, anywhere in the South, and the barbs of the times, perhaps any times, were compounded by the love lost in a life apart and the love lost in death.

In his grief and love, he turned to his academic tasks–the ones that Ellen Mays believed in so fiercely and that kept him from her side at the end of her brief days. Believing as he did that ignorance among the black men was actually a white design, Mays desperately wanted black institutions to instruct by setting high standards. Yet of course such institutions simply had to compromise on some things in order to survive at all. At the moment Morehouse College seemed to be at some considerable risk of folding. Hope appeared to be one of the figures best able to find money and other resources to save Morehouse in those parlous times. From 1921 to 1924, Mays watched the master and learned, like a smart substitute player paying close attention to the coach from the sidelines. Hope went among some of Atlanta's white leaders, those who would be famously described as the city's "power elite"; and Hope pressed them for money and help for the men of color studying at Morehouse. He failed on many occasions, but he succeeded often enough. Like all black educational leaders of the day, Hope relied on northern philanthropists, especially northern Jews, to help with the finances of running a school. Booker T. Washington had been first in finding the way to the hearts of northern Jews, who remembered the prejudice they had endured on their way upward, and Hope successfully followed Washington's lead. Like Washington, Hope was also adept at finding money among northern philanthropists, including those who had no memory of such prejudice. No less a magnate than John D. Rockefeller, the benefactor of the University of Chicago, was a fellow alumnus of Brown University, and he helped Morehouse College, though of course the largest portions of his wealth went to his Ivy League alma mater and to his own University of Chicago.[47]

Nor were these northern contributions strictly money alone, but also time, that precious time of the northern businessmen who first and most loudly among Americans proclaimed that time is money. For instance George Rice Hovey of the American Baptist Home Mission Society and Virginia Union College came to Atlanta and personally showed Morehouse College bookkeepers how to post bills in a modern, efficient, and accurate way. Hovey was among those who insisted to Mays that the black Richmonders were in all cases northerners and in no way southerners. That Hovey was so kind as to render the advice moved Mays of course; but that a fine, classical, educational institution was managed by people who until 1923 did not know how to record their business transactions moved Mays to something else again, something like disgust and even fear. Then, when he realized that the many students studying on scholarships were paid with funds taken directly from the operating budget of yearly receipts instead of from interest earned by a managed endowment fund, Mays's mathematical mind told him that Hope needed to exercise some prudence in finances if he intended to continue for a long time to train young men to be good citizens and good soldiers in the fights for justice.[48]

Hope surely did believe in the fight for justice for the people of color. and Mays thrilled to the president's rhetoric—high classical rhetoric that knowledge is power, that black ignorance decreases black power and increases the power of the white lords, and that Jim Crow was specifically designed not only to keep black people in ignorance but also to remind them publicly and often of their status. Hope preached—and Mays heard and held to it—that the Morehouse man must have a social responsibility and must work on behalf of black folk injured by the damnable Jim Crow.[49]

Because of Hope's encouraging words, Mays made it a point to meet Will Winton Alexander, the South's most prominent homegrown liberal of the 1920s and the director of the Commission on Interracial Cooperation (CIC), regionally headquartered in Atlanta with branch offices in each southern state. Dr. Will, as he was universally called, was also a trustee in charge of distributing monies for the Rosenwald Foundation, based in Chicago. Mays of course had yet to meet a single white southerner with much intelligence—and such intelligence as white southerners had was deployed as a weapon against black people. It was not only the lynch mob death dealers in Phoenix, his first real memory of any kind. It was as well the white Mayses directing the black Mays children to eat from the trough, a Jim Crow trolley driver strutting with his weapon, and above all Dr. Wallace Payne cuffing the child in the post office.[50] These were the actions by which Mays knew white southerners. Now he came to the CIC offices of a white Atlantan, one known to be intelligent, educated at Vanderbilt University and said by Hope to be sensitive and anxious to help the striving Morehouse students and faculty.

Alexander did appear to be intelligent; he did appear to listen to the professor; and he did appear to regard Mays as a human with a mind and a soul and a perfectible nature. Yet he also seemed nothing like the northern liberals Mays had known. For one thing Dr. Will did not even define the words the same way as a striving Morehouse man when he used the term "Jim Crow." An ordained Methodist minister who once filled a pulpit in Nashville, Alexander hated Jim Crow because it was violent and because it denied black people opportunities, and he intended to find opportunities for striving African Americans. However, the segregated aspect of Jim Crow, if it troubled him, did so only in an abstract and almost academic way. Alexander was looking at the formulation "separate but equal" and wanted to make the material things equal; he was evidently spending little time or thought on the "separate" side of the defense of Jim Crow as rendered by the U.S. Supreme Court. At least Alexander said nothing to that effect to Mays in 1921 or 1922 and instead talked only about making material things equal. Dr. Will, Mays decided quickly, had no intention of fighting segregation as a system of racism; instead he wanted to bring economic opportunities and social respect for African Americans while delaying for long years, perhaps forever, a day of meaningful integration.[51] Alexander helped a few a little, and he counseled everybody to go slowly. He so advised Mays on their first meeting. The dean of the Morehouse faculty listened politely and departed.

Mays went back to his quarters at Morehouse with proof of two things that he must "read, mark, and inwardly digest."[52] One lesson relearned was that southern white people at best had their limits. Another lesson newly learned was that President Hope had to play clever games merely to find the money to keep the college in operation at all. Black presidents had to smile and nod often as they heard stupid things, and they had to be mindful about saying anything at all in certain circumstances, lest they lie and prostitute themselves—or speak the truth and lose the money gift. Will Alexander had friends in high places, not only in Atlanta but in Washington, Chicago, and New York. He had to be placated, or he could become a dangerous enemy. The Morehouse dean watched with fascination as Hope played out the line with these "fish," whom Mays judged to be big and dumb but dangerous. Will Alexander was told that he was the white liberal of Atlanta. If he said to go slow, to find economic opportunity in the ghetto, to build social respect on your own side of town, and to live with the separateness and segregationism of Jim Crow, then the black president needed to smile and to nod his head and to tell everyone that Will Winton Alexander was simply the best there was in the white South, emphasizing that qualifying phrase in a way known ruefully among striving black academics in Atlanta.

At any rate Hope surely could persuade white people to part with their money, and he did so without irritating them with the truth. These naked emperors parading in their paunchy flesh needed to be reassured that they were dressed in finery and that they looked and sounded fine. Hope had learned from no less than the "wizard," Booker T. Washington, how to talk to such rich white men. Of Andrew Carnegie—notoriously "cranky" and unpredictable and thus "a very curious proposition" in his later years—Washington had told Hope: "He gets ideas into his head in his own way, and when they once get there, it is very hard to get them out. Almost impossible by direct means."[53] Yet Washington occasionally did by indirect means raise money from Carnegie, and Hope by similarly indirect means found ways to raise money from Carnegie's foundation and from other such men.

Nor did Hope miss opportunities for profit among African Americans. For instance, as a rural educator, John Brown Watson kept Louisiana and Arkansas public colleges afloat by judicious application of country-slicker politics with urban white donors and politicians of North and South. Yet Watson was also a sharp-eyed businessman who bought and sold realty in Atlanta, and he provided a house and at least two lots for use of the Morehouse administration. Hope and future Morehouse presidents could use the Watson home for a residence or could rent it out, and the value of the lots, one of the "sure buys" in booming Atlanta, was a significant addition to the tiny Morehouse endowment.[54]

Indeed Hope, the blue-eyed and blond-haired descendant of Scotsmen, had mastered the message of the much darker Watson, a message repeated for Hope's successor, Samuel Howard Archer. Watson kept saying to go slow and to be thorough, to be simple in life and living and work and to think for the long term. Watson liked to jog and not to run, both in the literal and in the metaphorical senses, because he thought jogging the more steady and more sure exercise, the one more appropriate for successful work over a long life. The slow progress, the occasionally painful pace of forward motion belied no false starts, no stumbles, no running a long way in the wrong direction. Hope, like Watson, put his institution into the long exodus away from slavery and toward the Promised Land, but even Moses's forty years might be too quick a pace for these travelers, given the obstacles of hard times and the cruelty of the white lords of the land. Hope, again following Watson, stayed true to his own name. He was too quietly confident about the long run to be put off the pace by the brambles and the mire of the stretch of pathway immediately before him.[55] Mays must have realized that. After he attained his Ph.D. and tried to run his own school for scholars of color, he used the same tactics, understanding the cruelty and determination of the evil white lords of the land and the extreme limitations of the so-called good white lords of capital such as Will Winton Alexander.

In keeping with the classicist's marching orders for sustaining a long campaign, Mays understood also a God-demanded duty that he preach to the dark folk of the neighborhood near Morehouse College. Some 125 plain and largely unlettered but hardworking and right thinking people gathered regularly at a little church called Shiloh Baptist Church. From his social context courses at the University of Chicago, Mays knew the significance of that name "Shiloh." North-northeast of Jerusalem and ten miles north of Bethel, it was the "ancient center of Israel," the place where Joshua set up the tabernacle, where the sacred ark was kept, and the "seat of the priesthood" for Eli and his sons. Then had come decline; the Philistines had destroyed the tabernacle; the ark was removed; and Shiloh "lost its prestige." Many chosen Jews were displaced, dispersed far away, much as sons of the mighty African tribes had been dispersed into southern Piedmont lands such as the valley of the Saluda, where they worked for other men on land not their own. Yet, long, long ago Shiloh had been the site of a dividing up of good land among deserving and believing people, much as Walter Rauschenbusch wanted land for deserving black people in the twentieth century. For Mays then, "Shiloh" signaled at once the ancient achievement, the current despair, and the long-run promise of justice when the good lands would be returned to the good and true people.[56]

Such good people, mostly country folk only recently come to Atlanta, asked Mays to be their pastor at Shiloh Baptist Church. Already licensed, he could preach to them well enough in 1921, but he wanted to serve as their ordained pastor, and so he went before Morehouse professor C. D. Hubert, both a faculty member and a practicing minister with a congregation in Darlington, South Carolina. Dr. Hubert got in touch with Ellen Harvin Mays's pastor, the Reverend Garrick, and they arranged a formal ordination in Sumter for the Christmas holidays in 1921. Thus on a happy day before her sudden death, Ellen Mays had been able to see her husband honored before the children of God in her own home church during Christmastide; and the people of the Shiloh Church began their new year of 1922 with their own duly ordained pastor.

From the first Sunday of 1922, Mays began to offer two Sunday services, one in midmorning and one in early evening. His morning service was always concluded by 12:15 P.M., which was different from local practice and much appreciated by his congregation of hardworking laborers and students from Morehouse and its sister college, Spelman. On occasion white people came to Mays's services, and as he put it in the era, they came "clothed in the skin that gives perpetual protection." Without revealing his resentment of them at all, the minister treated such white visitors with respect—but no more respect than he accorded the other worshippers. He always integrated any white visitors, refusing to set aside "choice seats" for the guests.[57]

Despite the presence of highly educated young men from Morehouse and equally well educated young women from Spelman and the occasional white intellectual, Mays did not attempt to preach the social context of Dr. Case in his sermons. Neither did he "whoop the benches." Instead he preached simply and directly from the Bible, emphasizing the themes of love, charity, respect, moral conduct, and hard work. He was paid one hundred dollars per month, but he gave twenty-five to fifty dollars of that salary to the organist, who played the well-known spirituals that were the balm for a dark Christian's hard life.[58]

The congregation seemed to appreciate Mays, and often a day laborer would press a quarter or fifty-cent piece into his big hand at the end of the service. The minister would swallow hard, knowing at once the great financial sacrifice being made if he accepted the money and the painful sense of rejection if he returned the coin. He always accepted, as was fitting. In that vein he actually saw in practice the biblical story of the widow's mite. This parishioner was Sister Reddick, an elderly widow who worked for a white family and lived in a small frame house at the back of the white family's lot. She worked for that family every day, including Sunday mornings, when she cooked and cleaned on their behalf. Because of her work schedule, she attended the Shiloh evening service, and she always contributed her coin when the collection plate was passed her way. One weekend she invited Mays over for supper in her simple home, and as he took bread with her he noted how little she had, marking in his memories the way she gave the better portion to Shiloh Baptist Church.[59]

Original sin also became evident, however, when someone stole the greatcoat of the striving minister and dean. As Mays recalled it, one bitter cold day early in his pastorate, he had left his hat and greatcoat in his study outside the sanctuary. The study was not locked during worship services. On this winter's Sunday, when 12:15 P.M. came around, Bennie Mays shook hands with his brother and sister worshippers and then went to get his wrap and his hat on the way to Sunday dinner between late morning and evening services. His coat was gone, though other things were left undisturbed. Possibly a transient passerby had taken it during service, but it was also possible that one of the worshippers had taken it. The cold and the pain Mays felt as he walked to his dinner was only partly the effect of midwinter winds. He could not afford a new coat, so he spent weeks looking in pawnshops in Atlanta until he found his old coat and bought it back for himself. He told that story as a parable of Jesus's sacrifice: "I made you, you were mine, I lost you, I found you, and I paid for you to have you back." His rendering, while his own version, followed an old Protestant sermon about a boy losing a boat that he had made, finding it in a store, and then buying it back.[60]

His congregation generally responded warmly to his sincere efforts to preach the biblical themes of love, charity, respect, moral conduct, and hard work. The widow's mite and the day laborer's coin were poured in by the bushel barrel, while theft and ingratitude and insults were added only by the pinch and by the trace.

To the pastor's work of making Shiloh Christians was added the schoolmaster's work of making Morehouse men. The saddened widower Mays went hard at the twin tasks. His measured Thomistic response to disagreements with John Hope proved prudent as Thomas Aquinas would judge it: Hope requested Mays to serve as acting dean for the academic year of 1922–23 and again for academic year 1923–24, and encouraged him to consider a return to Morehouse once he earned his University of Chicago degree. As the dean, Mays insisted on a general toughening of standards and raising of expectations in mathematics and psychology in particular, but in all instruction in general. Hope watched his young dean closely. He approved Mays's work and wrote at least one letter at that time showing how much he valued Mays's administrative acumen.[61]

One of Mays's most gratifying tasks was guiding the debate team, especially debaters James Madison Nabrit and Howard Thurman. The light-skinned Nabrit, like his namesake, was a man of elegance; but unlike the white Madison, he brought a confident style to his small frame. He wore his clothes well, and from early student days he looked the part he worked to become, the competent attorney who could beard the lion of damnable Jim Crow. By contrast Thurman was darker and fleshlier, with a high forehead already foretelling adult baldness and with large buckteeth, a front bicuspid conspicuously capped in gold. Despite Mays's strictures, Thurman could not wear a suit without quickly rumpling it, presenting a messy spectacle made more obvious when he lined up next to the dapper and trim little Nabrit. Yet there was brilliance in him too, and in the early days the large man with the almost burlesque gestures and wrinkled finery evinced the learning and the boldness that later made him a productive scholar, inspirational preacher, and dynamic lecturer in religious studies. The two made quite a team, Nabrit the counselor of controlled force and Thurman the neo-Romantic force in tune with an outraged Yahweh. Mays pushed both men along in their reading, in their reasoning, and in their forensic techniques.[62]

Thurman and Nabrit swept all before them, and on one occasion they had to do so against white oppressors who intruded themselves into the Jim Crow debates. Mays wanted Nabrit and Thurman to compete against white debaters, but the "very laws of the very lords forbade that" as the debate coach phrased it. Nor was Mays afraid of sending his team to be judged by white judges, as sometimes happened. Yet in the spring semester of 1923, at Fisk University of all places—that campus where no less than William Edward Burghardt Du Bois found stirring and striving the souls of black folk—qualified black judges were displaced from their appointed role solely because they were African Americans. Mays gnashed his teeth as his list of approved black judges was discarded, and he came to see that Nabrit and Thurman would be evaluated by white Nashvilleans, some of dubious qualifications and all suspect of the backhanded racism that favored local black people, "our niggers," over the "stranger" black men from Atlanta.[63]

Hewing close to his Thomistic training, Mays pushed the young men even harder than usual, insisting that only a superhuman performance could possibly win the trophy on this day in front of bigoted, and possibly unintelligent, white judges. Practice could make perfect; carefully developed habits were virtues in social ethics; and prudence distilled courage of a special sort. These men of the House could make perfection so obvious that even dull white bigots had to acknowledge it, however grudgingly. Indeed Mays rose to the challenge and began to thrill to the struggle, for he lived by words he liked to quote from Thomas Carlyle: "Like is not a May-game, but a battle and a march, a warfare with principalities and powers. No idle promenade through fragrant orange groves and green flower spaces waited on by the choral muses and the rosy hours; it is a stern pilgrimage thru the rough burning sandy solitudes, thru regions of thick-ribbed ice."[64]

On the day of the debate, Nabrit was seldom so pointed or precise, nor was Thurman so inspirited and passionate, and the two in combination overwhelmed the white judges, who awarded them the prize. Mays, normally proud of his tight control over his emotions, especially in front of southern white people doing an injustice, surprised himself when the verdict was announced. He shouted and jumped up onto the high stage, clearing the space between auditorium floor and stage floor much like a champion hurdler. He was at least as joyful as Nabrit and Thurman, for the Morehouse men had fought the fight so well that even detestable white people had to acknowledge that "the idea that whatever Negroes have built must die . . . is no good."[65]

For their part Thurman and Nabrit recalled Mays as a stirring coach, and they recalled their days at Morehouse as a period in which they forged strong characters and good habits through processes by no means always enjoyable even in the Aristotelian sense of the "good life." Most white academicians, and probably a good portion of black academicians, would not wish to be remembered as schoolmasters, with the connotation of the drill master, preacher, scold, and parental figure, but Mays accepted the label as a fair description of his role. In fact Mays began to speak in Calvinist terms about an appointed duty and station established by no one less than God. Some of this resolve to serve a providential task is a Calvinist and Augustinian reading of theology, but some of it as well reflected his best efforts at living without Ellen Harvin Mays in a land dominated by thuggish white men: "To be able to stand the troubles of life, one must have a sense of mission and the belief that God sent him or her into the world for a purpose, to do something unique and distinctive; and that if he does not do it life will be worse off because it was not done."[66]

Furthermore Mays concluded that happiness itself might well be impossible for those so chosen, and that in any case happiness, Thomas Jefferson notwithstanding, was overrated: "I do not know what happiness is," Mays stated, "and I do not think it is important that we be happy. But it is important that you find your work and do it as if you were sent into the world at this precise moment in history to do your job. If happiness can be achieved, it will be found in a job well done and in giving and not in receiving."[67]

It was likely that about this time the stirring dark men first began to call Morehouse College "the House," a term attaching itself casually both to the institution and to its leaders, especially John Hope, Samuel Howard Archer, and eventually Bennie Mays. Mays was shaped by the House, but he also shaped the House, and his debate coaching, mathematics teaching, psychology teaching, and deaning all happened as the full identities of the House and the Morehouse man were developing. The name was funny but serious too. The "big house" was where the white "lord," the lord of the land, made his home, occasionally taking to himself a pretty slave to lay with, occasionally treating some wrong-sheet offspring from such rape as a favored "high yellow." But mostly the white lord sat in his big house and presided over the struggling gangs of dark folk who worked his land, first as slaves, later as sharecroppers and renters. The big house, such as Henry Hazel Mays sat in back in the valley of the Saluda, was not always big in fact, as Henry Hazel Mays's was not, but it always had a front entryway for the white lords and a back door for the dark people and sometimes also for the poor white day laborers. When any sharecropper, white or black, got hold of a little money, he began to call his own place "the House." He began to let the small-town rich man know that a freeholding farmer could have his own house.[68]

The House in Atlanta under John Hope and Dean Mays became a dark man's House with its own front door. The front door opened up the library, and a stirring dark scholar must walk proudly through that door and read his classics, his sociology, his Bible and its concordances, his history, economics, and poetry. That front door opened also into a chemistry laboratory, and the stirring dark scholar must walk erectly through that door and apply the natural and mathematical sciences, the knowledge, to the test tubes there. That front door opened also to the debate hall, and the men of the House must walk through it to the podium to apply the classical rhetoric to the problems posed by the hated white lords. The House also had a paved pathway, a handsome paved drive, and that path led up and out, a direction lighted by the unfailing North Star.

One of the ways that striving black men at the House could show their manliness, professionalism, and leadership was to join Omega Psi Phi, a national social fraternity for men of color. Its college members were proud of their academic performance and campus leadership. Omega Psi Phi alumni were everywhere, North and South, and all were generous in helping each other in business concerns and in helping the communities of color in their own residential neighborhoods. The association was not only important to the young dean at Morehouse for its work with the students in his charge; it was as well his own balm in a strange land where stupid and vicious white men held power. It was a mountaintop from which he could see above and beyond the armed trolley and bus conductors on what were only lowly hills. Indeed it was even a height from which he could see beyond the river across which his own Ellen Harvin Mays had gone. In 1924 Omega Psi Phi was conducting a conclave in

St. Louis, and the Morehouse dean was traveling there, anxious to see and enjoy another city that proclaimed itself to be northern and not southern. Mays was also anxious to meet other Omega men and learn from them how to make a church, a college, a life work in a land where the untrue and the unworthy held sway.[69]

As he planned this trip, the schoolmaster thought again about the train that he would take to St. Louis. The Jim Crow law and the segregation prophets said that a black man must ride in the Jim Crow cars, not in a car with a Pullman berth. Mays was determined to start in Birmingham and travel first class to St. Louis, much as an Omega man could travel from St. Louis to Chicago or to Kansas City. He went to the Atlanta ticket agent and asked for a first-class ticket, with Pullman berth, from Birmingham to St. Louis. The white agent was suspicious and asked who the ticket was for. The dean gave the answer, "Mr. Mays," knowing that no ticket agent would ever call a black man "mister." The agent would assume that a manservant was on an errand for his white lord Mr. Mays. This strategy worked, and thus Bennie Mays owned a first-class ticket for the Birmingham to St. Louis leg of the trip.[70]

Using this ticket was quite another matter. When he arrived in Birmingham, he stood his tallest, which was very tall, and he marched onto the Pullman car to take his seat. At once he heard murmuring, and he could see white fingers pointing at him. His berth was directly in front of a dining car, and most cars in the train were full, so many passengers had to pass by Mays to get in and out of the diner. The Pullman porter, doing the job in the South that young Bennie Mays had done in the North, came by to warn him that his life was in danger. Mays retorted that it was the porter's duty to protect each passenger. The whole thing was nervous making and unsettling, and, when the train stopped at Columbia, Tennessee, Mays deboarded long enough to visit a friend, J. W. Johnson, also a black academic. Although Professor Johnson reassured him, Mays sought out the porter and took a berth in the "deadhead," that is, an empty Pullman car where he could sit with black members of the crew who were taking a break from their duties. Before he had settled into his berth, however, there was a summons at the deadhead door, and Mays found himself looking at three white men with guns pointed at his head. They angrily demanded that he go to the Jim Crow car. He complied, but they followed closely, scuffing his heels with their feet and poking their guns into his back, and their voices grew crueler, louder, and more insistent, no matter how quickly he moved his long and quick legs. As the group made its way toward the Jim Crow car, other passengers jumped up to join, until the whole thing began to look like the Phoenix lynching mob that was his first childhood memory. Once in the Jim Crow car, he was quizzed roughly as the vengeance men tried hard to find out what agent sold him his ticket. With great resolve, he stiffened his naturally stiff neck and said nothing. At last the angry squadron of enforcers left, though he remembered hate-filled backward glances and more loud murmurations long after all white men had exited the Jim Crow car. Indeed Mays remembered their looks and sounds fifty years later when he wrote his memoir.[71]

Afterward, he found a statement, and subsequently forgot its author but remembered and repeated the message, which fit this turn of events: "One of the tragedies of life is that once a deed is done, the consequences are beyond our control."[72] It all reminded him that a man had to plan carefully, choose his battles with some patience—and live to fight another day. He had gone into that campaign for the first-class seat without much planning or patience, and the result was bitter. He could have been killed; everyone saw it; and the humiliation was public. In classical terms he had made himself *mikrosukia,* a man less than he was, and he had let roughnecks diminish him in front of the polis in assembly. And he had bought that ticket through clever stratagem to demonstrate his dignity! The whole episode ruined his St. Louis trip and left a chalky undertaste in his cup over his next days as pastor at Shiloh and dean at Morehouse.

Nothing got any better when he talked about the trip with others. Above all, Will Alexander was a disappointment, insisting that economic opportunity and not integration was the prize in the sky. There it was, proof if proof were needed, that Mays could find no good southern white man, even and especially among the ranks of the Atlanta liberals. On this score President Hope understood his dean's emotions, for he himself had been cool toward Alexander's CIC. In fact, a white liberal of the CIC, Ashby Jones, had whispered discretely to the other white council members that the Morehouse president and creator of the Atlanta University system was "the hopeless John Hope." At any rate Will Alexander told Mays that these things did not much matter, and John Hope told him that the struggling Morehouse College, and not the Jim Crow Pullman car, needed the dean's attentions. Although Hope publicly and properly showed his pride in the Atlanta University system, in which black schools shared expenses and resources—including that consolidated heating system serving all campuses—he had to concede privately that the House gave more than it received in the system.[73]

If Hope was right on this score, then even the overrated Will Alexander was right for once, at least about the hierarchy of things, about what mattered most and what fight should be fought first. The people at Shiloh Baptist Church and the young men at Morehouse College did not, right now, need a leader who could ride first class to St. Louis on the Pullman. What they needed right now was a fully educated leader. Both groups in his life deserved a leader—pastor and dean—who could show the brilliant Yankees that he knew his stuff, that he knew his Bible, especially the historical context of the New Testament.

A striving man, a magnificent man, a man of *megalosukos,* no matter how determined, needed an example of what he should be. Somehow, even John Hope, for all his own high and fine qualities of *megalosukia,* was not in fact that manly exemplar for Mays. In the academic year 1922–23, the example at last came for the man who was named both for the patriarch Benjamin—whose seed was to inherit Gilead—and for the prophet Elijah—the man who never died but ascended straight to God's side. This exemplar, as Mays put it, was "called of God to do His work," and this exemplar was the great preacher, great scholar, and great community leader Mordecai Wyatt Johnson. The Reverend Johnson, almost golden in color and with "the face of an angel" spread across his broad and noble head, spoke with the voice of an angel darkened by the passions of struggle. The Reverend Johnson filled the pulpit of the First Baptist Church of Charleston, West Virginia. That land was known to Mays only by reputation but was a place that called itself northern and not southern, a place unlike Richmond, for it had no statues of Confederates and no cotton had ever grown there. Charleston, West Virginia, was a place where the lords of northern capital had built mansions for themselves high in the hills above the valley of the Kanawha and down in the valley they had built factories wherein worked dark labor as well as white labor.[74]

This manly example, this Mordecai Johnson, this black proponent of *megalosukos,* spoke in the Morehouse chapel at one of John Hope's required services. It is not recorded what the Reverend Johnson said, but there was a theme to which he often returned in such addresses to educators and students. At such times he spoke often about the need for romance in the medieval literary sense of imagining a fable so as to instruct about right and wrong in the audience's real world. Of black people and white people, the Reverend Johnson said, "It is a great romance to consider what they may become in this country in the next few years." Furthermore the minister liked to say that there must be more "inter-action between the white and colored people of the South; and the romance is in the observing—and imagining in advance—a new level of inter-action which is possible." Once the "inter-action"—this achievement of the prize of integration and opportunity—is romanced before an audience, it can become a goal, the prize in the sky to move toward. The romance, once dramatized, can become a guiding light, and then black men following the light can make the romance a reality.[75]

It also is not recorded whether the visiting minister moved the young men of the House student body, but it is recorded that the Reverend Johnson profoundly stirred the young dean of the faculty of the House. Here was a great black preacher who spoke the truth and who pastured his flock with justice and equity. Mays wished to be no less than Mordecai Johnson, so that he too could speak out with justice and equity. And beyond question such a man of *megalo-sukos* must be trained well, better even than Mays had been trained so far.

So to serve, so to build, so to lead, Mays had to be more soundly built, to grow. He needed to take leave from Shiloh in order to return to lead those good people well. From the brothers and sisters of Shiloh, Mays took formal leave, intending to return with master's degree from the University of Chicago—marked as such by no less than Dr. Shirley Case—in order to serve them more fully and lead them more fairly. To the men of the House, Mays bade farewell, not intending to return to their classrooms, but thinking to return some day to preach to them as a visitor to their campus chapel.

7

MY TIMES ARE IN THY HANDS

1924–1926

Chicago was much as he had left it. Yet more and more black people had come there from the valleys through its western and southern gates. Still the factories thrummed, and the bosses were paying. And still it was a city in which black people came and settled and labored and sang as strangers in a strange land.

The University of Chicago grew no less steadily in the eyes of the white man, but it remained a place where black folk were strangers. As before, Mays joined other dark students in their orchestrated demonstrations—sitting deliberately by white men at table in the cafeteria, speaking with studied friendliness to white professors on the campus footpaths, sitting up bolt upright in classroom while reciting lessons proudly learned and stating opinions proudly reached. This resistance did not receive any help from the dark Asian students who came to Chicago to study. In fact the Indian students soon picked up and employed the Chicago way of segregation, presuming the black people must be the American version of the untouchable caste and thus were to be shunned. For his part Mays and his fellow dark university students presumed that the Indian students wore their turbans not for religious reasons or for cultural traditions, but strictly in order to appear exotic and the opposite of African Americans. In a city of man where there were many kinds of peoples, the dark folk of the South were at the bottom of all the peoples at the university, and they were pointedly kept there even and especially by the most recently arrived newcomers from Asia. Yet the attitudes of all the peoples who were not black stiffened the resolve of Mays and his dark brothers and sisters.[1]

Mostly though he studied. Dr. Shirley Case and the other men of learning were finding out more and more about the actual lives of the men and women of the New Testament. Mays rejoined the graduate team of Dr. Case and his scholars, and all of them, master and apprentices, did research on "pagan survivals in

Christianity." When Jesus walked and talked, there was interaction among the disciples who walked with Jesus and the men who did not walk with him—and indeed there was interaction among the disciples and men of the era who never even heard of Jesus. After Jesus ascended, there was interaction among surviving disciples and other men and women who had never seen or heard the Jesus. And when most of the disciples were dead and gone, there was interaction among those who wrote down the New Testament records and still others who never saw or heard or even knew of Jesus. Hebrew law and Hebrew prophets were there before the Coming and were still there after the Ascension. These laws and prophets were well documented. But so too were pagan laws and pagan seers, some Roman, some Arab, some north African, some Greek, and perhaps even some Indian. These were less well recorded, but they were there, and traces of their footsteps and echoes of their voices were all through the recorded New Testament if only a person knew where and how to look for and listen to them.[2]

As Mays conducted his own research and as he outlined his master's thesis, he accepted Dr. Case's category in which Jews too were pagans. To consider the Hebrews as some sort of proto-Christians was unfair to a great religion of the ancient and modern world, and indeed it was unfair to the religion that Jesus professed. Judaism is separate and distinct from Christianity, and the great ancient religion continued on, following its own course. At the same time other religions followed their own courses, and these too had their own identities separate and distinct from Christianity. For Dr. Case, Judaism was more than Christians often made of it, since it was not part of Christianity but was sui generis. On the other hand, it was also less than Christianity because, as he defined it, it was non-Christian and thus pagan.[3]

All that was debatable, but Mays accepted it for purposes of thesis writing and proceeded to isolate pagan practices connected to Christian belief as recorded in the Bible and as recorded by early Christian fathers. Vital to the whole organizing scheme was Dr. Case's central theme, played and replayed by master and students: Christianity was able to survive in its early days of struggle partly because it contained many pagan elements that were familiar to and attractive to pagans. Most striking among many discoveries by the ordained Baptist minister was evidence that the practice of adult full immersion, the sign of the Baptists, was pagan in its origins.[4]

"In fact," stated student Mays on page one of his thesis, "In a technical sense, Jesus was not the founder of Christianity. There is no one moment in history to which we can assign the starting point of Christianity." Furthermore, he announced, Christianity was and is a "social movement." This "social movement" did not merely adapt old pagan forms and present them in new places:

early Christians were not "mere copyists." Instead, as their social movement gained ground over time and space, it reshaped old pagan practices into a new context given by the recorded teachings of Jesus Christ, his followers, and his later commentators; "in every instance, the same ideas were developed along Christian lines quite distinct from the original Pagan setting."[5]

The Bible, especially the earliest available texts, was surely precious but more so for what it showed about man's understanding of God than for what it showed about God to man. An evolving understanding, or progress, was vouchsafed to those who worked hard to read the Bible with care, because God is good, because God is revealing himself to believers, because God has granted the marvelous faculty of reasoning to man, because man is perfectible—that is, capable of improvement both individually and in society. For all these reasons, a man taking the ancient texts and taking all the research other men could perform about the time and the place in which that ancient text was written, could learn quite a bit about men in another time and in another place, and in such processes he could learn a great deal about himself and his own time and place while also learning much about any people in any time and any place. Like the Reverend Marshall back in the valley of the Saluda, Bennie Mays searched the literal meaning of each ancient word in biblical text as he searched the deepest and most spiritual meaning of the Word, the Logos, associated with God himself.[6]

Unlike the Reverend Marshall, the Chicago scholars regarded each of these words as man-made, imperfect, and quite specific to a time and a place. Each specific human word was at some remove from divine will, which could not be fully understood by any human and thus could not be rendered accurately for any human ear or eye. Where the people writing under the authority of the teaching of John the Evangelist wrote the word "logos"—and here Bennie Mays carefully wrote the Greek letters in his own hand because the typewriter he used and the one used by his hired thesis typist did not have Greek letters, but also because Mays felt a glory and a power in writing Greek words that now were his own as a scholar—they were trying to describe some things quite different from the lowercase "word" that humans used to refer to the signal about some things in their experiences.[7]

These writers, writing long after other men had spoken words in another time and another place were, in using "logos," talking about nothing less than the essence, the very being of God, the one who starts all things and finishes all things, the one who is everywhere and who always is, the one who at an important point was understood to be "I AM," and thus the Hebrew- and the Greek-speaking students render an important phrase to show that this being, God, exists outside time and in fact created time:

And God said unto Moses, "ı am that ı am," and he said, "Thus shalt thou say unto the children of Israel, 'ı am hath sent me unto you.'"

Jesus said unto them, "Verily, verily, I say unto you, Before Abraham was, I am."[8]

With Dr. Case, Bennie Mays looked at the ancient Hebrew texts, which he could not translate except for a word or two, and then at the Greek texts, which he could read, albeit slowly and with struggle, and he saw how different those marvelous English words were from the words recorded first in Hebrew and then in Greek.

He saw the profound need not only to offer better English words for those Greek, Latin, and Hebrew words, but he also saw the even more profound need to know, really know, just exactly what was going on in the lives of the men who wrote the original words in Greek, Latin, and Hebrew. Moreover he was intensely concerned to know just exactly what was going on in the lives of the men who originally read—and who originally listened to those who were reading—the words in Greek, Latin, and Hebrew. It was to some degree frustrating work, and yet it was not hopeless, merely difficult.[9]

The hope in all this work is still central to Baptist teaching, as Mays understood the teaching of his sect: a personal relationship sought by the Being with the believer, in which the believer is transformed and carried over into a new life. Having accepted the relationship—grace—without having earned it and having escaped punishment without deserving to be forgiven, the believer then has the duty, the mission, the calling, and the commission to bring others to the Lord. The believer has been shown the way by the Son of God, Jesus Christ, who is also the Son of Man and thus in human form suffers the mortal pain of the Passion.

To bring others to the Lord in this way, Christians had to use human words and human sentences to communicate, and the Bible as it evolved became a wonderful way to communicate among humans. Part of the Bible caught echoes and reflections and feelings from the essence of God's own Logos, but always as appropriate to a specific time and a particular place. In studying the Bible, therefore, Mays resolved to be a historian, looking for context, for what the human word intended to say at another time and in another place. He wrote that Christianity "was inevitably bound up with the environmental forces of the Roman world. . . . it is an evolutionary movement; and must be modified, as all movements are, by its environment."[10]

Faced with this challenge, many people, including those with whom Mays preached, got the duty of the interpreter exactly backward: "Many good meaning people try to make the New Testament modern by interpretating [*sic*] it in the 20th century thoughts and terms, rather than finding out what it meant to the early Christians and to the authors themselves."[11]

Most pertinent to Mays in his study of the social movement in its various dialogues and conversations were the Roman Stoics, especially as he traced them through the apostle Paul, who "accepts the first cause as the soul's return to it." As historian, Mays found the Roman translators of Diogenes the Greek Stoic to be especially prevalent and powerful during the Augustan Age, the time when Paul went to Rome. Mays was especially excited by the then-new discoveries of texts in an important library in Rome, including a manuscript in which the librarian lectured on Stoicism and described the sources available in his facility. For Mays, Paul did not speak back directly to Jesus Christ, but more to Diogenes and other Greek Stoics—and Paul spoke forward directly to Thomas Aquinas and not directly to Augustine. Both descriptions are somewhat eccentric among biblical scholars and intellectuals, and the major point is not whether Mays was right or wrong, but what he was thinking at that time. From the Roman Stoics, Mays adapted a renewed respect for the senses and for human reasoning, and he connected both faculties to Thomas Aquinas, thereby giving his old favorite a classical legitimacy among Christians because of Paul. He quoted the Roman Stoics: "Only in the reasoning man does virtue express itself in right action."[12] Like all Christians, Mays was struggling with the tension between an absolute declaration of radical and unearned grace—with its unconditional forgiveness—and its polar opposite—the obvious imperative to do good. Thinking non-Christians have always scored the believer for an unmistakable contradiction in belief—that one is saved by grace unconditionally and cannot save himself, but once saved must do the right thing (do the good). Thinking Christians have always been discomfited by the same contradiction. For his thesis and for his life, Mays resolved things by emphasizing actions, doing good, practicing good, doing the right thing, thereby coming close to the heresy of "works salvation." His rightness or wrongness in understanding Roman Stoics is not the issue here, nor is it the chronicler's place to resolve the ancient Christian dilemma of grace and works. The issue here is to see how Mays resolved things. The Stoics and Paul between them had resolved Mays's dilemma of grace and works. Pagans had spoken truth, which Jesus Christ had refined and purified, and then Paul had spoken that truth to still another generation with the help of the Roman Stoics.

Still another pagan survival was the value of land and the power of the landlords over those who worked that land. Those who looked to the Bible for a historical justification for slavery and for other abuses of labor were right in that the Bible clearly recorded the power and the privileges of the landlords. Yet Mays could find no celebration of landlord power in the Bible. In fact he found plenty of evidence that pagan prophets and early Christian leaders resented the power of the landed class and warned that class that its members must serve the orphan, the widow, the wounded, and others who did not own the wealth in land. Jesus in particular, Mays found to be preaching justice for those—widows, unmarried women, lepers, the outcast Samaritans, and other wounded and desperate people—who had very little at all. On these issues, Case could help his student find the social history: Who owned the land? Who worked the land? Who was dispossessed? What were the disputes? Even so, Case did not push his student to write a master's thesis concerning social justice, but rather a careful demonstration of the pagan practices that predated the preaching and teaching of Jesus but which were still involved in Christian practices once a recognizable church had been formed and set in motion.[13]

Working for and with Dr. Case, however, Mays did in his own way reaffirm his conviction that the social gospel must be brought into the black churches. The preachments of Walter Rauschenbusch and the studies of Henry George were with Mays on his second trip to Chicago and its university even more profoundly than on his first trip. This time he involved himself fully in the Forum, a student discussion group that met on campus and debated social issues. Sometime in the spring semester of 1925, Mays had an experience that was as close to a miracle as he ever had. It happened at a meeting of the Forum.

A sociology graduate student, William Oscar "Bill" Brown, stood up to speak, and as he did so revealed his Texas accent and other evidence that he was from the "white tribesmen" of the southwestern inner coastal plains. This sociology student was working with the famed Robert Park, but on first hearing Bill Brown's drawl, Mays immediately presumed southern white prejudice, and he suspected as well the other thing that the preacher saw often in southern scholars: lack of intelligence. Yet as Bill Brown continued to talk, Mays was pleased to hear certain things and then surprised to find himself drawn to the Texan, especially because of his country farm origins. Some of these revelations occurred at that first Forum, and others came more gradually, but all were set in motion for Mays by Brown's first standing up and speaking on that one occasion, the specific date of which is not recorded.[14]

Referring to the indisputably great Robert Park, Brown said that the sociologist was a great man but a man of only one part of the South. He knew only about the plantation lords of the land and nothing about the small freeholding farmers. Brown also complained that Park thought racial prejudice was "organic"; if this were so—if it were actually growing as part of the body of the South—then it was intractable and irremediable, save only by destruction of the white South. Indeed, Brown said with a quiet pride, his "socialist granddaddy Darling" back in Fayette County cotton and peanut land was a greater influence on him than the distinguished professor Park. Later Bill Brown spoke of his "emancipations," first from the hypocrisy of the white southern Methodist church, a freedom achieved after earning a bachelor of divinity degree from no less than Southern Methodist University in Dallas in 1922. Second came the emancipation from the caste system that put Mexicans and African Americans beneath and always apart from his own proudly Anglo family of Browns and Darlings. Hard study of the Bible, he credited for his first emancipation from the southern Methodists. His mother and his father he credited for his second emancipation. Mays the Baptist minister was intrigued that Brown had turned away from white Methodism in Texas, and he was powerfully drawn to a man who wanted to share cotton land with black men and Mexicans and who insisted that race prejudice, even among southern white men, was learned—and not naturally grown in the body and the soul.[15]

If Brown were right—and racial prejudice was learned from teaching—then young white children were not yet guilty of damnable racism and could be taught social justice, including racial equality.

He needed to know more about this William Oscar Brown, called "Bill" by students at the university, "Otto" by friends elsewhere, and "Oscar" by the professors. He learned the young man's personal history, finding that Brown's people hailed from farming stock in the tiny town of Cistern, near Brownsville, in Fayette County, Texas. The land there was sandy loam, fair for cotton, good for peanuts and cowpeas, and—as a native ruefully marked it—best for scrubby post-oak trees of no market value. It was sere and lonesome and yet fetching too. One in three of the people in Fayette County was black, one in two of the families was Anglo-American, and one in five was Mexican American, generally styled Chicano. His father, Will, was a Texas socialist of a kind once active in the farmlands, and his mother, Irene, was a schoolteacher among the Texas Methodist women who protested and, after decades, finally curtailed lynching in their land. Like Bennie Mays, Bill Brown was a man who had trouble paying for his Ph.D., and his progress toward the doctorate was slow and labored, punctuated by long spells of teaching for money far from Chicago. This was the man who spoke at Forum, the man who "emancipated" first himself from prejudices against people of color and then emancipated Mays from the dark man's own prejudices against southern whites.[16]

Mays was bound no less by the same rural poverty. Yet he intended to push on through to earn his own Ph.D. with no further delays. He sent his notice to the good and true people at Shiloh that he was resigning his pastorate. They needed to find a pastor who could serve them with full attention to their needs and not someone like Mays who required time away from the flock to study, reflect, and write at a faraway university center. It was hard to part from the people of Shiloh, but Mays did so, and in March 1925 the dark man proudly accepted his A.M. degree and even more proudly entered the Ph.D. program, taking doctoral courses in the spring and summer sessions at the University of Chicago.

But such was not yet his part to play after all. Like Bill Brown before him and many others after him, Bennie Mays was out of funds and could not continue his studies toward the doctorate after all. He knew he could run with Dr. Case and his best, but poverty took him out of the race at this time as it had earlier. It was not directly racism that denied Mays his chance but rather poverty; and Bill Brown, a white man innocent of the damnable prejudice that marked most southern white men, was in exactly the same position. Back behind all of it, somewhere and some way, was the Lord, who had a plan. The Lord chose the time for all things, frustrating as his decisions were for those who swore to do his work: "My times are in thy hand: deliver me from the hand of mine enemies, and from them that persecute me." These words are from Psalm 31, the lament of the faithful believer, in Dr. Case's words a pagan believer, whose expression of belief was carried forward all the same into Christian expressions of belief. Again Mays surrendered himself into divine hands, utterly unable to do what he intended to do when he intended to do it, frustrated and saddened but not embittered, for the same psalm concluded: "Be of good courage, and he shall strengthen your heart, all ye that hope in the Lord."[17]

So the man seeking magnificence in order to serve the Lord had to step away from the racetrack and work away from the contestant's field. The prize was still there, and a Ph.D. degree was not that prize. Yet the coveted degree was not a "graven image" either. It was a legitimate sign of the Lord's acceptance. That sign, however, was not to descend on Mays yet, as it would not descend quickly on the poor white Texan Brown. Each man, one black and one white, was finally and after all from the human family of Ha'adam (Adam), a man of the earth, and like the original Adam must return to the earning of daily bread before he could study the Word in the magnificent temple at the university presided over by Dr. Case.

The agent, if not exactly God's agent, in this time of deciding, was Dr. Robert Shaw Wilkinson, president of South Carolina State College in Orangeburg. Dr. Wilkinson was the man who had counseled young Bennie Mays against study at Virginia Union College in Richmond because the president then doubted the plowboy's competence to run with the "colored people of quality" in Virginia's capital city. Now this same man offered Mays a job teaching English at South Carolina State College. It was a sign of Wilkinson's respect, but at the same time a sign that Mays had to run at a slower pace on a different track. State College was also the place where a young lady of indisputable quality, Mabel James, had written in her own fine hand a note of congratulation to young Bennie Mays for academic achievement early in his struggles to survive the don't care boys and demonstrate prowess to the few excellent professors. Now Mabel James served as personal secretary to Dr. Wilkinson, and she wrote Mays again, urging that he accept the position. State College needed him, and Mays needed money. It was the Lord's will that Mays leave Chicago and go to Orangeburg, and, strengthened of heart and filled with good courage, Mays obeyed that will with hope in the Lord.[18]

A sure sign that Mays belonged back in Orangeburg was his meeting Sadie Gray, a recent State College graduate who now occasionally instructed in social work at her alma mater while seeking a master's degree in that field from the University of Chicago. She and Mays came together naturally enough, and they passed quickly from friendship into romance. Like Ellen Harvin, and unlike Mays himself, Sadie Gray was light skinned. Also like Ellen Harvin, Sadie Gray had a past marked with its full measure of pain—though the Gray family was prosperous and even privileged.

Almost yellow in color and buxom to the point of the comic, Sadie Gray tended to plumpness in her youth, and that physical fact made her appear shorter than her actual height, which was average. This short and wide appearance was emphasized by the striking contrast when she stood alongside the dark, straight-backed, tall Bennie Mays. Her face was wide and handsome and above all welcoming, with a prominent chin, a Roman nose, and smiling eyes set memorably under sharply etched eyebrows. As she aged, she lost some weight, more often wore her reading glasses, and began to look more contemplative and scholarly though still patient and welcoming. The contrast with her lover and then husband continued, for he seemed to grow taller and more angular as he aged. His prematurely white hair made his visage appear dark indeed, and at times his manly and grave authority made him seem forbidding, powerful, and a bit distant. Both Sadie and Bennie Mays were tough and demanding, but Sadie Gray was one whom the wounded could approach, especially if the wound had been inflicted by her man.[19]

As for her childhood and upbringing, Sadie Gray knew enough of prerogative to insist on respect from the people of power whom she met, and she knew enough about pain to insist on compassion toward those broken or at least bruised by the powerful. She was from the town of Gray in Jones County, Georgia, where the rolling hills of the Piedmont gave onto the flat pine forests with their occasional hillocks in the broad inner coastal plain. The Ocmulgee and the Oconee Rivers cut valleys on their paths from the highest Piedmont hills southward toward the piney woods and hardwood bottomland near Macon. The Ocmulgee in particular created a dense and richly tangled hammock of wildflowers and magnificent vine-covered trees, and the lands washed by both the Ocmulgee and the Oconee had fertile soil good for many crops, but especially for cotton. A daughter of the valley of the Ocmulgee, Sadie Gray, did not bear the name of the town as her surname by coincidence. Her father, James Gray, was a slave born to a dark and comely slave woman whose name is not recorded. This lady had been raped by her master, James Madison Gray, for whom the town was named.[20]

James Madison Gray, lord of rich lands and strong slaves, never married but instead came to the same slave woman at least three times, producing three slave sons. It seems likely that he came to her many times more than three, for the careful student of miscegenation notes that masters who lay with their slaves typically lay with the same slave often and for extended periods of time. For her part, Sadie talked about her white ancestor who gave the town of Gray its name and who named the local Confederate regiment and who gave her the distinctive yellow skin and gave her some status and gave her some shame. As she talked, Mays concluded and recorded that Sadie's unnamed paternal grandmother was "perhaps the reason [James Madison Gray] never married!" Mays also observed that in the antebellum days, "white men could father Negro sons 'without benefit of clergy' and still be respected and respectable pillars of society," an observation proven so by the official historical sign on Highway 18 that marks the accomplishments of James Madison Gray.[21]

Sadie Gray numbered white ancestors on her mother's side too, and there the story was no less complex. Her mother's father was Madison Blount, a skilled carpenter and son of his master, also named Madison Blount, who had raped one of his slaves. Slave Madison Blount was light skinned and in some ways privileged, for he was taught carpentry, and he could use this expertise to earn some money for himself that other slaves never saw. When freedom came, Madison Blount possessed a money-earning skill and the goodwill of white landowners, who readily hired him to make their furniture, construct additions to their homes, or even to build them entirely new homes. The black family of Madison Blount did not go hungry or get cold in the days of slavery and did not suffer privation in the new day of freedom. For all that, Madison Blount served as a slave and remained a slave until Federal troops freed him. Whether in the days of slavery or in the days of freedom, Madison Blount was never acknowledged as his father's son, not even in that backhanded way of little perquisites and special recognitions and occasional kindnesses and fatherly pats that a man like James Madison Gray showed his own wrong side of the sheet son, James Gray.[22]

Indeed Master Blount hated Slave Blount, as is recorded by the people of Slave Blount's family. And that hatred was returned full force by the wounded and embittered son of the rape. When freedom did come and Madison Blount was able to live the life of a self-employed skilled artisan, he moved as close to the status of bourgeoisie in the piney woods of southern Georgia as a man of color was likely to get in the late nineteenth century.

White masters had often taken black slaves of both genders, claiming the sexual conquest as a property right and denying in their statute books that such unwanted sex was a rape since a black person in the day of thralldom had little or no legal standing if the master pleasured his own body in preference to a slave's will. In contrast even in the days of freedom rape of white women by black men was avenged by the lynching mobs. Rape, in fact, could seldom be pronounced as a word in polite company, but the high-yellow offspring of white rape of black women were everywhere to be seen, outward and visible signs of an inward and thus invisible thrust and disgrace. And the black men accused of tasting white flesh were strung from trees and hung from posts and riddled with bullets and burned to fagots for their supposed actions—and sometimes for their supposed thoughts as understood by whistling or by looking or by not clearing the way from the sidewalk when a white lady rustled by.

Yet Madison Blount worried about his daughters and the possibility of their rape in a way that was extreme even in a time and a place when talk and fear about rape was widespread. Free women of color were not the legal objects of white passion that slave women had been because after 1866 there were laws against rape of black women. All the same, as the family of James Mays and certainly the families of James Gray and of Madison Blount marked it, white boys of landed families expected to come to black women to learn about sex, and the mature men of landed families expected to come to black women when they hungered for the "exotic" passion denied the white couples in their own class. Despite the new status of freedom for black women, conviction for raping a black lady carried a maximum of one year of prison while conviction of rape of a white lady was a capital offense. The difference in penalties was effective, and black men knew that it was to risk death to come to a white lady, while white men knew that they could come to a black lady with only light consequences. Results of the law were not surprising, for white boys continued to take black ladies for their pleasure and for their instruction. Madison Blount suffered great dismay at the offenses against neighbor girls and warned and warned his daughters to stay away from white boys.[23]

So angry was Madison Blount that he declared there was no god and that prayer could not protect his daughters; he would protect them with his own strong right arm. When Sadie reached the age of sexuality and became full breasted and broad hipped and attracted men, grandfather Blount agonized that she would be taken for sporting sex by an old white lord or for teaching sex by an anxious son of such a lord of the land. As Sadie Gray recalled:

I had advice from . . . my maternal grandfather . . . Madison Blount. . . .
Grandfather told his grandchildren that he hated his father, and that he was afraid of him until he was eighteen. After that he told us, "I have not been afraid of God nor the devil!" He often said, "I am an Ebo!" He resented the fact that his slave-holding master took advantage of his enslaved mother. He told us that he was a bastard. I think Grandpa Blount really hated white people. I remember his lecture to me when I was sixteen. It seems he would give this lecture when his daughters and his granddaughters reached a certain age. He told me that I was growing up, almost grown up to be a lady. He told me, "You must take care of yourself. You know your Dad and I are bastards, but we must be the last bastards in our families. Our mothers were slaves; they could not protect themselves. But you do not have to take insults from anybody. Your Dad and Granddad will spill every drop of blood in their veins to protect you little girls. I am not afraid of anybody; so if you are ever molested by a white man, you let me know. Remember, no more bastards. You must be as fine and clean as any family alive." Grandpa Blount died at the age of ninety-two. He never joined the church because he did not believe that God exists. Though unlettered, he arrived at this conclusion after seeing the injustices of slavery. When [Benjamin Mays] tried to get him to see that it was the justice of God that enabled him to escape slavery, he reminded [Mays] that many slaves, better men than he, died in the system, and some slaves were killed. "If there is a God, He is not just!"[24]

As a matter of fact, Sadie and all her sisters were careful around white men, but they were even more cautious about what Grandfather Blount might find out. Even when young, the girls knew that strong-willed men such as Grandfather Blount speaking of Ebo ancestry, working steady with a skill, and proud of a small savings account, were large and tempting targets for the white-robed Ku Klux Klansmen of their time and place, all the more so if they were light skinned and spoke disrespectfully about the Christian God. At the most practical level, Sadie Gray recorded the actions she took in the light of the advice from her mother, Emma Frances Blount Gray: "Once, when a trap was laid for me by a group of white men at the railroad station, I was tipped off by a Negro man who heard them making the plot. When I told Mother about it, she advised me not to tell Father for he would get himself into trouble. Mother told me to be prepared to protect myself, to carry a hatpin in my bosom and, if attacked, use it. As I recall, I carried a hatpin with me for a year or more."[25] With such practices and ploys, Sadie Gray and her sisters Emma Catherine Ware Gray, Julia Gray Burton, and Elizabeth Gray Blount survived Jones

County, Georgia, and attained educations and careers for themselves. Only her sickly sister, Lucia, was unable to attend school or develop a career. Three boys in the Gray family—Emory S. Gray, James Madison Gray, and Madison Blount Gray—also did well in school and in life. Only the sickly Cecil, who died young, was denied an education, and, as for Lucia, that denial was by the enemies of illness and debility rather than the more infamous Jim Crow. Of the nine children of James Madison Gray and Emma Frances Blount Gray, seven earned high school degrees from advanced preparatory schools sponsored by black colleges, and five went forward to study at college, with four taking baccalaureate degrees. Perhaps most impressively, three of the Gray children earned degrees from the elite white northern institutions Northwestern University and the University of Chicago.[26]

In Sadie Gray, as in Ellen Harvin, Bennie Mays had found a soul mate whose family expected academic achievement far beyond the norm at the State College in Orangeburg. Don't care boys were still there, but the president, Dr. Wilkinson, insisted he wanted high standards. And Sadie Gray insisted on her own high standards in social-work courses she taught, even as she encouraged Mays to set the bar of expectation as high as he could for his scholars of English. There was also a tough-minded young historian, Asa H. Gordon, who had been teaching at State College since 1919, after taking his baccalaureate degree at Atlanta University. Gordon, like Sadie Gray, had grown up in the valley of the Ocmulgee and the Oconee, and like Bennie Mays, had been educated at a city school far from his country home place in a similarly determined effort to rise above the Jim Crowed villages. Gordon had grand designs, an Ivy League Ph.D. in history, but for this season in the wilderness he studied on his own, adopting the term "New Negro" to describe himself. He spoke often and tellingly about this New Negro. Gordon had some trouble defining the term, but he said such a person rejected slavery and Jim Crow and held himself to extremely high standards in academics. He collected examples of slave resistance to the oppressions of the peculiar institution, and he kept notecards about South Carolina and Georgia black men who had achieved something. He insisted that a real scholar had to be a "Race Man," that is, a serious-minded academic dedicated to attack the "fatal weakness" that denied a black person a place in history. Gordon influenced Mays and Gray, both of whom began to use Gordon's term "New Negro." All three applied the term to themselves, thereby defining themselves as academics committed to the highest scholarship and as reformists committed to social justice. Bennie Mays also, somewhat confusingly, spoke about himself as a Race Man focused on winning maximum credit for good things accomplished by African Americans in the United States.[27]

The strong-willed English professor promptly clashed with the strong-willed president, much as Mays had clashed earlier with Hope. The issue was again professorial prerogative and academic standards. Mays, encouraged by his band of colleagues, insisted that the bookworms of the State College be honored and that the don't care boys be disciplined and dismissed. President Wilkinson, justly proud of his own training and degrees, said he wanted well-trained and fully credentialed professors who would hold the students at the State College to a high standard. What Mays saw, however, were many badly trained professors, some of whom sought popularity by assigning high grades across the board. Those such as Sadie Gray, Asa Gordon, and Mays, professors who demanded close reading, correct writing, clear speech, and thoughtful attitudes, could achieve these goals only by clearing from their rolls large numbers of students, perhaps one in four. As Bennie Mays could recall bitterly from his own student days, don't care boys sometimes actively intruded on the serious study of the bookworms; and this intrusion did not exclude threats with knives.

One young man in particular completely failed to meet Mays's standards in English. Neither did he come up to the standards of any of the scholars whom Mays respected, whose names Mays did not record in his memoir. Nor could this don't care fellow find a substitute for Mays's English course, and thus Mays stood before him to block his graduation. Yet at a faculty meeting, Mays was flabbergasted to see the student's name listed among the candidates for the baccalaureate. On this sort of occasion, the faculty routinely voted "aye" in assent to the dean's whole list, but this time Mays rose to speak, declaring that the particular student was absolutely unqualified for the degree. It seemed then and still seems so today, that an institution should follow its own standards for graduation. Mays told his colleagues that they were "degrading" their degree. Several members of the faculty spoke in support of Mays's efforts, but others spoke in support of the student, despite his failing mark on a required course. Wilkinson is not recorded as saying anything, but his silence suggested an "aye" vote for the candidate. The ensuing vote was won by the student and lost by Mays, and later the exasperated memoir writer recorded that the majority was "by one vote."[28]

The president's silence on this issue rankled Mays. At a small, black college with a weak faculty, the president had to set the standards for the institution. In time a president with high standards could recruit a solid faculty that could properly enforce its own academic expectations. But the standards Dr. Wilkinson set in 1925 were not high in Bennie Mays's judgment. Sometimes even a low standards bar was moved yet lower, or in the case of this don't care student, the bar was removed altogether.

There were outward and visible signs that the State College was further damaged by damnable Jim Crow. The college trustees were political appointees, and in that era they were always white. When board members made their occasional visits to the campus, it was both law and practice that they be served meals in a strictly segregated setting, even when there were no white voters around to see a white trustee breaking bread next to a black person. Thus the trustees took their meals in splendid isolation, separated from President Wilkinson, the dean, and other officials of the institution for which they were entrusted with oversight. With such an arrangement, Mays found it obvious that State College would continue to receive appropriations no better than 10 percent or so of the money spent on the four white state schools—the Citadel military academy, the Clemson agricultural and mechanical college with its own military training, Winthrop College for women, and the University of South Carolina. Specifically in 1925 the white schools received $1,057,324.71, and State College received $106,625.[29]

In that year, while preoccupied with such issues as a poor state with small resources yet again reducing even that pittance it spent on educating African Americans, Mays attended a conference in Columbia for white liberals and some black academics. The first lady of State College, Mrs. Marian Birnie Wilkinson, insisted that Mays attend the event, which was sponsored by the South Carolina Commission on Interracial Cooperation. Speaking on this day was the region's top commission official, Jessie Daniel Ames, who was known for her outspoken fight against lynching, which became largely successful in the 1930s, especially in Bill Brown's native Texas. Ames addressed not lynching but education, saying that, in order for black children to go forward one step, black parents and educators would likely have to accept white children going forward two steps. Mays's sense of classical justice and his mathematical way of thinking were equally offended. Taking the 1925 expenditures as "steps," two steps forward for the four white colleges would give them $3 million, while the "one step" forward for State College would give it $200,000. Continuing her projected budget, by the 1940s State College would not be getting 10 percent, but instead 5 percent of white appropriations. Ames was perhaps speaking more metaphorically than mathematically, but Mays was still incensed. He kept his calm demeanor among the white officials, but he later wrote sarcastically that "no doubt Mrs. Ames felt wildly and daringly liberal and magnanimous."[30] He never used "magnanimous" (which comes from *megalosukos*) lightly. His heavy sarcasm was born of disgust.

A sad truth settled onto his broad but burdened shoulders: "Negroes and whites often sat on opposite sides of the table and as often lied to each other." Yet, as he knew from the Bible and his beloved classics, "People truly communicate only when they tell each other the truth." By 1925 the only white southerner Mays knew who spoke in such a simple and direct manner was Bill Brown from Mrs. Ames's Texas, and Mays began to despair about meeting another such truth bearer of any color anywhere in the South.[31]

Of course Mays knew that there were truth bearers in South Carolina, even if none was white, and he was pleased that the Lord's will so unfolded that he met a courageous African American, indeed a New Negro, who gave him the chance to bear truth to young black students. In the winter of 1926, Mays had made a trip to Atlanta and was buying a ticket back to Orangeburg at the train station. As he often did, he attempted his solitary rebellion against Jim Crow trains, requesting a berth in a Pullman. The agent politely but firmly refused, claiming no berths were available. As he made his way toward the car, Mays was intercepted by Ralph Bullock, boys' work secretary of the YMCA, based in Columbia. Bullock was also black, and he had bought a ticket for the same black coach, on a train that would pass through Orangeburg on its route between the capital cities of Georgia and South Carolina. Bullock had watched Mays requesting a berth, and he was impressed. He stuck out his hand in friendship, as Mays recalled, and said, "I want to meet a Negro who has the nerve to ask for a berth in Atlanta, Georgia."[32]

They talked on the train trip and formed a friendship based on the goals of the New Negro—a label that again neither could define but could describe as an academic who rejected Jim Crow and stood up for the self-respect due black people, even and especially if only to be beaten down. Soon after he returned to his duties at the State College, Professor Mays was pleased to receive an invitation from Bullock to speak at a YMCA event, the Older Boys' Conference, to be held February 26, 1926, at Benedict College. The title Bullock suggested for the proposed speech was "The Goal." The audience would be adolescents from all over South Carolina, some of them considering college degrees and professional careers despite obstacles of poverty and Jim Crow. Mays determined to give them the goal of the New Negro, a man unbent and unbowed before the assaults of white tyrants such as Dr. Payne and a man who did not expect help from white liberals such as Dr. Alexander or Mrs. Ames.[33]

Asa Gordon made the trip with Mays, and he used the occasion of the English professor's speech as a chance to establish a building block in a Race Man's project, a book to attack the fatal weakness of black nonhistory and to brace the New Negro in the fight against damnable Jim Crow, which relied on the fatal weakness to justify itself. Gordon's first book was called *Sketches of Negro Life and History in South Carolina,* and he planned subsequent books for other states. He intended that Mays should write at least one chapter for the volume, and the chapter grew out of his remarks at Benedict College. Gordon's book celebrated the New Negro in South Carolina, and Gordon got Mays to add an introduction to his Benedict speech. The introduction gives context for his address and shows it to be a proud and quite militant presentation of the New Negro, who rebels against all aspects of the all-pervasive Jim Crow. Although it contains material Mays did not share with the boys in the auditorium, the essay shows Mays's thinking as he prepared to speak to them. In it he presaged a formal development of civil disobedience and gave clear personal examples from his own life of ways in which a man of *megalosukia* could stand up to Jim Crow oppression in a manly and militant but nonviolent fashion.[34]

He described a woman refusing to trade with a white salesman who entered her houses with his hat still on his head, and he described a couple who refused to buy inexpensive shoes at the local store from a clerk who would not let them try on the shoes. In the former case, Mays said the lady at home made no verbal response at all to the salesman, who left that day but returned on another with his hat removed properly and conducted respectful business. In the latter case, the couple made certain that the clerk understood that they would buy better quality Florsheim shoes through mail order rather than his humbler and less expensive offerings; in time the clerk would relent and allow the couple to try on the store's shoes, rather than lose his sales commission. Also the clerk and the store manager would also get the point and stock more expensive shoes that might be appealing to the New Negro. In some ways Mays's introductory essay presaged the call of E. Franklin Frazier for a serious-minded and substantive black bourgeoisie who could use thoughtfully applied economic pressure against Jim Crow instead of telling each other "myths" about a self-sustaining and segregated black financial empire that did not exist. In any case, when Mays met and worked with Frazier some years later, the two certainly saw these economic issues in the same way.[35]

The boys gathered at Benedict College were active in the African American chapters of the YMCA across the Palmetto State, and some of these chapters took part in civil rights campaigns against lynching and for black education. Other chapters, as might be expected, were carefully designed to assuage local white fears about "uppity" young black men who might threaten the order of Jim Crow. Above all, this audience comprised bright young men filled with hope for a better day, and Mays wanted to feed that hope with the "living waters" of Jesus Christ and also with the bread and wine—the flesh and the blood of a Savior committed to radical social change. The goal he held out for the boys was not a limed marker for a touchdown on the gridiron, but rather the goal of a full adulthood, full maturity as a New Negro trained at college and ready and able to lead in a world of industry and commerce, a world of economically and financially integrated markets, and a world of culturally and ethnically integrated groups. In the model of a biblical prophet, Mays offered hope rather than optimism, a hope based on determination before obstacles, rather than an optimism based on miscalculation of the power of damnable Jim Crow. The biblical distinction between hope and optimism among prophets was clear to Mays, who found the same spirit of determined and unblinking but realistic rebellion in the prophet Amos and in the reformist Walter Rauschenbusch. In later years the distinction was lost on some white reformists, who were overly optimistic about prospects, and in still later years the distinction was even lost on some black radicals, who looked back at Mays in this speech and saw gradualism, and even Uncle Tom acquiescence. Taken in context of his introductory remarks, his own career, Bullock's intentions for Christian prophecy and change, and Gordon's teachings, "The Goal" was bold. Mays delivered it—and it was heard by the audience—as a threat to the white order of things in South Carolina.[36]

A man of *megalosukos* needed a place to stand and people to stand with him. In the modern academic world, tenure and promotion were expressions of this ancient element, outward and visible signs of an inward grace. A regular position at South Carolina State College, the completion of a Ph.D. dissertation, and marriage were all component parts of the status and security Mays needed. He loved Sadie Gray, and she loved him, but the couple needed to formalize things and quickly. The handsome young professor was sometimes the subject of gossip if he danced with another lady at a gathering and when he was followed to bus stops by groups of excited female students anxious to win his attentions. Whether in Aristotle's time or in 1926, a professor and a minister not only had to look to his personal conduct, but he also had to pay attention to deportment, *to what he seemed to be* to the outside world. Bennie Mays and Sadie Gray set their wedding date for August 9, 1926, and planned the next phases of his academic career, the period in which he would finish his dissertation, attain his Ph.D., and then win tenure and promotion at South Carolina State College.[37] The New Negro fighting for the dignity and rights of all African Americans needed to find his place and take his stand. At this moment there was the sense that God's will, man's leave, and the Mayses' plans fit together on the Orangeburg campus.

Soon, however, in that spring semester of 1926, it became obvious that the foundations of their plans were not laid solid. President Wilkinson informed the professor that a married couple could not both work for the State College in its academic departments. This was a sharp blow to Sadie Gray's career and to her identity as a New Negro, but it also presented a real problem for the couple's budget—which was already stretched taut, for Sadie's proud father, James Gray, was in financial difficulties, and she was trying to help him.

Newlyweds Benjamin and Sadie Gray Mays. Courtesy of the
Moorland-Spingarn Research Center, Howard University.

In the agricultural recession of 1925 James Gray, so long the owner of his
own home and land, had borrowed money and secured the loan with his farm,
thus entering into serious debt in his senior years. As the regional recession
deepened, James Gray found his debt mounting while his revenues fell. The
Gray realty could well pass from his hands, and James Gray himself could pass
into homeless dependency after a lifetime of upright independence. Sadie Gray
had stepped into the breach and met the mortgage payments, something that
the couple intended to continue.[38]

Yet now President Wilkinson was insisting that Sadie Gray give up her position when she became Sadie Mays. The strong-willed president and the strong-
willed professor were once again in conflict, but of course the professor knew

he would lose to the administrator, and of course he did. *Umin* and *thumin,* said the Bible's ancient refrain: The lots were cast. The couple began looking for new livelihoods.

An opportunity developed in Tampa, Florida, where the Urban League posted a vacancy for executive secretary. That African American organization was in those days extremely self-conscious about the aspirations of New Negroes in cities, even and especially in southern cities. To work with the Urban League would be to serve all New Negroes and to do so as a New Negro. There was also a vacancy in Tampa for a case worker with the Family Service Association, a city-sponsored office housed at the local Urban League, and Sadie Mays was offered this position. The two jobs were defined by the Urban League as "work to improve the lot of Negroes in employment, recreation, housing, health, education, and juvenile delinquency, and, if possible, to reduce the friction between Negroes and the police." James Gray's mortgage could be met, his lands kept safe; Sadie Mays could have a career in a city with professional opportunities for women; and Bennie Mays could fight for the New Negro in a growing city of opportunity and hope.[39] The dissertation and the long-sought doctoral degree and the professorship vouchsafed by such a credential must be postponed yet again.

In the ancient call and response, the Aramaean asked, "How long, oh Lord, / How long?" The New Negro heard the Lord's answer: "Only a little while now, a very little while, / For come he certainly will / before too long."[40]

8

NEW NEGROES ON DETOUR

1926–1934

Mr. and Mrs. Mays spent the years 1926–32 at work in Tampa and Atlanta with some interesting northern trips. The husband and wife defined themselves as New Negroes working according to station and training to improve the lives of young African Americans throughout the lower South. The work kept each close to the academy. Indeed by 1931 Sadie Mays had earned her master's degree in social work at the University of Chicago, and Bennie Mays had completed most course requirements for the Ph.D. in religion there. This work was not a career, however, for the two were as often away from the academic campus as they were on the campus, and Bennie Mays looked back on the entire period, 1924–32 (including his service as professor of English at South Carolina State College) as a time of "detours" from their appointed academic route. Above all, these were years of economic privation set in motion by a sharp agricultural recession in the rural South in 1925 followed by the more profound and more infamous Great Depression that took the urban South and even the prosperous Northeast down to the level of the already prostrate South Carolina.[1]

Throughout these "years of detour," the Mayses walked paths some distance removed from the thoroughfare traveled by most academics, especially the way followed by most black professors and educators. These paths were rough, and the trip on occasion became lonely for the couple. Bennie Mays understood and accepted the reason for the difficult detour, and he often quoted the Protestant reformist Henry Van Dyke, who had written in "The Story of the Other Wise Man": "It is better to follow even the shadow of the best than to remain content with the worst. And those who would see wonderful things must often be ready to travel alone."[2]

The train trip to Tampa in 1926 was marked by hopeful predictions at its terminal point and by glad tidings at its genesis. Tampa, the Mayses were told, was not like the rest of the South but was instead a community guarded by "White Angels" who rewarded "Good Negroes"—terms Mays recorded in *Born to Rebel.* Older black people were said to be protected and indeed rewarded for their "Good Negro" behavior by the "White Angels," and younger black people who bade fair to become faithful "Good Negroes" were given opportunities because of the cooperation between mature "Good Negroes" and the ruling "White Angels." Only a few discordant cries against the all-white Tampa police force broke the reassuring and bright notes in the litany of praises sung for the city.[3] The terms "Good Negroes" and "White Angels," always problematical, were used in largely satirical sense by Bennie and Sadie Mays among themselves, but they used them in a simple and straightforward fashion in front of the white benefactors and the mature and local African Americans, for all of whom "White Angel" and "Good Negro" described real people in a real place and not caricatures. Some black people in Tampa might or might not understand the full meaning of "White Angel" and "Good Negro," but almost none of them would have understood that the New Negroes Bennie and Sadie Mays were on this scene only during a detour. The black folk in Tampa thought that the Mays couple had settled in for a long campaign for justice there.

The Urban League, whose full title was the National League on Urban Conditions among Negroes, was in those days the practical and focused Martha to the biblical sister Mary of the National Association for the Advancement of Colored People (NAACP). As historian John Hope Franklin marked it, "The NAACP included in its program a plan widening the industrial opportunities of Negroes, [but] it did not find time to do much in this area" as the NAACP "concentrated its crusade to destroy lynching, to secure the franchise for Negroes, and to put an end to all forms of segregation and discrimination." The task of finding jobs for young black people—especially those newly arrived in large urban centers—and the task of training them for industrial opportunities, even the lowly and mundane but vital task of getting rural black folk accustomed to the foreign ways of cities, all these chores fell to the Urban League. Formed by the merger of three black self-help organizations in 1911, the Urban League as Bennie and Sadie Mays found it was definitively an organization working for New Negroes. As Franklin noted further, "It did an effective job of bringing the employer and employee together and easing the difficulties of mutual adjustments. The League also developed a program for the training of young men and young women for social work. . . . Its program of training made possible the education of many of America's most distinguished Negro social workers in the next generation." It was Sadie Mays's job to train and organize social work in Tampa. Bennie Mays's role was less sharply defined and apparently was to be both grander and vaguer in this city of "Good Negroes."[4]

For his part, the Lord God had cast up gray skies and ireful clouds, as foreboding a day for starting a mission as Bennie and Sadie Mays could recall— and the weather became a nagging portent that lingered in their minds during a warm reception filled with hope and promises. They met the self-proclaimed "Good Negroes" John Hall and Father John E. Culmer at a welcoming for the Mayses at St. Paul's A.M.E. Church. The name of the specific "Good Negro" who handled introductions from the dais is not recorded, but the name of the "White Angel" certainly is: Mrs. Ruth Atkinson. This charming lady made it clear to the newcomers that she could and would protect "Good Negroes." In a special section set apart from the black congregation were the white special guests, the mayor, civic officials, and business leaders. Following the cue from the mayor, they nodded in agreement and smiled with admiration as the diminutive but forceful Atkinson spoke. There was withal a great deal of that overly polite and strained enthusiasm that Bennie and Sadie Mays marked from the warnings of old songs often redone on "race records" played for Race Men relaxing and also enjoyed by the sober couple who never went to juke joints: the pat on the back might hold you back.[5]

After some long weeks of kind wishes and warm regards, the Mayses were indeed patted on the back and held back. The job of executive secretary of the Urban League, Bennie Mays reported later, was both "the most prestigious position for a Negro in Tampa" and "almost impossible." The executive secretary had to be liaison between the segregated worlds of black and white. There were structural problems of poverty and race: flimsy housing, badly trained teachers in dilapidated schoolhouses, and a Jim Crow wing of a poor hospital. Natural and logical consequences followed such conditions, as "miseducated" boys with no prospects first pulled away from family and church and then took to drink and drugs, quick and violent sex, and sharp and nettled contests with each other. The executive secretary was told to think and to talk without limits, to "map out" courses of corrective action. Yet, much as had been the case in Orangeburg, the white and the black worlds did not talk much to one another. There were dinners and banquets, unending fetes, and there were smiles, unfailingly warm, and pats on the back, unremitting and vigorous. But there was no truth spoken, no issue addressed.[6]

Without question there were chances to do good work for people of color, especially the young men of Tampa. As executive secretary of Urban League, Bennie Mays could get the ear of the chief of police and could gain the favor of businessmen who might hire a young man Mays recommended. Judges and city personnel bent to hear his pleas on behalf of young fellows in various phases and stages of trouble. The public schools, in disrepair and served by under-trained teachers, could on occasion get some financial assistance from wealthy benefactors if Bennie Mays approached them at a propitious moment.

The director of Bennie Mays and all other such regional agents explained why the Urban League executive secretaries played such vital, if ill-defined roles. According to Jesse O. Thomas, field secretary for the Urban League in Atlanta and thus for the entire lower South:

> [In 1919] most of the churches had what they called a Social Service Department. The department functioned somewhat in this fashion. Each Sunday the pastor would take up an "after collection" and during his pastoral visits the following week he would divide the amount among the shut-ins or those on the sick list. This represented his conception of a social service. The establishing of the Atlanta Urban League brought to Atlanta, to the extent that Atlanta was the Gateway of the South, a new conception of social work. It was not long after the Atlanta Urban League got to functioning and had an opportunity to demonstrate a more scientific approach toward supplying the unmet needs of persons who were ill-housed, under-fed, unemployed or under-employed, or suffering from some other manifestation of maladjustment, that these Social Service departments of churches automatically disappeared.[7]

Mays was thus to supply "unmet needs," including many material needs once met by pastors of black churches. In different ways, but in the same office building, Sadie Mays could work with white people of power and wealth in Tampa to help youth of color. Few were more generous in financial support or more open in emotional support than Ruth Atkinson. Yet it quickly was made clear that the "White Angel" hovered to protect "Good Negroes" and not New Negroes. A series of incidents drove home to Bennie and Sadie Mays the message that "myne own familiar friend" the White Angel spoke with words "smoother than butter" and "softer than oil," and indeed "deceit and guile depart not from her streets." Although no face smiled more broadly and no hand patted more affectingly than Ruth Atkinson's, the Mayses found that no hand could more effectively hold back their corrective actions once "mapped out."[8]

It was the little things, the small but unremitting cuts that bled the magnificence and the newness out of an African American in Tampa. White people who called the case worker's telephone routinely asked for "Sadie," and white strangers who came into the offices casually addressed her as "Sadie" if they saw her name tag. As for the executive secretary, there were the many times he was addressed as "Bennie" by white people new to his acquaintance, and there was the general salute "boy!" that unknown clerks and service people used on first greeting. To complain made one sound whiny; to accept made one an officer in the court of Jim Crow and an accomplice enabling a racist addiction. The

Mayses sought to resolve these things for themselves. The coworkers in the offices said politely on the telephone, "I will go and find Mrs. Mays"; and for her part Sadie Mays then picked up the receiver to say, "This is Mrs. Mays. How may I help you?" In his turn Bennie Mays continued the New Negro stratagems of affecting the consumer's wallet, shutting his purse to the openly offensive, dealing in business by mail order and during trips up North. On official business for the Urban League in town, however, Bennie Mays often had to follow the practical if resented path of St. Paul, doing as the Romans did in Rome and thus playing the "Good Negro" in front of the "White Angels."[9]

One day Bennie Mays encountered the racist barb in a place where mail order and business travel were no remedy: The gasoline service station. Pulling into a station, he was brought short by the attendant, who called out, "What can I do for you, boy?" As Urban League historians record it, "Mays immediately backed up and drove away boiling mad. He wrote a hot letter to the filling station manager protesting the treatment, which he described."[10]

Yet this manager did not respond to the drawn purse strings. In fact he showed his own economic power by taking Mays's note and his own description and enclosing them in a letter to the Tampa Community Chest with the query about why should that omnibus charity help the Urban League, given the "uppityness" and untowardness of the organization's executive secretary? The Community Chest of that day, much as the later United Way, made a coordinated and combined appeal to the few well-disposed civic groups and business leaders on behalf of carefully selected causes, and the Urban League was a recently added beneficiary. In fact the Urban League could not do much of its assigned work without help financially and verbally from the locally powerful stewards of the Community Chest. Soon Bennie and Sadie Mays found that the manager's protest could go far indeed, all the way to the ears of the "White Angel."[11]

Before the service-station affair, Bennie Mays had fought a larger fight, and he thought it was the primary cause of controversy for him as an officer. There had been a benefit pageant for Urban League charities, and it was called "From Darkness to Light." According to Mays, it was "designed to portray the progress made by Negroes from slavery to 1928," and it was performed at the Tampa Bay Casino by students from Booker T. Washington High School. The city owned the casino and rented it to the American Legion, Tampa Post no. 5. The American Legion in turn rented the casino to Booker T. Washington High School but with the absolute proviso that Florida laws of segregation be enforced. White people as well as African Americans attended the pageant—in the parlance of the day, not segregated but separated, or as was also said, together but not mixed. Black people were sent to the balcony, much as at the cinema, and white benefactors were escorted to the spacious downstairs seats.

For this event the arrangement was a real problem because many black people were present to sit in the small space reserved for them, and only a few white people were there to sit in the large space designated for them. The balcony crowd grew cramped and uncomfortable and was perhaps even too heavy a weight for the structure to bear. Downstairs there were plenty of seats, the white benefactors forming a minor archipelago in a wide sea. Were it not dangerous for the crowd, and were it not such a cut to the soul, it could have been funny. Eventually a few hundred black audience members were permitted to fill in the side seats downstairs to left and right of orchestra—or main—seating.[12]

Nothing could be done, for the American Legion officials enforced the local Jim Crow law, as Bennie Mays recorded it, "so meticulously that the result was ridiculous." The music and the presentations were no fun for the black audience in the cramped and creaking balcony or in the side seats left and right of the orchestra seats. Surely some of their white friends knew of their discomfort and displeasure. It was not a shining moment for anyone in Tampa, and it was a terrible moment for a New Negro. Surely no New Negro could or should tolerate such abuse. Mays determined to declare a strong protest.

He wrote about the occasion of festivities, funds raised from which were to benefit African Americans in Tampa. And he thought about benefits in general, reflecting that no benefit came free but always came with a cost. The benefit at the casino was surely and sorely needed, but the cost was high. The New Negro had to behave like the "Good Negro" in order to win the "White Angel's" benefit. The benefit was good and its value mounted high indeed, but the cost was higher and indeed mounted toward the heavens. In fact, Mays decided, it cost too much despite what it gained:

> Were it not pathetic, it would be laughable that out of 800 or 900 seats reserved for white people, only 68 were present, including little children. . . . There is no denying the fact that these were the best seats in the house. To be mathematically exact 508 of the best orchestra seats were vacant all during the pageant and Negroes could not sit in them. The writer, wanting a good seat, attempted with his wife and a friend to sit in the orchestra seats in the rear. The [Negro] usher went up in the air and insisted that we crowd ourselves into the side seats. Our seats were so inconvenient that at times we could not see the performance. The balcony and sides were crowded while 508 of the best seats in the house remained vacant. Had I been allowed to sit in the rear of the main auditorium, I would have been fully 14 seats from the nearest white man (one) and much farther from the other 67. . . .
>
> . . . It cost too much. It cannot be justified by law; cannot be justified by tradition. Neither justice nor money can justify it. . . . It sets a bad example

before the ambitious youths of the city, does not help the Negro in developing self-respect, and does not increase the white man's respect for him.[13]

Mindful that the executive secretary of the Tampa Urban League never spoke for himself alone but always for all African Americans in Tampa, Bennie Mays called on the Negro Ministers Alliance, an association of which he was an active member but not the leader. He reviewed with them the events and then read his manifesto to them. Father Culmer—a self-proclaimed "Good Negro" and thus suspect in the Mayses' eyes to that point—spoke quickly and firmly in full support of the statement. So too did all the other ministers assembled. It was a show of courage, commitment, and solidarity. All sensed that something big was happening, and because of that sense, Mays had also fully informed Jesse O. Thomas, his field supervisor. Thomas recorded that he encouraged Mays to involve all members of the Negro Ministers Alliance and all relevant officials in the Urban League in Tampa, but Mays recorded that he had already done so before talking with Thomas. It is a fine point. What is sure is that all active members of the Negro Ministers Alliance and all relevant officials active in the Urban League agreed with the statement that "it cost too much." It is further agreed by all that the southern field director completely supported the minister's statement.[14]

The Reverend M. D. Potter, a member present at the meeting, was editor of the *Tampa Bulletin,* an African American newspaper. He was pleased to publish Mays's statement on the front page of his paper and to write a supporting editorial. As the Mayses marked it, most Negroes in town responded as did the preacher-proprietor and the other newspapermen setting the type. Yet there were problems at once at the school board; the white superintendent, J. G. Anderson, was vexed by Mays's statement and made formal complaint to Thomas in Atlanta. Bennie Mays was always convinced that Anderson was moved to action because of a "Good Negro," whom he did not name, who was active in the public school administration and who was set like flint against the New Negroes. Certainly Ruth Atkinson was back of everything and in front of everyone, and the "White Angel" sent word about a conference in special session about the Urban League, the Community Chest, and Bennie Mays.[15]

Thomas sent a telegram from Atlanta to Bennie and Sadie Mays and told them about the upcoming conference. He also surprised the Mayses by notifying them that it was not the bold stand on the Jim Crow benefit for which the executive secretary was impeached. Rather Mrs. Atkinson was focused on the gasoline service station incident and at the Mayses' insistence on decent manners toward female black office workers in general and specifically Sadie Mays. Mrs. Atkinson expressed her displeasure among white people and to Thomas, but to the Mayses she continued to be pleasant. Like the song on the race record played at the juke joint, the "White Angel" had a smiling face and patted you on the back, but in the mode of the back stabber. Thomas revealed to the Mayses that Mrs. Atkinson intended to fire Bennie and Sadie Mays, and this firing would not be for the noble gesture titled "It Cost Too Much," but rather for the New Negroes' insistence that they were adults deserving adult salutations. Meanwhile the "White Angel" flew to the courts of judgment in the offices of a wealthy benefactor, Mr. Brorein, chief executive officer of the Tampa Bell Telephone Company.[16]

Mr. Mays the student of the classics, had trained himself not to reveal weakness in his face or even anxiety, and he drove the car to the session for his supervisor, J. O. Thomas, holding the visage of a proud officer and the countenance of the dutiful servant. When he and Thomas arrived at Brorein's offices, Mrs. Atkinson was there, gracious and smiling, as was the school superintendent, J. G. Anderson. The "White Angel" suggested that Mr. Mays remain in the drawing room while Mr. Thomas, Mr. Anderson, and she attended the chief executive officer in the corporate board room. Jesse Thomas recorded that Bennie Mays was left to sit alone in the plush offices for at least fifty minutes. (Bennie Mays did not mention this incident in *Born to Rebel*.)[17]

Thomas wrote that the white "tribal leaders" spoke firmly in councils that Bennie Mays had misbehaved at the service station and that Sadie Mays had routinely misbehaved on the telephone, that both were wrong about proper treatment of black adults, and that both must go. The white chiefs produced a letter in which Bennie Mays referred to his three college degrees as evidence that he was not to be addressed as "boy." Thomas later said he stated regret that Mr. Mays had expected adult treatment because of his education and credentials. He asserted in these councils for the white chiefs that Mr. Mays and Mrs. Mays deserved treatment as adults because they were adults. Thomas went on to pronounce that all black adults should be addressed as adults and then declared that he would not discipline Mr. or Mrs. Mays on any of these issues about telephone calls, office manners, or the service station incident. He recorded further that Mr. Brorein, Mr. Anderson, and Mrs. Atkinson were displeased but as always scrupulous in their good manners and charm. In any case only Thomas could fire Bennie Mays, and the "White Angel" and the Bell Company executive were left with only their ability to eliminate the Urban League from the charity rolls of the Community Chest. The meeting ended thus. Mr. and Mrs. Mays were not fired, and neither was Mrs. Atkinson obliged to share her wealth to support the works of the Urban League.[18]

Such Urban League works included a major sociological and economic study supervised by the University of North Carolina sociologist Arthur Franklin Raper and completed in this same spring season. Raper, a native white man from North Carolina, bore a most unfortunate name.

In his scholarship and even in his conversation, Raper struck with the same purifying and poison-dispelling force and the surprise of the "first lightning" flung by the more happily named John Hope. Raper studied lynching, and he produced data to show that the death-talking mobs seldom had proof of a rape, sometimes did not even pretend that a rape had actually happened, and generally sought to prevent a trial in which the accused could be confronted by the accuser. In many cases, Raper found, the accused was already in custody, the victim secured and removed from further shame, and authorities in place for a speedy trial. The lynching mob was thus not established for retribution on behalf of a victim with no recourse, but rather as a signed assault on African Americans who sought the right of free association. Raper could cite these statistics, and he could narrate his many frightening stories of lynching actions. In 1933 he brought data, interpretation, and a precisely focused outrage into a memorable narrative that helped to sway thinking white people away from the practice—or even from apologizing for the practice—of the lynching bee.[19]

In addition Raper was making a careful study of the black folk who farmed the lands of dark soil at this moment when the working folk of all colors began to do other things besides farming. In particular Raper studied the farmers of depleted soil where cotton, tobacco, corn, sorghum, or any other crop no longer flourished, and there were few returns on their hard work. He announced that such people, white and black, found their feet set on a "path to peasantry"—not slavery, but while it was better than slavery, neither was it to be the one-time security of the old free-holding society. Absent some policy change, Raper prophesied, there would emerge a peasantry that would be beholden to the owner of the poor land they worked. And that landowner would be beholden to creditors in a far city, usually Manhattan, and those creditors and note holders would be frustrated by the poor return on their investment and by the low market value of their lien holding. Raper gathered these data, coming to focus on the plight of black farmers in two Georgia counties. He began to speak as an economic prophet warning everybody to set their feet down some other pathway to reform—or else join the story and play the miserable role that he called *Preface to Peasantry.*[20]

Raper was a thinker, and he provoked others to thought. At table he could be charming, but he could also fling his purifying lightning, striking and stunning a host satisfied with the economic life that so garnished his table. Mays established ties to Raper. Together they rode to the slums to take photographs and to talk with the New Negroes of Tampa, those who studied and strove for attainment in school and professions. Raper and Mays were unsparing and unblinking as their cameras captured images of open sewers and filthy cisterns, homes without running water, many more homes without power and light, one-room schools presided over by the badly trained, muddy mires of roadways, white folk's clothes hung in the bright sun behind the dreary house of the black lady who cried to see her own children dressed in unwashed cast-off clothing, and young boys with no prospects wandering the streets—and those wanderers, in the ancient refrain of the Spanish conquistadors of the doomed red natives of the selfsame Tampa Bay, were "without law, without king, without faith." Raper and Mays collected data at the University of North Carolina and the University of Chicago; and they used their mathematical minds to integrate their statistics accurately and usefully into their narrative. They included testimony of witnesses from among the victims. Both men, white and black, had won the confidence of Tampa African Americans, who talked and told and talked and told as Raper and Mays listened and wrote and listened and wrote.[21]

The Mayses enjoyed their working association with Arthur Raper, and they longed, even ached, to extend the friendship, to have another white friend from the South, in addition to W. O. Brown. To break bread at table in equal company and full companionship was the sign of friendship for the classicist, and Jesus was noted for reclining at table in equal company with suspect characters such as corrupt tax collectors and fishermen of simple speech. The Mayses welcomed to their table a host of similarly undistinguished folk, but yet there remained that longing to bring to their table the distinguished white professor from North Carolina. He was invited for the occasion of the launching of the study of black life in Tampa, but Raper found he had made other commitments for the evening. The Mayses declared their understanding but expressed their hope that he could find a way to come to the important event. Always Raper was politic, but the excuse was hollow. The Mayses expressed their sadness and declared their fears that the prominent white North Carolina professor did not intend to sit at table and break bread with them in equal friendship despite Jim Crow. Thus pressured, Raper canceled the other engagement and joined them at the dinner to launch the project, sitting at the side of his coeditor Bennie Mays. The Urban League official recorded that at meal's conclusion Raper turned to him to announce with poison-clearing lightning: "I didn't feel funny." It was his way of announcing that he had never before sat to take a meal alongside black people, and that he had avoided doing so because he had for long decades accepted as a fact the cultural assumption that breaking a taboo would actually hurt him, make him "feel funny."[22]

Another episode with Raper was funny. That is it was funny to recount once both men had allowed years and landscapes to pass. As the two investigated and wrote up their findings, they needed to rent a car. The rental workers put a temporary cardboard agency sign on the car; Mays signed the chit and climbed into the back seat. Raper took the wheel, and off the scholars went toward the muddy vales of the old Tampa black section. It was against Jim Crow for the two to sit together on the front seat, but permissible for a man of one race to serve as chauffeur for a man of another race, most of the time the chauffeur being black and rider white. Before they got far, a white Tampa policeman stopped them and berated Dr. Raper for serving as chauffeur to a black man. It was not against law, but it was so contrary to practice as to guarantee the wrong kind of attention from the official and from other white people. It put both scholars in mind of an old saw about Dr. Booker T. Washington, who once needed a taxi ride from the train station but could locate no black drivers and only one terrified white driver. Dr. Washington took the wheel; the cabbie gave his cap to Dr. Washington and climbed into the back passenger seat—so Jim Crow was followed to the letter. In the 1928 case with Mays and Raper, the two social science researchers bore the officer's chastening quietly but then went on their way, white researcher driving, and black researcher riding.[23]

At the unveiling of the report, Urban League people, New Negroes, and white liberals—including the "White Angel" and the Bell bosses, all came forward to review the study and to celebrate the ingathering of data by the co-editor social scientists. White newspaper reporters attended and took notes, but in the morning edition only the North Carolina sociologist, the white Raper, was named and discussed as author, and the University of Chicago scholar, the black Mays, was not mentioned. Surely the "White Angel," the Bell bosses, and other seemingly good white folk wanted it to be so. Perhaps too Dr. Raper had a hand in telling the story this way. Surely a man of *megalosukos* could not stay on with the Tampa Urban League unless he was willing to sink into the *mikrosukos* of the "Old Negro" and in so sinking hurt the standing of every New Negro in Tampa by accepting less than his earned portion of respect.[24] Classical understanding of an individual's magnificence commingled with the community image of the New Negro to make Bennie and Sadie Mays deeply humbled and shamed.

The "White Angels" and the Bell bosses did him no honor, nor did any black people in his native South Carolina. Yet Bennie Mays could take solace that others elsewhere honored him. He was not without resources. He could shake the Tampa dust from his sandals, and he could go someplace where people could appreciate and respond to his commission. For the writing of his dissertation at the University of Chicago, he could draw on the Rockefeller Foundation, whose General Education Board officers proffered him a full research fellowship. That purse could be set against the University of Chicago tuition and still allow him some living expenses if Sadie Mays could find employment in Chicago too.[25]

As they pondered that offer and thought about married life in Chicago, there came the chance to work with the reformist YMCA, or Y. (Mays usually referred to the Young Women's Association as the YWCA, not the Y). There was need for a secretary to oversee the Y's work on black college campuses in South Carolina, Georgia, Florida, Alabama, and Tennessee. The headquarters and base of operations for this much-traveling secretary were in Atlanta. If Bennie Mays took that job, then Sadie Mays could likely serve on the paid staff producing the Georgia Study of Negro Child Welfare. She could also provide some social work teaching at Atlanta University. Although the jobs for the couple were in Atlanta, the focus of work for Bennie and Sadie Mays was the rural countryside that produced the college students and the newly arrived workers in the towns. And these people in these villages were sore pressed as an agricultural recession had settled over the land and was in its third year, even as city people reveled in their final months of Roaring Twenties prosperity.

In order for Sadie Mays to gain this opportunity, however, Louisa Fitzsimmons, another "White Angel" of doubtful sincerity, must be served. The officers of the Georgia study needed to hear Mrs. Fitzsimmons's opinion of Sadie Mays's performance as a professional for the social work offices in Tampa. In the privacy of their Tampa home, the couple could rail against her, but in her presence and in the presence of the Atlanta staff of the Georgia study she had to be shown respect. Sadie Mays asked this "White Angel" for a letter of recommendation, and Mrs. Fitzsimmons received the request politely and appeared to accede. Long days passed, and the Georgia study officers reported to Sadie Mays that they lacked Mrs. Fitzsimmons's note. They could not proceed if the most recent employer and supervisor issued no opinion. With due respect and perhaps undue trepidation, Bennie Mays appeared before the powerful lady to ask if there was a problem in writing about his wife to the Georgia study. Mrs. Fitzsimmons declared that Sadie Mays was a good person and a good worker; but, she added, as a social worker, Sadie Mays did not understand white southerners and would get in trouble in Atlanta expecting to be called "Mrs. Mays" and otherwise expecting the civilities reserved for white ladies. Bennie Mays controlled his tongue. He asked Mrs. Fitzsimmons to be completely honest, and urged her to send in her honest evaluation quickly. Mrs. Fitzsimmons agreed, and she sent forward her words of support, noting Sadie Mays's good qualities but also warning that she would cause trouble by insisting on the respectful treatment accorded by white ladies. Officers of the Georgia study accepted Mrs. Fitzsimmons's evaluation and hired Sadie Mays, knowing as they did so that she thought of herself as a child of God and a lady and did not think of herself as a work mule or a lap dog.[26]

Going back to Atlanta, Bennie and Sadie Mays were returning to the capital of the segregated Jim Crow South, the city at once the center of southern black attainment and the center of white supremacy. As Bennie Mays marked it with carefully measured pride, Atlanta had Jesse O. Thomas of the Urban

League, black professors at Morehouse and the other colleges in the Atlanta University system, and the Y's black leaders: James Moreland, Channing Tobias, J. H. McGrew, William Craven, and Ralph Bullock. All of them were "able and admirable men, each demonstrating manhood and dignity in a highly segregated organization."[27] This Y section of the detour might well slow Mays's work on his dissertation, but it would keep him in the company of black men proud of their manhood and keen on their signs of New Negro dignity.

As it happened, this Y detour made Bennie Mays a better scholar. If it took him longer to attain the Ph.D. degree, then so it has been for many at the University of Chicago, especially students of Shirley Case. Working all the time with black and white church people, Mays was ever in mind about God's revealed Word and man's efforts to apprehend, to catch and to hold onto that Word, that divine breath, that holy wind. Dr. Case's teachings seemed to be more involved in the Mayses' own lives in Atlanta than in the seminary discussion room with its ancient maps and ancient manuscripts. The people of God, whether triumphant in Solomon's Jerusalem, exiled and enthralled in Babylon, huddled in catacombs, serving as lap dogs of the mighty Roman emperors, cloistered in monasteries, or reading in university—all, in all phases of time, read their holy texts with care, with devotion, with rapt attention to divine will. Yet again and again, something came up for which there was no literal guidance. Prayer and study yielded a sense of God's will, but Bennie Mays could acknowledge such prayer and study for what it was: inspired interpretation and not an exact commandment. As for those people of God, so it was for the believers at the Y in Atlanta, and so too it was as he gleaned it from his studies of a much earlier day for Dr. Case. Men had ever strained to find and to follow God's will; but always it was found in sources adding to the Bible and seldom was it drawn directly from Hebrew, Aramaic, Greek, or Latin words that had been blown across the decades by that powerful yet precious breath of God.

The impossibility of finding the precise word that exactly fit the divine word was by turns tragic, comic, frustrating, and inspiriting. Always some earthly crisis drove him to the Bible, but on each trip he was driven, blown by God's own breath, to historical sources around the Bible and to some historical sources around the moral problems that cried to be addressed. As at Bates College and at the University of Chicago and at the Y, Bennie Mays read his Bible in context of classical thought, especially the Roman Stoics, and thus the medieval scholars of classicism, Thomas Aquinas and Augustine, Romish and papist or not, were vital to this Baptist, as were the Chicago scholars and the modern thinkers, liberal or not. His foundation was divine; yet his Holy Bible, by definition of the word "biblio," was a collection, really a library, of sacred books and poems and songs in multiple forms—and the magnificent and awe-some collection was set firmly on the hard rock of pagan myth, and it was but-tressed by the flying thought of medieval scholastic divines and reinforced later by the engineering of Dr. Case. Of course Bennie Mays was not passively receiving the thoughts of Dr. Case, rather he was wielding his own shovel, exca-vating things for himself, and finally interpreting for himself in this reconstruc-tion of a collection of words about the Word.[28]

The main task for Bennie Mays, executive secretary for the college-student Y chapters, was in two parts. First he must "broaden the horizons" of the young men, usually rural and even if urban so newly come to town as to be deeply parochial. Second was to build up their confidence and "get them to be some-body" despite all that poverty and Jim Crow law and white practice did to beat them down and to break self-confidence. Crucial to the twin tasks were con-ferences in the fresh air of the western North Carolina mountains; but as the psalmist notes, the hilltops too are filled with enemies, and in looking at them one must ask God, "from whence cometh my help?" Jim Crow and its damn-ing proclamations were in force and fouled the otherwise fresh and bracing air of the tall Carolina pines and firs.[29]

African Americans were restricted to the Kings Mountain camp, while the white boys convened at the nearby Blue Ridge camp. In fact the Kings Moun-tain Y camp was integrated, for white leaders and white students were often brought there because Bennie Mays and his senior Y secretary, Frank T. Wil-son, believed that young black leaders needed to be in the company of white boys and men, especially in settings of free discussion and frank debate and fully cooperative teamwork. When white boys came to the black camp, they took meals at table with everyone, slept in bunks in the same cabins, brushed their teeth in the same sinks, showered in the same bathhouses, peed into the same urinals, and were led in devotionals and prayers honoring the same God. The Blue Ridge Y camp, however, was the more expensively appointed facility, with a bigger budget and bigger visitors and bigger programs, and it was strictly for whites only. The black Y youth at Kings Mountain were thus served only the scraps that dropped from the sumptuous feast at the table of the white lords of Blue Ridge.[30]

In 1928 some changes and improvements came, but they were a pittance. The Blue Ridge Y accepted five African American boys as "fraternal delegates"; and the white officials agreed to permit up to 5 percent of all attendees to be black—provided that the 5 percent did not amount to more than five boys. These fraternal delegates ate at a Jim Crow table, slept in different quarters, and showered, brushed their teeth, and attended bodily needs in a special bath-house. In such Jim Crow setting, the term was "together but segregated," and the effect on discussants was not integrationist, nor did it push toward brother-hood and equality despite the label "fraternal." Instead "together but segregated" conditions reminded all, especially the impressionable white adolescents, that black people were different, not the same at all, deserving of less, deserving of only the table scraps. It was the kind of thing Jessie Daniel Ames called liberal-ism and progress, the tossed scrap that made Tampa's "White Angels" and Bell bosses puff up with pride in self-contemplation. Frank Wilson and Bennie Mays protested, and in protesting they "strained the bonds of affection," as church people name such relations, but the rule of five and the rule of 5 per-cent and the rule of "together but segregated" stayed in place. Mays and Wil-son heard that it was better than nothing. They heard that change would take time. They heard truth, Mays and Wilson did, for the children of these chil-dren would live by the rule of five and the rule of 5 percent and live by the rule of "together but segregated," even unto a second generation at the Blue Ridge Y. Three U.S. presidents came and went, one of them elected four times, and much changed in the world, but the Blue Ridge Y through all those days held to its rule of five and its rule of 5 percent and its rule of "together but segre-gated" until a federal law imposed change in 1965.[31]

In such a mood, Bennie Mays chafed at things southern, ached to bring change, and resented the white lords even more than before—all of them, from the obvious cruelty of Dr. Wallace Payne to the subtleties of the landowning Bill and Nola Mays to the backstabbing of Mrs. Fitzsimmons and Mrs. Atkinson. It was hard to remember W. O. Brown from Texas, first equal white friend. When thinking about Arthur Raper from North Carolina, there was less mem-ory of working together and sitting at table and more memory of Raper receiv-ing sole author credit in the newspaper for the Tampa project. Mays bitterly called up the words of his mother, Louvenia Mays, who told him to stay away from white people and especially white girls: "They will get you into trouble."[32]

Then in 1929 came Ruth Lockman, the kind of great-looking white girl whom Louvenia Mays specifically warned her boys to stay away from. Mays and others were arranging a Kings Mountain conference for the YMCA and YWCA. As was the case for Kings Mountain camp, things were truly inte-grated, but even so Mays and his coworkers were surprised to find representing the District of Columbia Intercollegiate Association this "beautiful white girl" from the South. Equal friendship with Bill Brown and collaborative work with Arthur Raper were one thing, but working at a conference alongside Ruth Lockman was something else. Not only was she sleeping in quarters with black girls and peeing into their commode, but she was sitting at table right next to black boys and tilting her head and looking with blue eyes into their eyes while they talked. It was the kind of thing the law and the prophets of Jim Crow preached against, and the kind of thing proscribed in force by nothing less than Judge Lynch and his dreaded rope and fagot.[33]

There was suspicion of Ruth Lockman at once, and Bennie Mays was not entirely innocent of such suspicion. Young white women, those who in no way could be called matriarchs, were by definition a problem in a system built for two colors, especially where the dominant white people not only laid claim to the land but also to the black people and above all to sexual favors from the black women. With the freeing of the slaves, the law made the white lords press their claims more quietly, but press them they did on many an occasion, and the mulatto, high-yellow population kept growing, primarily from white men successfully prosecuting their sexual claims. However quietly the white lords pressed their claim to black ladies, they were extremely loud in announcing that white ladies were not to be touched by black men, and when the black youth were of the age of puberty and the white ladies were of the age of puberty, such white ladies were not even to be looked at by such black youth. A young white lady coming into a black campsite could not be told to go away, but if at any time she suddenly claimed a black youth had made an improper advance, much more if she claimed rape, then the entire black community at camp was in jeopardy. False claims of rape happened often enough that black ministers and counselors were cautious when a young white lady came around.[34]

Yet Ruth Lockman made no improper advances and inspired none at Kings Mountain camp. She looked directly at people and spoke plainly and listened patiently to people. She was not from the Deep South and came from different traditions than those of South Carolina and Georgia that Bennie used as his model for expectations of white southern women. She seemed a sister in Christ, in the notion of sisterhood as marked and written about by St. Paul: "These women were a help to me when I was fighting to defend the Good News. . . . Their names are written in the book of life. I want you to be happy, always happy in the Lord; I repeat what I want is your happiness. Let your tolerance be evident to everybody."[35]

Bennie Mays came to trust Ruth Lockman. In fact he began to inquire of her what her Virginia father knew of her activities in integrated settings. He was surprised to learn that her father was a native South Carolinian, a Methodist minister who had pastored churches throughout Mays's native state and who had been particularly active among black clergymen in Orangeburg, raising money for the private black Methodist Claflin College. The Reverend Lockman talked and acted around black people much as did Bill Brown or Dr. Case or the better professors at Bates College. Mays concluded that the Reverend Lockman had been changed forever working among church people for godly causes in places where the spirit was rich but the purse was nearly empty. Not only could Bennie Mays accept the Reverend Lockman as a native South

Carolina brother in Christ, but he could accept Ruth Lockman as a native Virginia sister in Christ. Moreover Bennie Mays could see that some of this problem was also a black problem, that African Americans had to give native white southerners—even and especially including pretty girls—the benefit of the doubt and give everybody the chance to be fully equal before the one true Lord God. Above all, the quaint notion that people could be grouped by "tribes"—fair enough in Rambo as the boy Bennie had found Rambo to be—was not only irrelevant but wrong, and dangerously wrong. He would not refer to all the groups as "tribes" except in withering sarcasm, and in such a way he tried thereafter to restrain such sarcasm. No man of *megalosukos* could talk in such a way, Mays realized, and so came a third epiphany about color: some white southern men were decent. He now learned and recorded in 1929 that he—and Sadie Mays—could trust some southern white women.[36]

There were thus these epiphanies about white people and justice. Learning the lesson to trust some northern white people from the Chases, Baird, Pomeroy and others at Bates, he kept touch thereafter with Bates friends; learning that Bill Brown of Texas was one of several decent white men from the South, he kept touch thereafter with Brown; learning that southern white girls were not of nature a demonic threat, he did not keep touch thereafter with Ruth Lockman, but he actually learned the more radicalizing and transforming lesson from her.

From now forward, Bennie Mays found his eyes opened to a marvelous potential in all men, all boys, all women, and all girls. Proud of his blackness, this New Negro could still be proud of the humanity in good people of all colors. At least one older white man who came to Kings Mountain camp changed during worship and began to call the minister and Y official "Mr. Mays" after earlier refusing to do so. The final chorus of praises among all the 150 psalms now sang for Bennie Mays himself:

> Hallelujah!
>
> Praise God in his holy temple;
>   praise him in the firmament of his power.
> Praise him for his mighty acts;
>   praise him for his excellent greatness.
> Praise him with the blast of a horn;
>   praise him with lyre and harp.
> Praise him with timbrel and dance;
>   praise him with strings and pipe.
> Praise him with resounding cymbals;
>   praise him with loud-clanging cymbals.

> Let everything that breathes
>   praise the Lord.
>
> Hallelujah![37]

The word "everything" was not a metaphor but an exact description: "this one invites every living being to praise Yahweh." Everything and everybody could come to sing praises at Kings Mountain camp. Perhaps it was time for nothing and nobody to come to Blue Ridge camp. Thus Bennie Mays decided for the African American boys on his campuses by 1930. Within a few more years, the nationwide YMCA and YWCA reached the same decision, ending all Y-sponsored conferences for youth of any color at the lovely Blue Ridge camp, where youth could be together only if they were segregated.[38]

God did not want one to see "tribes," Bennie Mays realized, because "tribes" did not exist. Or rather, they existed in the minds of mortal men at the lovely little segregated camp on the Blue Ridge mountaintop in North Carolina. Sadie Mays too was finding that "tribes" did not exist unless someone wanted them to exist. Bad white southerners, or perhaps just misguided white southerners, made themselves see "tribes" and then by law and by practice they kept black people in "nigger towns" and "black bottoms" and other vales of humility. Some black people came to accept the white perception, to think of themselves as "nigger," "darky," "Sambo," or "black boy." Such African Americans so accepted those white perceptions that they laughed and sang and made no threat to anyone. Still others came to think of themselves as "bad," to glory in the fear that they could cause in white oppressors, who perceived "bad niggers," "niggers in the woods," "tough niggers," or "niggers of the streets." African Americans accepting those white perceptions swaggered and yelled and made maximum threat to everyone. The first sort of black men shuffled and fetched it, smiled and joked, much as Hezekiah had when the night riders came to kill him and his son Bennie. The second sort built their muscles, sharpened their knives, moved their feet fast, and waited quietly in the shadows, tigers ever at the ready to attack the dumb white dudes, the damn fools who might wander over to the black side of town at the wrong time of day when no police and no witnesses stood near. Hezekiah Mays had in fact been both. Sometimes he had survived by laughing and smiling and shuffling and playing Sambo the clown—for "Sambo" was the African word for clown, and the word and the role were already there before Hezekiah was born. Yet Hezekiah had also drunk his liquor, had felt it good and strong, and had realized the strength of his arms, the muscles and sinews toughened from picking cotton, lifting bales of hay, and handling stubborn mules; and he had at those times felt his own badness. When totally "liquored up," in high spirits and enflamed by drink, Hezekiah was a terror to behold, and he could defend himself and indeed hurt others with his muscles and his knuckles.

The words of the poet and playwright John Dryden had caught it all, had described Dr. Wallace Payne and Hezekiah, had described the "White Angel" and the Bell bosses, had described the officials of the lovely segregated Blue Ridge mountaintop:

> All, all of a piece throughout:
> 　　Thy Chase had a Beast in View;
> Thy Wars brought nothing about;
> 　　Thy Lovers were all untrue.
> 'Tis Well an Old Age is out,
> 　　And time to begin a New.[39]

Many men, many women, were playing in a play, many were playing roles established by bygone myths—and the roles no longer worked at all because the play was over. It was time to begin a new play, a new life: "'Tis Well an Old Age is out, / And time to begin a New."

The new role to play on this leg of the detour was to step back from making policy in order to study the other African American men and institutions that dominated the black side of making policy. The ordained minister agreed to study black ministers and churches. Again it was Rockefeller Foundation money that paid the freight. The foundation had created the Institute of Social and Religious Research, based in Chicago, and this institute offered Benjamin Mays and the Reverend Joseph William Nicholson stipends to produce a study called *The Negro's Church*. Nicholson, from Springfield, Missouri, was an ordained Methodist minister trained in philosophy at Howard University and in divinity studies at Garrett Bible Institute of Northwestern University. He was completing a Ph.D. in education at Northwestern in 1930, and his dissertation, "An Occupational Study of the Christian Ministry among Negroes," was closely related to the study he would conduct with Mays. Firmly committed to integration, Nicholson eventually became an ordained Episcopal priest, the only African American priest in a large diocese that included the city of St. Louis. He made a name for himself in the St. Louis area for economic activism and for integrating the public schools. Also a leader in the St. Louis Urban League, the Y, and the NAACP, Nicholson worked hard for justice, integration, and opportunities. Like Mays, Nicholson also became a member of the board of education for a major city at a time in life normally given over to retirement, travel, and rest. No less a scholar than Mays and no less an activist, Nicholson was genuinely a full partner, but the voice heard in much of the study is Mays's.[40]

Of the fourteen months he was involved in this research and writing, from mid-summer 1930 to September 1932, Mays wrote in *Born to Rebel* that the work, "if not heaven-sent, must surely be heaven-bent," for it forced the scholar and minister to understand his role as a man of the cloth for a group described by the sociologists as "over churched," that is, poor people spending too many precious resources on tiny church buildings in which badly educated ministers struggled to serve small congregations, each of which was likely to split off again into still smaller congregations demanding their own building in which to meet. The data show that, for every one thousand souls, there were twice as many black ministers as there were white ministers, and the verdict seemed to be that these black ministers were less than half as effective for their tiny congregations as their white colleagues of the cloth were for theirs. Mays and Nicholson were saddened but not surprised to gather data showing that fewer than four of one hundred black seminary students came to their seminaries with a baccalaureate degree. As for educated African Americans, Mays and Nicholson found in their survey that "few college men are looking forward to the ministry as a career."[41]

One thing beyond dispute was the extreme Jim Crow nature of American churches, their dramatic segregation, their complete difference in wealth and financial resources. More like Old Testament prophets than Chicago scholars, Mays and Nicholson stretched out God's plumb line to take the measure of black and white churches. Like Amos, they found things to be far from plumb, in fact to be built so unsoundly, crookedly, and carelessly as to be on the verge of collapse. Mays and Nicholson did not mince the phrases: white people never wanted black people to worship as brothers and sisters in Christ, and they had used their gold- and their cotton-backed bonds—as well as the lash and the knout—to keep black church experiences impoverished and segregated, again "together but separate." In the long dark night of slavery, the Methodist and Baptist ministers had served the planters who paid their salaries by pushing the slaves into the balcony to be lectured at and even hectored about God's will that they be slaves beholden to God's chosen white folk. This occurred despite the firm antislavery preaching of Methodist founders John and Charles Wesley and despite the equally firm antislavery preaching of the original North American Baptist, Roger Williams. Then the planters had published in their statute books that black people had to attend the white ministers' worship services and could not worship on their own unsupervised. The white men of the cloth preached the untruth that God disdained his black children and favored his white children. And the white lords of the land rounded up African Americans to force them to listen to the preaching of the untruth. How easily, how naturally, and how obviously black people could sing the ancient Hebrew lament at being strangers in a strange land, languishing by the river in Babylon.[42]

When freedom came, independent black churches established themselves, with Nicholson's Methodists and Mays's Baptists being particularly early and particularly prominent in forming national organizations to serve freedmen. The bad old days of preaching untruth about slavery were done and gone, washed away by the blood of a million casualties, at least sixty thousand of whom were black soldiers. However, the freedmen were absolutely not welcomed to the white churches, despite the famous example of Robert E. Lee going forward to kneel at the Lexington, Virginia, communion rail next to a black parishioner. That church was an Episcopal congregation that attracted few freedmen—and only a certain class among the white Christians. The Episcopal Church that Nicholson chose to serve came years later, after revolutionary change. The far more popular postbellum Methodist and Baptist churches kept black worshippers at bay, largely by ensuring that their worship and activities would have absolutely nothing to do with the needs of the destitute and displaced freedmen. Mays and Nicholson insisted that Jim Crow was at play, that a practice of consciously excluding African American parishioners kept white Protestant churches white. In case someone might miss the message, Mays enumerated the simple steps: first black worshippers are told they are not wanted; second they are shown that they will never be served.[43]

As Nicholson and Bennie Mays gathered their data, another short stay in Chicago became possible for the Mayses: a few months in the spring of 1931, during which time Sadie Mays could complete her master's degree and Bennie Mays could touch base with the university divinity professors. Generally these were happy times, as the academic community at the great school began to recognize both Sadie and Bennie Mays as accomplished professionals worthy of regard and respect.[44]

There certainly were moments that spring when Bennie Mays took the chance to stand out to great scholars and good reformists and to show that his ongoing research with Joseph Nicholson was fruitful. He accepted an invitation to speak at a conference called "Whither the Negro Church," to be hosted by a black academic honorary society at Yale University Divinity School in New Haven. Yale, the epitome of scholarship in the old East, had integrated its divinity school early in the century, and by 1931 there were seven black Ph.D. candidates there. These seven, while pleased that Yale was integrated, were yet troubled that there were not more black students there and were also generally vexed as they contemplated the low level of training for most black ministers and the lack of discernible direction for most of the black churches served by these badly trained pastors. The seven had formed the honorary fraternity Upsilon Theta Chi in hopes of inspiring and guiding "a new type of leadership for the black church," and they had gotten support from some white professors, especially Jerome Davis, to conduct a conference each spring.[45]

To the conference of April 13–15, 1931, the men of Upsilon Theta Chi invited Mays and A. Philip Randolph. On this occasion the labor leader and new head of the Brotherhood of Sleeping Car Porters could meet firsthand and talk with Bennie Mays, the Pullman porter activist of a previous era, whose exploits in organizing, while unsuccessful, remained so legendary as to be mythic for the now powerful unionists of the 1930s. Also speaking was the sponsor, Professor Jerome Davis, and Mays was pleased not only to learn from the great scholar but also to find in Davis a man willing to learn from others. Mays gave the conference the fruits of his research with Joseph Nicholson: African American ministers needed to be better educated, better focused, and above all dedicated to social improvement for their race. He gave the distinguished audience a combination of raw data on ministers and churches and an inspiriting call to mission: new men—and indeed a new kind of men—were needed, for Mays showed that the brightest black scholars of this era were not entering the ministry. The ministers of this new time, he proclaimed, must be "prophets of the new day, fearless and courageous."[46]

Conscious of the wealth, power, and prestige at Yale, Randolph for his part called on the ministers to "take a working class view" and develop a "working class . . . program" for their congregations. Those African Americans who had migrated from the South had briefly found opportunity in the factories in New Haven and other northern cities, but now the Great Depression had landed with full force. Black workers were "first fired because last hired" and in dire straits, now without their familiar rural churches to give guidance during still another time of troubles. Randolph, like Mays, wanted more from ministers than solace. He wanted activism, including risk-taking actions by black ministers on behalf of black labor, a combination of efforts for civil rights and labor rights—and all as duty in a Christian mission.[47]

Then Jerome Davis spoke, and Mays was deeply moved, for Davis accepted what Randolph and the University of Chicago scholar had said and then added the insights of Mohandas Gandhi. It is the first recorded instance of Mays's hearing anything substantive about Gandhi's "soul force" and "militant pacifism." Davis urged all to read Gandhi and to adopt his techniques. At this early date Mays heard a careful articulation of the concept of peaceful resistance, of breaking the law but always taking the consequences and accepting the results, including imprisonment and punishments. Most wondrously, Mays heard the concept of understanding and loving one's opponents, fighting their sins but not them, seeing the oppressors as a people themselves oppressed by other injustices. This last Gandhian teaching most affected Mays and most changed his actions as a New Negro and Race Man seeking justice. He had come to know that all men are brothers, that even southern white men and pretty southern white girls had souls and the potential for good. Yet here was Gandhi being quoted as saying that even fools such as Dr. Wallace Payne, knaves such as the Phoenix night riders, hypocrites such as the "White Angels," and tyrants such as the Bell bosses must be loved and changed, their sins fought to be sure, but not their persons. Davis's speech was stirring, but in particular it explained some things about activism that had troubled Mays. Davis insisted that people at the conference should go to India to see Gandhi, and Mays vowed to do so, apparently in response to the call from this white scholar in 1931 and not to Mordecai Johnson in 1935.[48]

Davis used Gandhi's term *satyagraha,* and this concept immediately became part of Bennie Mays's vocabulary some years before he had the chance to meet in person the one called Mahatma—or the spiritual and high-minded one. In 1920 Gandhi had taken the Sanskrit word *satya*—truth—and combined it with the Sanskrit word *agraha*—persistence—to create a new word accessible to all peoples, especially the millions of the unlettered. The new word described long-persisting, never-yielding, ever-patient, dogged, and intrepid—but never aggressive—pursuit of truth. To be a *satyagrahi,* a practitioner of *satyagraha,* the committed reformist must reflect deeply on his own self and on his own flaws in order to examine an injustice in society, seeking to encounter and then apprehend—capture—the underlying evil during a pacifist, unthreatening and patient search for essential truth. Once capturing the evil, the *satyagrahi* must inform the agents, the evildoers, what he knows about them and about himself and must be completely aboveboard in confronting them in their evil, always making it clear that the evil is shared by all and must be dispelled by all in all. The confrontation must never be violent, must never be secret, and must always be deployed and carried forward with extreme forbearance. All these qualities are divine, and they appear in the practitioner as a gift from the divine. The whole process is not only spiritual but very much part of Buddhist revision of Hindu meditation. Any consequences of the *satyagraha* strategy of confrontation—such as the oppressors exercising verbal abuse, physical beating, jailing, or even executing the *satyagrahi*—must be accepted as the necessary outcome for the *satyagrahi,* and the suffering of the *satyagrahi* is essential to the *satyagraha,* for it finally will awaken the divine understanding in all people, even and especially the divine understanding deep in the oppressor's self.[49] Mays in his understanding of these new terms remained essentially a Baptist reformist with classical training and modes of social science research, and he did not use the vocabulary as skillfully as others present, or as did believers in other times and other places. But he did adapt much of the strategy and techniques, and evidently spoke to those present with great effectiveness, just as his remarks, recorded in the printed proceedings from the conference, inspire today.

The seminarians at conference passed two resolutions, and Mays had a hand in both; yet he could say with full *megalosukia,* and nothing of *mikrosukia,* that he had brought away more from this session than he had given, even though he gave much. The resolutions said first, as Mays put it, that "Negro ministers must be 'prophetic and fearless' in technique in making applicable the implications of the religion of Jesus in relation to our social order," and second that "every Negro church must discover and develop a style of leadership that could do for America and the Negro race what Gandhi has done for India and what Jesus has done for the world."[50]

At once Mays spoke to Randolph about a different way to seek justice for black labor by using *satyagraha,* and he also began to formulate strategies for seeking African American rights and broad social justice by using such tactics without necessarily becoming a believing *satyagrahi.* He in no sense abandoned his reformist American Baptist beliefs, nor his Roman Stoics—and none of his Socratic idealism. After long years of struggling to find the best way to apply classical thinking to a contemporary problem, Mays had suddenly found a concept fully relevant to a people of color in his own era resisting white colonial oppressors in which they did not—whether in India or in the Carolinas and Georgia—have arms and other material power sufficient to engage a white oppressor who monopolized arms and manpower and the other weapons needed in a violent protest of injustice. So unbalanced were the military weights in this contest for justice that the old Thomistic neoscholastic knew that armed rebellion could not be justified. As he often noted, one could not go into a war in which there was simply no prospect of survival. However, African Americans could and should take up the *satyagraha* under the understanding that the process of finding justice by seeking truth would be long, arduous, physically dangerous, and morally exhausting—but also under the classicist biblical assurance that the fullness of God's time was literally on the side of the protesting and suffering believer.

It is said by wags that Thomas Aquinas baptized ancient Greek philosophy, and certainly Mays in his turn had baptized Thomas Aquinas in the Saluda River. Now he was baptizing Mohandas Gandhi in American rivers. Of course the Mahatma in metaphorical sense and in literal sense declined such baptism— as likely would have Aristotle or Socrates. To the extent that Gandhi offered a moral technique for effecting social change, then Mays was following him, but he was in no sense claiming to be a *satyagrahi* of the Mahatma. Thus, from this point on, Mays preached nonviolence and pacifism, but he did not attain an intellectual or a moral consistency on the issues, as for example would his most famous pupil, Martin Luther King, Jr. Instead Mays persisted in applying the "just war" rubric to potential conflicts, concluding when it came that World War II was indeed a just war—and concluding at least initially that United Nations intervention in Korea was justifiable within the same Thomistic rubric.

As for domestic issues, especially given the preponderance of weapons available to white oppressors, Mays from this conference onward always insisted on pacifist resistance as the practical and the moral way to carry on the campaign for the exceedingly long run. Unlike Gandhi, Mays continued to hold a highly specific economic agenda, Henry George's single tax on realty; and he continued to hold a highly specific political agenda of civil rights and social justice learned largely from Walter Rauschenbusch through University of Chicago divinity school studies and Chicago Forum discussions. What changed was Mays's adoption of some specific techniques of pacifist resistance to brutal police tactics embodied in the broader term *satyagraha*. Thus, for all his enthusiasm for Gandhi's policies and means of resistance, Mays remained wary of Gandhi's own cultural tone toward the darkest peoples in India and elsewhere. He also remained unimpressed by Gandhi's socioeconomic programs. Mays was in no sense hypocritical or unthoughtful, but he was simply never fully convinced by Gandhi; and he never relinquished the Western thought and rational analysis that he brought with him to the conference in New Haven. In time Bennie Mays expressed his disappointments to Gandhi with regard to substantive change in race relations and with regard to structural change in economic conditions. Above all Gandhians in time disapproved of Bennie Mays on issues of war and peace.

Of course Bennie Mays shared all with Sadie Mays, and she too found Gandhian insights into the issues involved in the social services she was trying to provide. Returning to Atlanta that summer of 1931, the Mayses all but soared home, for each was affirmed as a useful professional and duly recognized scholar. Moreover each now had a vital insight, a prophetic view for and from modern times, into the long fight for the right in the church and in the world.

The detour had shown much to the pilgrim and the prophet, and in processes the detour had made him a better scholar of the Bible because it had taught him much about life. In particular the Word had unstopped his ears and opened his eyes, and had restrained his tongue. God did wonders, his children to teach, and Bennie Mays, while a dignified man of *megalosukos,* was yet and would be forevermore a child of this one true and just God. Divine breath had blown into his ears, and he was able to hear the cries of the unschooled and unskilled young black boys who must be saved from the mean streets with their hard, quick, hot violence as surely as they must be saved from the Bell bosses and the "White Angels" and the backstabbing liberal talkers who intended to keep most African American boys forevermore boys. Jesus had spit and made a paste of the divine spittle and the mortal clay and had rubbed it over the eyes of the believer, and the believer could see, and suddenly Bennie Mays had learned that a pretty, white Virginia girl or any white female, could as well be following God's plan to help as could anybody else and that the old white talk about "tribes" and peoples and special groups was all wrong, that God had made all people one and Jesus Christ had died for all people, died instead of all people, had made an oblation and propitiation, once offered, for all and for each. Jesus Christ did not make this sacrifice for some particular "tribe" but for all. There is "one fold, one shepherd," as St. John the Evangelist, or at least his Greek-speaking students, had written that truth.[51]

Bennie Mays had done well to restrain his tongue, that one small part that could do hurt quickly and yet keep hurting for long days, even unto generations. He had not at once spoken what he first thought, but had watched and waited in order to see and to hear. He had done well not to blurt out an early perception of human error that would wound a white southern girl or a white southern man sent by God. Nor would he let his tongue snake out and strike and wound even deeper a black child of God who had as yet had no chance to "hear them, read, mark, learn and inwardly digest" holy scripture "written for our hearing."[52] Only after so learning could one come to believe and then go to seek the cross. Those who prevented such learning in effect condemned a soul—and one could prevent such learning as well with a cleverly placed insult as with a physical barrier.

Aristotle and Thomas Aquinas both said to use the senses, trust the senses, and learn from the senses—and then to act on the knowledge so gained. Singers of African American spirituals sang a soulful version of the old Hebrew Psalm 34: "Taste and see / Taste and see the goodness of the Lord / Oh, taste and see / Taste and see the goodness of the Lord."[53] Bennie Mays had tasted and seen, and now he knew how to digest and use whatever else he might yet learn from Dr. Shirley Case. He would return to the University of Chicago, would taste more and see more, earn his Ph.D. from the toughest and most demanding seminary in the world, and then go forth to lead by serving.

The detour had brought him painfully yet gloriously back to the foot of the cross, and he believed more deeply than ever he could have imagined. While Jesus had died once instead of all, there was thereby no guarantee that troubles would end. Indeed Jesus's Gethsemane, the pathway of pain and punishment on the way to oblation and propitiation, must be repeated by the believer. From the toughened Scot Thomas Carlyle, Mays had tasted and now saw that a man had to suffer not only his own Gethsemane, but a "sea of Gethsemanes."

And a poem by Paul Laurence Dunbar now spoke to him more fully as he tasted and saw the poet's verse celebrating the Gethsemanes of challenge and conflict:

> Long since, in sore distress I heard one pray
> "Lord, who prevailest with resistless might
> Ever from war and strife keep me away,
> My battles fight!"
>
> I know not if I play the Pharisee,
> And if my brother after all be right;
> But mine shall be the warrior's plea to thee
> Strength for the fight.

Dunbar sang the need for the fight, and cried not to escape the fight, nor even for God to fight alongside, but rather for "strength for the fight" whose duty could not be avoided.[54]

From all of these, Aristotle and Thomas Aquinas, Carlyle and Dunbar, and most of all St. John's Gospel, Bennie Mays built his prayer:

> Dear God, we need thee—
> Every hour we need thee.
> We need thy poise.
> We need thy patience.
> We need thy grace.
> We need thy forgiveness.
> Dear God: Great is thy peace:
> Please God: In His name we pray.[55]

THE GREAT COMMISSION
AND ITS FILLING

1934–1936

> Jesus came up and spoke to them. He said, "All authority in heaven and on earth has been given to me. Go, therefore, make disciples of all the nations; baptize them in the name of the Father and of the Son and of the Holy Spirit, and teach them to observe all the commands that I gave you. And know that I am with you always; yes, to the end of time."[1]

In this verse the Savior in whom Bennie Mays believed charged his followers with the duty to convert and thus bring nonbelievers to him. The passage is known among preachers and divinity students as "the great commission." To serve the commission as he understood it, Mays needed to complete his graduate work and begin ministry to students at a black college. To finish the graduate student phase of his apprenticeship and begin the commission in earnest, there was a third long stay Chicago during 1934 and 1935. This time Sadie Mays went along, living and working there as well. This third mission accomplished the goal, the writing and the defending of his dissertation, and with that accomplishment came the outward and visible sign, the Ph.D., a degree earned by no more than a score of African Americans in the year 1935.[2] Writing one's dissertation was the great challenge for scholars at Chicago, and the university was notorious for its demands on Ph.D. candidates in this phase of its program. If accomplished, the University of Chicago dissertation allowed a man to announce himself as a scholar. The University of Chicago scholar could likely publish a monograph based on his dissertation. Yet many never finished this task, and many had to step away from the contest and watch others take the prize. That an African American would fail to write a dissertation was fully expected by friend and foe of the race, and Bennie Mays—the New Negro, the Race Man—thus had the broadest possible social goals in mind when he went back to the university.

In his third Chicago residency, Bennie Mays for good reasons focused on his dissertation, aiming sure to do research and to write and to finish the task begun ten seasons ago and postponed twice. In so writing, he brought together different, even conflicting, parts of his being, "strands of his life," as he phrased it.[3] His classically defined vocation, calling, or mission for his entire being was the ministry; and his ordination for this ministry, in his mind, was incomplete until he had made his statement in his dissertation, "The Development of the Idea of God in Contemporary Negro Literature." There was also the "strand," or aspect of his being that was the University of Chicago social scientist, the investigator doing his research and rooting out his facts without sentimentality, making his diagnosis by discovering truth, however daunting that truth. Above all there was the strand of the New Negro, the one who would propound the question of the greatness of his people. He knew the essence of that greatness was in the relationship to God, even and especially as some African Americans of the era were questioning this relationship and looking for other gods. There were even some prominent black leaders, the most important being W. E. B. Du Bois, who were questioning the idea of a divinity at all. Mays always insisted that there was a God and only one God and that the different religions were expressing different ideas about facets of the same God and not actually describing different gods. This third strand, the New Negro, was Bennie Mays's lifeblood, but for him it must be a New Negro who remained spiritual in relationship with the idea of God. All these strands are throughout Bennie Mays's whole life, but in his dissertation the three strands are pulled together most self-consciously—as the Chicago theologians would say, "with intentionality," by which the Chicago scholar intended to describe a focused purpose whose driving intention came from God's will and not from man's will. Ever the historicist of Dr. Case's seminars, Bennie Mays in this scholarship was also the ardent student of two University of Chicago men dominant in this new era, Edwin Ewart Aubrey and Henry Nelson Wieman.[4]

Shirley Case had demonstrated unforgettably that all aspects of religion, especially the Bible, happen in time and place and are thus by definition historical. The meaning of the words and phrases and the meaning of the actions, all must be studied in context by scholars functioning essentially as historians. Bennie Mays accepted these insights and took some delight in teasing out the facts of the surrounding environment, as he had done in his master's thesis on the pagan origins of Christian religious practices and beliefs. Without at all abandoning historicism, he now took Case's insight still further: it was not only the people writing the canonical chapters of the Bible in one era and the people reading those chapters in that era who had histories; but also people today have histories and read their Bibles with a new historicism different from the one in which it was written. Taking things even further, Mays wanted to look closely at how his people, his race, used their own times and places to receive and to apply God's truth. Of course Mays was a liberal theologian, committed to interpretation as the only possible route to meaning in the Bible. The University of Chicago in 1934–36 was increasingly and self-consciously modernist; it was paying attention to plural voices and plural points of view, noting and using ironies of all kinds, and questioning deeply all authority. Bennie Mays was by no means a thoroughgoing modernist, for, as Robert Penn Warren said in another context, Mays remained quite sure that there was Truth to be found, and he remained quite sure that that Truth resided in a living God, a good God who had sent his only Son, not as a prophet but as the Messiah bringing salvation. Mays then and later had no truck with moral relativism—or with any suggestion that there was no God. And he was a Trinitarian, who believed in the divinity of Jesus and the continuing presence of the Holy Spirit after Jesus ascended.[5]

Mays wanted justice for all people, and he remained a Race Man only in the mortal struggles in his Georgia and Carolina, where a black person had to struggle literally for mere survival and then struggle to be treated as a human. When locked in these fights in the Deep South, Mays was a Race Man jealous to claim each credit for all black people and determined to shift each blame away from all as well. When not in this Race Man defensiveness, however, Mays worshipped and spoke to a God of and with no color at all—or more properly a God of and with all colors. By epiphanies variously arrived at, Bennie Mays had concluded that God had no color, that God loved all, and that God could save all—or could destroy all. After his work with Nicholson, Mays had an up-to-date sense of black congregations and their relationship to black ministers, now he wanted a more truly historical approach, one that traced the beginnings of the long road that gave us these many small churches with their many badly trained ministers, who turned so often and so predictably to "whooping the benches" and who so seldom sought the social justice that Mays insisted the historical Jesus sought.[6]

In Professors Aubrey and Wieman, Mays found the right guides for this latest voyage. In later years Wieman's reformist Unitarianism and committed peace and justice activism set him in a high place for many theologians involved in the civil rights movement of the 1960s. However, for Bennie Mays in this movement, this New Negro phase of the long march, Aubrey was the important figure. As a believing Christian, Aubrey was deeply relevant to Mays. He was, after all, an ordained and practicing Baptist preacher, for whom Jesus was divine and the Bible—at least as interpreted—was *vital,* that is living. Besides being a superb scholar and a consummate professional, Aubrey was an activist, prominent in the reformist wing of the YMCA and also in the Federal Council of Churches, a group increasingly committed to the fight against southern Jim Crow laws and northern Jim Crow practices, especially in strife-ridden, segregated Chicago. Beginning in 1934 the council became important to Bennie Mays, and his dissertation director was at least partly responsible for that involvement.[7]

Born in Glasgow in 1896, Aubrey was a pro's pro and a man's man, and both attributes appealed to Mays. With his open and level gaze, his broad forehead, and his wavy but carefully barbered hair, Aubrey looked the part of a square and solid soldier, a well-organized military man. He in fact served during World War I, driving ambulance trucks in France and Italy only a few years after leaving Scotland for the United States and some months before he was naturalized as a citizen. With war's end he earned a philosophy degree from demanding little Bucknell University in Pennsylvania and then enrolled in religious studies at the University of Chicago, earning three degrees in that field, including a Ph.D. in 1926. He was thus a Chicago student working under Shirley Case during some of the same seasons as was Bennie Mays. Indeed, like Mays, Aubrey had worked in the academy full time while taking courses and preparing his dissertation; unlike Mays, of course, he worked at elite white schools: Carleton College, Miami University of Ohio, and Vassar College. In 1929 Shailer Matthews, Shirley Case, and the religion faculty invited their former student back to the university, where he immediately became not only a valued colleague but also an important national leader. He began to review books for the *Journal of Religion,* and he came to be reviewed in that publication as well as in the widely read *Christian Century.*[8]

Of particular importance to Bennie Mays was Aubrey's remarkable ability to do what Mays himself intended to do; that is, to move easily and effectively between the research seminars of Dr. Case and the workplaces of the practical-minded ministers who were men of general intelligence but not specialists in language, archaeology, and religious history. In 1931 Aubrey participated in a Chicago conference, Church Workers in Colleges and Universities, whose sessions intended to establish a "vital," or living, alliance between secular and religious educators and their schools. Aubrey addressed a trend among white college students, and Mays was finding the same trend among black college students: the kids had real doubts about the messages of the Bible and whether organized religion could be of any help to intelligent people. In fact college students of all races expressed suspicions that organized religion was not actually trying to help intelligent believers, and they sometimes expressed a deeper and scarier suspicion that ministers wanted their flocks to remain unlettered and therefore more pliable. The Communist Party (CPUSA), particularly active in providing coal and food and other necessities for black people and to addressing all the needs in parts of Chicago, loomed as a group that could help God's poor and at a moment when God's ministers were not always focused on the needs of the poor. Unfortunately for Aubrey, Mays, and other believers, the CPUSA proclaimed that there was no God, and its members pointed to ineffective and corrupt ministers as part of their proof. Aubrey warned there and then about two bad trends among ministers and divinity students who intended to become ministers, "a devitalized modernism" and an "impossible obscurantism." The first trend by definition took the life out of faith and all belief in the good by introducing so many doubts that any belief—above all the belief in achieving the good—seemed silly at best and wickedly misleading at worst. The second trend took the best communicators, especially among God's chosen speakers and leaders, and set them to talking only among themselves about the most specialized meanings of long dead phrases—and all this while unemployed workers rummaged in the trash piles for food and sought guidance from the ungodly and even the antigodly.[9]

If indeed Jesus came to build a hospital for the sick, then Aubrey the old ambulance driver intended to drive them to the Lord so they could drink the living water and eat the saving bread, exactly what the best Baptist minister of any color was about.[10] During Mays's third Chicago season, Aubrey published several important books, some of them while directing Mays's dissertation. In all of them his messages were the same: modernism is an attitude, not a guide, "a method and not a creed"; communism is about power, and when it denies God and God's good it is only one more idol, one more golden calf built by willful and sinful man. Revelation—the sudden and blinding understanding of who and what God is—will not happen, and thus religion for the crisis of this Depression must be "religion without revelation." In hard times, Aubrey said, people most need the "ultimate meaning" to be found only by deep and reflecting prayer and by careful application of science and logic to problems, but that science and logic must be guided by a living and real spirit of the Divine. A creed is needed, and man is helpless without a creed, but the creed must be informed by science and by reason.[11]

In his books and lectures, Aubrey criticized the self-styled naturalism of his famous new colleague Henry Nelson Wieman and of the even more renowned Karl Barth. Aubrey thought their efforts to find a material truth as revealed in the world ignored the spirit, the living water and the life-giving bread of Jesus Christ. Wieman thus was only a new and more attractive example of the old error, reason without faith. On this score Mays in this era and all the days of his long life stood more closely to the Scots dissertation director than to the brilliant thinker and modernist Wieman. Also Aubrey scorned the supernaturalism of that era's Dean Inge and Rufus Matthew Jones as being a new expression of the opposite old error, faith without reason. Aubrey then made a gesture that Mays understood and saluted, but critics of the 1930s era could not accept it or even comprehend it. Aubrey declared admiration for Thomas Aquinas as a man who used God-inspired logic and an Aristotle-inspired research to find the saving balance between faith and reason. Drawing on Thomas Aquinas's *animarum nexus*—the bond of souls—Aubrey called on reform ministers to reach back to their poorly educated and desperate congregations, but also to reach forward to the highly educated but also desperate modern theologians. The bond of souls, *animarum nexus,* was nothing less than the committed scholar determined to unite faith and reason in a new age. Thanks to Aubrey, Mays took on himself this bond of souls and attempted thereafter to link modern scholars, traditional parishioners, deprived poor, the depraved wealthy, and black and white all in this *animarum nexus.*[12]

By 1935 Mays was a fully formed thinker, and his blend of Chicago social science and Thomistic logic with classical philosophy and Baptist passion was of his own making, but in Aubrey he found exactly the kindred spirit to direct him in a dissertation that aimed to diagnose what was wrong with African Americans' religion and to prescribe remedies so that the flock could be guided safely out of the wilderness of modernism and away from the Gehenna of the CPUSA back to Jesus—a Jesus who was, however modernist and historical for Chicago scholars, still the divine Jesus.

What then of Henry Nelson Wieman? He was a man of considerable interest to Mays and a man whom Mays often talked about. Born in Missouri, Wieman was a son of a father who was Presbyterian minister and a college-educated mother who was deeply spiritual and knowledgeable about religion. It was a home where all aspects of religion were discussed and where the young Henry Nelson was encouraged to ponder the mysteries of God and the duties of the believer. It was also a home in which doctrine and the Bible took distant second and third places behind prayerful reflection on the "absolute self-giving" that is "at the heart of the best faith." The athletic and popular boy was given time and space by his parents and teachers to think deeply about "the problem assigned all." In 1907, Wieman said, he first understood: "The problem is not to discover what people actually do commit themselves to in religious faith, but what should rightfully command it. . . . My problem was to get more reliable knowledge about the nature of the reality, whatever its character, that should command religious faith, whether or not we in fact actually do give it [our] supreme devotion. Obviously, that which should command our faith is what, under favorable circumstances, progressively creates man and all the good that he can ever have."[13]

The search sounds Unitarian, and in his golden years Wieman became Unitarian, ending thereby long decades of reflection and even agony about the nature of Jesus Christ by concluding that the Christian doctrine of the Trinity was a hopeless confusion and that the miraculous resurrection was a red herring drawn across the path of men called to serve and save. And then he dismissed the Hebrew Tanak, law and prophets, as an earlier superstition and futility. Thus Wieman took from the Psalms of David only the rhythmic *maschal* as it called to service, and from all Jesus's teaching, he took only the parables as guides to the sacrifice of a self-centered will to the broader needs of the world.[14]

Wieman did not read the Bible in order to "contextualize it" in time and place, as the men around Shirley Case did in their research to understand the faith of the early Church. Rather Wieman read the Bible within the task of bringing good to a suffering world, especially a world suffering in the twentieth century from the incredible power of nation-states and empires, man-made things armed with overwhelming weapons of destruction. Of course Wieman set off on this antiwar mission when the great weapons of World War I were artillery and mustard gas and rather crude dynamite, machine guns, and an early and clumsy propaganda. In other words Wieman was committed to shield the powerless against the awful depredations of the powerful before the powerful gained the ultimate weapons of intercontinental missiles guided by lasers and bearing atomic explosives that could level the factories and businesses in a city and then spread radiation in all directions to kill slowly the people far, far from the factories and workplaces.

Wieman was exercised not only by the mighty empires and their abuse of terrifying weapons but also by the way misguided religious faith—including the teachings of Jesus Christ—could send men to war: "Human power has become so great and is growing so rapidly, that error in matters of religious faith will be suicidal if not corrected."[15] From Wieman, Mays surely took a double portion of the passionate campaign against modern warfare, and he took the logician's shield against the superstitions that called themselves doctrines, just as surely as he took the researcher's sword against the confounding and conflicting clouds of mysticism that obscured imperialist ends. Already Mays had been stirred by the mission of Gandhi and the concept of waging peace as an active, engaged and vigorous campaign, fully as demanding as war but without shedding the blood of others. Wieman gave some of the Gandhian inspiration a logical structure and foundation. For all that, however, when he said that the revelation in Jesus Christ "cannot mean the first entry of God into human existence," nor even the most important, Wieman went too far for Bennie Mays. To Mays, Jesus Christ remained the miraculous Being, the One with God, living and guiding in this life, the Being whose teaching must be discerned by study and prayerful reflection.[16]

Generally Mays was fascinated by the self-proclaimed modernism sweeping the Chicago campus, and yet he also remained the Baptist minister with the commitment to understand the Word of Jesus Christ as a living and vital word, more important than the teaching of others.[17] Mays paid attention to Wieman, followed his career, and encouraged students to read and think about him, but Mays did not become a Unitarian Universalist. His interest in Wieman was academic—in the best and worst senses of the word. In following with fascination Wieman's thoughtful peregrinations, Mays did not follow Wieman anywhere in terms of a new religious expression. Agreeing that man should "seek a better understanding of that which should rightly command" the "absolute self-giving,"[18] Mays yet kept his commitment to Shirley Case and to Edwin Ewart Aubrey "to discover what people actually do commit themselves to in religious faith." Wieman was riding the wave of something that must be understood, and Mays eagerly sought to understand Wieman and that wave of modernism. However, it was Aubrey—like Case before him and Rauschenbusch even before him—who provided Mays the tools—and the personal contacts—for ministry of the social gospel that combined classical disciplines with Jesus's parables and the Golden Rule.

Determined to finish his dissertation, Mays pushed along the writing. He set himself the goal of explaining how his people, black people, understood the God of all. He came to this task as a social scientist who knew how to conduct field research and how to take polls in big-city ghettoes and rural-black bottomlands. He also came as a believer in a time of much unbelief; furthermore he was a believer whose forebears had believed much superstition and even nonsense. He needed all his classicist resolve, all Thomas Aquinas's steady and unblinking logic, but he needed as well a full complement of Augustine's passion for the vitality in the personal relations between God and believers. This New Negro drew on modernism for the weapons of a new science, and he agreed with the modernists that many in high places were only authorities of muscle and not of virtue. However, his heart beat to the drums of the Baptist missionary abolitionists seeking justice alongside a living God who cared for his people even when he allowed them to be exiled into Babylon. His dissertation was strung in creative tension, the classicist's *syzygy,* pulled between powerful attractions. Done right and with God's favor, the work could unite different strands of black being, or even soul, as he understood that identity. Done wrong, the dissertation might well anger believers while being damned by social scientists as unacademic.

Because of this tension, Mays employed carefully measured phrases. Cautious and precise, he abandoned the rhythms and tones that he used in his preaching, teaching, persuasion, and other communications. Despite his love for the classicist rhetoric of force and fire, he wrote with great restraint on this controversial subject matter. He adopted the practice of looking at the people who wrote—whether as novelists, poets, educators, politicians, or public officials, people who happened to be literate and who happened to be among the few whose writings were preserved. He knew full well that this method could never capture the ninety and nine, a large portion of whom could not write and even if they could, had no place to publish or preserve their written thoughts. For all that, he had to start somewhere—and he retained the suspicion that it was the intellectually and literarily active who most deserved study.

The social scientist thus split his people into groups that formed a trinity. The first group thought God created all people "from one blood," a sign that race is political and not biblical. God is just, and people of any tribe or other group can "enter into his courts with praise and thanksgiving." The second group answers that black people's cause is just and that "God is on our side," not only protecting them from harm but even attacking the "other" ethnic groups who are not part of "us" and not on the side of "Our God." The third group, in the most recent days, concluded that there is no God.[19]

Mays noted that these are groups, or "strands," of attitudes inside men and women and not groups of entire peoples. More than one strand could run through the fabric of a single person, and thus a teacher or a preacher or other writer could well contradict himself or herself when trying to explain the idea of God. While Mays found that the great majority of black writers considered God to be God of all, almost none of these novelists and poets, or even the ministers, had serious scholarly training and thus the "Negro's ideas of God grow out of his social situation, and they are derived neither from teleological nor cosmological thinking." He could not accord his ancestors or his contemporaries much regard for their background and training to build systems of analysis either for the teleological—that is, conceptions that explore *whither*—or for the cosmological—that is, conceptions that explore *why*.[20]

Mays began his study with the poet whom he quoted more often than any poet of any race, Paul Laurence Dunbar. He named Dunbar's days, the period between 1867 to 1914, "classical." He omitted from his discussion early writers, including Phillis Wheatley, Benjamin Banneker, and Frederick Douglass. Indeed he stated that, except for Dunbar, black writers working before 1914 did not justify study.[21]

In spite of his admiration for Dunbar, Mays lumped him among traditional writers who treated of strictly "compensatory patterns" of theology. In other words Mays found that people of Dunbar's era wrote in "naive" fashion about a God who compensated for natural deficiencies in African Americans—a damning observation from a New Negro who conceded no such natural lackings. From a theological standpoint that compensatory approach was sorely wanting, because writers often compensated for "God's deficiencies," explaining away injustice and even evil because God could not do much better or because people could not appreciate what they actually had. Mays also criticized the compensatory perspective because it was "used to support a shallow pragmatism." Such a God became merely a "useful instrument" for making an oppressed people feel better and "sleep better at night," but this viewpoint also encouraged a belief in magic and discouraged initiative, investigation, and energetic self-reliance. At its worst the compensatory view of God made a man accept social injustice, that is Jim Crow, because superstition made the black man believe himself created inferior by a magical and unsympathetic, possibly even white, God.[22]

In this long night of the compensatory period, Booker T. Washington called for self-help and self-reliance and above all diligent study and hard work. Mays understood that Washington "did his most effective work in this period" by forcing black people to turn away from the folly of compensatory worship and to take up instead the tasks of feeding, clothing, schooling, and otherwise improving themselves—but of course doing so in segregated settings safely removed from racist white politicians. As an integrationist, Mays was unhappy that Washington thus denied striving dark men and striving dark women the chance to compete with white people. Yet Mays preferred Washington's self-help and initiative to the defeatism and complacency of the compensatory main current running at full force in that day. Mays considered Washington a kind of Moses guiding his people out of slavery and through a wilderness, pointing them toward a Canaan for the New Negro, but not able himself to move beyond Mount Horeb, well short of the Promised Land. Dunbar, who wrote poems now of despair and now of great resolve, reflected in his great but imperfect art Washington's great but imperfect leadership. Always the social historicist of Dr. Case's seminary, Mays measured the context and thus appreciated the difficulties against which Washington struggled and thereby judged that the Wizard of Tuskegee had moved his people a long way forward despite an army of oppressors.[23]

Mays opined that Dunbar at his best was a Hebrew prophet singing songs of sadness to his God, holding back nothing of his pain or his shame from Yahweh Lord Sabaoth. Dunbar knew that God already knew everything, and the poet knew as well that God would not reject "a broken and contrite heart," even and especially if the heart belonged to a black man. Dunbar was thus in this right relationship with his God, acknowledging his inability to save himself and thus coming to God begging for balm and begging that his tears be put into our Lord's bottle. Locusts, floods, droughts, pharaoh's army, Assyrians, and Amalekites in one epoch; middle passage, soul driver, lash and knout, and rape by white masters in another epoch; lynching bees, denial of voting rights, Jim Crow trains and toilets, and exploitive sharecropping in still another epoch; even in the North there were rats in ghetto walk-ups, confidence men, numbers runners, pimps, crooked cops on the beat, Irish bad boys roaming the alleyways, and snide Bengali students at the University of Chicago—with skin bronzed in India and never in Africa or Alabama—who made clear that they were brown and not black. Dunbar's poetry told Mays that his people had been chosen to suffer, and he laid that suffering before his God:

> Lead gently, Lord and slow,
> For oh, my steps are weak,
> And ever as I go,
> Some soothing sentence speak;
>
> That I may turn my face,
> Through doubt's obscurity,
> Towards thine abiding place,
> E'en tho' I cannot see.
> For lo, the way is dark,
> Through mist and cloud I grope,
> Save for that fitful spark,
> The little flame of hope.
>
> Lead gently, Lord, and slow,
> For fear that I may fall;
> I know not where to go,
> Unless I hear Thy call
>
> My fainting soul doth yearn
> For thy green hills afar;
> So let thy mercy burn—
> My greater, guiding star.[24]

Mays wrote of Dunbar in this and similar poems: "Dunbar wants comfort when lonely, strength when weak, and companionship when the battle of life is fierce; he wants to be free of sorrow and vexation; he wants protection when the skies are dark and protection from harm; he yearns for righteousness to prevail; he wants grief and poverty eliminated; he wants security from temptation which comes to one who has won renown; it is implied that he wants security of existence after death; he craves for strength to face bravely the struggles of life and strength to fight; he yearns for clear vision; he wants status and privilege for the Negro race and friends for the race; he desires a complete life and he craves for a heaven on the earth."[25]

Yet this poem and the many hymns like it are "compensatory" in a "traditional way" in that God will bring salvation in another world. That much was true enough, but Mays detected therein a suggestion that it might not be worth fighting, or even fretting, the injustices of this world. If so, Dunbar could make his brothers and sisters think of themselves as God's only people, and their unique suffering would be to bring unique rewards. Worse, Dunbar, if misread, could be heard to say that the pains of other peoples did not matter to a God who was strictly in love with the black soul. Reading only Dunbar, and only part of Dunbar, a black person could be so "naive" as to sin by excluding whites and other nonblacks from preaching and prayer. Even the kind lady who never spoke hatred, who yet prayed for a dollar to give her granddaughter, was sinning by expecting God to take care of her particular desires to the neglect of the general needs of all. This strand of black belief thus was a problem, even evil in its effects.[26]

Still a greater evil was something uncommon in Mays's youth in South Carolina, but now it was often seen—especially among the thinkers and researchers and the best trained professionals, including leaders whom Mays expected to work alongside to vouchsafe the justice prophesied. This evil was unbelief, atheism, not the misguided worship of false gods nor the honest confusion and fretting of agnosticism, but the heresy of unbelief, the specter of nothing less than real atheism. This strand was not commented on before the twentieth century because it was not much seen and not much heard before those years. In the 1930s, not only was atheism present among some of the best educated New Negroes, but it was even the distinguishing mark of the brightest and best scholars researching, writing, and speaking in the Great Depression, notably W. E. B. Du Bois.[27]

Already Du Bois had caught Mays's attention with his deeply spiritual *Souls of Black Folk,* his social science monographs, and his good work with the NAACP for integration. Indeed one had to respect Du Bois for his words and actions whether one was a Race Man stirring for political power and authority or a New Negro striving for spiritual teleology. Du Bois was a fervent believer in what an African American could be and do. But Du Bois's spirituality was born of Georg Wilhelm Friedrich Hegel, and Du Bois, like Hegel, was no Christian. He was what believers called the idealistic heretic; that is, one who claimed to take a supernatural inspiration for direction—and then save himself by his own energies and works.[28]

Du Bois was no believer in any Christian version of Jesus the Christ, and although not yet a Communist, he was already proclaiming himself an atheist.

This unbelief in Du Bois affected black intellectuals, and the unbelief of the Communists on the campus of University of Chicago affected the intellectuals. Such unbelief among thinkers vexed and even haunted Mays. Organized religion had failed its black churches, Mays acknowledged from his research with Nicholson and from his fieldwork with Arthur Raper. Black churches had failed their black members, Mays agreed, and had said so in his book with Nicholson. The result, especially in Du Bois, was a strand of atheism in many black intellectuals and writers, and this strand of unbelief also ran through the thinking of Christian believers, even on occasion affecting Mays and his friend and colleague Nicholson. In response Mays and others could only cry aloud the words of the distressed father of an afflicted child as that cri de coeur was captured by St. Mark's gospel: "Lord, I believe, help my unbelief!"[29]

The final strand to describe is the first one Mays had noted: the belief that God had created all people from one blood and loved all people equally. The strand was found in the best of Baptist faith, for Mays saw and taught that the Jesus of the Bible and the Jesus of history was savior of all. The Baptist dissertation writer saw and taught as well that each was saved by one confession and baptism, that necessary act taken consciously one time and thereafter forever sufficient for salvation. The strand was true to his own integrationism, because the Jesus Mays found in the Bible and in history was no respecter of color boundaries or class lines. Yet even for himself in days of trials, Mays found that this belief in one God of all was often entangled by and all but lost among the strands of compensatory belief and unbelief. Only by a "strong pull and a long pull and a pull altogether" could believers remove the one true God of all strand from the entanglements of the sinful world and then follow that strand to its end in justice. As the ordained minister preaching, he had to prophesy the right prophecy, to walk the right walk, and to lead all peoples in the right pathways. As the University of Chicago social scientist, he had to be forthright about how obscured was the one true God of all strand and how prominent were the obscuring strands of compensatory faith and unbelief. As the New Negro, he was called to find the right way to move his people into full brotherhood—after which time they must ignore color and class and follow the strand to salvation for all. Despite his measured language, his dissertation spoke as passionately as an inspired preacher at a protracted camp meeting back in the valley of the Saluda.[30]

The broad patterns of his dissertation were set by early 1934, and Mays could look for a permanent academic position. He could also reflect some on his skills and his opportunities. After much scholarly reflection on why things were the way they were between the races, now he could spend some time pondering his own case. Having done the conceptual work for Aubrey about the history of African American thought about God, having done the fieldwork alongside Arthur Raper and Jesse Thomas about ministers attempting to find economic justice for God's black people, and having done his study alongside Joseph Nicholson about contemporary black churches and their ministers, Mays arguably knew as much as anyone about black ministers, black congregations, and black believers' approaches to issues of racial problems. It was hard to find anyone in print who had performed as much research as Mays had. All that work, spread over ten years of jobs and graduate work, reaffirmed for him his own great commission: to train the best New Negroes to be ministers who actually led their congregations toward social justice. The vaunted imprimatur of the University of Chicago, especially with a letter of introduction prepared by Aubrey, gave the final needed academical approval to a career of published research and a career of fieldwork for reform.

In some ways he was what he always had been ever since baptism in a body of water in the valley of the Saluda: a Baptist who believed that his confession and baptism saved him that one time for all time and that no churchly rituals or priestly words could change that precious once-and-forever salvation. For many Baptists, the surety of that knowledge made one conservative or perhaps apolitical because no one was saved by works that he himself performed. On the other hand, once saved a person could certainly take some chances, even death-defying chances, and Mays intended to lead his Baptists to take chances on behalf of racial justice. He paid attention to the revelation by the prophet Isaiah that God did not expect burnt offerings or sacrificed animals or other rituals. Isaiah said that God wanted justice for the poor, the afflicted, and the oppressed. Some theologians, especially among white Baptists, would disagree and say that Mays was seeking works salvation instead of the divinely granted onetime-and-forever grace marked and witnessed by the onetime-and-forever adult baptism back in Greenwood County. But Mays would reply that St. Paul, St. Augustine, the Wesley brothers, and in fact a "mighty cloud of witnesses" expected the saved believer to save others and to work for social justice—or else the sacrifice of Jesus on the cross and the miracle of redemption would seem unappreciated by the beneficiary. This Baptist of the social gospel believed that one was saved in order to do justice.[31]

In his final time at the University of Chicago, Mays confronted those who ran the residential dormitories on behalf of handicapped students. Yet he set his face firmly albeit coolly against the CPUSA members in town and on campus, even when some of that party loudly spoke on behalf of the poor on the south and west sides of town and when they loudly spoke on behalf of the university's handicapped. Before the Great Depression descended, Big City opportunities for jobs had given hope to black ghetto residents, hope that economic opportunities would simply outweigh Big City racism. Now the disappearance of the jobs and the dampening of economic hopes made the ghetto meaner, especially as Mayor Edward J. Kelly cut benefits for the unemployed and demonstrated to President Franklin Delano Roosevelt that Chicago was his town and not a property of the New Deal. Trapped in two corners of a city with no jobs and little food, many black people turned against each other in random crime and others turned to the CPUSA, the only Chicago organization that seemed able to deliver coal, blankets, and food to folk in the ghettoes in this time of troubles. Yet Mays disliked and distrusted the CPUSA even more than he disliked and distrusted Mayor Kelly and the local white Democrats. In the Communists Mays beheld godlessness and a fascination with power that repelled him. He was convinced that men such as Jesse Thomas and Philip Randolph could work alongside labor leaders, the Urban League, the YMCA, and mainline New Deal Democrats to save the day on Chicago's southern and western sides. He gave the good, gray liberals his support, and he set himself apart from the Reds and their promises. In *Born to Rebel* he wrote, "Then as always, I was wholly unsympathetic to the Communist ideology."[32]

On the campus Bennie and Sadie Mays watched all behaviors closely, ever alert to the realities of racism. Determined to do research and to write, Bennie Mays was still a fierce battler if injustice intruded and faced him squarely. Robert Maynard Hutchins, then president of the university, was not only a leader in things intellectual and academic but also a left-wing reformist intent on improving all social relations. Hutchins grandly announced that his presidential door was open to any student who witnessed racial incidents. When Sadie Mays was ready to march to take her master's degree in social work from the university, she and her Bennie received tickets for the balcony. The couple remained near the ticket agent and watched with sharp eyes as every black person received balcony tickets and every white person was handed tickets to seats in the spacious and largely vacant downstairs auditorium. This result was too much like Tampa for the Mayses to brook, and they accosted the ticket official. In talking with that lady, the Mayses soon concluded that her actions were a particular woman's practice and not university policy. They told her of their intent to report her to President Hutchins, and she quickly gave them downstairs seats, promised to seat other black people downstairs, and begged them not to report her. These supplications convinced the Mayses that the woman had acted on her own. Most important, her words convinced them that she was changing her behavior.[33]

On the issue of civil rights for the handicapped in residential dormitories, Bennie and Sadie Mays saw and protested mistreatment of their own, Sadie Mays's sister Emma Gray. Gray suffered both because she was dark and because she was crippled by the amputation of a leg during her Georgia childhood. She came to Chicago to earn a master's degree in English, and because of her disability she requested a room on the first floor of a dormitory near the department in Cobb Hall. William J. Mather, a Quaker, was in charge of the dormitory housing, and he refused Emma Gray's request, opining that southern white women in the dormitory could be offended. Bennie Mays pressed the case for Emma Gray with vigor, going by often to see Mather about the issue. In a sarcastic sort of epiphany worthy of St. Paul, Mays recorded: "I had not known any Quakers previously, but I had heard of their involvement in the abolition of slavery and their liberal policy on race. I was now learning the hard way that Quakers—like other groups—have members whose actions are a far cry from their professed religious beliefs."[34]

When Mays attempted to involve President Hutchins, he discovered that the reformist was traveling in Europe for several weeks. Dean of Students George A. Works answered the graduate students' call, and Emma Gray was assigned to the first floor of Gates Dormitory, convenient to her classes and her professors in Cobb Hall. Yet the stiff-necked Quaker Mather reasserted his own power and reassigned Gray to the top floor of Gates.[35]

There ensued a little Mays-Mather war, and CPUSA students offered to help the handicapped in the fighting. Still "wholly unsympathetic" to the Communists, Mays avoided publicity beyond the graduate school hallway gossip and kept the war small and focused. Emma Gray lost the battle for a first-floor room and still won the war by completing her academic work in good order. Southern white women in Gates Hall befriended Gray and helped her up and down the steps in the dormitory and also ran errands for her. Some of the white women became Emma's friends and she theirs, disproving Mather's opinion about race relations among his charges. Director Mather, erstwhile fighting Quaker, never bent, but neither did any of the female students bow, and the Mays and Gray families in their reminiscences concluded that these experiences were more good than bad. As the summer quarter of 1934 concluded, Mays successfully stood his written and his oral comprehensive examinations and completed his dissertation. He had only to defend the dissertation before Aubrey and the good doctor's committee of scholars at a time that suited the prerogatives of those gentlemen. Emma Gray had finished her graduate work in English; Sadie Mays held her master's degree in social work, and it was time for the dark southerners to leave Chicago, missions "magnificently fulfilled" as Mays marked it.[36]

The great commission to train black leaders could be filled several ways and in several places. The final weeks of Chicago's hot Depression August were spent pondering exactly what to do. A church in St. Louis called Bennie Mays, and he and Sadie Mays thought long and hard about that opportunity before

Dr. Mordecai Wyatt Johnson, the first African American president of Howard University. Courtesy of the Moorland-Spingarn Research Center, Howard University.

declining. Then Thomas E. Jones, president of Fisk University in Nashville, called with an academic opportunity to teach and to lead and to teach teachers to lead. Mays gladly accepted and began his preparations for the move. Then an unexpected call came from his hero and exemplar, Dr. Mordecai Johnson, first black president of Howard University.

Dr. Johnson wanted Mays to come to the nation's capital to build a great school of religion at that national university—one that by charter served all races. Yet Howard had done little to train ministers of any color, despite charge and charter. It produced attorneys, physicians, and business leaders, and these were good lay leaders in churches, but its mediocre faculty and its badly designed curriculum in religious studies stood in sad contrast with the fine law and medical staffs and facilities. Mays could repair to the work of training ministers, especially black ministers, the work that he and Nicholson had demonstrated convincingly needed to be done. However, there was the moral commitment to Jones at Fisk, and Mays could not go to the District of Columbia unless the good Nashville president gave him his leave and his blessings.

Dr. Jones graciously assented and blessed the plan, and the Mayses were bound for the school set on a hill that was once part of the John Smith farm north of the old Washington City boundary and purchased by a combination of Con-gregationalist money, a federal appropriation, and the personal generosity of the so-styled Yankee stepfather and college namesake, the Federal abolitionist General Oliver Otis Howard.[37]

10

IN THE NATION'S CAPITAL

1936–1940

Black professionals were proud of their colleges. Even in the nineteenth century, some had attended Brown University, Oberlin College, and Wilberforce University. These alumni spoke with pride and gratitude of the academic "mother of their soul," the college that had challenged and pushed and yet loved and nurtured them too. These few schools, all in the North and each abolitionist in its nineteenth-century identity, had integrated themselves with a precious few dark people whom W. E. B. Du Bois called the "talented tenth." Bennie Mays was bathed in such feelings, and from more than one spring: from Bates College and from the University of Chicago. In their different ways, George Colby Chase, Dr. Shirley Case, and Dr. Edwin Ewart Aubrey had challenged black students—and especially Bennie Mays—to reach for the same stars as aspiring white scholars.[1]

For all the New Negro's gratitude and pride in integrated schools, however, Bennie Mays was most grateful to and most proud of the historically black colleges. It was memorable how he had learned life lessons as taught to the "quality Negroes" at Virginia Union College in Richmond and the far more difficult lessons at least attempted at the beleaguered and besieged South Carolina State College on behalf of black people, many of whom could never be called "quality Negroes." Far above these and other historically black colleges there were three—Morehouse College, Fisk College, and Howard University—and their alumni attorneys, physicians, and professors spoke with an entirely different kind of emotional, almost visceral, pride about the good things assayed and accomplished at those schools.

In the New Negro pantheon of 1934, Howard University in the nation's capital could make claim to be the most important, the only place to train black attorneys and for long decades the only place where black medical students could train at an important research hospital. This university was led by a man of magnificence, Mordecai Johnson, one New Negro whom Bennie Mays held in the greatest respect. The first African American to preside over Howard, Mordecai Johnson was determined to make the university more than a great place for black students. He wanted the university to fulfill its charter and its mission to be a national university that trained men or women of any race or creed or nationality. Indeed, from its earliest days, Howard had trained black and white students, and some of its first credentialed physicians and educators were women as well as men. The Reverend Johnson was a great preacher, especially about social justice under the social gospel. He was upset that the Howard School of Religion was not producing ministers or scholars of divinity who were anything like the kind of attorneys and physicians attaining degrees in their fields at his school.[2]

Johnson had committed himself to bringing all parts of Howard into a new era, nothing less than the dawning of an age of the New Negro, as proclaimed for Howard by the polymath Alain Locke, poet, philosopher, and publicist who called for the school to be nothing less than the vanguard for a Negro Renaissance in cultural expression and spiritual development. As important as Asa Gordon had been for defining black identity during another era in Carolina and Georgia, Bennie and Sadie Mays soon judged Locke to be the true master at such defining and redefining. Locke looked at culture, at all moral and aesthetic expressions of values among his black people, and his term "New Negro" was as much a goal as a description. His New Negro drew as much as possible on African culture and strove for power with a sense of racial dignity that is at least as much African as American. It is not, however, Pan-African, nor African-centered, although it is informed morally and aesthetically and materially by African experiences and values. Thus Locke insisted that the New Negro is part of America—distinct, recognizable and valued at once for being different —but also remaining part of the larger cultural whole. No single part of the New Negro identity could be called especially American at all, but all parts of the cultural whole—actively together with New Negro and other evolving identities—make a new American identity.

In fact university historian Rayford W. Logan insists that Mordecai Johnson became the first black president of Howard at least partly because of the publication and discussion of *The New Negro,* the bold manifesto by Locke. This collection of literature and philosophy and political opinion featured the polymath Locke, artist and philosopher, who redefined what "Negro" means, at least in America. For his efforts Locke was promptly fired in 1926 by angry white administrators, but before he had missed a semester, Johnson arrived in June of that year and reappointed Locke while praising the work as well as its author. For himself Locke insisted on his academic rights, and he won on that

Alain Locke, the Howard
University professor who
coined the term "New
Negro." Courtesy of the
Moorland-Spingarn
Research Center,
Howard University.

issue. For the New Negro, he insisted that all people of color stand up for their
rights as men because they deserve it—but also because American culture deserves no less than the full recognition of the African American as a vital and
contributing part of the whole.[3]

As for Race Man imagery and claims, part of being a New Negro was to
stand up for fellow black people, always to be conscious of and responsible to
the right of each man of color to full credit and full opportunity in all settings
in America. Race Man was an obvious part of being a New Negro, but it was
hardly all that there was. Someday, a long way down the line for the black race,
there should be justice and peace, and on that day, the Race Man was no longer
needed, since all would recognize the accomplishments of men of color. Yet
even in that long-distant day, there would still be the New Negro, proudly recognized as a distinct and vital part of the American whole.[4]

Because of Locke, because of the cultural debates and discussions associated with part of the District of Columbia involving statistician and social scientist Kelly Miller, because of dialogue among thinkers and publicists writing in the *Pittsburgh Courier,* because of Carter Godwin Woodson, the historian of the race, and especially because of Dr. Johnson, Bennie and Sadie Mays could continue to refer to themselves as New Negro, and arguably they would never abandon the intentionality expressed in that term, even in the late-1960s as they somewhat reluctantly began to replace the signifier New Negro with the word "black." The nation's capital, especially the part occupied along Shaw Place by Howard University, became for the Mayses nothing less than a New Jerusalem, the chosen center for New Negroes who would save not only their own people but all American peoples. Surely it would be a long, long, long march punctuated by fighting and wounds along its winding course. And always there would be the words of Jesus lamenting the original Jerusalem: "O Jerusalem, Jerusalem! You who kill the prophets and stone those sent to you."[5]

The newly appointed dean of the School of Religion had to look with the longest range and with the most hopeful vision to see anything promising. Since 1867 the School of Religion had been called the neglected stepchild by campus wags. This was despite its beginnings as the dream of idealistic abolitionists, themselves ministers and members of the Gideon's Band of northern educators, who understood the vital role of the black church in all eras. Howard-trained educators, attorneys, and physicians were rightly proud, and they paid fitting tribute to the mother of their soul by their good and prominent works. But Howard-trained theologians were another matter, especially when Bennie Mays compared them to the men who studied under Dr. Case or Dr. Aubrey.[6] There was no real library of primary sources; the scholarly periodicals were lacking; even the professors were wanting in their personal training.

Dr. Aubrey had said again and again that the scholars in schools of religion, men of *animarum nexus,* must "reach forward to" the cutting edge of research, but at the same time the researching scholars must also "reach back" consciously to lay people, nonspecialists, and especially skeptical and unbelieving nonspecialists. It was a tension created by the circumstances, but this tension must be converted into a good thing, "creative tension"—a term associated with Mays's greatest student, the Reverend Dr. Martin Luther King, Jr., but a concept and practice created in the 1920s by Aubrey and established and taught at all the schools where the Scotsman taught, not least the Crozer Seminary, which Aubrey created and the one where Dr. King began his first serious theological studies. In his research for Aubrey and Case, Mays had certainly reached forward in his studies, and in his preaching in churches he had certainly reached back in his ministries. Much to his chagrin, Bennie Mays saw no such sense of creative tension at Howard, and in fact he saw little serious research and even less reaching back to lay people. Where was the bond of the souls? Mays and Joe Nicholson had gathered the data on where black professional scholars of religion were trained and where they were practicing—and it was clear in 1934 that the men of Howard were not distinguished in the field of religious studies.[7]

Mighty King David at a moment of similar tribulation had cried words that now served Dean Mays: "May my vindication come from you, / May my eyes see what is right!"[8] The new dean looked hard at his students. There were only twenty-eight of them, and half were undergraduates. He wondered too what the Lord saw in the faculty, none of them a research scholar, none trying to help his poor brothers of any tribe, and none a social gospeler. There was the small Carnegie library building with outdated and even amateurish texts, and the School of Religion itself was housed in a sagging frame building unworthy of the noble Frederick Douglass whom it honored with its name. It was hard for human eyes, even the most determinedly hopeful and optimistic, to see what was worth saving. How did the Howard folk ever let the School of Religion decline to this sad state? Yet Mordecai Johnson had acknowledged these conditions and had called on Bennie Mays to fix these problems.

Dean Mays applied his University of Chicago social-science analysis to the situation, much as Dr. Case had taught him. One problem was structural, for Howard was in part a federal creature, supervised by the Department of the Interior, and it was in part private, started and supported by the evangelical Protestant American Missionary Association. There was a federal appropriation each year—around two hundred thousand dollars when Dr. Johnson first arrived in 1926, and even that small appropriation was opposed vigorously by white southern congressmen during the budget debates in each session of Congress. These some seventy congressmen objected most loudly in 1928, after the African American Dr. Johnson became president of the institution. Mississippi's John Rankin and B. G. Lowry, along with Georgia's Malcolm C. Tarver, spoke with particular venom, and Bennie Mays was not surprised that in the U.S. Senate Coleman Livingston Blease of his native South Carolina had taken occasion during a debate on a joint resolution of both houses to inject his own Negrophobic poison into the wounds already opened by others.[9] Even with Senator Blease now departed, his words echoed in the corridors, and each year for decades southern congressmen rose to decry Howard University and Dr. Johnson.

Still a different structural problem for the School of Religion was caused by the federal and public part of Howard's character and creation. However large or small the federal appropriation, federal monies could not be applied to a School of Religion. Moreover the basic accrediting agency, the American

Senator Coleman L. Blease of South Carolina, one of the southerners who opposed
congressional funding for Howard University. Courtesy of Library of Congress.

Association of Theological Schools, did not certify theological degrees granted
by Howard, and no theologian there was a member of professional or reformist
organizations. Only Bennie Mays was attending conferences of scholars, and
only Bennie Mays was a member of the Federal Council of Churches. A great
portion of the new dean's tasks was thus to find money from private white
donors in the North and from institution-building white scholars at the University of Chicago and elsewhere to help in his endeavors. His time of study
with and the observations he made alongside the institution-building and
extremely political Dr. Aubrey were thus vital to getting started with the heavy
load Mays had to tow at Howard.[10]

As before in other places, Mays closed his eyes to what existed at present and relied on divine vision for a sense of what could be. Again David gave him the words for the coming journey: "Show the wonder of your great love!" And most important was the supplication, "Keep me the apple of your eye, / Hide me in the shadow of your wings."[11]

Almost at once Bennie and Sadie Mays liked most of the Howard faculty whom they met. As the couple came to know these professors, several began to confide how much they distrusted President Johnson. Some found him autocratic; some thought he expected too much from the faculty; others considered him too secretive. Bennie and Sadie Mays could not follow the bitter critiques back to any logically connected source of genuine grievance. What the couple beheld in their new president was a dynamo charged with "supra human" energies, who was building by pushing his people to show performance and then holding up that performance to potential donors and above all to northern congressmen. Donations came in from philanthropists, and the federal appropriations grew, attaining the magic million-dollar mark in the Great Depression year of 1930 and averaging three quarters of a million dollars throughout Mays's stay with Johnson at Howard.[12]

Indeed in 1928 Dr. Johnson had campaigned for and had gotten a virtually guaranteed annual appropriation from the federal government as part of the Department of the Interior budget, thereby replacing the yearly fights over small and varying appropriations with a relatively generous line item in a federal agency popular even among many in the white South. The budget for the Department of Interior grew dramatically during the presidency of Franklin Delano Roosevelt, and with its growth came corresponding increases in Howard's line of appropriations. Salaries increased for professors; a new library went up; and Public Works Administration monies built dormitories, classrooms, and lecture halls. The much-improved School of Social Work employed Sadie Mays as instructor and involved her in interesting studies of the District of Columbia black community during the early years of the New Deal, before war preparations drew away domestic spending. The school was also connected with black scholars and politicos who crowded into "Dee Cee," as the capital was called by the many southerners who were newly arrived. Sadie Mays became friends with Mary McLeod Bethune, who was active in education and reform during the New Deal era, and who served with Sadie on the National Council of Children and alongside Sadie with the National Youth Administration, which actually found some jobs for Dee Cee youth of color and also provided some technical training, and the reformist wing of the YWCA. Sadie Mays's school also put her in touch with the diligent social science demographer Kelly Miller and the historian Carter G. Woodson, who meticulously collected and cataloged all materials and resources about African Americans.[13]

Prominent on the busy campus was another handsome structure, the Howard Law School, a fitting site for its founder and dean, Charles Hamilton Houston, whose well-trained attorneys were winning case after case for the NAACP campaigns to improve the segregated public facilities in the South, and to find some relief for the many young black men who were on weekly basis locked up in some southern jailhouse on little evidence and with scant legal basis for incarceration. After New Deal and private money had combined to build a new cafeteria, the old cafeteria was gutted and completely redone inside and outside for Dean Houston. In that era few public or private law schools admitted African Americans, and Howard was the only historically black school fully accredited to offer the degree in jurisprudence. Houston was consequently mentor to almost all black attorneys properly licensed to plead before the bar, and above all Houston was the coach and model for the NAACP and other civil rights lawyers gradually emerging. There was just cause for rewarding Dean Houston and his successful school with the new site.[14]

Yet Bennie Mays reasoned that it was relatively easy to prevail upon the Roosevelt administration to reconstruct a building to house a law library, lecture hall, seminar room, and departmental offices fit for Dr. Houston and his scholars. After all, it was clearly in the federal purview to provide a national center primarily for training African Americans in the law but open to all qualified applicants. Such funding was as logical as the relatively generous support already offered for the research hospital that trained medical students from Howard. By contrast, Mays noted again, no federal funds could be directly expended on his School of Religion: a very prominent clause in Representative Louis C. Cramton's act authorizing the appropriation was that no federal funds could be so used. Dean Mays pondered his own case for a new building and library resources in the midst of all the construction. All schools on campus were needy and worthy, but the new dean alone lacked ready access to New Deal monies. In any case there was some immediate good news: President Johnson agreed to hire Howard Thurman, the dean's old debate student at Morehouse and a man who had become a brilliant theologian. Dr. Thurman became dean of the chapel and professor of religion.[15]

No matter how much Bennie and Sadie Mays admired and liked Dr. Johnson and no matter how much they liked their new colleagues, the fact was that the grumbling and mumbling betrayed serious dissension in the ranks. The biologist Ernest Just, who had developed a technique for preserving blood plasma for transfusion, disputed the terms of a planned retirement and insisted that he was being mistreated after years of poor pay and laboratory conditions that were inadequate. Even more bitter in dissent was their new friend Kelly Miller, whose studies of black education and demographics Bennie Mays and Sadie Mays used in their own research and even in their own daily work. The polymath humanist Alain Locke, theorist and artist of refined definitions for the New Negro, could not abide any of the Howard administrations before, during, or after Dr. Johnson's tenure. Nor could pioneer scholar Carter G. Woodson, who was long ago mistreated by Johnson's white predecessors. Woodson was never reconciled to the black president and thus avoided the campus proper, keeping the base for his important studies near the campus and making them accessible to the scholars there. Rayford W. Logan, who arrived in 1938 to bring professionalism to the history department, chronicled the discontent of the talented tenth with something like glee and kept a cool, even icy, personal distance from Dr. Johnson. Indeed Bennie Mays's prize recruit, Howard Thurman—whose chapel services Dr. Johnson admired and whose soulful publications Dr. Johnson loudly publicized—felt antipathy toward the hard-driving president and stayed on-site only as long as Dean Bennie Mays was on campus. Inside the handsome wrought-iron gates and along the "long walk" across the rapidly growing campus, then, there was much unease expressed by the hardworking and talented faculty.[16]

Beyond the gates and uptown on Capitol Hill, southern congressmen found new occasions to insult the university and its black leader. Unable to stop the joint resolution of 1928 that installed Howard University as a line item in the Department of Interior's budget, these men bitterly resented the idea of a black bourgeoisie and a black academy, and they watched with sharp eyes and keen hearing for the chance to attack. Opportunity came quickly as Howard students and faculty, encouraged by the otherwise resented Dr. Johnson, protested racial injustices such as lynchings and continuing Klan violence, gross racial inequalities in the late phases of the New Deal social programs, and racist court cases. Among the court cases, the cause célèbre was the Scottsboro Case, wherein black teenagers were herded through a sham trial in northern Alabama and convicted of rape in a case that became even more sensational after one of the "victims" not only recanted her accusations but began to campaign on behalf of her "attackers." Because the International Legal Defense Fund of the CPUSA had boldly jumped in to defend the Scottsboro Boys, southern congressmen could focus on Communism and Reds rather than on social justice, and they could with a stretch of logic claim that all civil rights activities were Communist inspired. Quickly the southern congressmen seized on the false charge of Communism as an effective new weapon to launch at Howard and its professors and students. Given Bennie Mays's disdain for the Communist Party in Chicago and especially at the university there, this cut went deep. Yet the social scientist in him also recognized the red baiting for what it was: congressional speechifying popular among the Negrophobes back home and a criticism that could draw attention away from the fact that Howard University was making great strides and training a cadre of fine leaders proud of their blackness even as it trained white professionals liberal in their toleration.[17]

Through the southern congressional sniping on Capitol Hill and the grousing professors at the faculty lunch table, President Johnson was unbowed. Bennie and Sadie Mays judged that no white man could have accomplished what Mordecai Johnson accomplished. The Race Man dean saluted the Race Man president, who understood the politics of the New Deal and the art of raising money in order to build a truly national university. In their estimation, the time had passed for white paternalism, whether smiling benignly as in the years after Reconstruction or sneering and overtly holding back as in the early 1920s. Furthermore, in their continuing education by observation, it was surely from Mordecai Johnson that Bennie and Sadie Mays drew the classic Stoic aphorism recast in the modern colloquialism of Race Man boxer Joe Louis, the Brown Bomber: "Sometimes a college president just has to take it on the chin."[18]

There was thus much for the new dean to do. Yet first he had to learn still more, especially if he were to be a proper man of magnificence in a university in the nation's capital. Given the attacks by the southern congressmen and the murmurations in the faculty, a dean of any school in the District of Columbia needed to look and act the right part on all occasions, but especially on occasions of high ceremony. A social faux pas in such a highly public setting redounded to the damage of Howard University. Senators Richard Russell of Georgia and Theodore Bilbo of Mississippi joined with Congressmen Tarver and Rankin to watch intently for chances to find social missteps, but so too did a goodly portion of the faculty. Indeed Rayford Logan noted that some faculty members were not above feeding congressional or cabinet staff anti-Johnson information for their speeches and committee investigations. And sadly sometimes officials uptown were all too willing to dine at the table of rumors set and tended by these black faculty members.[19]

Thus Bennie Mays had still another lesson to learn. Sadie Mays understood some important things about public appearances, and he needed to follow her lead and not his own on such matters or put at risk his hard-won but easily lost magnificence. The lesson came at a dinner arranged by Harold Ickes, who was the prime Howard supporter in the New Deal. Ickes determined to answer southern detractors by hosting a black-tie dinner at the fashionable Willard Hotel to salute Howard University and Dr. Johnson. It was an occasion to honor the triumphs of the university and its president; the dean of the School of Religion was one of the triumphs and was thus given a seat on the dais. For all his insistence on elegant and appropriate demeanor and dress, an insistence enforced—in fact *actualized,* he could quote Aristotle and Thomas Aquinas to

say—against varied and sundry clothier's stores and their clerks, Bennie Mays
had never bought a black-tie dinner suit, or tuxedo. Nor did he see any reason to rent a tuxedo, something hard to do in the nation's capital, where the
rental outfit businesses and their clerks behaved as unhelpfully and even dis-
dainfully toward black men as did such attendants back in South Carolina. The
dean dismissed his wife's suggestions and made his plans instead to wear a tidy
business suit proper to an academic or a church occasion. However, Sadie Mays
did not accept her husband's decision, and soon her words were forcefully
repeated by Avis Robinson, the formidable secretary to Dr. Johnson. Ms. Robinson was a lady thoroughly familiar with the expectations of "quality Negroes"
and the behavior of racist store clerks. Mays soon came to see that President
Johnson himself expected his dean to wear the proper black-tie outfit, and thus
the humbled academic leader submitted to his wife's demand and went shopping for a proper tuxedo of his own. On the evening in question, he looked the
part, as did *all other* male attendees, and he realized how inappropriate a business suit would have been. The Chicago scholar of the sociology of the Bible
could interpret the record from St. Matthew's Gospel in which Jesus told the
parable of terrible punishment for those who came improperly attired to the
king's banquet, "for many are invited but few are chosen." The small lesson that
he needed to dress for success fit precisely inside the large lesson that he needed
to heed Sadie Mays on such issues.[20] In later years Mays could recount the
episode with gentle self-chiding, but he did so knowing that he came close to
an unacceptable public mocking of his own person, of Dr. Johnson, and of
Howard University. The little things mattered in this job, and no little thing
was insignificant.

Learning enough to be trusted in a little thing, Bennie Mays addressed himself to a large thing. A federal appropriation vouchsafed by Harold Ickes built
a spacious new library, the Founders Library, central to the campus. The creation of the Founders Library left the handsome Carnegie Building vacant and
available. Although too small for a main library, the Carnegie Building was a
fine structure with ample space for a specialized library collection and plenty of
room for departmental offices, a lecture hall, at least one seminar room, and
other instructional space. Given the weaknesses of the School of Religion and
the crying needs among all the striving departments, there were good reasons
for rewarding some other dean with the Carnegie Building.

In his best Aubrey style, however, Dean Mays put together his case for presentation to Dr. Johnson. He noted for at least the third time that federal
monies were specifically excluded for the School of Religion because Congress
could pass no law establishing any religion. This status helped this time, however, because the Carnegie Building had been erected with private funds, so it
was among the few places on campus where the School of Religion could be set

up without using federal funds in some way. Bennie Mays believed that Dr. Johnson expected his deans to fight for such prerogatives, and thus he pushed his case hard. Whether by virtue of his logic or by his "persuasion, pressure and persistence," Bennie Mays prevailed, and Dr. Johnson worked with the trustees to find private funding for the renovations needed to convert the Carnegie Building into the new School of Religion, which was accomplished in October 1939.[21]

So overjoyed were Bennie and Sadie Mays at this turn of Fortune's wheel that the couple arranged for all divinity students to join with them in a special day of moving the school's library books by hand from the old wooden-frame building across campus to the beautifully reappointed Carnegie. It is not recorded, but it seems probable that Sadie Mays hosted a party on-site to reward the workers with a propitious feast and, more important, with just the right words of encouragement and appreciation. Her habit was to make these kinds of labors into family fun.[22]

Yet another opportunity burst upon the dean, and almost at once, before the academic year of 1939–40 was concluded. Dr. John Moore, a friend and theologian at Swarthmore College, sent word to Dean Mays about the chance to buy an entire library collection of divinity school books, and to do so at a price profoundly discounted by circumstances leading to the sale. In the processes of delivering this message, Moore reminded his associate of the deep truth in Aubrey's insistence that the scholar of religion must reach back and must reach forward. In order for Bennie Mays to reach forward and improve his School of Religion at Howard University, John Moore had to reach back to help his friend. It was again the bond of souls, the *animarum nexus,* that sense of connectedness in pursuit of the common goal of improving the training of ministers, which was there always in the students and associates of Dr. Aubrey. The specific opportunity came because Auburn Theological Seminary, a Presbyterian school in New York State, was to merge with the much larger and more nationally based Union Theological Seminary in New York City. Union's famed library was so large that "only" some eleven thousand volumes from the Auburn library were needed there. (The Howard seminary library in 1939 totaled ten thousand books!) Thus the Auburn seminary prepared to close its library and planned to auction off some thirty-nine thousand specialized volumes as one collection to another seminary that wanted to buy the lot. Several small Presbyterian seminaries were attempting to bid, but Dr. Moore believed ten thousand dollars would buy the collection for Howard, provided that Dean Mays and President Johnson acted promptly.[23]

Although ten thousand dollars was enough to pay salaries for several professors in those Depression days, it seemed to Mays a relatively small sum to pay for such a full theological collection. It would take much time and quite a great deal more than ten thousand dollars in expenditures for Howard to build a collection equal to this one now up for auction. Bennie Mays traveled to Auburn to examine the collection himself, and he subsequently made a forceful presentation to President Johnson, even sending a telegram notice that it would be a "colossal blunder" not to buy the books. Yet there was the difficulty that Dean Mays had just pushed his president hard to give the School of Religion the Carnegie Building and then he had pushed him equally hard to raise the money for the needed renovations. Now he was asking for still more money. Again the money could not come from any federal appropriation, and it could not come from the operating budget of Howard, for most of that money also came at least indirectly from federal funds. In other words Dr. Johnson would have to raise the money himself, just as he had done recently for the renovations to the building. There were real concerns in the matter. Besides the additional work for Dr. Johnson, there was the worry that other schools and programs on campus might resent the fact that Dean Mays's school was favored yet again. Even so, Bennie and Sadie Mays realized that the chance to acquire such a library was an opportunity that would not likely come their way again, and thus a team of persuaders and petitioners went to work on President Johnson. That team included the formidable Avis Robinson, who saw the telegram and repeated with her own emphasis that ignoring this opportunity would be a "colossal blunder."[24]

After much discussion, it emerged that the largest concern for the president seemed to be the actual value of the collection. He wanted an expert opinion that it was worth ten thousand dollars. Dean Mays in his *megalosukos* considered himself to be a scholarly expert on the value of such a collection, and he had the evaluation from Dr. Moore of the prestigious Swarthmore. However, in order to placate his president, Bennie Mays arranged for personnel at Colgate Rochester Theological Seminary and at Union Seminary to set a value on the collection. The Union experts thought it a bargain, but the Colgate Rochester experts opined that the collection was not worth ten thousand to them. Dr. Johnson was much influenced by the opinion of the experts at Colgate Rochester, and things hung fire for "tantalizing" days while Dr. Johnson made his own assessment of the risks and rewards. Bennie Mays became apprehensive, even anxious. He did not know how much more expert testimony he could get, and for that matter he did not know how much more he should have to get. Recalling that the president liked debate, Mays went back in to see Dr. Johnson, pointing out that two expert teams, Union's and the president's *own dean* (Mays's italics) agreed, while only one team disagreed. Furthermore, Dean Mays noted, the experts at Colgate Rochester possessed a large library of their own and had only said the collection was not worth ten thousand *to them,* a nice but possibly important distinction in their valuation. The social scientist and mathematician dean also showed Dr. Johnson that, at its current rate of buying books, it would take Howard seventy-five years to build such a collection. Once again Mordecai Johnson came down on the side of his persisting and pressing dean. He found donors, and he bought the books.[25]

Before this transaction was completed, the American Association of Theological Schools concluded its rigorous assessment and fully certified Dean Mays's school as an accredited institution. The Howard School of Religion thus became the second African American school, after Gammon Theological Seminary in Atlanta, to be so accredited by the national-ranking service. By academic year 1939–40, Dean Mays had accomplished many of the goals he had set for himself. His "strengthened faculty" included Howard Thurman; student enrollment had increased in size and in quality, especially in the graduate program; library holdings had increased 290 percent with one large accession; the Carnegie Building with its renovated classroom and office space was a handsome building; and now there was full accreditation. Still to seek was a significant endowment of several million dollars whose interest-bearing securities and other holdings could be dedicated specifically and only to the School of Religion. In Dr. Aubrey's sense of institution and bridge building, then, his doctoral student Bennie Mays was boldly and successfully reaching forward.[26] As proper for a student of Dr. Aubrey, however, it was time to reach back as well.[27]

Oppressed African Americans and other people of color needed reaching back in the worst way, not only in the ghetto of Shaw Place surrounding Howard University's handsome and expanding campus, but also throughout the United States and into colonial possessions in the world beyond the nation's borders. To reach back to the oppressed people of color, Bennie Mays operated at the same time in two theaters of battle—like Napoleon, the grand strategist of the art of war, who simultaneously operationalized campaigns on more than one continent. The two theaters of war for this black Napoleon were the domestic front of race relations in the United States and the faraway front of foreign relations in which the people of color were oppressed in Africa, Asia, and Latin America. The language may seem far-fetched, but by 1937 Bennie Mays had concluded that peace had to be "waged" and "strategized" and "fought for" with the energy and ambition that Napoleon had brought to military affairs. Publicly at Howard in 1937 and increasingly so in every year thereafter, wherever he was, Bennie Mays adopted a Napoleonic stance of vigorous, far-reaching, and unremitting campaigns for peace and justice. Mindful that it sounded odd to "fight for peace" and to compare pacifists to imperialistic warriors, Bennie and Sadie Mays were equally mindful that war had to be conducted by a few great minds working in coordination and that peaceful pursuit of global justice needed no less energy and no less greatness. Peaceful pursuit also needed endless committee meetings and posturing and posing among the planners no more than the generals did with their battles. The Mayses concluded, and thereby acted on the conclusion, that democracy comported poorly with war strategies and no more successfully with peace strategies.[28]

Mays was not afraid to be described as elitist, but he preferred to treat of the language of merit, virtue, worthiness, and—above all else—*megalosukos.* He was opposed to mob rule that brought unreasoning violence, as in the Phoenix Riot of his childhood. He was opposed to inexpert and even anti-intellectual forces making decisions as they had done in South Carolina, and as he could still observe uptown in the halls of Congress, where badly informed and sometimes badly educated racists among the senators and representatives perpetuated Jim Crow policies with their bills and resolutions. In speaking of "democratic reform," as he often did, Bennie Mays spoke strictly in terms of an improvement for the demos, the numbers of people. The processes—the means by which such "democratic reform" would come—were to be directed by elite of intellectual merit and moral rectitude. Mays was like both W. E. B. Du Bois and Booker T. Washington in his expectation that a "talented tenth" of educated and morally righteous people would direct the nine-in-ten who lacked the required competence and the required moral direction to save themselves.[29]

The nation's capital chronically shared in the national sin of racism, demonstrating many slights to black people laid on by those who could not conceive a dark man as an equal. In that way the District of Columbia was much like Chicago, a great urban center with economic opportunities unmatched in the rural South but with social injustices in force everywhere outside the ghetto. And in the lingering Depression, economic opportunities were dried up, leaving black people trapped in a ghetto in a Babylon that was a strange land indeed. More acutely the District of Columbia was Virginia and guilty of the southern sin of Jim Crow, that particular set of rules laid on by a people who were so expert in manners that they could use every occasion to establish practices—some refined and nuanced, some crude and blunt, but all carefully and brilliantly executed—to drive home a disdain and contempt for African Americans through every major practice and every tiny gesture.[30]

Bennie and Sadie Mays shopped for clothes and found primarily Jewish shop owners near the campus. Some of these Jews considered black people to be fellow sufferers and companion wanderers, all children of the real Lord and all persecuted by worshippers of a false god. Many Washington Jews, however, accepted southern perceptions of color and sometimes outdid Protestant Virginians—or even the Protestant thugs back in the valley of the Saluda—in their abuses. In fact such a large number of Jewish store owners and clerks treated the Howard black people and the Shaw Place black people with such searing Jim Crow cruelty that the redoubtable Jesse Thomas privately asked Bennie Mays if Jews might by nature be prejudiced against African Americans![31]

The question—put forth in a private letter and likely repeated in confidence during travels or visits to the Mays house—stunned and stung Bennie Mays, who knew Thomas to be a good man who wanted all to be brothers in Christ. Of course Jews were not Christians, and Bennie Mays had often seen anti-Semitism among badly informed black ministers, but here was an educated friend of the best sort taking an anti-Semitic stance to ask about Negrophobia in a whole people. Had someone else posed the question, Bennie Mays might well have exploded or perhaps responded with that academic brand of sarcastic dismissal practiced by scholars. But in personal dialogue with a trusted coworker, he took the leading question not as an intended insult but as an hypothesis that could be tested by the bountiful evidence carefully marshaled in the University of Chicago way of empiricism. Building his case for his friend with care, Bennie Mays enumerated enough Jews who were by his observation kind and decent to convince Jesse Thomas—and perhaps himself—that nothing in the philosophies or the traditional practices of Jews was springing from a predisposition in that ethnic group to err in treatment of African Americans. Such a belief would return one to the discarded error of thinking of black people, Jews, and white southerners as distinct races with the implication that each had a distinct god for his race—an error in moral vision that Bennie Mays himself had only recently laid aside but to which he would never return. He also reviewed the Hebrew writings, especially the Tanak and his beloved Psalms of David to find proof of Jewish openness to non-Jews and Jewish conception of a real Lord for all peoples. He considered that he had saved his friend Jesse Thomas, perhaps his closest friend, from sinking into anti-Semitic nonsense, but he did note in his sorrow and anguish a personal regret that southern Jim Crow in Dee Cee was so effective that it could transform many an otherwise good Jew into a narrow and foolish bigot who could and did hurt the heart of God.[32]

These abuses of African Americans were noted by some good-hearted northern congressmen whose liberalism and activism kept their eyes open as they moved around the capital city. Representative John J. O'Connor of New York spoke with commendable force, an almost Ciceronian vehemence: "Right in the shadow of the Capital you have segregation and Jim Crow." O'Connor called forth moral outrage to end the practices at the individual and face-to-face level and federal laws to end the group practices at the societal level. But O'Connor was answered by the sneering Richard Russell and John Rankin, who talked again of Communist plans to establish some sort of "Negro Communism" in a southern state. Theodore Bilbo was again clownish with heavy humor about northern politicians seeking black votes. It was Georgia congressman Malcolm Tarver who spoke most pointedly: "the high ranking Democrat attacks segregation [in order to show] his favor for coeducation of Negroes and whites and for their co entertainment in hotels and theaters." The time had come, Representative Tarver said, "for people of the South to act themselves." He asked plaintively, "What protection have we [against male black assault on white women]?"[33]

Bennie and Sadie Mays were sickened by still more references to the Communism, but they were even more disturbed by Congressman Tarver's and Senator Richard Russell's smarmy references to the sexual threat posed by black men to white women in a coeducational schools such as Howard (where female white students of medicine had always studied) and other institutions, where coeducation could slide into "co entertainment" in sleazy hotels. Bennie Mays knew that in Sadie Mays's family and in Ellen Harvin's family, it was *white* male intrusion on black women that produced the "high yellow" and other complexions among African Americans with "a lot of white blood." As poet Langston Hughes wrote in a memoir, the light brown skin of the mulatto was a reproach to white rapists. Eventually Mays heard and then came to know that back in South Carolina young Strom Thurmond—who eventually became the longest-lived and the longest-talking of the segregationists—had in that very decade fathered the child of a teenage black maid in his father's house, even as the grandfathers of the segregationists had raped household slaves sometimes in the selfsame houses.[34]

Always active in public campaigns for the New Negro, Bennie Mays was a member of the Urban League, the NAACP, and the reformist Federal Council of Churches. The status of the Federal Council of Churches as an integrated organization thoroughly enraged Senator Russell, who spoke often against it as a Communist agency that should be suppressed. Long decades after the Federal Council of Churches lost some of its membership, power, and standing, Southern Baptist churches continued to list in their published guidelines a ban on employing any pastor who had ever been a member of that organization. Of course Bennie Mays—as dean of an accredited school of religion with charismatic Howard Thurman preaching on how to preach for justice—certainly could prepare many good, young men of *megalosukos* for reformist pastoring. Yet he wanted to reach back with tools and techniques that could defeat Senators Russell and Bilbo in that day and defeat in a new day Senators Thurmond and Jesse Helms, powerful southern lords in Congress, who cowed President Roosevelt—and later cowed Presidents Kennedy, Johnson, Nixon, and Reagan. To secure his ends, Dean Mays followed the lead of Yale theologian Jerome Davis and traveled to India to confer with Gandhi about militant pacifism, in which protest was peaceful yet radical with part of its strategy to submit to beatings and imprisonment in public theaters of civil rights war in order to show nonsegregationist, but otherwise uninformed citizenry, what the segregationists really were. Another public tool was to write for and work on behalf of the *Pittsburgh Courier*, Robert Lee Vann's nationally circulated newspaper that came to the mailboxes of most educated black businessmen, academics, activist ministers, government servants, and elected officials in that era. Pullman porters "routed the national editions so that . . . U.S. rail lines could quickly distribute them to hundreds of thousands of readers East, West, North, and South." From Gandhi, Mays drew inspiring words and a newly cast message; from Vann and his successors, Mays found a vehicle for spreading his message everywhere.[35]

Ever since the session with Jerome Davis in New Haven during 1932, Bennie Mays had been fascinated with the techniques and the actions of Mohandas Gandhi. Perhaps before his exposure to Gandhi's teachings, Mays had realized in a vague way that violent uprisings by black people—New Negro or otherwise in identity—would end only in bloody defeat at the hands of white racists. After learning of Gandhi's teachings, however, Mays had gradually evolved in his thinking so that he embraced nonviolent protest no longer as a practical approach but rather as God's chosen way, as the stuff of "soul force" and the expression of sanctified suffering, whose ends were vouched safe by the Divine because of their means of pacifism.[36]

Between 1932 and 1938 Mays intensified his expression of Gandhi's principles, and then in 1938 he determined to signify and magnify his pacifism by going to India to meet in person the human author of the divine concord in Asia. It was a fitting climax in Mays's journey of epiphanies to find justice for black people and to find and express his own personal excellence in magnificence. As Aubrey had showed him, even Thomas Hobbes—usually quoted to the effect that life was nasty, brutish, and short—had announced that a man's personal excellence lay in his "peaceableness" and specifically in his ability to bring a peaceful resolution out of societal afflictions. Having learned that some northern white men could be trusted to do good, Mays had proceeded to learn that even some southern white men could work with black men to do good; and then most spectacularly he had come to the realization that even southern white women could be trusted to do good rather than play the role of Potiphar's devious wife in the Bible (she who lusted after the Hebrew slave Joseph and when rebuffed arranged to punish the captive for her own lust: essentially the way Bennie Mays observed lynching amid all the passionate white talk about protecting virtuous white women from black beast rapists). Yet successive unveiling of God's justice had shown that, even among some southern white women, was a soul invested by the Holy Spirit, and that some liberal southern friends, however few, were set in place by God to help in the cause of justice. There was indeed no other way to understand the sudden announcement by Ruby Bates that the Scottsboro Boys had not raped her, and her subsequent campaign to help the young men out of Alabama's twentieth-century criminal form of slavery in its penal system.[37]

Yet, as spectacular as were the earlier epiphanies, the full realization that the righteous warrior must be a man of peace who actively struggled for nonviolent solutions to injustice—that which Mays's most famous student, Martin Luther King, Jr., later called "marvelous militancy of pacifism"—this revelation came upon Mays with such force that he determined to go to meet Gandhi and seek an audience so that some of the magnificence of the non-Christian crusader for peace and justice would radiate onto him in portions sufficient to send him forward in the greatest struggle of all, the struggle by all people of color for justice in a world where the white people had the guns and where, whether British or French or German, the commanding officers of the white battalions had no more sense of justice, or even decent governance, than thugs such as Dr. Wallace Payne back in the valley of the Saluda. The concept of *satyagraha,* the full-blown nonviolent but in its own way aggressively militant technique of resistance to oppression, Bennie Mays had studied and reflected on in New Haven when he met Dr. Jerome Davis. There were parts of it that left him in a questioning frame of mind, and he wanted to press Gandhi for specific answers before he adopted a non-Christian strategy.[38]

Opportunity to meet the man who had become known as Mahatma (great soul) came in 1937 because of Mays's membership in the YMCA, whose leaders selected Mays and eleven other representatives to attend sessions of the World Church Congress, which was set to meet in India for several weeks in June, followed by a grand session at Oxford hosted by reformist interfaith theologian George Padmore. Gandhi had already served some time in jail, and he had long ago reconciled himself to the probability of a violent death, possibly from British colonial officials, possibly from overzealous rebels who accepted the radical nature of his protest but did not grasp or did not accept the absolute rule of nonviolent resistance to imperial rule, or possibly from rival claimants to leadership in the drive to independence. Indeed in 1919 the tactics of *satyagraha* had once resulted in a British massacre of some four hundred unarmed and remarkably well-disciplined Gandhians at Amristar. Thereafter some rebels had talked about and occasionally committed retaliatory violence against colonial officials. Yet at that time Gandhi had made his point forcefully, not violently, by fasting to protest any armed resistance by his followers, and the tactic had held together his movement while pushing the British toward many piecemeal reforms of policy and eventually relinquishment of the valuable territory. Even so, Gandhi was jailed at least once more after 1937, and after many close calls with assassination his life ended in 1948 after an angry Brahman shot him three times at the conclusion of a fast.[39]

For all the danger thus involved, there was yet something mystical and moving for Mays in his "ninety minutes with Gandhi," a length of time for which this most dedicated of University of Chicago social scientists allowed an arcane significance that the men of Dr. Case's seminary would normally find amusing if not dangerously misleading. In the exotic and timeless city of Mysore, however, Bennie Mays avoided any such mysticism. Mays the social scientist had two carefully focused questions to ask of the great leader. First he probed exactly what the nonviolence in *satyagraha* entailed in terms of consequences for what resulted when the oppressed struck back. Second the dark-skinned Mays wanted to know exactly what Gandhi thought about the caste system, in which the darkest peoples were consigned to handle the refuse of all other castes and were thus labeled untouchables.

On the first question, Gandhi gave the social scientist an answer reaffirming what Mays had already absorbed from Jerome Davis's notes on *satyagraha*. No violence is ever acceptable; especially not short-term violence in retaliation for killing. Indeed the violence that comes in response to militant protest may well get one killed, but that is the price to be paid for principled protest in the cause of justice. One must accept the consequences of protest, including the duty to pay the price with one's life in disobeying a law that is unjust. To avoid the punishment, whether jail or shame or death, is to dishonor the cause by living beneath the stated ideals of the soul force. In slightly different language, acceptance of such consequences was exactly what Mays the classicist of Western traditions had always believed from his study with Dr. Aubrey of Plato, Socrates, the Stoics, Thomas Aquinas, and the Protestant expression in Walter Rauschenbusch and the Chicago social reformists. As Mays noted in *Born to Rebel,* this message of breaking unjust law while expecting to suffer the full consequences of violating that law, in both its Western and Eastern forms of expression, was always hard to explain and in fact was never accepted even by prominent followers of his student Dr. King. Yet, as Mays also noted with the pride of an academic father, Dr. King himself completely grasped both Socrates and Gandhi and went to his own death with dignity and discernment.[40]

As he asked the second question about caste, Mays was only partly the social scientist boring in on a presenter at seminar. He was more the dark boy cuffed about and cursed by the cruel white folk back in the valley of the Saluda because of Jim Crow. And the man of whom Mays asked this question was a privileged member of the *vaisya* merchant caste, whose members were taught that even to gaze upon a dark untouchable was to risk damnation in the next reincarnation. Gandhi answered that he did not believe the dark peoples were truly untouchable, and in fact he ministered to them and included them in the call for the justice of *satyagraha* and its soul force. On the other hand, the soft-spoken Gandhi defended the caste system as an economic policy, and said that he made no protest against that economic policy and the caste system neces-sary to it. Like Jesus the historical actor, Gandhi thus made no protest against the existence of economic injustice, and on the score of caste the Mahatma ministered to individuals and offered healing and solace without making social protest against economic institutions of slavery. Radical enough to touch the untouchable, the Mahatma was not great souled enough to call for economic equality. Justice and peace in *satyagraha* for Gandhi were not economic issues. As he later recorded the disappointing answer, Bennie Mays was characteristi-cally deferential, but he did make clear his delight that subsequently the color-coded caste system of the political economy was attacked by other people in all valleys of all rivers, from the Saluda to the Indus.[41]

The trip to Bombay, Mysore, and Oxford functioned as a public ceremony in which a New Negro could show all people his new public stance on a tech-nique for attaining justice. There hardly seemed time for Gandhi to say or do anything that Mays had not already heard and accepted beforehand in schol-arly and intellectual forums. Instead Mays could be seen and observed increas-ing his own personal excellence in this most public, and quite dangerous, way. To speak so openly of racial justice all over the world was to risk the ire of the men of the South, who at home could call him a "nigger" and be candidly racist for their racist local audiences and constituencies; yet in other places such racist men could hide their racism and gesture at the unorthodox international move-ment started by Gandhi and label this exotic and much misunderstood teach-ing "Communist," thereby bringing nonracist disdain down on the heads of those campaigning for justice and peace. Mays was already a victim of scatter-shot essentially aimed at President Mordecai Johnson by racist congressmen. In making this journey, however, Mays made himself an explicit and direct target for Senators Russell and Bilbo and Congressmen Tarver and Rankin. The new danger was that in traveling south of the Potomac, a black man so publicly a target for rhetorical "shot" could be literally shot by bullets aimed by overtly racist voters stirred to fever pitch by the wild and unrestrained rhetoric of the congressional champions of Jim Crow.[42]

Taking nothing away from the public and ceremonial elements of this jour-ney and making no claim that Gandhi actually said anything new to Bennie Mays, the fact of Gandhi's magnetism—almost in the biblical sense of Elijah's "double portion of spirits" given Elisha—cannot be gainsaid. Mays had already drawn on techniques and direction from Gandhi; during the ninety minutes he drew also a personal, intimate, inspiriting, and encouraging "heart to fight," as Thomas Pettigrew would call it. But for Mays it was "heart to fight" socio-economic campaigns never imagined by Gandhi at all.[43]

With such an invigoration, Mays could enter more fully and with even more effectiveness than beforehand in making a particular kind of Howard University ministry, a special kind of scholar activism that demonstrated commitments to world peace and justice by supporting Gandhi's anti-imperialist campaign. That same scholar activism organized the ward or beat in the northern ghetto and the chancery court or county court in the southern countryside to improve schools, protect against lynch mobs, help people register to vote by paying property taxes and passing literacy tests, and invite good white people, especially in the South, to join in the campaign in the church pews, the chancery court, the schoolhouse, and the local feed store.

To be Gandhian at the local level was to bring a discipline and a focus to protests for Bennie and Sadie Mays, who were already disciplined and focused in the classic Stoic way of Marcus Aurelius. The crucial Gandhian insight now put into their practice was one they had already seen in Plato's version of Socrates but had not known how to employ in their own lives: The moral protester of injustice accepted the mortal consequences of his actions. Jesus accepted crucifixion as the consequence of his teaching and preaching and healing in Judea. Socrates drank hemlock as the consequence of his teaching in the Athenian agora. St. John the Baptizer accepted first imprisonment and then beheading as the consequence of his teaching and preaching in the wilderness. Even bumbling, misspeaking St. Peter, after missing the point so often—fighting inappropriately, running away, and denying he even knew Jesus—even and especially Peter, when it really mattered, accepted imprisonment and then accepted a horrible crucifixion, made more horrible because he was so big and strong that it took long hours to kill him in that fashion. Bennie Mays knew he might have to die, and he certainly knew he might have to go to jail. Indeed imprisonment of some protesters was crucial to the Gandhian appeal to civil rights: go to jail for trying to ride in the Pullman car or for trying to sit in the nice seats of the trolley car or for trying to register to vote. Let the attorneys trained by Charles Hamilton Houston demonstrate the unconstitutional nature of your imprisonment exactly because you had legal standing through incarceration. Let the *Pittsburgh Courier,* the *Chicago Defender,* the NAACP *Crisis* and someday soon the *New York Post* publicize your case so as to reach those quiet good people who did not lynch and who did not curse black people and who even did good and decent things for them on the sly away from the attentive eyes of the racist majority. Make your plight so obvious that these decent people have no choice but to end their silence and declare the good and stand alongside you.

On the vital Gandhian issue of war between nations, however, Bennie Mays had not thought things through at all—a gap in his social science and his moral philosophy that later cost and cost dearly. For the nonce, Mays's foreign policy was anticolonial and anti-imperialist, a nonviolent and marvelous militancy of pacifist protests against the old white empires of the British, the French, the Dutch, and the Spanish. Even as he visited Gandhi, however, there were "colored" troops, the Japanese, scorching the good earth and bayoneting "colored" peasant farmers in China. Mays had not thought through how to apply soul force and the marvelous militancy of pacifism to colored-on-colored imperialism. Nor had he thought through what to do about real Communists, not Senator Russell's bogey men conjured up for the congressional chambers, but the painfully real and the painfully evil Joseph Stalin and Mao Tse-tung seeking alliance against the evil of racism and injustice, the Nazis of Adolf Hitler and the fascists of Tojo Hideki. This moral quagmire was yet to come, and when Bennie Mays and his friends marched into it and could not extricate themselves, it took his best student, Martin Luther King, Jr., to show the moral way out of the trap created by not thinking things all the way through in the face of a growing and overwhelming evil.

But all that pain was faraway in time, and nobody other than Gandhi was actually thinking about it in the mid and late 1930s. In this period Bennie Mays as a pacifist could salute the U.S. policy of nonalignment and neutrality and even isolationism at a time when the great majority of Americans wanted nothing that looked like World War I, no matter what the issues. Whether confronted in the southern countryside or in Dee Cee, the problem in Mays's face was Jim Crow in his native South and economic apartheid in the urban North, and for these foes he now had the Gandhian weapons of the principled protest and imprisonment, especially in conjunction with his longtime labor rights friend and coworker A. Philip Randolph, who was developing mass gatherings of activist pacifist resistance.[44] While his questioning attitude had not been fully resolved in his personal interview with Gandhi, it had been inspiring as to method but disappointing as to socioeconomic aims for the New Negro, who retained commitments to goals established by Walter Rauschenbush and desired from Henry George.

In the task of reaching back to the persecuted people of color at home by speaking at forums, writing feature pieces, and otherwise publicizing the New Negroes' demand for justice, there were several important outlets for black protest and reform in the 1930s. Harlem of course was the cultural center, and it spawned literary and journalistic organs, many of them associated with, if not sponsored by, poet and activist Langston Hughes. There was the important *Amsterdam News,* since 1935 the personal project of entrepreneurs and self-conscious New Negroes Dr. C. B. Powell and Dr. Phillip M. H. Savory and the major outlet for publishing about black culture and expression and achievement downtown. Still downtown but among white people in New York, the

New York Post became involved in civil rights reporting and advocacy, and in its pages the New Negro Ted Poston became perhaps the greatest and certainly the longest lived of the journalists crusading for racial equity. In Chicago, Robert Sengstacke Abbott and then his nephew John Sengstacke, along with reporter Frank A. Young, created a populist working-class herald in the *Chicago Defender.*[45]

Yet in the 1930s arguably the most important African American newspaper was Robert Lee Vann's *Pittsburgh Courier,* based in the steel city but circulated by the hundreds of thousands all over the United States. Its publisher was significant because Vann was active in persuading Pittsburgh voters to support Franklin Delano Roosevelt, thereby abandoning abolitionist loyalties to the Grand Old Party (GOP) and joining the Democrats, whose southern wing featured Senators Blease, Russell, Bilbo, and James Vardaman as well as Congressmen Tarver, Rankin, and Hill. In fact, it was Vann who came up with a widely repeated directive for African Americans still loyal to the Republicans because of Abraham Lincoln: "Go home, and turn Lincoln's picture to the wall." In Vann's opinion the GOP had turned its back to his race after Reconstruction. He encouraged what he usually called "The Race" to support Roosevelt, primarily because of his wife, Eleanor Roosevelt. Pittsburgh black people supported Roosevelt vigorously in 1932, setting the stage for the eventual transformation in racial identities and political allegiances in which much more than 90 percent of black people became Democrats. The *Courier* was the first black newspaper to feature national editions as well as a host-city edition, and eventually it reached some two hundred thousand readers in some fourteen editions, with many rural southern readers subscribing by mail. True to Vann himself, the *Courier* represented a particularly upbeat and business-oriented approach, in contrast to the *Chicago Defender*'s self-consciously working-class reformism. For all that, Vann's newspaper publicized lynchings, voter registration fraud, residential discrimination in the nation's capital, and inequalities in spending on public schools as well as a gracious plenty of features on successful boxers, footballers, singers, show business people, and prosperous entrepreneurs.[46]

Vann had an interesting story. Extremely light in skin color, he could have "passed" over into the white world had he so chosen. He was from Hertford, North Carolina, related to a prominent white family, the Vanns, another branch of whom produced the great historian C. Vann Woodward. Very much the entrepreneur, Robert Vann was a dapper dresser and knew how to present himself to maximum advantage. For instance he used the *Courier* to publicize his availability and suitability to serve on the U.S. Supreme Court—in spite of the fact that other black men with real legal training were better qualified than he, to say nothing of the fact that the Roosevelt administration was not seriously considering any black candidate for such a post. In some ways Vann was an unlikely candidate for reformist, especially for those using radical techniques of protest. However, the *Courier* gave full and fair coverage to CPUSA efforts against lynching, gave Bennie Mays and others their chances to describe *satyagraha* in feature pieces, and above all, provided space for full panoply of opinion among its columnists from W. E. B. Du Bois on the left to George Schuyler on the right. Other interesting *Courier* writers included the self-educated J. A. Rogers, who searched out and publicized African roots, often in graphic or cartoon format; social scientist Kelly Miller, who was permitted many column inches for occasionally dense statistics; writers on special assignment, such as Samuel Daniels, who covered the Italian invasion of Ethiopia; or J. R. McCoy, who carefully followed and chronicled the long story of the Scottsboro Boys as their individual appeals wound their ways through the courts from 1937 to 1972.[47]

And Benjamin Elijah Mays, dean of the Howard University School of Religion. From his arrival on the Howard campus, Bennie Mays was regularly featured in *Courier* news stories, sometimes quoted for facts about black churches in substantive features, other times noted in the "Purely Personal" column devoted to publicizing the doings of Dee Cee's black leaders. In late April of 1938, Bennie Mays was given major space for a news feature concerning the YMCA liberal integrationist efforts of "interracial goodwill" dedicated to the chance for "boys in our community [to] develop to full manhood not only physically, but spiritually, morally, and educationally." From that point onward, Bennie Mays was in the *Courier* most weeks, gaining his own opinion column, originally called simply "Mays," in 1942 and continuing to write for Vann and his successors until 1981.[48]

As Bennie Mays wrote for the *Pittsburgh Courier* and as he began to speak before the professional businessman's fraternal and service club Omega Psi Phi, and as he worked with conferences of the YMCA, the Urban League, and the NAACP, he was less the University of Chicago social scientist than he was the reformist social-gospel Baptist minister. He did operate at more than one level, and again Aubrey's useful images explained those levels. With academics, writing in scholarly and refereed journals or speaking at conference sessions with moderators and critics, he was the University of Chicago social scientist, cool and analytical, assuming nothing, taking nothing for granted, carefully assembling models to predict behavior based on observations made a posteriori, and such observations made most accurately and thus most usefully by keeping one's emotions in check. However, when speaking to integrated groups meeting at the YMCA events or when speaking to other reformist organizations, he was quite different. Then he was as passionate and as emotional as the Reverend James F. Marshall back in the valley of the Saluda, although of course

Mays's agenda was different from the Reverend Marshall's. Mays could operate at either level by compartmentalizing his activities. He accomplished this so successfully that it is only with the vantage point of looking back over many years that one can see the art and the artifice in what at the time seemed "natural" instead of carefully learned and painstakingly practiced.[49]

Photographs and memories of friends and students capture Bennie Mays the Baptist reformer, big hands clasped tightly, veins protruding on his neck and forehead, sweat rolling off him, and eyes wet with the sharpness of the pains expressed. He moved such audiences to tears, to laughter, and finally to action—that was the social-gospel Baptist reformist with the style of the Reverend Marshall but with the message of Walter Rauschenbusch. By contradistinction, the cool and detached observer tried to be sure that he got his observations in an accurate and scientific way by keeping his emotions out of sight. This detached observer may be heard in his formal writings and academic addresses. In his correspondence, and apparently in his social interactions in day-to-day life, he could shift from one compartment to the other with amazing speed. By the time of his deanship at Howard, Bennie Mays had perfected his rhetorical arts and could use the techniques most appropriate to the audience.[50]

In the midst of this happy buzz of activity and recognition, Bennie Mays was brought up short in April 1938 with the news that his mother, Louvenia Carter Mays, had passed on out of this world. He hurried home to lay her to rest. This was the woman with the suspiciously light complexion who had taught her ebony child that no one was better than he, that he was as good as any light-skinned or white child, that he was "as good as anyone." She had told him that his dark skin was in its own way beautiful. In the same way, Louvenia Mays had nurtured all the children. For her own part, she had endured a remarkably cruel master, Henry Hazel Mays and his wife and the even crueler plantation overseer S. C. Deel. Then Louvenia Mays had endured much in the days of freedom both from the new and brutal Jim Crow laws and from the occasional but always memorable drunken cruelties of her husband, Hezekiah Mays. Now Louvenia Mays was dead, worn out from a long and wearying road. Bennie Mays, the prized son, could celebrate what she had done, and he could regret that his busy schedule had kept him far from the valley of the Saluda in these final days, much as a similarly busy schedule had kept him far from the valley of the Santee when his "pretty girl" wife Ellen Harvin Mays had reached the end of her much shorter road. Besides her simple and unshakeable pride in race, Louvenia Mays was powerfully spiritualistic and took balm against the pains of South Carolina life in her Baptist faith. It is written that she had talked about heaven and her intention to meet Bennie Mays there "not long, not long, from now," as the psalmist says and as the choir responded on its hard benches. Her son had moved on intellectually beyond images of angels floating in clouds, but like his Louvenia, Bennie Mays believed that a gracious God had prepared many mansions, however metaphorical such mansions, for departed believers such as his good mother.[51]

As for Hezekiah Mays, the widower of Louvenia, the father of Benjamin and the son of James, much is left unsaid and in *Born to Rebel* Bennie Mays was vague about late-life relations with his father. He suggested vaguely that in this late spring of 1938, he and his father made some kind of rapprochement and reconciliation. He noted that Hezekiah Mays knew how to behave around the white lords of the land and the white peasants and mill workers, and he knew how to protect his family by being careful never to challenge the presumptions of the white folk, whether high and grand like the landowner Bill Mays, who had taught him basic literacy, or high and mean like Dr. Wallace Payne, who liked to cuff the dark children, or low and threatened like the mill workers who voted for Pitchfork Ben Tillman and Coleman Livingston Blease and Cotton Ed Smith to Jim Crow everything that mattered. Bennie Mays also knew that his father hated white people and wore the mask of the happy and unthreatening fool purely for survival.[52]

Whatever rapprochement or reconciliation developed, the period of such a relationship could not have been long. After burying Louvenia Mays, Bennie Mays returned to the demands of his deanship, and *Born to Rebel* records no major trips back to the valley in the month of May. In June came news that Hezekiah Mays had passed on.[53] For a believer, and especially a believer whose profession was to train ministers, Bennie Mays faced a confoundment with his father's demise. Hezekiah Mays had not been able to accept the idea of a just God or an afterlife, and he remained dubious about ministers and church people as he remained dubious about the divine. For a believing Baptist, there was an inevitable piquancy in the death of a loved one who denied belief. There was pain for any man whose father died, especially when there had been as many conflicts as congruencies in their relationship. But Bennie Mays, despite some considerable modernist thinking, remained a good and true Baptist who believed in a salvation for those who had truly confessed and accepted forgiveness. He could find no spiritual or intellectual explanation for salvation for this one who resolutely declined to confess and resolutely denied God. By his belief, Bennie Mays had long ago cast aside any notion of a devil with pitchfork amid flames of hell, but he did define hell as a state of being removed from God, and he knew that Hezekiah Mays had lived a life removed from God. It followed that Hezekiah Mays faced an afterlife. The next logical statement could not be made aloud, but of all the mysteries about God and man, what happened on death was the largest and murkiest enigma. However one twisted and reorganized and compartmentalized and skipped steps in the thinking, there was no logical reason and certainly no factor based on faith that could make Hezekiah Mays's afterlife a story of hope. In the fourth week of June Bennie Mays again left on a second lonely return trip home that closed out a chapter in a career and in three lives.

As the year 1940 dawned, Bennie and Sadie Mays could look with satisfaction at great accomplishments at Howard and for New Negroes in Dee Cee: the School of Religion fully accredited; important new faculty, especially Howard Thurman, in place; Bennie Mays with speaking and writing outlets where he could make a nationwide influence on educated or "talented tenth" of African Americans; growing interest among some northern liberal congressmen in trying to ease the plight of black people in the South; some evidence of at least minimal progress in the South toward spending money on black schools; and even some minimal steps in the South to end the extreme violence against young black men. Even farther beyond Howard's gates at Shaw Place, but still because of the university, Bennie and Sadie Mays were to spend a sabbatical year— September 1, 1940–September 1, 1941—working with the YMCA among the Bantu peoples of South Africa on an educational project in the land where Gandhi first came to world notice as the Mahatma. The long walk through the Howard University campus was, by its definition, a march of progress, and much of that self-definition seemed justified by facts that the social scientist could amass.

For all that, the glass was at least half empty and maybe worse. Bennie Mays thought that the move of the School of Religion with its enhanced library collection to the renovated Carnegie Building was a temporary move, auguring a future move to far more spacious quarters with a still more dramatically increased collection. Increasingly, however, he thought that Dr. Johnson considered the move as permanent, not temporary. Bennie Mays was not making much headway in building a separate and dedicated endowment for the School of Religion on his efforts, and Johnson was far too busy raising money in other places for other purposes to address the school's dedicated endowment. There would remain that anomaly that Howard was a federally assisted university, and any funds coming in from the New Deal programs must be carefully kept away from Dean Mays's department.

The world was fully at war by 1940, and while Bennie Mays saw good reason for the United States to stay out of this war, the fact remained that New Deal social programs were being reduced and eliminated as President Roosevelt prepared for the possibility of U.S. entry into this struggle. As cartoonists and other wags noted of Roosevelt's rhetoric, "Dr. Win the War" was taking precedence over "Dr. Fight the Depression." Furthermore, as Dr. Win the War began his "treatments," the employment picture for white people finally brightened. The economy moved forward smartly, but none of this growth made great impact in the black ghettoes, and black unemployment remained stubbornly high. If indeed the United States entered war, the impact on the School of Religion would be damaging. Mays's best students would be drafted out of their study carrels, and potential recruits for his school would not even come because of the draft and volunteering. In many ways and for many reasons, the School of Religion in 1940 was as much a stepchild at Howard as it had been when the tedious succession of indifferent white presidents held sway fifty years before President Johnson arrived on scene. Mays appreciated what Johnson had helped him to get done, but lately it seemed that the president was celebrating as if the major work were all over.[54]

Thus pulled by conflicted emotions, Bennie Mays strained forward to improve the many things still wanting at the Howard University School of Religion. He did feel some sense of accomplishment, but as a proper man of *megalosukos,* he did know above all that this was not the time to rest in the shade and look back at the long way he had come. He knew that this was the time to press forward. He knew also that it would be harder and harder to do so because he saw little evidence that Dr. Johnson intended much more improvement for the School of Religion.

In terms of his personal magnificence, however, Bennie Mays's star was still ascending. He shone brightly among the New Negroes in Dee Cee, brightly enough to be noted many places north and south of the Potomac River. It is not recorded exactly when, but sometime in January 1940, he and Sadie Mays entertained a visitor who changed the course of their lives. In some secrecy John Hervey Wheeler of the board of trustees of Morehouse College asked to call on the Mayses at their home on a confidential matter. When he arrived and settled into a seat in their living room, Wheeler said what the Mayses—and all talented tenth readers of the *Pittsburgh Courier*—already knew: Morehouse needed a new president, and a search was underway. Wheeler talked candidly about problems at the House, its small endowment, its small enrollment, the poverty of many of its students, and the extreme difficulty of getting students to make tuition payments in timely fashion or to repay loans from the college. Wheeler also talked about the school's possibilities, above all its tradition of developing leaders not only for the Deep South but for the nation. Bennie Mays could assure Wheeler that his own memories of a season teaching at the House were golden, above all since it was there that he had worked alongside John Hope and had coached James Madison Nabrit and Howard Thurman in debate. Wheeler inquired if Bennie Mays would be interested in taking the presidency, and the Howard dean answered affirmatively. Wheeler then cautioned the couple to say nothing about this conversation, and he also warned them against any assumption that the presidency would be offered. After Wheeler left, Mays later recorded, he was convinced he would not be offered the presidency, but Sadie Mays was quite sure it would be offered.[55]

A considerable time did pass, but on May 10 the Morehouse trustees, probably meeting in New York, voted to offer the presidency to Bennie Mays. Trustee Trevor Arnett, onetime member of the Rockefeller-funded General Education Board and a man with whom the Mayses had often dealt on professional matters, made a telephone call announcing the board decision. Trustee president Kendall Weisiger sent a formal letter, apparently on May 30. Largely because of Sadie Mays's "intuition," Bennie Mays had been thinking about how to respond to such an offer since at least February, and thus he could and did respond both warmly and with great precision. On May 31 he Mays sent a note of conditional acceptance, contingent on agreement with the trustees about six points. First point was the acceptance of his sabbatical year in South Africa for the YMCA; the next five points had to do with structure and finances at Morehouse with regard to its relationship to the Atlanta University system, with regard to its independent governance, and with regard to a major reform that would bring the college treasurer into college infrastructure answerable to the college president. The Mayses were relying on Wheeler's own strictures about secrecy to give all concerned plenty of time to negotiate particularities of detail.[56]

Negotiations were not simple, and time and quiet were needed, especially since the Morehouse trustees were a heavily white and heavily New York group of Spelmans and Rockefellers and other wealthy northern philanthropists. One black trustee, Hattie Rutherford Watson, was concerned primarily with Spelman, the college for women with which Morehouse had an interlocking trustee structure, but she was a close student of educational policy, being married to the reformist Deep South educator John Brown Watson. She was also a close student of college and other finances, being the child of a talented tenth Dee Cee legal accountant who was the first black man to preside over the legalities and bookkeeping of a major liquidation of a failed insurance company, which was otherwise white owned and white run. Hattie Watson took careful notes on proceedings and could share with Bennie and Sadie Mays that most of the businessmen on the board of trustees agreed with the dean's observations and accepted his conditions. She could and did share with the couple that some ministers on the board were suspicious of Mays's University of Chicago training and that other ministers were known as "sky pilots" because of their refusal to pay attention to the issues of budgets, endowments, enrollment, and other "earthly and mundane things." Getting all stakeholders together physically in one place was a challenge, and getting all stakeholders together in a basic sense of agreement was a time consuming, though not particularly contentious, affair.[57]

Any hopes for careful and quiet negotiations were destroyed by the friendliest of nemeses, Robert Lee Vann, who on June 29 proclaimed in the pages of his *Pittsburgh Courier* that Bennie Mays was the new president of Morehouse. Vann evidently had a good source on the board and wrote about the trustee's call; on the issue of the negotiations, Vann either did not know much or found it too tedious to describe for his readers. In that world of some half-million black readers, Vann had "scooped" his fellow black publishers, and he had even scooped liberal white journalists, who might find such things newsworthy for the *New York Post* or the *Cleveland Plain Dealer*. Mostly what Vann did cemented the deal. Mays could hardly walk from the job now without appearing to be a hopelessly self-absorbed careerist angling for every nickel, and the trustees could hardly break off negotiations without appearing to be captives of "sky pilots" and reactionaries.[58]

Finally there really was not much to consider. Bennie and Sadie Mays strained at their tethers in Dee Cee. Morehouse offered marvelous opportunities, especially for one like Sadie who, doomed to childlessness, seemed almost made in heaven for the guiding role of first lady on a campus of young men. Bennie Mays's fund-raising might be constricted at Howard, but he would be the main fund-raiser at Morehouse. Above all, there would be no president above him to frustrate his plans. The academic year 1940–41 would be based on travel and on-site reform in apartheid-ridden South Africa in preparation for a long career in the Jim Crow-ridden Deep South.

IN MY FATHER'S HOUSE

1940–1947

Bennie and Sadie Mays had been shocked to find the sad state of affairs at Howard University's School of Religion in 1934. Part of their dismay was caused by the way in which the unkempt Douglass Building sagged and slumped in the midst of a campus otherwise building happily through campaigns sponsored by Harold Ickes and the first New Deal. Imagine then their sensations as they moved their possessions to Atlanta in order to live and work at the much vaunted Morehouse! It had been sixteen years since Bennie Mays had lived in a dormitory room and instructed mathematics at Morehouse, and his fond memories of what he had found then were in bitter contrast to what he found now. Before agreeing to be president he had looked hard at the college's accounting books, and he had made an inspection of the physical plant, concluding that much work—long, tedious, and hard work—stretched ahead for the next president in the purely physical and material plane of life. Yet, when the couple actually occupied the president's house and took up residence and duties, things looked gloomier than when they were being pulled by *Pittsburgh Courier* cheerleading and Sadie Mays's "intuition" and pushed by Dr. Mordedai Johnson's "stepchild" treatment of the Howard University School of Religion.

Unlike at Howard, nothing was being built at Morehouse in 1940. A redoubtable faculty servant, theologian Charles DuBois Hubert, had stepped in as acting president during the crisis occasioned by the grave illness and retirement of President Samuel Howard Archer in 1937. Hubert could report that Archer was a fine leader and teacher of men, as all had presumed, but he had been no student of financing an institution of higher education; and Hubert had inherited paper mountains of uncollectible student bills and even larger mountains of outstanding debts. Hubert was relieved to hand over these problems to the new president, pledging his full support to Bennie Mays even while bluntly passing on the bad news. For his part the ill and weakened Archer gave Bennie Mays a full report on the ill and weakened institution that he had left.[1]

During the last season of Dr. Archer's presidency, "loyal House alumnus" and fearless Deep South educational leader John Brown Watson had sent in a blistering note after a long weekend visit to his "beloved alma mater." He said that the dormitories and the classrooms were not maintained and that student comportment was not fitting for African American scholars; rather, he wrote, "you will know that NIGGERS [*sic*] live here." Moreover, Watson warned anyone who would listen, as long as "sky pilot" ministers and disengaged old, white millionaires supervised the place, Morehouse would and could produce nothing substantive, nothing good. Bennie Mays did not use the word "nigger" even in intimate correspondence, and he disagreed with Watson's dismal forecast about private black schools, but he otherwise found that Watson had painted a true picture.[2] Where Dean Mays had presided over a stepchild on a campus of privileged heirs at Howard, President Mays had come to preside over a stepchild campus at Morehouse.

For all that, it was still "the House." As he recalled fondly from his stint teaching mathematics there, the King James translation of the Bible called heaven "my father's house" in which there were "many mansions." The imagery was vital to Mays in his preaching, especially in "reaching back" to the non-scholarly lay people with whom he sought the "bond of souls." The House, fallen on hard times or not, was still the home of striving New Negro men who intended to become fathers of a New Negro talented tenth that would lead all people of all colors and all ethnic groups to justice and peace in the United States—with a starting point in the capital of the modern South.[3]

Facing "so much with so little and so few," as he later recalled, Bennie Mays approached things like a proper University of Chicago social scientist. Gathering his data, he identified four overarching goals for the House, and then under each guiding goal he established measurable, indeed quantifiable, objectives to mark progress toward it. The first goal had been established by the American Baptist Home Mission Society shortly after the end of the Civil War in a church basement in Augusta, Georgia, when the school was founded as Baptist College: the training of men who would march in the first ranks of the talented tenth, leading the race to become New Negroes. Since the relocation of the college to Atlanta and the renaming of it in 1911, such men had always been called Morehouse men. In fact Dr. Mordecai Johnson had received his baccalaureate degree with highest honors in that first year that the Baptist College was called Morehouse. Morehouse men such as Doctors Mordecai Johnson, John Brown Watson, John Hope, and Howard Thurman were as sorely needed now as they were at any time in southern history, even considering the grave crisis in leadership created after the Civil War by sudden freedom and sudden citizenship. The second goal was an enrollment sufficient to produce such leaders at the Atlanta college. Enrollment had drifted gradually down toward a couple hundred students, and not all were well qualified or pursuing their degrees in orderly fashion. The third goal was an endowment that would enable the school to give scholarships and other assistance to members of the talented tenth who, like young Bennie Mays, did not have the wherewithal to pay the Morehouse tuition and expenses. The endowment was barely over one million dollars; it was unwisely invested; and scholarship money sometimes came from the operating budget and sometimes came from the principal of the endowment. Despite its connections with the Rockefeller family finances, the House had an endowment that was small, diminishing, and lacking any guarantee that a dedicated endowment would survive at all. The fourth goal was for Morehouse College to become a full partner in the consolidated Atlanta University system, largely created by—and for some years presided over by—John Hope, once president of the House. In 1940, with John Hope deceased, Samuel Howard Archer deathly ill, and Rufus Clement focusing on the total Atlanta University system of black colleges and universities, Morehouse was distinctly the junior partner among the member institutions, whose consolidation was after all the dream child of Morehouse men.[4]

The making of Morehouse men could be broken down specifically into three subsets: better physicians, better attorneys, and better ministers. Of course it was necessary for all graduates of the House to lead, but physicians, attorneys, and ministers were the necessary *and* the sufficient portions of Bennie Mays's mission. The House did not actually train professional physicians, attorneys, and ministers, rather it fed the professional schools for African Americans: Howard University and Meharry College of Fisk University in Nashville. It also fed students to a handful of liberal northern institutions willing to accept fully qualified black applicants into their professional programs. Having presided over and having won accreditation for a professional graduate school in religion at Howard, Bennie Mays knew from painful experience what happened when well-meaning black colleges sent forward men who were not prepared for the rigors of the next level of study and scholarship. He knew too how much difficulty Charles Hamilton Houston had encountered with similarly well-meaning black college deans and presidents who had sent forward poorly prepared men for the serious study of the law.

The physicians were most profoundly needed, and it was their training that was most problematical. The expenses of a law library or a divinity school library, and the salaries for law professors and for theologians were scant compared to the expenses of the laboratories, the professional journals, the salaries of teaching physicians, and above all the research hospitals attached to Howard or Meharry. Also medical students studied much longer than did students of law or students of divinity. At a great northern institution, to give a chair of study for six years to a badly trained African American, who then had to leave the program and abandon his studies, was to waste precious resources in a way not likely to be forgotten. President Mays had to be able to assure admissions committees at those few northern institutions that his graduates had mastered the principles in biology, chemistry, and higher mathematics and had established the practices of long and steady hours of applied study and work to survive the rigors of medical training. The same assurances had to be given to the committees at Meharry and at Howard, but those committees after all were brothers of the blood who could be forgiving of the occasional error in a way not to be expected at the University of Rochester, Brown University, or Case Western Reserve University. Nowhere was *megalosukos,* or *magnanimatatum,* more vital than in the reputation for preparedness for a Morehouse man arrived for study among brilliant white northerners at a medical school with its own research and teaching hospital.

Despite or even because of these problems, it was physicians who were most needed among the Morehouse men, and they were needed for several reasons. More than any other group, the physicians would earn large salaries and thus would have more disposable income than other Morehouse men, and they could assist the House and other charitable and reformist works such as the Urban League, the Federal Council of Churches, and the Y. At the level of mission, the physicians could go into segregated communities, especially in the Deep South, and bring decent health care to rural communities where white doctors would not deal with black injuries and illnesses. Indeed, in such remote communities, there were white doctors such as Dr. Wallace Payne, whose competence was doubted and who were as likely to bring violence on black children as to provide any care. In Bennie Mays's image of the Morehouse man, and in what ensued over the decades, it was really the physician who best embodied everything that the new president wanted for and from his charges. For President Mays, the physician who started academical training at Morehouse must emerge as a believing Christian and believing citizen who gives back to the black community. Very much at play—and fully credited to him—was Dr. Aubrey's image of the scholar with the "bond of souls" reaching forward to develop the newest techniques and gain the latest knowledge while reaching back to help those in the community who lacked knowledge and basic services.

Only some serious financial help with scholarships for worthy premedical students could possibly enable Morehouse College to produce the kind of serving physician that President Mays demanded. In finding money for the expensive apparatus to teach the premedical students and finding money to pay the right biologists and chemists to train them, Mays had to raise tuition, but then he had to scramble to find scholarship money to provide most of those academically worthy but financially strapped premedical students. In that quest, he surprised himself by approaching none other than Margaret Mitchell, author of the 1936 novel *Gone with the Wind* and legatee of its 1939 cinematic version, which immortalized actors Clark Gable and Vivian Leigh but also romanticized slavery and provided disastrous images of Reconstruction, when a few African Americans politicos enjoyed a modicum of power based on black suffrage. Mitchell did not create the stereotypes, but in her novel and in the cinema based on her novel, slaves were depicted as well-treated and happy folk in a benevolent thralldom where no Henry Hazel Mays or his overseer S. C. Deal beat or raped them. Her novel's depiction of freed slaves was even more disastrous, showing them as completely irresponsible and occasionally bestial; and the cinematic portrayal of the streets of Atlanta given over to drunken thieves and rapists was as memorable as anything Bennie Mays had seen on the screen since that terrible evening back in Lewiston, Maine, when he squirmed amongst an appreciative white crowd reveling in images of the bestial and virulent freedmen in *The Birth of a Nation.* Over time Bennie Mays was pleased to see historians revising images of slavery to convince at least some thoughtful white southerners that the institution was not beneficent; but no amount of scholarship could budge the majority-white opinion that Reconstruction was a time of irresponsible and even dangerous black rascality at the freedmen's first opportunities to vote and serve. This Margaret Mitchell, who had so wounded black people with her false portrayals, Bennie Mays now approached secretly, and he did so by suggesting to her that her preference for Jim Crow could be best served by helping Morehouse College.[5]

An astute biographer of Margaret Mitchell has shown her to be something of a rebel in Atlanta and has pointed out that elements of her novel are quite rebellious, especially her portrayal of the iconoclast and materialist Scarlett O'Hara, who defies the softness and dependency expected of the southern lady. But the same could be said for Jessie Daniel Ames of antilynching campaigns, and Bennie Mays had found Ames to be a major obstacle in matters of integrated education. Mitchell had money and an inclination to help African Americans so long as they remained separated from her white people; rebellious inclinations on some scores to the contrary, the novelist harbored profound doubts about black competency in an integrated setting. Approaching her discreetly, Mays told her that there were not enough black physicians to care for black patients, forcing an unwanted integration in services onto white physicians and white patients. Increasing the number of black physicians, he told Mitchell, would alleviate pressures for integration, leaving white physicians to treat Mitchell's people but still ensuring that qualified care could be provided

Bennie Mays's people. In this context Mays said nothing about integration as a favored goal for the development of the New Negro. Instead he approached her with the assumption that all people of all colors deserved decent health care, and he found to his relief that she fully agreed. He also understood that Mitchell was a shrewd enough businessperson not to throw her charitable gifts to the irresponsible. He presented her with a carefully laid-out plan for establishing scholarship endowments whose interest return was dedicated to financial aid for qualified black premedical students, and he promised to show her good results as the premedical students won admission to and earned medical degrees from Meharry, Howard, and certain liberal universities "at the Far North." Above all, he assured her, he would respect her wish for anonymity and privacy in the matter. He would not associate her name in a public way with a black institution, nor would he reveal her identity to other black fund-raisers; the last promise being especially easy to keep, since he did not want competition for her funds.[6]

Margaret Mitchell enthusiastically supported this plan, albeit in complete anonymity, and she was personally responsible for enabling at least fifty Morehouse men to become qualified and competent physicians. Her death in a traffic accident in 1949 ended her personal involvement, but by then a solid base had been established for such financial help to men of the House, and other benefactors could be successfully approached by pointing to the good performance of Morehouse graduates. In his memorable work as "schoolmaster to Negro leaders," Bennie Mays was most successful with the physicians, who became the living symbol of Morehouse men who were able to inspire boys in the most remote southern villages and to make some useful influence on at least a few white souls even in the most benighted of Deep South communities. During Mays's tenure at the House, the doctors and dentists among his alumni reached 350, better than a dozen per graduating class—and in graduating classes whose total number was never larger than three hundred and sometimes was as low as fifty. Particularly prominent were Peter Chatard, who earned the M.D. in surgery from the University of Rochester and became a plastic surgeon with a much-respected clinic in Seattle, Washington; and Henry Wendell Foster, Jr., one of the first African Americans to earn the M.D. in obstetrics from the University of Arkansas and who then became head of obstetrics and gynecology at Meharry as well as presidential adviser on medicine to President Lyndon Baines Johnson in 1965–68, and then medical adviser to President William Jefferson Clinton in 1995, after failing to win Senate approval to be surgeon general; and David Satcher, who earned the M.D. at Case Western Reserve University and became president of Meharry for seventeen years before becoming the first African American surgeon general of the United States in 1998. In fairly short order then, Bennie Mays had accomplished what he wanted with the premedical training program. In a major 1955 Harvard University study, it was found that most Meharry medical students came from Morehouse, that the House was number three in producing Howard medical students, and that Morehouse men were by far the largest number of black enrollees at northern medical colleges.[7]

In molding Morehouse men, producing ministers and attorneys was financially much less of a challenge than finding the financial wherewithal to produce candidates for medical school. In fact Morehouse College had never stopped producing attorneys and ministers, even and especially in the declining years of President Archer. The ranks of attorneys and pastors included many Morehouse men emerging in every decade of the college's operation in Atlanta. Bennie Mays the young mathematics instructor had coached in debate the future theologian Howard Thurman and the future attorney and jurist James Madison Nabrit; and he had been able to look on with satisfaction as the latter became a highly successful attorney, legal scholar, and college administrator and as the former flourished as preacher and teacher of preachers after Mays hired him at Howard. Yet, Bennie Mays suspected that there might be slippage, and that the quality of the preparation for these men might have dropped in the most recent years. He was determined to bring a Phi Beta Kappa chapter to the House. Doing so would give both students and faculty nationwide recognition—and continuing expectations nationwide of performances on both sides of the professorial desks. However, Phi Beta Kappa would not authorize a campus chapter until Bennie Mays brought the financial state of the House into proper order, and it also required a general improvement in the number of earned Ph.D.s on the faculty—not doctor of education (Ed.D.) degrees and not the honorary degrees sported by some beloved professors and administrators and ministers. Phi Beta Kappa also required evidence of publishing scholarship, something once taken for granted at every member institution of the entire Atlanta University system in the days of W. E. B. Du Bois, young Rayford Wittingham Logan, and John Hope, but now something wanting in most departments at Morehouse.

In other words the new president announced that the faculty members would have to show tangible proof of their scholarly backgrounds and their scholarly careers: earned Ph.D.s and publications in scholarly and refereed academical journals. Finding and promoting such high-quality scholars for the professoriat should then attract a higher quality of applicant for study at Morehouse. As he explored everything that was involved in bringing a Phi Beta Kappa chapter to Morehouse, some old racist personal wounds were uncovered and reopened yet again. At Bates College years ago, Bennie Mays had been denied entry into Phi Beta Kappa despite the heroic efforts of George Millett Chase. Mays was awarded his own key at approximately the same time the

University of Chicago had awarded him the Ph.D., as if only by winning approval at the world's greatest graduate-training center could a black man force recognition from the white New England school. Those selfsame forces of racism haunted him again. Black schools did not have Phi Beta Kappa chapters. Indeed not all Georgia's white schools had chapters at their privileged Jim Crow campuses. In that day only the University of Georgia, Emory University, and the well-heeled Presbyterian women's school Agnes Scott had been awarded chapters.[8]

As he studied the processes of institutional application, Bennie Mays could see why southern black colleges made poor candidates for the honor. More than half of a college's faculty needed to hold earned Ph.D.s, and President Mays found that at Morehouse barely a third of the professors held this academic doctorate. In fact Fisk and Morehouse still had some instructors who held only baccalaureate degrees, something unheard of at the University of Chicago, Bates College, or even across town at Agnes Scott College. Mays came to realize that having a Phi Beta Kappa chapter was an important long-term goal, one that could inform his actions in hiring, promoting, and firing. But it was truly long term, and he reconciled himself to a campaign not of semesters or even of academic years but of decades.[9]

Crucial to this long-running campaign was his faculty, and as he took a hardheaded University of Chicago social scientist's look at his faculty, what struck him the most was their low pay. After all, the Chicago economists, whether left wing or right wing, all insisted that "you get what you pay for." The House paid little, and in at least certain cases it got little in return. Fortunately Bennie Mays made friends early with Florence Reed, a neo-abolitionist and inspirational New Yorker who ran Spelman College. Talking with her and with Hattie Rutherford Watson, Mays looked at the compensation for the Spelman faculty, and he could see why that sister faculty was superior to the staff at Morehouse. The compensation at Spelman was as follows: an instructor holding a master's but with no experience earned $3,500 to $3,800; an assistant professor with one year's experience beyond earning a master's, $3,900–$4,400; an associate professor who had served five years as an assistant professor and "showed evidence of doing research," $4,500–$5,400; and a full professor who held a Ph.D., had served seven years, and showed "evidence of doing research," $5,500. In that day Spelman's salaries were not far from southern white-school salaries. (Although projected into the twenty-first century, the lower ranking professors barely earned 80 percent of today's modest South Atlantic small-college scale adjusted for inflation; and the full professors earned barely 58 percent of that same scale adjusted for inflation.) The Spelman faculty was demonstrably better off than the men and women at most small, liberal arts colleges of the region, regardless of historical racial composition. Also

Florence Reed, president of Spelman College, and Benjamin Mays.
Courtesy of the Moorland-Spingarn Research Center, Howard University.

Spelman faculty benefited from the annuity pension Teachers Insurance and Annuity Association (TIAA), created by Andrew Carnegie; but TIAA, while available at the House, was not then institutionalized with regular matching contributions from the college.[10]

By contradistinction the pay for Morehouse faculty members was thousands of dollars beneath Spelman at each range—with some full professors making do on a few thousand per year, and one instructor actually receiving only nine hundred dollars. Even worse, there seemed to be little system for measuring years of service in grade, evaluating teaching, or demonstrating evidence of research and publication. As Mays began to search for and to cultivate donors whose gifts could improve Morehouse, he talked passionately to such benefactors about better pay for his faculty. He told his new faculty he would pay them more, but that he would expect more in return. He also told them he was imposing a rational system for tenure, promotion, and academic advancement up the ladder of rank. In many cases Mays's procedures resulted in anger when long-serving instructors who considered themselves ready for advancement and a raise were told that their educational training was wanting, because they lacked the Ph.D. Most controversial of all, Mays with his University of Chicago expectations told some who held the Ph.D. and had served seven years that their complete lack of publications made them ineligible for promotion until such time as they did publish in a scholarly venue.

News of these standards went down hard with the veteran faculty, and initially President Mays was no more popular in Atlanta than he had found President Johnson to be at Howard. He stuck with his standards, however, and he was eventually able to lure good faculty members. Moreover he was able to get from those faculty members the good scholarship and the good teaching he demanded. Among veterans, Charles DuBois Hubert and George Denis Sale Kelsey published in refereed journals and taught their students—especially Otis Moss, Jr.; Lerone Bennett, Jr.; Floyd McKissick; Harvey E. Beech; and M. L. King (then Michael, later changing his name to Martin Luther, Jr.) to do serious research and writing while the professors and their young charges were active in protesting Jim Crow and getting Atlanta black people to vote. Kelsey, who had interrupted Ph.D. studies in divinity at Yale University in order to help out his mentor, Dr. Hubert, was especially pleased to see that he could be rewarded for completing his doctorate and rewarded again for publishing his dissertation on social ethics among southern Baptists. Hubert labored nobly for civil rights and for improving scholarship, and the new president had formal occasion to memorialize both men in special addresses in which he characteristically drew on Periclean traditions to salute them and to "exhort the living to emulation of the virtue of the deceased."[11]

Given the reality that only a few institutions offered black students the chance to earn a Ph.D., Bennie Mays could proceed only by hiring at least some white scholars. After his own long years of being denied for various honors and opportunities because of his skin color, the president set his face like flint against any black scholar, trustee, friend of the college, or other associate who dared to complain about the white hue of some of the new staff. Transition for some faculty members was painful, as they took on white colleagues, as well as expectations of scholarly production and better instruction, but were compelled to wait several seasons for promised increases in salaries. Despite some awkwardness and some almost comic moments, instruction at Morehouse improved by all qualitative and quantitative measures. By judicious hiring and firing and by imposing challenging but obvious and open standards for promotion, Bennie Mays was able to build a worthy faculty, one that could reach back to pull forward their young student charges and still reach forward to compete with the best scholars at Howard, Fisk, Spelman, and in some cases at predominantly white institutions of some privilege.

Gradually building a good faculty, Mays set about bringing his teachers enough good students to teach. He was bold if not reckless in his actions to raise enrollment and thus achieve his second overarching goal. Initially enrollments had slipped because Morehouse was too expensive for many black youth in New Deal days, and neither Dr. Archer nor Dr. Hubert had been able to find enough donors for the many needed scholarships. By midwinter of 1941–42, however, enrollment was sapped by a different problem. Now still another world war threatened enrollment figures. Although Mays had not thought all the way through the full implications of the rise of the racist Axis of fascists and the possible need for war to stop them, by December 7, 1941, Bennie Mays had to face squarely the reality of another terrible war. He would support this war despite his attraction to Gandhian pacifism because the Axis seemed bent on destroying minority races and ethnic groups if left unchecked. Despite his speeches and reflections, sincere as they were throughout the 1930s, in this phase of his intellectual development, he still believed that there were some "just wars," that this war against Hitler, Tojo, and Mussolini was just. He thus remained more a student of Thomas Aquinas than of Gandhi. To the point for the House, World War II involved yet another draft of men of military age, and black men of military age were also men of college age. Good students were being drafted out of Morehouse or even before they could apply for admission there. Mays boldly decided to recruit for the House young men who were too young for the army or the navy. He came to believe that fifteen-year-old boys of good will in proper environment could manage college—and indeed could flourish there.[12]

Bennie and Sadie Mays personally recruited some of these young men, most famously the teenaged M. L. King, son of Morehouse alumnus and Atlanta minister M. L. King, Sr. Approaching the prominent Atlantan, the Mayses persuaded "Daddy King" that young Michael was a good candidate to get started early in college work. The fifteen-year-old was duly enrolled. Over his time of study at the House, M. L. King was persuaded by the "schoolmaster" himself to abandon his plans for law school and enter the ministry, proof that President Mays was not putting his divinity studies second to law and medicine even if the House needed to increase production of doctors and lawyers. Others who came in during World War II included the journalist, publisher, and popularizer of black history, Lerone Bennett, Jr., who hailed from the Mississippi Delta; the journalist Robert E. Johnson, who, after earning a master's degree in journalism from Syracuse University in 1952, eventually became associate publisher and executive editor of *Jet*, a popular magazine founded by the successful black publisher John H. Johnson in 1951; and North Carolina activists Floyd McKissick and Harvey E. Beech, who became reformist attorneys. With this single step, Morehouse gained a group of hardworking and challenging students whose numbers pushed enrollment up to five hundred and who gave and took in the classroom in a way that reinvigorated most of the teaching faculty. There were challenges in the dormitories as much younger teenagers took their places alongside students who had reached their majority, and there were challenges in the classrooms as the bright and inquisitive, but unevenly prepared, scholars met the leavening that comes to such yeasty elements in a uniform general-education core of liberal arts curriculum. Harvey Beech did not own pajamas and had never seen them until a kindly upperclassman gave him a pair. Some boys drifted into religion classes with the idea of gaining a minister's deferment from the military draft, and these young scholars were astonished to discover that they were expected to learn to preach. For all that, this wartime group acquitted themselves quite well as students and spectacularly well as alumni. Bennie Mays was able to attain an eight-year funding for scholarships for the early-admit students from the Ford Foundation. When that grant expired, he was able to fund such early-admit scholarships—some 194 of them from 1948 to his retirement in 1967—through the generosity of trustee Charles E. Merrill, Jr.[13]

Beyond the campus, the experiment—also conducted in less thoroughgoing ways at white institutions—raised important questions about the appropriate age for serious academic challenge in learning to write and to speak, conducting laboratory research in applied sciences, studying higher mathematics, and discussing weighty philosophical and theological issues. Subsequent educational experiments in such programs as the international baccalaureate studies, concurrent enrollment in high schools and colleges for certain courses, advanced placement in some secondary schools with college-level exit examinations, governor's schools for increasing challenges for public-school students, and charter schools have essentially reaffirmed the wisdom of a step taken at Morehouse as much out of desperation and genius as from planning and forethought. Later Bennie Mays, while presiding over the Atlanta Board of Education throughout the 1970s, came to rue most of those programs conducted on behalf of white children in the most segregated schools of a major city, when he himself had presided over the granddaddy of such experiments and had done so for black students and on pennies before the birth of most of the white education leaders in a self-consciously new era of schooling for the gifted and talented.[14]

Benjamin Mays (right) at a Morehouse commencement with Wall Street financier Charles E. Merrill (left). Courtesy of the Moorland-Spingarn Research Center, Howard University.

All students were treated in a radically new way with regard to their finances. Although sympathetic with the poverty he remembered vividly from his own teenaged years and although dedicated to finding scholarship money for his charges, Bennie Mays had no truck with students who committed themselves to a payment plan and then failed to pay up. Among his first actions and among his actions continued longest was a tightening down of the bill accounting and collecting system for tuition, room and board, and books and equipment fees. Fred Gassett, longtime bursar at Morehouse, was delighted to cooperate by bringing the books into order and throwing out the "deadbeats." Gassett, who was so light skinned that several students presumed he was white, could be a formidable character for a young fellow who was arrears in his payments. Actually Gassett was also kindly and helpful and often found jobs for those who could not meet their payments. In many cases Gassett, with Mays's approval, worked out alternative payment plans for many destitute but sincere scholars. Yet the bills did have to be paid, and dozens of delinquent debtors who could not or would not work for and with Fred Gassett were turned out of the House. Disgruntled students, parents, some faculty, some administrators, and alumni began to call the president "Buck Benny"—as Mays later recorded in his memoir. The nickname was nasty. The memoir writer noted that the sobriquet referred to his obsession with dollars or "bucks." What he did not note is a deeper slice into the skin and psyche of the New Negro. Buck was country-white talk for a young and virile black man (sometimes rendered "buckra" or other variants), and the name always operated among white southerners as an insult intended to do the same harm as "nigger" or "jungle bunny" or "black ape." Among black people, "buckra" was shorthand for "belt buckle," and certain authorities were never to be looked at in the eye, only at the belt buckle. For white people, "buck" and "buckra" were derisive; for the black people the terms were much resented. Famously dark and tall and powerful in his youth, Bennie Mays had heard himself called "buck" before; he had heard it from people of both races. Drawing on his reading and reflection on Marcus Aurelius, he resolved always to keep his temper and never allow others to see how the words hurt. Drawing on Gandhi if not for a response to Hitler and war, then at least for a response to societal interaction, he resolved never to label other people with such words. It took Sadie Mays's kind counsel of her besieged husband at home and Sadie Mays's equally kind counsel of aggrieved young men—in combination with Fred Gassett's many make-work jobs—to banish the term "Buck Benny" from the talk in the halls and on the lawn.[15]

In any case, from desperate beginnings in 1940, Bennie Mays in 1967 could hand over an institution with more than 1,000 students—whom Morehouse wanted and who themselves wanted to be at Morehouse—and each student was either able to pay full fare of actual cost or able to attain scholarship help from the endowment. Anybody looking at Morehouse in 1940 could conclude at once that the place needed more students. Nevertheless it should be marked that Bennie Mays was quite perceptive in choosing the magic number of 1,000 for the size of his student body. By the end of World War II, Morehouse counted 418 full-tuition payments, more than double such actual payments per annum before the war. Also there were 230 newly admitted students ready for matriculation in fall 1946. However, rather than celebrate an enrollment of 500 or 600 students, Bennie Mays insisted on a target of 1,000 full-tuition payment students, even though such a number could only be accommodated by building more dormitory and classroom space. It was the right size for the dimensions of what he wanted in liberal-arts instruction at the House, and it was a specific size affirmed by a legion of scholars working in a major study financed by the Carnegie Foundation fully four decades later.[16]

To maintain a college endowment properly and to build it significantly, as had been done at Spelman and at Howard, Bennie Mays had to go on the road, specifically the railroad. He estimated that he spoke at least thirty times per year outside the Atlanta area, and he reached most of those destinations on the Southern Railroad, riding in Jim Crow discomfort until he could reach Dee Cee or St. Louis, where the Jim Crow procedures were dropped for passengers heading north and west. Given his pride and his intent to be a New Negro fighting for the "Double V"—victory over fascism abroad and victory over racism at home—these trips became draining emotionally. He often fell into disputes with white passengers or with sable Pullman porters who valued their job security over the rights of black passengers. When he arrived at his northern speaking destinations—Cleveland, Manhattan, Chicago or Detroit—Bennie Mays lived a different kind of life, toasting millionaires on Houston Avenue or at the 21 Club in Manhattan and shopping for expensive shoes and suits in the best shops in Chicago. The speeches supplemented his income and indirectly endowed Morehouse. On a remarkably small base salary of less than $5,000 per annum, Bennie Mays often earned an additional sum of $2,500 to $3,000; yet his annual charitable giving was seldom less than $2,500 to $3,000, suggesting that his speaking fees essentially went right back to the House. In fact he could report to donors and potential donors that he and Sadie Mays had sold their most valuable possession, a piece of real estate in Dee Cee, and had donated the sales receipts to a matching fund in a major endowment campaign. It was an extreme act, but one true to the conception of the magnificent man dedicated to his mission at Morehouse.[17]

Mays's travels also brought new donors to the House and occasionally added new trustees, hard-driving financiers and industrialists who leavened the "sky pilots" who fretted that Bennie Mays was too modernist to be a Baptist, that he was too often gone from campus, and that he was too dangerously activist in politics. Besides Margaret Mitchell, generous donors included F. A. Toomer, Calvin Singleton, Dr. and Mrs. Nathaniel P. Tillman, and the renowned financier and philanthropist Julius Rosenwald, a Jew whom Bennie and Sadie always mentioned favorably if their black friends made anti-Semitic remarks. Besides members of the Rockefeller and Spelman families who sat on boards at Morehouse and at Spelman, Bennie Mays was pleased to bring aboard Wall Street financiers: Charles E. Merrill, Jr., head of the giant brokerage firm Merrill Lynch; and from the Danforth Foundation, founder William Danforth, his daughter, and his grandson. Despite his misgivings, Bennie Mays also developed and maintained warm relationships with Will Winton Alexander—the best-known white-liberal Atlantan of a previous era, now removed to semiretirement in Chapel Hill, North Carolina. Never entirely convinced that Alexander was a genuine civil rights man who respected the aspirations of the New Negro, Bennie Mays yet found Alexander indispensable in opening doors to benefactors for the House. The result was that Mays could raise funds for major construction, especially for dormitories to house his rapidly growing enrollment, but also for building facilities, even for the Maroon Tiger footballers whose role in a good school he continued to doubt since his beloved University of Chicago had done so well by abandoning gridiron play altogether and since his alma mater Bates College had done so well by ceasing to give athletic scholarships while dramatically deemphasizing football and other sports. Coaches and players generally doubted that Bennie and Sadie Mays liked football and basketball, but anyone attending a contest at the handsome facilities would never guess it. The corpus of the enrollment proper, which he kept strictly separated from any capital campaign funds raised for dormitories or stadia, grew at a steady rate— and did so at a time when stock market returns were low because of low interest rates and small-investor fears of a return of the great crash of October 1929. Although Mays's successor, Hugh Gloster, later eclipsed all Mays's fund-raising accomplishments, Mays did record a remarkable twenty-seven-season record of endowment growth greater than inflation and greater than typical returns on investments for the period 1940–67. He could make such a record only by steady travel, persistent and patient development of friendships with wealthy white people, and astute investment of the funds by the team of endowment managers and investment experts that he employed from the companies of Rosenwald, the Danforths, and Merrill.[18]

The new friends among the trustees, at least some of them, expressed wisdom too when the classicist president forgot the Greek maxim to do all things in moderation. Finally admitting to Samuel L. Spears and to F. A. Toomer that he was "quite certain that I have been driving too hard" and was in fact "beginning to feel the strain," Dr. Mays submitted to orders from counsel—likely

Rosenwald, Merrill, and almost surely Hattie Rutherford Watson—and agreed to limit long trips per year to thirty, to make no speaking appointments farther ahead than three months, and to take a total of at least four weeks vacation each year. Although this was still a crushing schedule, especially considering his many engagements at black Baptist and Methodist churches within driving distance of Atlanta, "local" visits not counting as part of his quota of thirty, Bennie Mays restored enough classical moderation to his presidency to be able to do the job over three different and trying decades instead of wearing himself out in one hectic and heroic spurt of seven fat years.[19]

To achieve the final goal of full partnership in the Atlanta University system involved one in problematical ironies, not least the contrasting legacies of John Hope, the onetime Morehouse president who had largely created and then for long years had operated the unique system. Clark College, Spelman College, Morehouse College, Morris Brown College, and Atlanta University were close enough to each other in distance and in mission to create one coordinated system in which certain resources belonged in common to all members. At the foundational level, all schools got their heat in wintertime from one integrated steam-pipe network, and these savings, while appreciated in the heady times of the 1920s, were essential in the hard times of the Great Depression. A student or faculty library card for any member institution gave one the chance to use scholarly resources at any of the four institutions, and the Atlanta University Graduate Center became a connected but independent institution that could serve any qualified graduate from a member institution. Graduate instruction in laboratory sciences and in divinity studies were early offerings at the center, but in time almost any graduate or professional study could be pursued there. Such a great deal of this concept and of its operation was owing to the personal drive of John Hope, he of the "cleansing lightning" and flashing blue eyes, that Bennie Mays still associated the university system with him.[20]

Although Mays's most acute memories were of the vigorous John Hope of 1922 and 1923, other Atlantans recalled a different legacy. Between 1925 and his death in 1936. Hope had moved away from "creative pessimism"—his term for a healthy skepticism about any project—into a debilitating pessimism that led Will Alexander and others to call him "John Hopeless." With regret and never loudly, Bennie Mays had to concede that much of Morehouse's downward slide was the responsibility of the John Hopeless side of his hero and mentor, who had begun to think of reasons never to attempt any innovations in his Depression era Atlanta University system. A dying man such as Samuel Howard Archer and a harried interim president such as Charles DuBois Hubert grew understandably reluctant to send forward suggestions for experiments to John Hopeless, and soon the university system was running on memories as much as anything else. The long and steep climb back was hard, but merely by starting to repair things at Morehouse and merely by expressing his infectious optimism and evincing his characteristic determination, Bennie Mays invigorated the member-institution Morehouse and reinvigorated the entire Atlanta University system.[21]

Morehouse men were everywhere in the university system, and each was anxious to bring his alma mater back into full partnership in the integrated system—as each was anxious for the system to step forward smartly on its own as it had before the Great Depression. Samuel Nabrit needed only a few encouraging words and a few enabling funds to run hard in the graduate-science laboratories that he supervised. Brother of successful attorney James Madison Nabrit, Morehouse graduate Samuel Nabrit had been the first black person to earn a Ph.D. at Brown University. In short order Dr. Nabrit was not only offering intensive review and drill for Morehouse men and others preparing for entrance examinations at medical schools, but he was also demonstrating laboratory research to other black teachers and educationists. In similar fashion Rufus Clement, erstwhile Morehouse theologian, was soon preparing divinity students for the demands of modernist religion—that is, the Walter Rauschenbusch combination of detached scholarship in textual analysis and thoroughly engaged activism in causes of social justice, not what all meant by "modernist religion," but what the University of Chicago and the Atlanta University system men meant by the term.

This kind of partnership between aspiring students and the graduate center was one thing, but another aspect of full partnership involved a major change in structure. As Bursar Fred Gassett reminded Mays often, Morehouse College finances were all but hamstrung by having one treasurer, who kept the books and signed the checks for Spelman and Morehouse, so that the House in its ongoing campus finances was not so much a junior partner but a child who had not reached majority and was not entrusted with responsibilities. Among Spelman leaders, Hattie Rutherford Watson and Florence Reed understood and supported Bennie Mays at once, and he was able to establish autonomy in the financial sphere for Morehouse.[22]

By 1967 Morehouse was again indisputably the best of the institutions in the Atlanta University system. That long climb back was begun by Bennie Mays and his allies, who labored to reestablish status for the House throughout World War II, attaining the specific goal of full partnership by the end of 1947.

The terrifying world war expanded everywhere, but Mays, like most Americans, was looking at Europe—at France and above all at England. He and Sadie Mays scarcely noted the fighting in Asia and concerned themselves with possible U.S.

entry into a European theater of World War II. By 1941 it seemed unlikely that the United States could avoid entanglement in Europe, and indeed Mays— both as *Courier* news figure and Morehouse chapel leader—was not particularly focused on *satyagraha* in context of this war. Instead he served largely as a Race Man concerned that black people be treated fairly as President Roosevelt's Arsenal for Democracy produced weapons and ordnance—and high-paying jobs to make such materiel. Mays was shrewd enough as logician and still enough of a Chicago social scientist to know that the fevered preparation for possible combat was itself likely to make combat probable if not inevitable. Rather than protest American involvement in providing weapons, Mays insisted instead that the Arsenal for Democracy hire black laborers. He also insisted that if war came, the army and navy do right by its black soldiers and sailors.

The issues for Mays in 1941 were not only issues of civil rights for black folk, but also issues of justice and equity for all labor, of whom black workers were only one much-abused group. Such issues as always revolved around A. Philip Randolph. Where Randolph in one era had looked back at Mays as the storied figure who fought for the Pullman porters almost alone, now Mays looked to Randolph as the spokesman for fair practices for black people in the rapidly growing labor movement. Organized labor had a big role to play in this phase of New Deal politics, and Randolph intended that black workers be fully part of the organization efforts. Mays supported Randolph completely, even though such issues were not central to the many challenges of running a college for black men in Atlanta. Less directly, but still important, Mays understood that the Morehouse man must work with—reach back to—noncollege working-class blacks in the "bonds of soul" to gain and hold moral leadership in the war that was surely coming, and in the postwar modern South that one could dimly, however hopefully, perceive out there after victory over the fascists.

Randolph had specific plans to pressure Roosevelt. Troops continued to train in segregation with limited opportunities for black advancement in rank, and their treatment at the many southern bases where troops trained was indistinguishable in racial practices from the Jim Crow mistreatment in their host towns. Different but related was the issue of local southern businesses that served army and navy needs at the military bases. These industrial-defense companies that held federal contracts were generally segregated and otherwise discriminatory in their practices. Randolph insisted such firms be integrated— and treat black workers fairly. Mays fully agreed. Randolph saw an opportunity. This war, even more than World War I, was one where all peoples were needed to fight, and an army without black troops was unimaginable—proof was in the way men of the House were drafted in large numbers. This war was an industrial one, a combat in which the ability to supply soldiers and sailors with rifles, helmets, jeeps, bandages, and canned food played a major role in winning or losing. In industrial wartime production, factories without black workers were also unimaginable; proof was in the way black farm labor was pulled toward the assembly lines of the Northeast and the upper Midwest. At this time Race Men had an advantage in the propaganda wars being waged. It was a world of color, and colonial people of color were part of the conflict and part of the postbellum resolutions of the conflict. In that theater, where people of color actually mattered, military Jim Crow and industrial-defense Jim Crow could be publicly protested as a way to embarrass the president's Arsenal for Democracy. The obvious need to win friends and influence people of color in Africa and Asia and Latin American, and the crying need for black soldiers and black factory workers could be used against administration officials, including the commander in chief himself. Much-needed black troops and workers must be treated fairly, given opportunities Randolph called "fair practices."[23]

In spring of 1941 Randolph planned nothing less than a bold public march featuring at least one hundred thousand African Americans gathering in Washington on the grassy mall between the soaring Washington Monument and the brooding Father Abraham of the Lincoln Memorial. Such mass demonstrations were regularly staged by the Nazi Germans, but nothing of such size and scope had been attempted in the United States—and of course the Nazi demonstrations were orchestrated by the Third Reich against minorities and other enemies, while this proposed demonstration would be orchestrated *by* people of color against the powerful U.S. government of the Arsenal for Democracy. Bennie Mays supported the concept at once, demonstrating to Randolph that the Morehouse president was still a man of labor activism. Risk was profound for all concerned, especially a college president already suspect among some alumni ministers and among Atlanta whites exactly because of his social-gospel activism of the sort preached long ago by Walter Rauschenbusch. The risk was rewarded, however. On June 25, 1941, President Roosevelt wrote out Executive Order 8802 rather than submit to such a huge demonstration of protesting black people. The order mandated nondiscrimination in employment among industrial-defense companies that held federal contracts. In addition the president established a Fair Employment Practices Commission, whose task was to bring fair treatment in the private sector of businesses so involved, even and especially in Dixie. In the working-out of things, the commission had limited practical effect on hiring and treatment, and black labor continued to suffer discrimination, but the sign and signal of the commission and the sign and signal of the proposed March on Washington had established valuable "heart to fight" for people of color in other venues.[24]

To drive home his political ties with Randolph, Bennie Mays brought the labor leader to Morehouse to deliver the commencement address of 1945, after victory in Europe but before victory in Japan. Speaking to a small but engaged group of Morehouse graduates, Randolph praised the Mayses' Christian activism and reminded the young men of their duties to the race in terms of justice for the working class. It was the same message heard often in Tuesday chapel services, but in this case it came from the nation's most prominent labor activist who worked for civil rights. True to his own and the Mayses' views, Randolph also took a hard line against the CPUSA, not only for their assault on religion but for what he called the interference with labor and civil rights activism. For his part Bennie Mays made sure that everyone who could not be there learned about the "lovely" message. In that audience of young Morehouse baccalaureates, M. L. King was appreciative, and he looked back on such things to say that Bennie Mays had brought to the campus a "distinctive . . . militancy" that produced a graduate who was an "innovative, politically engaged scholar" as well as "prophetic, social-gospel religion teach[er]."[25]

While the Mayses were engaged in this labor campaign, World War II wrote its own story. After the Japanese attack on Pearl Harbor of December 7, 1941, Hitler declared war on the United States, and Americans found themselves in war on all fronts. Following established personal patterns, the sometimes pacifist Mayses supported the war effort and concentrated on materialist Race Man issues about power and wealth for people of color.

The bloodletting was unprecedented, especially for civilian populations near industrial centers or in port cities, and the new weapons of destruction brought maiming and something close to torture for the casualties, whether uniformed or not. In the fervor of wartime propaganda, the Japanese in particular were described in ways that could only be called what they were: *racism.* The internment of Japanese Americans in California, as well as the wholesale confiscation of Japanese American possessions in real and personal property, seemed painfully close to the early phases of Hitler's treatment of Jews—with portentous foreboding that the United States could even slide into the later phases of Hitler's racism. Bennie and Sadie Mays had to remind themselves that New Negroes had only recently joined the Democratic Party, largely at the behest of *Pittsburgh Courier*'s Robert Lee Vann, and thus Franklin Delano Roosevelt remained suspect, especially as he curried favor with racist southern Democrats such as Richard Russell, Theodore Bilbo, Cotton Ed Smith, John Rankin, and Eugene Talmadge—well-armed champions of Jim Crow, who resegregated every major New Deal works program while blocking federal legislation to bring a modicum of physical protection from the atrocities of lynch mobs. When Roosevelt had attempted a campaign aimed specifically at racist and reactionary southern congressmen—at least against the extreme Georgians Talmadge, Tarver, and Walter George and the extreme South Carolinian "Cotton Ed"

Smith—the voting white southern public rebuked the effort spectacularly, and the great president retreated from such derring-do in order to maintain what he could of the New Deal and in order to retain executive power.

That still left First Lady Eleanor Roosevelt as a White House champion for New Negroes, and Bennie and Sadie Mays as well as A. Philip Randolph began to speak of themselves as Eleanor Roosevelt liberals. The so-styled Popular Front of World War II antifascism, despite its rather left-leaning name, was marked by a social conservatism that kept insisting "not now" and "wait until Hitler and Tojo are defeated" in response to black cries for justice. There was, however, the United Front, which even included prominent members of the CPUSA as well as Eleanor Roosevelt liberals, and Bennie and Sadie Mays—as well as Randolph and J. O. Thomas and white southern allies such as Frank Porter Graham and Paul Eliot Green—joined the United Front, which insisted on fighting Nazis abroad without giving up the fight against extreme racism at home. Indeed Thomas was convinced that no country could fight under Franklin Roosevelt's proclaimed Four Freedoms without fighting Jim Crow and the lynching violence as part of the broader campaign. Bennie Mays brought this message eagerly and passionately to his Tuesday chapel services and to his increasingly militant "Mays" columns in the *Pittsburgh Courier.*[26]

With the ascent of the largely unknown Harry S Truman, Bennie and Sadie Mays were initially sanguine and quickly gratified. The Missouri Democrat immediately extended the spirit of Executive Order 8802 and anxiously sought black support for his administration even when such efforts cost him dearly among the Richard Russell–John Rankin–Eugene Talmadge southern Democrats. New racial battle lines formed almost at once, and Truman made the right decisions, although he lost the state battles. With black people voting in Atlanta, Bennie and Sadie Mays had organized Morehouse men to get out the vote and to move voters to support candidates who would fight Jim Crow in the rapidly growing city. Georgia Democrat leaders countered quickly with the infamous white primary, a declaration that the Democratic Party was in fact a private entity that could choose its own candidates however it wanted in primary elections opened only to white voters. Black people could vote without hindrance in the main elections in November, Talmadge, Russell and others assured people, but of course the Democratic nominees would be "solid"—that is racist—on Jim Crow issues. In his column, Bennie Mays saluted President Truman's noble, if losing, fight against this strategy. Furthermore, if there were any doubt that Sadie Mays was full partner in the reformist team, it was completely dispelled in fall season of 1945, when she campaigned on her own against the white primary in Georgia and as she cooperated with W. W. Thomas to fight against a coordinated effort to hold a white primary in South Carolina. These were battles lost in a long war that Bennie and Sadie were sure they were going to win—and they were taking the Morehouse men with them into the fray. Indeed, before the war ended, the U.S. Supreme Court in *Smith v. All-wright* ruled that black people must be permitted to vote in the Democratic primary. Again a sign and signal were laid out for the future. The appreciative M. L. King marked this reformism as he went off to divinity studies at Crozer Theological Seminary, newly headed by none other than Bennie Mays's mentor Edward Ewart Aubrey. Young King noted that the Mayses together had made Morehouse and its environs "experiment stations in democratic living" and had challenged their students to fight all injustices as part of Christian faith.[27]

In biblical terms Bennie Mays's first seven years at Morehouse were certainly fat years. He was able to raise money, and more important, he was able to build and maintain a culture in which Morehouse raised money and then managed the body of its endowment in such a way that its resources grew steadily and dependably. He was able to recruit students by taking bold and innovative steps that involved considerable risk, and then he put into place policies that gave those students real structure, real challenges, and better education in all phases of scholarship and life than they had been getting before 1940. As Lerone Bennett has noted, Bennie Mays became the main "schoolmaster" with his chapel messages, his many messages in churches, and his "Mays" column in the *Pittsburgh Courier.* Merely by reestablishing the definition of the Morehouse man as a leader, by increasing enrollment and by building an endowment—merely by starting in a serious way to attack each challenge—Bennie Mays and Sadie Mays had moved Morehouse College into position to be a full partner in the Atlanta University system.

These were then good years, fat years, years of growth and years of achievement. Mays's many accomplishments on behalf of Morehouse, the Urban League, the Federal Council of Churches, racial justice at the Y, and black people voting in Atlanta caused the leadership of the Federal Council of Churches to offer him the presidency of that organization in 1945. From what is written and preserved in his correspondence, it is hard to tell how seriously Mays took the offer. Certainly he declared that he had much more to do at Morehouse and that he could not abandon his labors there. Of course the offer became known to important trustees and financial donors of Morehouse, and these individuals concluded logically enough that Mays's great leadership was being affirmed yet again by still another group outside the House. The not inconsiderable group that was unhappy with Mays—those ministers who thought Mays too much the modernist, those faculty members who thought him too much the "Buck Benny" and too much the hard-driving tyrant, even those students who found it hard to keep up with the newly raised expectations—all these individuals had to face the fact that important leaders beyond Atlanta in colleges, churches, and reformist councils throughout the nation were in fact extremely happy with Bennie Mays. Those unhappy groups also had to face the fact that trustees and presidents and other leaders at major institutions were recognizing Bennie Mays as well. Between 1945 and 1947 he garnered five honorary doctorates: doctor of law degrees from the prestigious white Denison College in Ohio and from the Richmond home of "quality Negroes," Virginia Union; doctor of divinity degrees from his own Howard University and his own "little college with the big heart" Bates College; and a doctor of letters from his beloved if much-abused South Carolina State College.[28]

As 1947 came to its close, there remained plenty of problems at Morehouse. Problems of racism and Jim Crow, economic problems, problems of an exclusionary society, and problems of a warlike society all assailed Bennie and Sadie Mays—and each Morehouse man who strove to become a leader for the New Negroes. And the Mayses wanted more than Race Man material gains. They wanted spiritually substantive New Negro advancement. What Morehouse under Bennie and Sadie Mays had done was to start on a long, long road. A solid foundation was built, and not on sand. The House sat on a place where it could survive a terrible storm. The Mayses and their allies had set up plans and established procedures in a systematic way that could bring victory, even the longed-for "second V" of domestic racial justice in the Double V of the United Front. Surely, this second "V" was way out there, a long way off. At every level, the making of the Morehouse man, the increase in enrollment, the building and managing of an endowment, and the entry into full partnership in the Atlanta University system, the college remained less than Bennie and Sadie Mays wanted it to be. By all quantifiable measures, the glass of the House remained half empty. Sturdy optimists and firm in their resolve, Bennie and Sadie Mays insisted that the glass was half full.

12

"TO YOUR TENTS"

1948–1967

"To your tents!" is a refrain of the tribe of Benjamin recorded in most translations of 1 Kings and 2 Samuel in the Bible. The speaker was the Benjaminite Sheba, and his words were exciting, affecting—and blasphemous. It was the worst part of having the name "Benjamin" and thus owning Benjaminite history in the Bible. By 1948 Bennie and Sadie Mays no longer used images of "tribes," and this passage helps to explain why. The northern "tribes" all but disappeared, and their leave taking so weakened the southern "tribes" of Judah that the Hebrew kingdoms could not stay together to defend their disparate portions against enemies. Finally the Jews were carried off into Babylonian slavery. What the Mayses wanted instead was a stirring cry to fight for all God's people and not only one race. "Call forth the mighty men," King David had responded to Sheba. Bennie and Sadie Mays wanted to call forth the mighty men on behalf of God's mission on earth. In chapel on Tuesdays, at Georgia churches on Sundays, and at interracial conferences on Saturdays, Bennie Mays called the Morehouse men out of their tents and into the fray: "All men are brothers," and "all men must fight injustice without a gun."[1]

As he spoke in chapel, as he prepared the men of Morehouse for civil rights marches and for lives of activism, as he counseled interracial groups, as he planned in his study, Bennie Mays throughout the period 1948–67 talked about consequences. He noted two things. First he told audiences that no one can control the consequences of his actions. Second he said that a man absolutely must be responsible for facing the consequences of his actions. The contradicting and ironic juxtapositions of the otherwise simple statements were known to the Stoics, to Epictetus and Marcus Aurelius; and they had been understood by W. E. B. Du Bois when that great scholar accepted full-blown Marxism and the Soviet expression of Communism as his personal resolution of the dilemma. Bennie Mays and Sadie Mays wanted a Christian—therefore non-Communist and probably anti-Communist—resolution of the old Stoics' dilemma, and they found it in the Gospels, especially as Aubrey and Case applied Walter Rauschenbusch to the Gospels. According to the Chicago modernists, there really is a controlling God with a largely inscrutable plan; and a Christian must struggle for justice knowing he will fail often, and he must be content that an honest struggle itself is redeeming and confident that finally God will work justice out of the many conflicts between good and bad men. Mays's amendment to this old resolution was Gandhian: war cannot be an agent of justice, and the consequences of war cannot be worked out—even by the Divine—into a just end. Bennie and Sadie Mays had thought World War II would be an exception, but its consequences had only demonstrated the uncontrollable, even demonic, aspect of war.[2]

World War II had unleashed a wild nationalism, and the Cold War was now boiling up a kind of "supranationalism" that bade fair to destroy God's plan for a unified and just kingdom. For a few months during the days of the United Front with all the talk of the "Good War" and "Double V," Bennie and Sadie Mays had put Gandhi on a shelf and ceased talking about nonviolent resistance in international issues. But the firebombing of Dresden and wholesale butchery of civilians in German and Japanese industrial cities had set the agenda for the sheer horror of the two atomic bombs dropped on more than one hundred thousand civilians. The consequences of entering World War II were so evil that even God could not work it out: "Not even an omnipotent God can blot out the deeds of history," Bennie and Sadie Mays quoted from an eighteenth-century popularizer of the Stoics. There must never be another world war, and Gandhi absolutely must come down off the shelf. Christians must apply Gandhi. Furthermore there could be no isolationism, no retreating to the American tents by noncombatant pacifists. Bennie and Sadie Mays insisted on the sternest of commandments: all conflicts everywhere must be joined and none can be avoided, but none can be responded to with military force. Everyone must be saved—and all together in a pacifist's version of a mighty worldwide campaign. After a season of abandonment, the Mayses returned to a pacifist's version of Napoleonic ambitions for global justice—one without the military.[3]

The only answer the Mayses could find, was for a truly effective United Nations, one that would preside over the freeing of old colonies and mediate any conflicts involving the militarily aggressive Communism of the Soviet Union and the militarily aggressive anti-Communism of the United States. The Mayses understood that the UN must have armed forces that could intervene as peacekeepers, but their limited "police action" must be discussed, voted on, and then deployed as multilateral foreign policy. Consequently and consistently thereafter, such ongoing policy must be reviewed in the same councils of debate. The use of UN force must be minimal and focused and arranged after "reasoning together," as the Prophet Isaiah put it. Then it must be carefully monitored. Above all, civilians must be kept out of harm's way, even and especially in UN police action. More to the point, the grinding poverty of the one-time African and Latin American and Caribbean and Asian colonies must be addressed by the privileged and wealthy United States and its allies through the UN. Root causes of internal conflict in former colonies lay in poverty, the Mayses reasoned, and the UN must be the agency that provides health care, education, technological expertise, road building, and other help from the advanced industrialized countries. Root causes of conflict between nations came from the greed of rich nations and the resentments of poor nations, the Mayses reasoned, and again the UN must be the agency to provide the forum for prophetic discussions about justice and peace. It sounded idealistic because the Mayses were idealists. Yet each insisted that the alternatives, the pursuit of self-interest among nations armed with atomic weapons, were the real impracticalities despite clever labels such as "realpolitik" and "geopolitical realism" and even the hoary "balance of power" being discussed among academics at the time. While idealistic and optimistic, Bennie Mays could be and was quite blunt in his public prophecy in the *Pittsburgh Courier:* "When a people become unjust, it needs no atomic bomb to bring about its downfall."[4]

This was Eleanor Roosevelt liberalism, and the Mayses became convinced that Harry S Truman and his foreign policy people agreed with this perspective on the United Nations as that organization convened in San Francisco for its first sessions. As for Republicans, the Mayses judged presidential candidate Thomas E. Dewey to be unenthusiastic about the UN; and many midwestern Republicans seemed to the couple to be "reactionary Republicans" with the isolationist mindset of "To your tents!" The self-proclaimed Progressive, Henry Wallace, appeared to the Mayses to be too close to some CPUSA members and other communists, and thus inclined toward a left-wing version of isolationism. Then there was the Dixiecrat Strom Thurmond of South Carolina, already notorious for his strident Jim Crowism and his suspected philandering with an underage black girl, and now Thurmond was sounding like a rabid anti-Communist who would fight them in unilateral fashion while ignoring the "caste and color" causes of injustice in the world. Surveying the disappointing field from left to right, the Mayses chose to campaign vigorously for Truman in the 1948 election. In his *Courier* column, Mays wrote that Truman's Fair Deal platform was about reformism and civil rights, far more so than had ever been the case in the four presidential races of Franklin Delano Roosevelt. In

northern cities black votes helped put Truman barely above the Republican
Dewey and above the Progressive Wallace. In Atlanta black people had been
able to vote, and their votes had helped bring Georgia into Truman's Democratic electors box while the other Deep South states—where black people were
largely prevented from voting—had placed their electoral votes in the box of
Dixiecrat Thurmond. The newly elected Truman did the right things about the
UN and African Americans in the military, and he was saying the right things
about racial justice in terms of voting rights, fair employment, equal housing
opportunities, and protection in the collective bargaining processes of labor
unions. Even more to the point, Harry Truman owed obvious and public debts
to black voters for his stunning election victory in 1948.[5]

The election was nothing if not complex and confounding, and recent
scholarship questions the importance of black votes in 1948, especially in Georgia. Outside the South, a plurality of white voters may have supported Truman
because he was close to the New Deal, and this election may have been a kind
of "posthumous plebiscite" for Roosevelt. "At the North" big-city black votes
went to Truman and helped him, but perhaps they were not the deciding
weight. As for the South, of course, Deep South states, minus Georgia, went to
Thurmond and Dixiecrats. In Georgia and in upper-South regions where black
people were permitted to vote, a working majority of white farmers and factory
workers may have supported Truman out of lingering fondness for the New
Deal, personal affection for Roosevelt redounded onto Truman, and traditional mistrust of the GOP. In fact one brilliant student has opined that—
beyond Mississippi, Louisiana, Alabama, and South Carolina—most white
southerners continued to see the Democratic Party as a strong supporter of
white supremacy and voted accordingly, especially in Georgia. Perhaps if
Bennie and Sadie Mays had done nothing at all and if black voters had stayed
home on Election Day, Truman would have won in any case. For all that,
the Mayses and their allies thought that black votes weighed heavily in the
precarious balance—and the Mayses heard from Truman's people how the
president considered that he owed black voters general support and specific
favors. Certainly Truman, supported by Eleanor Roosevelt herself and by
Eleanor Roosevelt liberals, went forward with futile but quite brave civil rights
legislation.[6]

Bennie and Sadie Mays intended to follow along with Truman on a grand
campaign in which the hated Communism would be resisted peacefully by
offering an alternative so attractive that people of color, whether in Georgia or
in sub-Saharan Africa, would come to the Democrats' Fair Deal. Few years had
begun with more hope for Bennie and Sadie Mays than did 1948. With Truman's surprise victory in the final months of that year, few had ended with
more hope.

"Call forth the Mighty Men!" It was time for the most important and certainly the most hope-filled era for the man and the woman of magnificence.

True to his profession and his career, Bennie Mays emphasized education, specifically college education and postbaccalaureate training as keys to fulfilling his hopes. Writing for a black audience in the *Courier* or speaking to the young men of the House in the handsome new chapel, President Mays was as abrasive as the most committed prophets in the Bible: "We must become more competent." Mays's New Negro was a man of great competence as well as great courage. Almost no one else was talking this way. Friends in the Urban League and the NAACP and the relatively new Southern Christian Leadership Conference (SCLC) were talking about rights and opportunities and were protesting injustices and things taken away—about barriers and burdens. Bennie and Sadie Mays supported such protests and demanded opportunities, but their focus was different. The Mayses preached and practiced the development of extreme competence and a sort of self-help to be developed on the black side of Jim Crow borderlines until the accursed boundaries were removed. Sometime in the 1950s, the terms "New Negro" and "Race Man" disappeared from most conversations, and in that decade the Mayses dropped the terms too. Yet the couple continued to think in this vein. Most black leaders emphasized assimilation and full integration while a vocal but focused minority emphasized a specifically black power drawing strength from specifically African sources of cultural strength. Neither of these competing concepts attracted the Mayses, as became painfully obvious in the period after 1968. Their insistence on building up a set of obvious qualifications and then demanding entry into mainstream American life was still essentially the stuff of Alain Locke and Carter G. Woodson and above all the stuff of Benjamin Elijah Mays and Sadie Gray Mays. The couple marched among former students and current colleagues in the same causes without at the time acknowledging how different the New Negro ideals were from those of the new integrationists and from the new separatists of the postwar period.

In the late 1940s and continuing until 1953, both Mayses used "New Negro" to mean an idealist neo-Hegelian fulfillment of racial potential, and both used "Race Man" to mean a political figure fighting battles tightly and even narrowly focused on issues about power to insure opportunities for black people. Abandoning such terms sometime after 1953, both Mayses still prosecuted the same two campaigns—the one spiritual and the other material, the former cultural and idealistic, the latter political and practical, but both of course related. They never formally announced the ending of the old terminology, but they fought the same fights the same way, adopting the new language about black power and sometimes even soul power and thereby often confusing people of both races in campaigns during the late 1960s and leaving a written record confusing and problematic for students looking back.

Withal, the Mayses passed seamlessly from early campaigns for self-help and integrationist accommodations into a self-proclaimed civil rights movement noticed by white liberals in 1953, 1954, 1955, and thereafter—but with antecedents stretching back to the founding of the NAACP and Urban League in 1908 and 1909. Bennie and Sadie Mays adapted Walter Rauschenbusch and Henry George to their early work and then adapted the Cold War words of the multilayered and multidimensional Reinhold Niebuhr. By contrast their most prominent student, the Reverend Dr. Martin Luther King, Jr., had nothing to do with Rauschenbusch and George and paid attention only to the lesser-known antiwar writings of Niebuhr. The Mayses also adopted Gandhi inconsistently, ignoring him completely in the prosecution of World War II and awkwardly claiming that UN action in Korea was consistent with the departed Gandhi. Their more-famous student King much more consistently and thus more radically adapted Gandhi to all foreign policy. Recent scholars have used "the long civil rights movement" to describe the twentieth-century struggle certainly beginning in 1908 and 1909, and their term, although never used by Bennie or Sadie Mays, seems fully appropriate in their case. After all, both of them self-consciously fought on behalf of full civil rights for African Americans long before white liberals noticed and named a "movement" in the 1950s.

Throughout 1949, still using the term "New Negro," Mays told *Pittsburgh Courier* readers, students in chapel at Morehouse, and worshippers in congregations that there was a serious racial problem of "brain power." He said it was a "shortage of brain development." Writing for an audience of some three hundred thousand well-educated and essentially bourgeois people of color, Bennie Mays actually said, "I hope there is no shortage of brain power." Yet, he noted, "some Negroes are too cursed lazy" to develop their brain power, while others "work hard but cannot see the short term sacrifice" in money (the salary foregone) to gain a college degree and thereby gain greater wealth and power over a long period of time. Girls needed college degrees, and married couples needed two careers in order to make it in the new postwar world, he told these readers. It was a mistake for girls to leave high school or college in order to start families. Such early marriages and young childbirth "cost *two* good minds" from the ranks of the New Negroes. Nor should everyone seek law degrees and medical degrees, much as he emphasized such professions at Morehouse. He quoted Dr. Mordecai Johnson, who said that black colleges needed at least 125 full professors to teach college students, but there were only 74. Furthermore he flung statistics at his readers: fewer than 80,000 black people were attending college, comprising only 3 percent of the U.S. college population. Yet African

Americans made up 10 percent of the U.S. population, so there should be 265,000 black students on campuses. For Mays one reason for the low number of black college students was poverty; more often it was segregation and other instances of overt racism, but the greatest reason had to do with willpower among African Americans: "Let the Negro fight segregation or discrimination with every ounce of his strength. But let him never forget that he must become competent enough to survive in the dual civilization."[7] "Dual civilization" echoed Du Bois's old term "twoness," and emphasized that the Mayses expected no quick end to de facto segregation in many things. There would still have to be much, much work on the black side of town before the Jubilo of full integration and full opportunities.

With that understanding of recent legal and educational history, Mays saw a threat to education of black physicians because of a complex—and superficially innocent—plan to give regional Deep South funding to the Meharry Medical College of Fisk University, where most men of Morehouse matriculated to become medical doctors. There was a proposal that at least two and perhaps as many as five Deep South states pay for black medical students to matriculate at Meharry, transforming that elite private institution into a partly public institution. Although the much-respected Howard University was such a hybrid of public and private institutions, Bennie Mays was instantly suspicious of this proposal. First of course it was clearly a plan to delay if not prevent forever the entry of black applicants into white public institutions for the training of doctors. In 1948 the University of Arkansas had admitted a woman of color, Edith Irby, into its medical school, and in the same year the University of Arkansas law school had admitted six men of color, including George W. Haley from the Morehouse class of 1948. The processes of integrating public law and medical schools were speeding up, "even at the South," and Mays was in no mood to slow things down because of this Deep South plan to "regionalize" the private Meharry. It would be no more difficult for Alabamians to open up their medical and legal schools to black students than it had been for Arkansans to do so. Mays wanted to keep the pressure on Alabamians in particular but on all Deep South states in general.[8]

There was another concern, and it came from the perspective of a dean and a president who had worked to gain accreditation of two different institutions. He was much concerned that white officials in Deep South states might be haphazard in their procedures for admitting black applicants to Meharry. He worried that the committee of admissions at Meharry might come under political, financial, and other pressures to let in badly prepared students—that "the standards of Meharry will fall below those of Howard University Medical School and other medical schools throughout the country." He had a real stake in this issue, for most of the students pursuing the M.D. degree at Meharry were from Morehouse, and, a different statistic, a majority of the Morehouse premedical students entered Meharry. Although Morehouse graduates were gaining admission to Howard and predominantly white public institutions in the North, Bennie Mays did not want vital Meharry opportunities to be watered-down for his premedical students. He campaigned vigorously against this regional plan, and it never came to full realization. At least in this period of time, there was no diminution of standards at Meharry. Pressures for integration of graduate and professional schools in Deep South public institutions continued to build, as Mays hoped.[9]

Bennie Mays took a different stand from those of other activist black academics and politicos of the era. His concern, if not obsession, was with "extreme competence" in New Negro candidates for medical and legal degrees. These applicants were to win entry by demonstrating a "supracompetence" that only the most committed racist could deny. Mays was uninterested in, and in fact opposed to, swelling the numbers of black doctors and lawyers if to do so involved dilution of talent. He wanted the best learning environment, namely excellent competition from the best and the brightest, for his Morehouse men going off to Meharry, Howard, Brown, the University of Arkansas, or any other medical school. He expressed an extreme reluctance to accept any kind of politically mandated "social promotion" or quota that would damage the educational experience for highly qualified entrants or that would diminish their eventual capacities on graduation. African Americans deserved the best from their doctors and lawyers, and the best could only come as the result of excellent undergraduate training, careful selection by medical school committees, and then thorough preparation in medical school [10]

Nor did Mays merely preach the need for much larger numbers of black baccalaureates, who would become candidates for professional training and then become leaders in business and church. He actively recruited men for Morehouse and women for Spelman. Yet he realized that the two colleges alone could not fill the need to increase enrollment of black college students by more than 180,000. For that reason in particular, he became a major player and fundraiser in the United Negro College Fund (UNCF). Always close friends with fund president F. D. Patterson, Bennie Mays began to coordinate activities with Patterson for both the UNCF and the Phelps Stokes charitable fund, which his friend also managed. Also Mays joined the Hazen Foundation, a liberal-reformist group focusing on the needs of African Americans, especially in education. He hosted a major UNCF conference in Atlanta early in 1949 and urged fellow presidents of predominantly or historically black colleges not to compete with each other for the relatively small number of black high-school graduates applying to college but rather to preach the message of attending college to all high-school students, so that all black colleges could draw from a large pool of applicants. In order to convince fellow black-college executives of his sincerity, Mays increased his travel and speech giving so that he could work for UNCF and all member colleges and not only for Morehouse. These trips for UNCF were in addition to the agreed-upon limit of thirty trips he made for the House.[11]

Also in 1949 Mays and his development team set and met a goal of three million dollars for the Morehouse endowment and a similar goal for Spelman. Both goals were reached before the new decade of the 1950s arrived. Throughout the period 1947–67, with his bold campaign of college building and education enhancement, Bennie Mays clearly established himself as the man of *megalosukos* and *magnanimatatum* in black education. The work with all these interlocking foundations—UNCF, Hazen, Phelps Stokes, and others—paid off. The best schools—Spelman, Howard, Morehouse, and Fisk—owed at least part of their continuing success, or "thriving," to the indefatigable Bennie Mays; rapidly strengthening or "surviving" schools—such as Central State (Ohio), Lincoln (Pennsylvania), and North Carolina Central—owed much of their growth and development to him; and weaker sisters—such as South Carolina State College, Ellen Harvin's Morris College, and Benedict College—might well have perished outright without the UNCF assistance for which Mays was largely responsible. For all that this chronicler notes a certain nagging concern. Had Bennie and Sadie Mays focused more tightly on the specific fund-raising needs of Morehouse, would not that fine college have been set on a firmer foundation? Perhaps more like the solid rock underlying the University of Chicago, or at least more like the foundation of Bates? Possible losses at the margins, even the deaths of some weak colleges, might well have been outweighed by a dramatically strengthened Morehouse.

Bennie Mays was determined to make an effect on white middle-class opinion, even and especially at the South, and he eagerly sought places to declare the message of Christian, indeed Baptist, racial justice. Obvious places were Y conferences, Y camps, and church camps, meetings of the Urban League and the NAACP, and meetings of selected Jewish, Roman Catholic, and Baptist congregations. He traveled and spoke extensively at such gatherings. Yet he wanted to reach farther, to gain the ear of decent white southerners, not intellectuals and not anti-intellectuals, but the quiet "middle brow" person who read novels at the seashore and did charitable work and had declared some support for Eleanor Roosevelt liberalism, albeit without declaring any sympathy for civil rights activism. Such believing people—separated out from large crowds of screaming Negrophobes and given a few moments to focus quietly on several paragraphs of prose at their kitchen table or in their reading room—did not routinely read minister's essays in *Christian Century* and certainly did not read scholarly journals such as *Phylon* or *Journal of Negro Education* or scholarly monographs from university presses. Nor did such individuals routinely attend church conferences or camp sessions that advertised civil rights themes or themes of racial justice. Yet they were susceptible to surprisingly liberal statements in *Reader's Digest* or *Life* magazine or *Time* magazine or even a rare liberal statement from columnist Ralph McGill in the *Atlanta Constitution.*

The audience of potentially reasonable people Mays had in mind was largely white females, women settling in the tract houses of the suburban communities developing beyond the southern towns on abandoned cotton fields. Unlike the black females whom he preached to at Spelman and in churches, these white women generally did not pursue careers; their incomes were relatively high and growing, and they had some leisure time for reading and reflection. To some degree he had in mind women not unlike the late Margaret Mitchell, only of course without her wealth and without any public display of eccentricity. He certainly had in mind women who had read *Gone with the Wind* several times and seen the cinema version; women who harbored many racist assumptions—and yet were not haters and would never cheer at the sight of a lynched black man hanging from a neighboring oak tree. He knew also from personal experiences at conferences and in other settings that sometimes a thoughtful suburban housewife could persuade her businessman husband to look at a photographic essay in *Life* or to read a brief piece in *Reader's Digest,* and that on occasion such an otherwise racist businessman could decide to do the right thing in a matter of social justice. He might even agree that it was wrong to let their teenaged son "nigger knock"—that is, to hurt a black boy purely for the joy of watching him suffer pain—and, even more, that husband might agree that the local black school should have a decent roof and new desks and new books or that black taxpayers and army veterans in a nearby town might deserve lighted and paved streets with police who protected rather than abused the families there. It was incremental, and it was slow, and thugs such as Dr. Wallace Payne could not be persuaded by a good wife; but Bennie Mays the Baptist minister had to believe in the principles of confession and redemption, and he had to believe that some of those white men sitting in the church pews and on metal chairs in Sunday School discussion groups were capable of persuasion through popular journals and publications put before them by their trusted wives.

The teaching of these souls in such gradual and gentle persuasion was brought to a new level of art by his favored student, the Reverend Dr. Martin Luther King, Jr., who took the concept and brought it to the incredibly powerful venue of network television evening news. In those suburban living rooms, with a few melodramatic images appropriately in black and white, Dr. King could catch not only the thoughtful housewife and her possibly educable businessman husband but also the curious and energetic teenage son or daughter, who possessed a mind yet plastic and yet to be hardened into attitudes of hatred and resentment preached by Senators Richard Russell or Strom Thurmond, attitudes yet flexible and not yet forged into the racist weapons developed by journalists James Jackson Kilpatrick and Jesse Helms. Almost everyone in those evangelical Protestant families watching the evening news was to some degree racist and was capable of racist hatred and even racist action, but the Mayses considered them souls shaped by a benevolent God, and as such they could be led toward the well of justice to drink the living water and to eat the bread that gave perpetual life.[12]

In the immediate postwar years, that kind of television news was not yet available to Bennie Mays, as he learned when he attempted unsuccessfully to involve himself in the production of a television feature about segregated travel. Widely read periodicals were available, however, and he made careful and concerted efforts to get himself and his message into such slick magazines for the middle brow. In the end it was not his part to accomplish such direct proselytizing and popularizing. He traveled with Edmund O. Cerf, a widely read editor and middle-brow writer, who acquired manuscripts and wrote pieces. Cerf was an Eleanor Roosevelt liberal on civil rights issues, but Cerf never actually published anything by Mays. He was the darling of various theologians' publications, but he never cracked the shell of *Life* or *Time*. As to Ralph McGill, Mays gnashed his teeth when the popular columnist of the *Atlanta Constitution* continued to insist that no white southerners supported integration, and Mays at last persuaded managing editor William H. Fields to consider the possibility that some white people in the "city too busy to hate" could be persuaded to integrate some facilities.[13]

Denied these arenas, Bennie Mays in 1950 took a step sideways and tried to reach the white suburban families in a more modest and less direct way by producing books that might be bought by such families. He began in the 1950s to take notes for a memoir that he early on gave the title *Born to Rebel.* Yet he quickly realized that work on this project was an extended process, one to be perfected and then proffered to the chosen audience of the white middle-class some years later, perhaps even a decade. In the meantime he chose to bring out a collection of essays written by Walter Rauschenbusch about Christianity and social justice. Rauschenbusch had died in 1918, but Bennie Mays found his essays and sermons perpetually fresh and engaging, and above all, easy to read and comprehend. As developing modernist theology became more profoundly involved in the multiplex and often self-contradicting and sometimes self-absorbed scholarship about changes in meanings of words—and as more of the self-consciously modernist scholars began to doubt publicly that there was a God—Bennie Mays attempted to return the discussion, at least at the middle-brow level of adult Sunday School and Y conference discussion, to the focused social gospel of the committed believer. He wanted white Protestants to see and reflect on these words of Rauschenbusch: [The Lord's Prayer ascribed to Jesus] "is not the property of those whose chief religious aim is to pass through an evil world in safety, leaving the world's evil unshaken. Its dominating thought is the moral and religious transformation of mankind in all its social relations. It was left us by Jesus, the great initiator of the Christian revolution; and it is the rightful property of those who follow his banner in the conquest of the world."[14]

Even this middle-brow project was a bit too scholarly for popular presses, yet far too middle-brow for any university-monograph series; but Bennie Mays was not to be denied on this one. As a leader on the board of the Hazen Foundation, he had helped publish several books on religious themes through arrangements with Haddam House, Women's Press, and the Association Press. In fact for some years, the Haddam House Series republished reprints of classics by Fyodor Dostoyevsky, John C. Bennett, and Roger Shinn. Whether a new edition of the Dostoyevsky's *Grand Inquisitor* or Bennett's extended Christian essays attacking Communism, each book in the series featured a highly readable condensation with a preface written by a theologian or journalist, a brief biographical sketch written by a knowledgeable journalist, and selections compiled and arranged by social-gospel theologians to lead to a message of social justice through principled and pacifist activism, "the marvelous militancy of pacifism," as the admiring King put it memorably. In the case of the Rauschenbusch essays, the editorial board's Paul M. Limbert explained briefly in the preface why a long-dead theologian was worth reading in 1950, and theologian C. Howard Hoskins, author of several social-gospel volumes, described Rauschenbusch's life in the introduction. Limbert and Hoskins made clear what is found in the papers left by Bennie Mays at Howard University: the Morehouse president personally "committed" himself to a life of Rauschenbusch's lived theology, and these commitments guided him as he personally selected and arranged and gave subtitles to each piece in the slim volume. It received fair reviews, and sold fairly well for several years, but the handsome volume simply could not do the things Bennie Mays ached to do for the justice movement in the 1950s.[15]

It was going to take political action to repair the damages created by Jim Crow. To stir the controlling middle class, even Truman supporters, into action against Jim Crow, it was going to take civil disobedience and public demonstrations that compelled attention to the unfairness of southern racial practices. Bennie and Sadie Mays's friends and colleagues A. Philip Randolph, Mordecai Johnson, J. O. Thomas, Rayford Logan, and F. D. Patterson—like the Mayses themselves—were not only speaking but putting their bodies on the line to integrate passenger cars on trains, public facilities at transit stations, church camps, Y camps, and other such facilities. On at least three different occasions in as many different eras, Bennie Mays had been pursued through dining cars by enraged mobs of white people who struck at and cursed him. In his actions and in his preaching, he insisted that neither he nor any other African American should accept the law saying that black was inferior to white. He always coupled that militant message with the difficult stricture that a man was subject to Caesar's law, and when one broke Jim Crow's color line, he had to submit to the legal authorities, again taking the consequences of his actions. Bennie Mays worked with NAACP attorney Thurgood Marshall on one case in particular, in which the president of Morehouse was roughly treated in a Southern Railroad dining car near Greenville in his home state. Mays's historian friend Rayford Logan of Howard University actually won a major court suit against the Southern Railroad for his own mistreatment, and Mays continued to preach to his young charges in chapel to defy the unjust law, to trust in God not to be killed by a crowd, never to strike back physically, and to take the fine or even jail sentence as consequence of the just protest.[16]

As the 1950s continued, the Morehouse president was pleased to see his students take his chapel message into the streets of southern cities, where they employed Gandhian techniques of protest in front of newspaper reporters, magazine feature writers, and in special cases the venue of evening-television news that had been denied Mays himself. James Farmer had abandoned his plans to become a Methodist minister in order to pursue the no-less-prophetic task of leading protests against voting restrictions and Jim Crow facilities as the head of the Congress of Racial Equality (CORE). Bennie and Sadie Mays supported Farmer's decision, judging his task to be God's ministry as much as the pulpit. Martin Luther King, Jr., had done well in Dr. Aubrey's new divinity school at Crozer and then had been inspired by Howard Thurman and others at Boston University's divinity school; Mays had tried to get King to join the professoriat at Morehouse, but his student had pleased him by turning down that offer in order to take command of the SCLC, after carefully orchestrating peaceful resistance in 1952 to the segregated bus system in Montgomery, Alabama. Neither King nor Farmer nor Andrew Young nor any of the great leaders of protest who emerged from Mays's Morehouse was responding only to broadly inspirational sermons. In chapel services and in dormitory lounges and in his own offices, Bennie Mays carefully instructed his students how to conduct a protest, and he worked with other presidents at historically black colleges to make sure that none of their students was penalized by a UNCF institution because of jail time served as consequence of Gandhian protest. These techniques included the nonviolent sit-ins, in which students took seats

at segregated cafeterias or drugstore lunch counters in defiance of Jim Crow
state law and accepted verbal and sometimes extreme physical abuse from white
toughs prior to the acceptance of incarceration by the police. In addition the
theologians at the House, following their president's lead, taught students the
technique of the integrated "Freedom Ride," in which northern-white college
students and southern-black college students rode buses together and attempted
to integrate waiting rooms and other transit facilities, again enduring verbal
and physical abuse from local white toughs and again enduring jail time for
violating southern state laws.[17]

The activist, protesting president was mindful of the wry comment that it
"takes millions to keep Mahatma Gandhi in rags," and Bennie Mays used every
foundation lever and every wealthy white source to funnel money to Ralph
David Abernathy and King in SCLC, to James Farmer in CORE, and to Thurgood Marshall, James Madison Nabrit, and Harvey Beech in legal court battles
for the NAACP. Mays's correspondence with King, Abernathy, Farmer, and
Marshall shows that many times an extra donation of money from the Hazen
Foundation or from Hattie Rutherford Watson or from Charles Merrill kept a
protest in motion. Not surprisingly, there were costs for Bennie Mays, especially in the state that produced Richard Russell and Mays's home state when
Strom Thurmond was most abusively racist. Both Russell and Thurmond
accused Mays of being a Communist agent, and it was good that Morehouse
was a private institution with funding from outside Georgia, because Russell's
and Eugene Talmadge's allies back in the Georgia General Assembly often
punished the University of Georgia and Georgia Tech for the mildest forms of
social activism by cutting their funding or by trying to muzzle their faculty
members. Throughout the tumultuous 1950s, when civil rights protest was
especially fraught with danger and obstacles, Bennie and Sadie Mays enjoyed
support from Eleanor Roosevelt, Harry Truman, and Hubert Humphrey, even
though these Democrats lost power after 1952, when Dwight David Eisenhower
assumed the U.S. presidency with important debts to "reactionary Republicans," especially in the Upper South, where the GOP was gaining strength
among the middle class but still beholden to Jim Crow among traditionalists.[18]

As Mays continued to teach the techniques of nonviolent protest, his chapel
addresses and his *Courier* column, now called "As I See It," reiterated the
imperative to accept consequences, even when no one knew what those consequences would be. His old students and his colleagues used his funds to fight
the good, pacifist fight; he turned over some of the funds he raised to the
NAACP; and he turned his ability to generate publicity to note some interesting heroes in his native South Carolina in the campaign to integrate the
schools. In Manning, county seat of Clarendon County, where his pretty girl

Ellen Harvin lay buried, Mays's new friend Kenneth Bancroft Clark had begun psychological experiments in 1949, showing black and white dolls to rural black children and asking them questions about the dolls' beauty and goodness. Many of the children most admired the white dolls; almost none declared that the black dolls were beautiful, and one particularly memorable little boy declared the black doll to be a "nigger" and declared himself to be a "nigger." In his own childhood, Bennie Mays had been schooled and reminded constantly by Jesse and Louvenia that he was "as good as anyone" and told he was certainly a "Negro" and not a "nigger." Yet here was a child telling a good role model, the distinguished Dr. Clark, that "nigger" was the best word to describe Bennie Mays's color, whether that color was shared by a doll or by a Clarendon County boy. These psychological results seemed to Dr. Clark and to Bennie Mays to show the extreme emotional damage directly created by Jim Crow schools. The president of Morehouse made sure that people knew about Dr. Clark's research into Jim Crow and its damage to schoolchildren.[19]

Mays's old debate student James Madison Nabrit brought such evidence to bear as he argued a school segregation case in Manning. South Carolina, before the Eastern District Court on May 28, 1951. Now an NAACP attorney, Nabrit offered a different approach to issues of segregation and public schools in *Briggs v. Elliott.* The South Carolina General Assembly, following the lead of Governor James F. Byrnes, had been putting more money into schools for black children, trying to show that the concept of "separate but equal" was a fair one. Nabrit showed that the black schools remained inferior in material terms, but he also provided evidence from Dr. Clark that the act of segregating children brought damage to the minority race. A three-judge federal district panel heard the case and then heard it reargued, with additional arguments by Nabrit's NAACP colleague Thurgood Marshall; two of the judges ruled against the NAACP, but one of their number, J. Waties Waring, was much moved by Dr. Clark's evidence and much unmoved by state expenditures on physical facilities, writing a twenty-eight-page minority opinion that remains important to jurists today.[20]

Several attorneys and legal scholars had worked on the NAACP's new approach for several ongoing cases, and the *Briggs v. Elliott* case was appealed in a group of appeals of other cases, all called *Brown v. Board of Education,* decided famously by the U.S. Supreme Court on May 17, 1954. Additional evidence was presented to show that segregation of public facilities was less traditional than white southerners pronounced it. A team of historians including John Hope Franklin and C. Vann Woodward provided historical data to show a relatively late development of segregation, with Jim Crow laws coming in South Carolina about the time of the Phoenix Riot in 1898. In considering *Brown v. Board of Education,* the Earl Warren court reexamined Waring's minority opinion and paid much attention to Dr. Clark's psychological data and to the historical record proffered by Thurgood Marshall. The justices ruled unanimously that segregation was doing damage at all levels and that integration of public schools must proceed "with all due deliberate speed." Surely the most famous Supreme Court case of the twentieth century, *Brown v. Board of Education* brought the integration movement into the consciousness of the white middle class, and it brought the struggle for school integration and improvement to the southern public schools in a way that gave renewed attention and publicity to the pacifist campaigns at all levels. Indeed, in the apt words of another psychologist investigator, Thomas F. Pettigrew, the Warren court's decision gave all black people the "heart to fight" in the long-running struggles for justice.[21]

Besides telling his readers about Dr. Clark's research, Bennie Mays also drew attention to Waring, a white jurist from an old Charleston family. Judge Waring wrote and spoke firmly about the issues, and in doing so, he gave the lie to Ralph McGill's opinion that no white southerners supported integration. Of course Waties Waring also suffered consequences, enduring the kind of emotional abuse that only polite South Carolinians can lay on fellow members of the elite when one of their number steps out of accepted lines. Among other things, Waring's marriage cracked apart; he remarried; and critics could in biblical sense "scoff" and "slander" and "wag their heads," claiming that the crazy old fool had no business on a federal district court since he could not "handle his wife" properly. Bennie Mays was so touched by Waring's boldness and so disturbed by the attacks on him that he wrote about the judge in his *Courier* column, and was largely responsible for arranging some honors for the much harassed justice enduring sudden unpopularity among white people of "quality." The man of magnificence knew that noble acts were not always regarded as such, and he wanted a record for posterity that people of color had marked the courage of Justice Waring. In any case Mays warned those who would listen that the South had "exhausted all of its tricks in the [*Brown*] decision, but Negroes must keep pressing" in order to solidify the gains.[22]

On November 10, 1955, several hundred professional historians and fascinated citizens gathered in Memphis at the popular Peabody Hotel and nearby sites for the Southern Historical Association (SHA) conference. Black scholars, especially W. E. B. Du Bois, had presented at SHA conferences, but the association's formal dinner had been segregated until three years earlier at its meeting in Knoxville, when it was dramatically integrated after historian C. Vann Woodward refused to deliver his presidential address in a segregated setting, either at the Farragut Hotel or in the restaurant at the University of Tennessee, and instead arranged for the historians to travel to an integrated private restaurant in nearby Whittle Springs. Not long afterward had come the *Briggs v. Elliott* case and then the *Brown v. Board of Education* ruling. At the 1955 SHA meeting, the professional historians not only included a baker's dozen of black scholars in the audience and in dining halls but a session dedicated to a consideration of the issue of Jim Crow segregation. The panel for this session was arranged largely through the work of Mississippi historians Bell Irvin Wiley and James F. Silver, and it featured Nobel laureate novelist William Faulkner, distinguished prosegregationist attorney Cecil Sims, and Bennie Mays. Since the audience included teaching historians, public schoolteachers, and good hearted "lay people" as well as publishing scholars, Mays was especially anxious to make a strong case for integration, for he was hopeful that the audience would not only agree but teach their students in the light of what he told them.[23]

Attorney Sims gave a properly measured legal brief, citing the many precedents that vouchsafed Jim Crow. He made his case thoroughly but of course with respect and even sensitivity for Dr. Mays at his side and for the black scholars in attendance. Faulkner could be unpredictable in public and was capable of saying wild things about segregation and black people generally. On this occasion the better nature of the novelist prevailed, and the Mississippian firmly defended integration while strongly attacking Jim Crow and its injustices. The opportunity for the strongest statement fell to Bennie Mays, who preached so effectively that "all the white women in the audience wanted to join his church." In University of Chicago fashion, he spoke of a "strong dominant group" that "possesses all the power, political, educational, economic, and wields all the power" in such a way that it imposes "heavy burdens, grievous to be borne, upon the backs of the weak," exactly the kind of oppression of the poor that every prophet declared to be a sin. Taking his social science language immediately into the Baptist pulpit, he then denounced anyone who would use Jim Crow for aggrandizement of white power and then claim to be a Christian. Drawing on Rauschenbusch and Aubrey, Mays repeated that Jesus Christ was a social revolutionary, and that it was time for Christian revolution in the South. Mincing no words, he said to the largely Protestant and churchgoing historians and others gathered there that the oppressions of Jim Crow were "tantamount to saying to God, 'You made a mistake, God, when you didn't make all races white.'" Raising the ante still higher, Bennie Mays told his audience that they must obey what the Supreme Court had ruled or destroy the U.S. Constitution, that they had to institute racial justice or abandon the pretense of being believing Christians and Jews. Mays reached the climax of his speech with characteristic optimism: "The Supreme Court has given America an opportunity to achieve greatness in the area of moral and spiritual things. . . . It is my belief that the South will accept the challenge of the Supreme Court and thus make America and the South safe for democracy."[24]

Mays had held his own alongside Faulkner, no small feat when the novelist was sober and focused. Also Bennie Mays had made an emotional appeal that was yet grounded in historical research and legal reason and thus had held his own with the scholarly jurist. It was a day remembered well by southern historians, and largely through folkloric traditions. The *Memphis Press Scimitar,* hardly a liberal organ, complained bitterly that their journalists were unable to get photographs of the historic occasion with the black scholar seated next a local segregationist attorney and the great novelist; and that their reporters had difficulty gaining access to the meeting room in order to record what was said. Indeed Bell Wiley, who had organized the entire SHA, arranged to print the remarks of Sims, Mays, and Faulkner so that there would be a record beyond the golden memories of the audience. The man of *magnanimatatum* had also to acknowledge the role of the pagan force Fortuna on this occasion: Jim Silver and Bell Wiley had originally invited the great black sociologist Charles Spurgeon Johnson, who backed out late in the planning of the meeting, and the great moment came because the Morehouse president was available as a late substitute.[25]

During this time Sadie Gray Mays suffered physical ailments, problems that she and Bennie Mays did not discuss with officials at Morehouse or with friends. Bennie Mays was careful to keep no particular record, but Sadie Gray apparently suffered some form of cancer, and her husband could not help but remember the failure of Atlanta physicians when his first wife, Ellen Harvin, needed specialized care and treatment. The correspondence does not show Bennie Mays confiding in friends and associates, but it does show him working with physicians at the Mayo Clinic in Rochester, Minnesota, where he had befriended the occasional donor and the brilliant specialist Dr. Harold Habein. As Bennie and Sadie Mays traveled discretely to the clinic for examination and treatment—Bennie Mays apparently submitted to an examination as well—more difficulties struck. In midsummer Sadie Mays's crippled sister, Emma Gray, who had already endured a great deal but had become a successful professional with a University of Chicago master's degree, perished in a car crash. Without mentioning his wife's illness, Bennie Mays did confide in some correspondence that the loss of this courageous and trusted sister brought even the ebullient and optimistic Sadie Mays into the valley of despair. The examination by at least one coroner official was marred by racist language, and Bennie Mays demanded and received a full apology from the man and from the entire staff. By the late autumn of 1958, Sadie Gray Mays was pronounced cured and fit by Dr. Habein—apparently cancer free, if that was the problem. The first lady of Morehouse, physically hale and sufficiently revived in health and heart to host the men of the House and distinguished guests, reentered her long-running campaign to rid Georgia and other Deep South states of their various Jim Crow schemes to prevent black people from voting in the hustings beyond Atlanta.[26]

As to the strictly academic side of things at the House in the late 1950s and early 1960s, Bennie and Sadie Mays continued to travel extensively to raise money, and the endowment continued to grow apace as financier Charles E. Merrill and others labored to invest wisely and to write grants to build buildings and establish programs. With bittersweet memories of the "stepchild" status of Howard University's School of Religion, Bennie Mays was determined to train ministers well, if not strictly at Morehouse, then in full and effective cooperation with the Atlanta University system. Gammon Seminary in that system was the first black seminary to be fully accredited by the American Association of Theological Schools, but the Morehouse president wanted to expand Gammon's reach considerably; and he wanted scholars at the House to be part of the expanded mission to train the best ministers. He was particularly exercised because he learned that the Candler School of Theology at Emory University stood ready in the early 1960s to integrate its fine divinity school, and he knew that realistically, many black divinity students would choose Candler over Gammon if given that choice. Wholeheartedly integrationist and committed to preparing black scholars for entry into professions by training them at historically white institutions everywhere, Bennie Mays was still nervous about being "integrated out of existence" and did not want to have a few black scholars emerging from predominantly and historically white divinity schools, while a lower quality and a smaller quantity of black preachers emerged from the Atlanta University system.[27]

Going into action, Bennie Mays worked with the John D. Rockefeller Sealantic Foundation to develop the Interdenominational Theological Center (ITC), a nondenominational degree-granting seminary for the training of ministers. From discussions dating back to 1956, Bennie Mays had raised the money for an official charter by 1958 and by 1961 had raised enough funds for the bricks and mortar to make the ITC a physical reality. More important, he had cooperated with the faculty at Morehouse, Spelman, Morris Brown, and Clark to make the ITC a divinity school fully accredited by the American Association of Theological Schools. Sealantic alone had put forward about a quarter of a million dollars, and the General Education Board contributed one million dollars; in 2010 terms the Bennie Mays team had raised more than 8.8 million dollars for the new enterprise. Not neglecting either the ITC or his own baccalaureate School of Religion, Bennie Mays was able in 1961 to have both the ITC graduate-training center and the baccalaureate Morehouse School of

Religion fully accredited by the American Association of Theological Schools, remarkable accomplishments given the short time period in which he and his team had to work.[28]

Such achievements caught the attention of young John F. Kennedy as he ran for president. Relying as he did on Harry Truman for a legacy and for campaign help, Kennedy determined to use Fair Deal rhetoric to make a bold play for black support in the 1960 campaign, and he was pleased to see Bennie Mays on his side early. The Kennedy people made a strong civil rights platform in the New Frontier electioneering, and they scored President Dwight David Eisenhower for doing too little on every front of civil rights, especially in the integration crisis at Central High School in Little Rock, Arkansas—a situation that stunned everyone because Arkansas had early and peacefully integrated its law school and medical school and even a couple public high schools. In his *Courier* column, now renamed "My View," Mays encouraged the three hundred thousand readers to support Kennedy for the Democratic nomination and then to support the Kennedy-Johnson ticket against Richard Nixon and Henry Cabot Lodge in the presidential election of 1960. In the close race, the Democrats prevailed, and Bennie Mays was marked for reward.[29]

Kennedy met with Mays and discussed a major appointment, proffering a seat on the National Advisory Council to the Peace Corps, with special duties in Ethiopia but also holding out the possibility of an official position with the Civil Rights Commission of the Department of Justice. Kennedy promised that, unlike Eisenhower's civil rights agencies, his agencies would be vigorous in support of civil rights for African Americans, with enforcement of existing regulations about discrimination and with plans to persuade Congress to pass a major civil rights act and a voting rights act—both with enforcement "teeth." Bennie Mays was quite excited by his personal interview with Kennedy, and he readily consented to the Federal Bureau of Investigation (FBI) background check requested by the White House, so that he could be cleared for congressional consideration. Of course he must have known that Senator Russell remained a real force, especially on committees but even within the councils of the New Frontier administration. More than once, Bennie Mays and Senator Russell had sparred in newspapers, with the senator invariably charging that the Morehouse president was a Communist. The investigation, plus Bennie Mays's own rather blunt anti-Communist speeches and records, could easily clear up that charge. In due time, Kenneth O'Donnell, special assistant to the president, collected and filed 239 pages of testimony from FBI agents, whose summary conclusion stated: "Investigation revealed Mays in the past affiliated with a number of Communist-front organizations. Persons interviewed stated that his activities along that line in connection with his desire to raise the social standing of the Negro race [*sic*]. Reliable informants having knowledge of communist activities had no information indicating Mays had ever been a member of the Communist Party. All persons interviewed highly recommended Mays for a position of trust and responsibility."[30]

No less a "witch hunter" than FBI director J. Edgar Hoover signed summary statements clearing Bennie Mays as to his loyalty and character, but this fight was personal as well as racist for Senator Russell, who had been attacked as recently as 1959 in Mays's "My View" column. The Georgia senator succeeded in preventing any consideration of Mays for the Civil Rights Commission. A White House assistant, possibly O'Donnell, called Mays back in, apologizing and offering some appointments that did not require congressional approval, including a trip to Ethiopia to discuss education throughout Africa and the relationship of such efforts to the new Peace Corps. Bennie Mays was deeply hurt, but he blamed Richard Russell rather than Jack Kennedy, and he remained committed to the New Frontier. In addition, despite the longstanding relationship between Vice President Lyndon Baines Johnson and Senator Russell, Bennie Mays made friends with and declared his admiration for the onetime Senate majority leader Johnson. Convinced that Attorney General Robert F. Kennedy, the president, the vice president, and most Democrat federal officials were now firmly on the right side of the civil rights movement, Bennie Mays stood on the sidelines of such action again, still raising funds, still teaching students how to protest nonviolently, and still working with NAACP attorneys to help various young men, especially Morehouse's Horace Ward, attack segregation at state universities. Whether President Kennedy misrepresented himself to the Morehouse president or was less than fully competent in dealing with Senators Russell and Thurmond, as is sometimes charged by scholars, Bennie Mays grieved when the president was shot, and he said nothing in public or in correspondence that was other than enthusiastic support.[31]

Despite Bennie Mays's initial enthusiasm for Lyndon Johnson, there were good reasons for worry when Kennedy was assassinated and Johnson suddenly became president in November 1963. As Robert Caro has noted, Johnson was much closer to Richard Russell than Bennie Mays seems to have acknowledged. Johnson had become Senate majority leader because the Georgia senator had "anointed LBJ as his successor" and had done so largely because of the way the Texan had played the committee games and other inside politics of the senior chamber. In 1957 the Eisenhower administration had passed a weak Civil Rights Act. Symbolically important, it had no real way to enforce anything, said nothing about voting or fair housing, and was generally a fine statement of principle with no enabling elements—and it was Johnson who had modified the bill to the point that it threatened no actual change in Jim Crow. Thus southern moderates could vote for it as a gesture toward the mainstream, but an empty gesture.[32]

In meeting Bennie Mays, Johnson had retained him as a special adviser and was personally warm in his dealings with Mays, though the man of magnificence knew enough to realize that Johnson was always warm and kindly in initial encounters but could be devious behind the scenes. Johnson's White House assistants arranged still another FBI investigation, reexamined the Kennedy investigation, and again cleared Bennie Mays fully. However, it is worth noting that Johnson staffers continued to investigate the Morehouse man throughout Johnson's presidential terms and that the FBI continued its investigation until at least October 10, 1969. For all that, Johnson had impressed James Farmer of CORE with the force and vigor that he employed to pass the 1964 Civil Rights Act in honor of the martyred Kennedy, and Farmer had reported as much to his old mentor. Dr. King for his part began to expect much from Johnson and began a series of long conversations with him in hopes of cooperating with a man who would bring major civil rights legislation to bear in the Deep South and in the entire nation. Some activists were disappointed that the 1964 act was again weak on housing provisions and again said nothing about voting, but Bennie and Sadie Mays were heartened by Farmer's and King's reports that voting legislation was coming, as was fair-housing legislation. In fact Farmer announced almost breathlessly that he was witness to Johnson's "cajoling, threatening, everything else . . . whatever was necessary to get the voting rights" legislation through committees and onto the floor for vote.[33]

Bennie Mays the classicist Stoic was hard to read at the time, and the record left behind has been no easier to interpret. As usual he was optimistic, never wanting to appear weak and unfocused in public countenance as his hero John Hope had appeared during his final "Hopeless" phase of running the Atlanta University system. Whatever he thought in private, Bennie Mays continued to declare his optimism that a voting rights act and a housing act would be passed and signed largely because of the Texan. He did not name his old University of Chicago friend Bill Brown, but the column "My View" told readers that Johnson was like the unnamed Bill Brown, still another white Texan who had learned bitter lessons, paid a dear price, and now stood solidly with people of color on issues of justice. In any case the time was ripe for action. Some six million people of color were eligible to vote; yet no Deep South state had even half of its black people voting. Indeed, in looking at statistics for Mississippi, Dr. King noted that only 6 percent of voting age African Americans were registered to vote, and progress was so slow that it would take 135 years for Mississippi to have half its eligible black people voting. King had plenty of young Morehouse men marching with him into the bloody reprisals in Selma,

Alabama, on exactly this issue, and young John Lewis, inspired by King, had left Fisk University to direct voting drives in Georgia.[34]

On March 15, 1965, President Johnson gave a memorable speech in which he demanded that Congress produce a voting rights act. Most melodramatically, he quoted Dr. King and the men of the Morehouse by repeating King's line "I have a dream." Dr. King is said to have burst into tears while watching this speech on television, and those who saw the tears also reported that Dr. King was not seen crying in that year in context of any other event. As emotionally wrought as Bennie Mays could become during a prophetic call for people to come to justice, there are no memories of his crying, no matter how happy. In any case the Mayses accepted Johnson's speech as a genuine call by a mighty man, and they declared their thanks rather than their astonishment when he was able to sign the bill into law. At this moment of great triumph, one especially poignant for Sadie Gray Mays because of her own vigorous and personal three-decade involvement in campaigns for black voting in Georgia, the Mayses expressed their gratitude and, like good students of Marcus Aurelius, noted that the promised fair housing legislation was still to come. Salute the general and give him his earned triumph, but move forward to the next battle, albeit nonviolent.[35]

The early summer of 1967 marked a personal ending that coincided with public and institutional endings. A proper student of the classics and a careful student of the Bible, President Mays looked not only at the ending of a career at Morehouse in June 1967, but at the ending of a career that comprised several phases of progress in twentieth-century civil rights. Honored almost to the point of embarrassment, Benjamin Elijah and Sadie Gray Mays were not only the "first couple" of Morehouse, but "*the* Negro couple" in higher education, and were now generally called "*the* black couple" of historically black colleges and universities. Morehouse College was *the* place for the training of male leaders at the undergraduate level, *the* place for training doctors, lawyers, professors, teachers, and statesmen as they began their careers at the fine, little, properly sized liberal arts college. Morehouse was *the* liberal arts college that worked hand in glove with Meharry, Howard, and other medical colleges now even in the Deep South. It was *the* college that worked with the best law schools everywhere, not only in Chapel Hill but now including Athens and Baton Rouge. Bennie Mays could leave Morehouse in an honored processional, appropriate to a man of *magnanimatatum* or *megalosukos* in ancient of times: Simple, yet regal, and above all with full dignity. He knew he would remain as elder adviser to the bright young men at Morehouse and at other historically black colleges and universities; many of those bright young leaders he had personally coached at the "training ground for college presidents" and every one of whom he knew. The successors would need counsel about new policies and would need his memories for policies that he himself had set in motion. Above all, these new leaders whom he personally trained and those whom he personally knew would surely carry themselves forward with a style that Benjamin Elijah and Sadie Gray Mays had created. Surely, these bright young leaders following his example would move not only the black colleges and civil rights institutions but indeed the whole country in directions whose path he had marked clearly.

There would be opportunities now. He saw time, precious time, to spend with his beloved Sadie Gray Mays, time when they could travel together, now not having to travel separate from one another on hasty political campaigns and fund-raising treks—and above all no longer traveling under the onus of damnable Jim Crow dishonor and disfigurement. There would be no more hectic pace of making six speeches in five cities over some long weekend. Rather the Mayses could take their time on trips, traveling for leisure and amusement in any public conveyance through any place, not to exclude Mississippi or his native South Carolina. There would also be time for reflection and writing. The memoir he had been scratching out for perhaps three decades could be shaped into a coherent narrative that he could share in a way that would instruct other people. The memoir might finally be his chance to meet that middle-brow female audience of thoughtful white citizens to whom he had gestured but whose ear he had never caught and whose vision he had never attracted. The numbers of such white people seemed to be growing all over the South, not only in Atlanta but even in the once benighted remote burgs of the valleys of the slow-moving southern rivers. He could take some more time with the columns he wrote for the *Pittsburgh Courier,* perhaps collecting the best ones into a book, a collection of essays aimed at that growing, yet elusive, crowd of decent white folk in his native region.

It bade fair to be a glorious ending to a magnificent career. Relaxing in the shade of the lovely campus over which he had presided, he could be excused for a long and appreciative sigh as he reflected on what had been done, how hard won everything was—and how satisfying would be the remaining autumn of recognitions and celebrations. Not only the ITC with a properly accredited masters and doctoral training for black and other ministers in John Hope's old Atlanta University system, but accreditation for a first-class undergraduate School of Religion at Morehouse. Not only a decent endowment for the best little black college in the United States, but a worthy presidential successor, Hugh Gloster, who had mastered the pathways of his mentor and would keep the House on the highest moral and material planes of progress. Bennie Mays could hand over to Dr. Gloster not only his personal reputation and the reputations of all the men of Morehouse, but he could also hand him farewell gifts:

Phi Beta Kappa, once denied to Mays the student at Bates College, for long decades denied all black institutions, was fully installed in 1967 at Morehouse; and Dorothy Danforth Compton gave the House $150,000 for the endowment—in 2010 a sum worth nearly one million dollars—and perhaps more important made it clear that she would stay on as a trustee and benefactor for the college.[36]

But as proper student of the classics and the Bible, Mays knew perfectly well the fleeting nature of honorable moments. He knew how David, after building a powerful kingdom, in his old age lived not in comfort but in extreme danger and threat, unable to warm himself in his bed except with a young lover perhaps not to be trusted. Members of David's own family ripped apart the kingdom from the inside. And there was Solomon, who—not long after the greatest triumphs—was compelled to use his wisdom to cling perilously to power through clever negotiations with the unrighteous and alliances struck with the evil ones. Solomon's God-granted wisdom was turned to clever tricks that angered at last the Deity and presaged the destruction of his kingdom for his posterity. Among the beloved pagans, Aristotle described well the best aspects of Athenian democracy, but he wrote most of this description on behalf of a dictatorial emperor from Macedonia, who was busy extending the borders of Greek rule, taking Greek ideas to new worlds, and yet ignoring Aristotle's best teachings of Greek moderation and dignity and justice. Aristotle lived in some public honor in the palace of Alexander, and yet the philosopher's most honorable instructions were dishonored by his most important pupil, his benefactor the emperor. Thomas Aquinas, so vital to the men of Morehouse, had developed his *Summa Theologica* despite, rather than because of, his often disdainful students at the University of Paris, who called him "The Dumb Ox" behind his broad back because of his size and visage. And despite all the accolades that came with his sainthood, it was hard to see how Thomas's most important prescriptions for proper Christian habits of behavior were in play at his beloved university or in his beloved Roman Catholic Church. Marcus Aurelius and Epictetus, whom Bennie Mays had baptized in his own mind in the waters of the Saluda River and then displayed for worshippers at the Morehouse chapel, these men in their temporal lives had yet lived hectic, frenetic, and often dishonored days, especially at the ends of their careers.

Yes, the classicist's record showed a high probability that a good man of *magnanimatatum* and *megalosukos* was apt to spend his final days alone and ignored, perhaps "unknown or known only to be despised."[37] At the moment that President Emeritus Mays rested in the calming shade of career glory with well-won acclamation for the hard-fought campaigns, Benjamin and Sadie Mays, optimists still, knew quite well that they were not headed into a final, restful, and quiet period of honor and relaxation.

13

"MYNE OWNE FAMILIAR FRIEND"

1968

"Myne owne familiar friend." The psalmist in a major mood switches voice with this melancholy note marked by bitterness, recalling a friend—"after my own heart," with whom he "took sweet counsel together"—who turned against him. The psalmist then returns for solace and life itself to the Hebrew God Yahweh, the one personal relationship—whether blood family, ethnic, tribal, national, or fraternal love—that can always be counted on reliably. "I will put my trust in thee." With the years 1968 and 1969 came a series of deaths, each one amounting to a powerful blow to any realistic hope for peace and justice. Old friends departed. Surviving ones, especially younger friends, seemed less reliable than before, treacherous at worst. And Sadie Gray Mays's cancer apparently recurred. Whatever her ailment, it was a condition that the couple again kept secret, but her reduced horizon bore down heavily on each of them.[1]

Besides the loss of the truest and oldest friends, Bennie and Sadie Mays found it hard even to talk with many of their younger friends and associates. Such folk laughed at the Mayses' language, or worse, they were stiffly polite and then laughed behind the Mayses' backs. Young activists used a variety of terms, sometimes all at once, and it was hard to know what these terms were intended to mean. "New Negro" had been vaguely redefined and then abandoned as a term sometime in the optimistic months after 1953. The Mayses accepted the disappearance of this term, as they had accepted and indeed welcomed the disappearance of "Race Man." But what term could describe the person of color who sought justice and peace? Indeed what term could describe any person of color? What once was New Negro was now variously called "black, sometimes capitalized self-consciously as "Black," later called "Afro-American" and then "African American." New leaders disputed the correct term, but reached consensus on rejecting "Negro." There were competing and conflicting goals for people of color, and Bennie and Sadie Mays were suspicious of every one of those new terms because they were deeply suspicious of the new leaders proclaiming new goals.

In thinking back over it, especially looking through correspondence and publications, the plain term "Negro" was discarded with a haste and a derision that seems stunning. The slain hero Martin Luther King, Jr., had proudly called himself a "Negro," and while he lived, the term was fully accepted from his lips. Yet mere months after his death "Negro" became nearly equivalent to "Uncle Tom." In fact the insult "Uncle Tom"—sometimes now rendered as a wry "Tom"!—would be laid on Bennie and Sadie Mays in spite of their decades of courageous campaigns against white oppression. For a University of Chicago couple, the imprecision and sloppiness of the language about social policy and social science was a problem. For veterans of the most dangerous days of the "long" civil rights movement, the insults from the uninformed and the inexperienced were gall and wormwood. In this mess there remained the task of training young men to lead, and for that there was the legacy of Morehouse. Yet in the period after 1967, the House itself was threatened and from within, by folk shaking their fists and yelling and dismissing everything that Bennie and Sadie Mays had built between 1940 and 1967. And while the young folk danced their dances and did their drugs and shouted their insults, the sly white folk resegregated everything—at least as far as the Mayses could see. None of this morass was completely unexpected, but Bennie and Sadie Mays were remarkably alone and lonely in the face of the current version of race relations as the 1960s, a decade of achievement and progress, ended.

Soul, black pride, black power: initially Bennie and Sadie Mays thought they understood these words, and sometimes they used them. Initially, they considered themselves marchers continuing in the same long campaign because they had understood the post-1967 world as an extension of their own continuing and career-long marches. They came to find, however, that new leaders were starting entirely new marches. Integration with its opportunities for power, wealth, and influence for young men of Morehouse, and an integrated society with opportunities for all people of color were now rejected, even at the moment that a real middle class was being formed and material well-being was increasing for most minorities. If the new leaders wanted to call the Mayses "Tom," the president and first lady emeriti for their part came to regard some of the striving young black people, especially in the faculty and student body of the beloved House, not only as arrogant ingrates with no appreciation for the blood sacrifices of their forefathers, but also as reprobates who worshipped false gods of violence, drugs, and sex. The Mayses' grand hopes were dashed, and it seemed dangerous to take "sweet counsel" with anyone, for all seemed to whore after the idols of untrue deities. Perceptions on both sides of this divide were exaggerated. This chronicler is trying only to capture the stated and written perceptions of Bennie and Sadie Mays, who—whatever else—in 1968 considered themselves to be in a dwindling cadre of reasonable people committed to pacifist reform of economy and society on behalf of the most oppressed minority in the republic. Where the angry young kept pointing at the glass half empty, Bennie and Sadie Mays, as they had throughout their long married life, persisted in showing that the glass once nearly empty was now half full. And the couple kept demanding that everyone work together, black and white, to "come fill the cup"—a goal they considered at once Christian, pacifist, and quite radical.

While still in the warm glow of the last commencement at the House, Bennie Mays had gained the title president emeritus. Strong allies on the board of trustees—including securities expert Charles E. Merrill, major foundation benefactor Dorothy Danforth Compton, and Nobel Peace laureate Dr. Martin Luther King, Jr.—had made it clear to him that the title was no signal to go away, but rather an acknowledgment that he had continuing duties at Morehouse. The inspiriting new president, Hugh Gloster, made it no less clear that he counted on the Mayses to help him in still new adventures for the beloved college. During that triumphant commencement, Bennie Mays was also presented with an honorary doctor of humane letters degree from the House.[2]

As for the campaign to bring Bennie Mays's memoir before the long-sought audience of educated and tolerant white people, Dr. DeLand DeVinney of the Rockefeller Foundation arranged for major financial help for research and travel and for paid time to edit the manuscript begun decades before. Whatever he needed to check records and search archival depositories, to pay typists and editors, and to catch up on scholarly reading, Bennie Mays had three full years with a regular stipend to do so as a Rockefeller Fellow. Other honors came. Already the holder of seventeen honorary doctorates, Bennie Mays was pleased to receive four more in his final academic year alone. Besides the doctorate from Morehouse, he traveled to receive doctor of laws degrees from Harvard University and from historically black Morgan College in Baltimore. There was also a doctor of letters degree from Grinnell College, a demanding liberal arts college run by neo-abolitionist social gospelers in Grinnell, Iowa. There he had the honor of introducing as commencement speaker his student Dr. King, whose frenetic schedule caused him to arrive almost ninety minutes late, but whose combination of eloquence and sincerity moved the Iowa crowd to round after round of applause for the slow-to-start celebrations.

Mays continued to write his opinion/observation column for the *Pittsburgh Courier*, a mission supremely important for formulating black reformist responses to the 1968 election campaign that pitted the reliable Happy Warrior, Hubert H. Humphrey, against Richard M. Nixon and his southern strategy for a revised Republican Party that included the old Dixiecrat Strom Thurmond and the old radio- and television-racialist Jesse Helms. Whether critiquing Kennedy-Johnson liberals from within the Democratic tent or critiquing the southern strategists from well outside their tent, Bennie Mays spoke boldly in his *Pittsburgh Courier* forum "My View," especially about the new term "backlash" that was employed to describe white anger at recent gains by black people in schools, the military, all professions, some large corporations, and city politics.[3]

Some hope emerged when Lyndon Johnson withdrew from the 1968 presidential campaign largely because of liberal dissatisfaction with his Vietnam War policies. Bennie Mays remained a supporter of Johnson but was sharply critical of the war. He was hopeful about a new presidency featuring Hubert Humphrey, whom he had known fondly since 1948, when the youngish Minneapolis mayor had spoken with eloquence on behalf of a Fair Deal for black people—and had helped move Harry Truman toward a boldly integrationist and pro–civil rights platform. Yet backlash set many voters alongside Richard Nixon, and anger about the war made some of Mays's allies reluctant to support Humphrey. Then the long-feared but unthinkable happened during Easter weekend 1968, when Dr. King was killed by James Earl Ray in Memphis during a controversial campaign on behalf of sanitation workers—the Memphian version of Gandhi's untouchables—and following a series of increasingly unpopular and rancorous trips to once-liberal areas of the upper Midwest.[4]

Bennie Mays sensed terrible problems coming at once. He knew enough about political dynamics and the reliance of a mass movement on a charismatic figure to expect awful consequences in the wake of such an assassination. Dr. King had held disparate groups together by the gravitational pull of his eloquence and his willingness to sacrifice for others. There was no other figure like Dr. King, and inevitably the movement became smaller and at the same time less focused. Owen L. DeVaughn, Jr., Morehouse 1949 and director of the Western Christian Leadership Conference based in Los Angeles, noted with wry regret of his old classmate and friend: "I am impressed with the fact that Dr. King had made for himself a role that only he could fill." The Reverend DeVaughn spoke for many in terms of an emotional response, but he also predicted what would happen. Nor was DeVaughn merely being defeatist: He and like-minded Morehouse men convened at once to search out and elect a successor for head of SCLC and otherwise to support those such as Jesse Jackson,

Ralph Abernathy, John Lewis, Vernon Jordan, and Shirley Chisholm who would continue nonviolent activism. DeVaughn himself soldiered on for an additional twenty years in Los Angeles before returning to his native Alabama to continue radical pacifist work. For all that, DeVaughn and the others knew full well that the loss of Dr. King had changed things completely.[5]

Bennie and Sadie Mays essentially agreed with their shrewd former student. Yet even the Mayses with their University of Chicago training in demographics and trends were surprised by the intensity and, above all the speed, of the change in the civil rights movement. Some surviving leaders spoke of violence, and they celebrated the riots that destroyed black living space in cities for the stated reason that riots gained attention, and politicians responded to the spotlight that such violence and destruction cast on urban problems. Others spoke of resegregating, restoring black dignity, pride, and room for achievement and accomplishment by leaving the white world; some even spoke of gaining a Deep South state as a black-only haven, and many more spoke of the urban ghetto as power base that should be reserved to blacks. Still others spoke about returning to Africa, almost like Marcus Garvey from Bennie Mays's youth. In his memoir revisions the astounded Mays reviewed Garveyism and proclaimed its 1968 version to be even more fantastical than the original. Still more fantastical, and to Mays self-destructive, was the talk about Pan-Africanism, a campaign to get African nations to unite with African Americans in the United States to bring justice both in those besieged lands and in the besieged streets of American cities. To Bennie Mays none of these alternatives seemed workable, and in fact each seemed to offer the certitude of death and destruction for a people recently on the rise. Full integration into the flawed United States, while not logically sufficient, still seemed to Bennie Mays the logical analyst to be the necessary first step to racial justice and the necessary second step to economic equity.[6]

For his part in responding to Dr. King's assassination, Bennie Mays remained truest to his own Gandhian principles of activist-but-pacifist protest and to his own integrationist dreams. In doing so, he thought that he was in fact truest to the ruling principles for the slain giant. Dr. King of course was by far the most famous of all the famous men of the House, and he was by far the most famous man that Bennie Mays had mentored. It could be understood if there had developed a degree of resentment that the student was recognized as such an accomplished master, sometimes to the exclusion of the mentor. Indeed sometimes the student Martin King was thought of almost as the mentor to the mentor Bennie Mays. Yet, if Bennie Mays harbored such notions, he never revealed them in his public utterances, in his correspondence, or to any on the intimates in whom he confided. Mays was pleased to deliver the benediction at the 1963 March on Washington. In fact the Mayses had gone out of their way to make sure that Dr. King was honored on every occasion that was afforded at Morehouse; and there is no way to overstate the genuine thrill the Mayses expressed when Dr. King received the Nobel Peace Prize in 1964. Nor was there any overstating the gratitude of the Mayses, long campaigners for voting rights, when the Montgomery-to-Selma march made such obvious impact on the Voting Rights Act of 1965. Sources for the Mayses' attitude toward their more famous and more honored charge were in the Bible: those who follow the law revealed by God are "wiser than all [their] teachers . . . and have more understanding than the aged . . . because [God himself] . . . instructed" them. It was the part to be played by student King that he see most clearly the divine "light on [his] path" and thus rise far above any of his mortal mentors. Like the Hebrew prophets Bennie Mays studied at Chicago, King had brought every believer back to the truth that they had forgotten. Such prophecy must be given fullest respect, and the divine light it revealed must be followed by believers without fretting over status or age or even personal virtue. The man of Thomistic magnificence must always respect revealed wisdom from God, whether the divine wisdom elevate student above mentor or carry away the student early and before his work is completed.[7] In this case both catastrophes had happened, and both had to be accepted as God's will—as both had to be accepted as God's charge that those remaining behind must carry on the work of the chosen prophet.

With the murder of the prophetic King, the Mayses responded for their public much as they had before in special commemorations for their student. They helped to arrange the most honorable and dignified kind of funeral that there could be. In the Sale Hall chapel at Morehouse and in public statements, Bennie Mays took the long view and spoke it: "Dr. King is one of the latest prophets to die to make men free." Furthermore the slain leader "was willing to suffer for a righteous cause in the firm belief that this kind of suffering was redemptive." To militants who condoned and even seemed to celebrate violent protest in the days after Dr. King's assassination, the eulogist pointedly said, "Let it be thoroughly understood that our deceased brother did not embrace nonviolence out of fear or cowardice. . . . I make bold to assert that it took more courage for King to practice nonviolence than it took for his assassin to fire the fatal shot. . . . Perhaps he was more courageous than soldiers who fight and die on the battlefield. There is an element of compulsion in their dying. But when Martin Luther King faced death again and again, and finally embraced it, there was no pressure. He was acting on an inner compulsion that drove him on." Mays concluded his chapel memorial by citing "the immortal John Fitzgerald Kennedy" in paraphrase: "Martin Luther King, Jr.'s unfinished work on earth must truly be our own." In his column Bennie Mays wrote what he said in several places: "the world moves forward on the feet of those who walk the high road of justice, fair play, and brotherhood."[8]

Even while the "schoolmaster of the movement"—the man Dr. King called "my spiritual mentor"—was speaking, riots broke out throughout population centers North and South. The spectacular exception to the norm of urban riots was Indianapolis, where the news of the assassination was delivered by presidential candidate Robert F. Kennedy, who pleaded successfully to the crowd of black listeners gathered in the ghetto for a peaceful and not a violent response in memory of King. Atlanta was not Indianapolis, and the Georgia capital had its own days of destruction, but at least at Morehouse Bennie Mays was able to speak memorably to a respectful crowd of peaceably mourning students and alumni. It was quite otherwise elsewhere in Atlanta and in some sixteen other cities from south to north. At least thirty-nine people, only five of whom were white, perished in the April riots, and the damages to African American property adjusted for inflation amounted to more than $265 million while displacing at least twelve hundred black people from their homes in Washington, D.C., alone. Surely, the Mayses reasoned, Robert Kennedy's words and actions reflected common sense and practicality as well as idealistic pacifism considering the terrible toll in blood and treasure for African American communities outside Indianapolis. Were not the black people of Indianapolis—still housed safely and still holding jobs and still harboring undamaged black businesses—better off than the twelve hundred homeless African Americans in the nation's capital—to say nothing of being alive, compared to the thirty-nine people who died in the violent riots? How could militant young folk look at such results and declare that it was impractical to respond nonviolently and that only violence begat results?[9]

Beyond the need to rebuild the cities whose black neighborhoods and business centers lay in smoldering ruins after the riots, there was the question about just what would happen to the movement with its most significant leader removed so viciously. King was only the most prominent and most recent in a long line of civil rights leaders who had been killed. Leaders Medgar Evers, Jonathan Myrick Daniels, Viola Gregg Liuzzo, and James Chaney, and many followers—including Addie Mae Collins and three other young children attempting to learn lessons about Jesus in a church basement on Sixteenth Street in Birmingham—had preceded Dr. King in that line. Soon Robert Kennedy followed Dr. King in the same procession of martyrs. Some could make a strong case that these people were martyrs to the technique of nonviolent protest, which was losing rather than winning. Despite Bennie Mays's congenital optimism and despite real material success that could be measured and shown for black people, one could be forgiven for thinking that a host of fine people were dying for a peaceful cause while the opposition was not constrained by any compunction about using violence.

Certainly other voices could drown out Bennie Mays's still ringing voice and could drown out the recordings of the more famous King's: From W. E. B. Du Bois—who called on black men to get up off their knees and who had sat through the Atlanta Riot of 1906 with a loaded rifle to protect his home and family—through Malcolm X's call in 1965 for racial justice achieved "by any means necessary," to Stokely Carmichael, who in the fateful year of 1968 told those seeking the vote to arm themselves and fight on behalf of black power, there were attractive heralds of an armed and militant, indeed paramilitary black power movement. None of these spoke about Socrates or Gandhi, and when they spoke about "soul force," their emphasis was on force as a physical and material thing—and finally such force was a violent thing. By like sign, when the mature Du Bois and when young Malcolm X or Stokely Carmichael spoke about soul, they did not mean anything ethereal but rather they designated the specific ethnic group African American. All at once "soul force" was not Dr. King's term at all, but rather a term that specifically marked black violence.[10]

When diverse personalities and characters such as H. Rap (Hubert Gerold) Brown, Eldridge Cleaver, Bobby Seale, and the Black Muslims' Elijah Muhammad were included among those loosely called advocates of black power and the soul movement, there was certainly a new militancy afoot in the land. It was not the "marvelous militancy" of the pacifist who knelt in prayer at the Rankin chapel at Howard or the Sale Hall chapel at Morehouse any more than it was the soul force of those who marched alongside Dr. King. It was instead a strident militancy that bespoke violence, and it attracted many young people. Most stunning was the transformation of Student Nonviolent Coordinating Committee (SNCC) in 1967 under Rap Brown. Founded on Easter weekend in 1960, SNCC included among its progenitors Julian Bond, then a junior at Morehouse, who served as its communications director and edited its newsletter *Student Voice* as he worked with voter registration in the rural Deep South. Now, barely six years later SNCC, had moved from a model of pacifist student activism to become a group that included no currently enrolled students, no lingering commitment to pacifism, much outwardly directed violence, and so much inwardly directed mayhem that the term "Coordinating" in its name was also inappropriate. Furthermore, with all the confusing talk about language for people of color, Brown adopted and used the term "nigger" in his powerful and aggressive rhetoric.[11]

Eldridge Cleaver celebrated the Black Panthers, who to the Mayses seemed to be mostly armed gangs in ghettoes on the East and West Coasts, a notion underscored by Cleaver's *Soul on Ice,* a collection of essays that included discussions of his own practice of rape as a "revolutionary action." In fact. in the month of April 1968, after Dr. King went down, a teenaged Panther was killed, and Cleaver was wounded in an Oakland shoot-out that brought a felonious-assault warrant for Cleaver, and self-imposed exile in Communist countries whence he sent back enthusiastic communications about justice in Cuba and Algeria. From this base of operations he ran for president the following November as the candidate of the Peace and Freedom Party.[12]

As for the Black Muslims, the Mayses as students of world religions could not countenance the way Elijah Muhammad changed the doctrine of the original prophet Muhammad, and they were ruefully reaffirmed in their view when Malcolm X actually made the pilgrimage to Mecca and returned to renounce the so-called Black Muslims. Then Malcolm X was killed, leaving the American leadership to Elijah Muhammad and the people whom the Mayses judged to be charlatans and not true Muslims at all. However, Malcolm X's late-life taking up of a nonracist and arguably nonviolent Muslim religious worldview was equally unattractive to the Mayses, who remained unsympathetic to the many black followers of Malcolm X even after Alex Haley and M. S. Handler and others had pointed out the leader's growth and development as an activist. Bennie and Sadie Mays were suspicious of and antagonistic to the new group of militants who were attracting followers at Morehouse and in the city of Atlanta, and the couple made no real distinctions among the rather different types of advocacy of these post-King proponents. So too were the youthful followers of the new phase of black power and the soul movement antagonistic to the Mayses, and there was no dialogue between them.[13]

Yet there was plenty of continuing dialogue between the elders of the academy and the Mayses. Still another honor came for Bennie Mays on May 3, 1968, when liberal and long-serving Michigan State University president John A. Hannah brought the couple to the East Lansing campus to award him the doctor of laws degree in special ceremonies. Arrangements had been made before King's murder and before the awful riots in Detroit. The occasion was bittersweet, with the Mayses grieving over the loss of a favored and prophetic son and liberals on the campus grieving and in shock over the wreckage of the Motor City, whose Woodward Avenue muscle cars and danceable Motown music had until the day before yesterday symbolized such hope for integration, industrialism, and onrushing improvement for all Michiganders. President Hannah, who had taken over at East Lansing only one year after Bennie Mays took over at Morehouse, had also requested that the president emeritus deliver the main address before the thousands of graduates at commencement exercises scheduled for June 9, 1968. Obviously the commencement was a fitting occasion for Bennie Mays to review the nature of the civil rights movement and remind liberals in the graduating class about the opportunities—and the duties—that still stretched before them all.[14]

On his return to Michigan State for the graduation remarks, Bennie Mays drew on the recent experiences in Memphis, Indianapolis, and Detroit as marks of emphasis for what were career-long assumptions and attitudes about the pursuit of justice on college campuses. Injustice had not started yesterday, and it would not be banished tomorrow. The prophet reminded his people about justice and led the way back against frightful odds, and murders of prophets were close to the norm in the Bible and in the history of the civil rights movement. Bennie Mays reminded those assembled about still another principle in *satyagraha;* that is, Gandhi's insistence that soul force meet physical force, that suffering is in fact ennobling, that violence is to be left to the oppressors and never to be taken up by those who seek justice. One had to be willing to die for justice, but one must never kill. It was a theme uttered only a few months before by Dr. King at Grinnell College, but it seemed to work as well on a campus of secular humanists at a research university. Again Bennie Mays reminded an audience about the damage done by riots and violence: Only the already desperately poor had died or lost their homes in those seventeen cities, in whose number Detroit figured prominently and for whom Robert Kennedy's leadership in Indianapolis stood as spectacular, but also hopeful, exception. As for city riots and urban violence and the early-spring reports of campus violence, Bennie Mays returned to the classical theme of accepting responsibility for one's protests, following the model established by Socrates. It was important to break an unjust law, but it was also important to suffer the consequences of breaking a law. Such incarceration, whether for Socrates in Athens or for Dr. King in Birmingham, showed that the principled protestor retained respect for the rule of law. "If [Dr. King] had violated the law and then called for amnesty," Bennie Mays told his audience, "his actions in a sense would have been irresponsible and would have indicated disrespect for law." Although the words paid highest tribute to Dr. King, they also scored the student protestors of the day, since most of their demonstrations quickly moved into negotiations for amnesty for their campus actions.[15]

This and other addresses by Mays drew some white liberal response. Senator Ralph L. Yarbrough, Democrat of Texas, was one white liberal who was much moved by Mays, and he arranged to have the eulogy to King printed in the *Congressional Record,* along with the Texan's own words of praise not only for King but also for Mays's principled pacifism. This support was interesting. Yarbrough was breaking with his traditional ally Lyndon Johnson and also breaking with what was surely the majority prowar and anti–civil rights expression among his fellow southerners. Likely a more typical example of the current regional mood among white folk was provided by that reliable bell-wether Senator Strom Thurmond—so crucial to Nixon's southern strategy—who on the same day placed in the *Congressional Record* a South Carolina daily newspaper's editorial complaint about the physical damage caused by demonstrators, with implication that the late Dr. King had at least indirectly inspired the damages, both in demonstrations that he led while living and in those such as Resurrection City, the tent city set up in Washington, D.C., to honor his memory and his causes. Of course in the development of time, Senator Yarbrough left the political scene and became one more footnote, and Senator Thurmond became respected for his role in building a powerful new Republican Party in his region.[16]

Demonstrating their approval of public demonstrations true to the *satyagraha* of the late Dr. King, Bennie and Sadie Mays hurried to support surviving leaders Ralph Abernathy, Hosea Williams, Jesse Jackson, and Bernard LaFayette. These and others intended to convert the sanitation workers' demonstration and methods into a Poor People's March on behalf of the "Fifty-First State of Hunger." This march, featuring mule-drawn wagons and many pedestrians, was to wend its way from Memphis across the Upper South to Resurrection City in Washington. The long and slow-moving trek would compel otherwise comfortable Americans to see the faces of poverty and hunger on the move. Then, Resurrection City, within sight of the grand monuments and the center of Great Society government, would compel national leaders to look into the same faces encamped in the capital. Before Dr. King's assassination, Hosea Williams had become the field director of the planned march, and he was assisted by campaign manager Bernard LaFayette. Abernathy, as King's closest associate, took up the overall leadership of the SCLC, and oversaw Williams and LaFayette. Jesse Jackson brought his inspirational preaching to Resurrection City at the end of the march and the beginning of the encampment. Correspondence with these leaders and with King's widow, Coretta Scott King, makes it clear that Mrs. King wanted Bennie Mays to appear at the Poor People's March and to take a major role in it.[17]

The heightened and closely focused emphasis on economic oppression was set within context of stopping the war in Vietnam, and this too reflected Dr. King's concerns in his final weeks. Bennie Mays agreed with Coretta Scott King that it was necessary to commingle antiwar and antipoverty with civil rights partly because he now pronounced all war wrong without exception, partly because a disproportionate number of black troops died in Vietnam, and partly because money for the war drained away funding for poverty campaigns. Coretta Scott King called for this holistic and pacifist protest against poverty, racism, and the Vietnam War because such a protest had been the final and most impassioned call from the dead prophet. Bennie Mays concurred with that vital claim. Immediately he sent Abernathy and the Poor People's Campaign $100 out of his own modest pension, which was supplemented by a modest stipend. (In twenty-first-century dollars Mays's gift was more than $600.) Mays also personally raised some $1,454—in twenty-first-century dollars some $8,800—from such disparate sources as black professional businessman C. R. Yates (who also agreed to collect from friends and associates), Mayor Ivan Allen, and even Ralph McGill, the *Atlanta Constitution* columnist not hitherto sympathetic to integration and antipoverty causes. In this period Bennie Mays eulogized Dr. King in many places, both in public speeches and in print and each time he connected the Vietnam War with poverty and racism, calling for a thoroughgoing pacifist campaign against these connected ills. A line he used several times was: "Let us not riot, but let us remove the causes for riot."[18]

In order to find more money for the expensive Poor People's March and the Resurrection City encampment, Bennie Mays worked with the popular Motown Records groups the Temptations and the Supremes to set up a benefit concert in Atlanta, with proceeds going to the Poor People's March. Sadie's poor health kept her from making this trip, so Bennie Mays went by himself to join the Poor People's March in the third week of June 1968 as the sad and bedraggled caravan made its way into Washington. Abernathy and Jackson and certainly Mays were not without their own charismatic gifts, but—like prophets before them in other places—each functioned "without honor" on this occasion. Few white people expressed solidarity with the movement, and the black citizens of the District of Columbia, already crowded out of living space and with unemployment aggravated by the ravages to the central business district, responded with violent and destructive protests against poverty, racism, and the war. The District police, still all but traumatized by the riots in April, responded to violent demonstrations aggressively, probably an overreaction that resulted in the wounding and jailing of many demonstrators. By June 19 Resurrection City looked much like Gehenna, the smoking refuse dump that was biblical destination of the wicked. Much black living space destroyed by the riots was obviously not going to be rebuilt; many businesses were obviously gone forever; and the protestors limped away without much to show for their strenuous march and their wet and muddy encampment. Indeed the whole episode seemed to contribute to the rapid retreat to the Maryland and Virginia suburbs—"white flight"—that had already begun before the inner-city riots of April, May, and June.[19]

For all that, Bennie Mays's speech at Resurrection City is enlightening, especially for those who would call him "Tom." He agreed with Coretta Scott King that "people were hurt and dispersed," and that living conditions in black

Dee Cee, already bad, had worsened. Yet he also agreed with her that "it was good to demonstrate solidarity with the March." His remarks before the dispirited crowd—literally rained on by the weather and spiritually rained on by white liberal nonresponse—were the best he could offer in the way of Baptist reformist rhetoric and *satyagraha* resolve. He connected the antiwar campaign to the antipoverty campaign, and he tried to reach beyond a narrow color-consciousness to bring in all poor people oppressed by war and poverty. While journalists of the day and historians of a later day cannot recall Resurrection City as a success, Bennie Mays and Coretta Scott King did. He carefully preserved news notices and flyers and mementos, and he regarded the Resurrection City protest as a shining moment in his own career as well as a fitting tribute to the memory of the chosen prophet King.[20]

Amid this turmoil Bennie and Sadie Mays were compelled to face her physical difficulties. By the normal reckonings of the medical profession, Sadie Gray Mays was a survivor of the cancer that had apparently been diagnosed by family physician Dr. James B. Gilbert in 1954 and then treated at the Mayo Clinic over the following two years. She had made it a little beyond ten years cancer free. In the terms of the medical profession, five years without recurrence makes one a "cancer survivor." However, in 1965 a recurrence of her cancer had evidently been confirmed by the experts at the Mayo Clinic. This time there could be some treatment, but no operation would be attempted given the extensive spread of the cancer and her advanced age. Thus no hope for a cure was offered. To the public she remained the buxom first lady with an unremitting smile on her beautifully rounded face, but the couple realized that an end to her times was coming sooner rather than later. Among other activities, Sadie Mays busied herself helping to raise money for and otherwise assisting at Happy Haven, a nursing-home facility in Atlanta to which she could repair if need be some day. In their fashion the Mayses never complained, and they never explained. They certainly did not utter the word "cancer" among associates.[21]

As for Bennie Mays, he was in remarkably good shape in many ways, but his heart was weakened and his blood pressure was high. He took medication to regulate the sometimes erratic patterns and rhythms of his heartbeat and to lower the pressure on the walls of his seventy-year-old blood vessels. Never a drinker or a smoker, he stayed trim, weighing a bit less than when he manned the defensive line at Bates College. As he had for five decades, he continued to take vigorous walks for exercise. African American men of the late twentieth century tended to suffer hypertension, or high blood pressure, to greater degree than white men of the same era, and black men often perished from undiagnosed and untreated hypertension. There was disproportionate hypertension, diagnosed or otherwise, among men of all races who held high-stress jobs in the academy, as corporate fund-raisers, and as political activists—the tasks Bennie Mays intended to pursue as before. Determined to live out his own time to the fullest, Bennie Mays monitored his health and paid close attention to what his physicians told him. When his end came, it was not going to be because of something that had never been diagnosed or properly treated. He approached his late-life health almost as he approached a social problem, compartmentalizing segments of the physical problems, analyzing, measuring, and planning methodically—and with as little emotion as possible.[22]

The Mayses faced their health problems with the same signature determination and characteristic optimism with which they faced the various campaigns they intended to pursue in the late 1960s. The couple made virtually no public acknowledgment that anything could or would slow down or stop either of them. Indeed, not only did Bennie Mays agree to travel, to write his memoir, and to continue raising money for Morehouse, but he also agreed to move to East Lansing, Michigan, for the entire academic year of 1968–69 to serve as visiting professor and adviser to President John Hannah. Although interested in making such a move herself, Sadie Gray Mays determined to use the political rights for which she had campaigned over a career. She had decided some years before that what public-school education—and specifically Atlanta public schools—most needed was some black educators to serve on the Atlanta Board of Education. In her limited time remaining, Sadie Mays announced that she would run for the board, setting in motion a campaign that officially began in the spring of 1969 before Bennie Mays's Michigan State assignment was concluded.[23] Thus Benjamin and Sadie Mays began the academic year 1968–69—only their second one as retired president and first lady of Morehouse—with full schedules.

On the campus of Michigan State, there was personal triumph and much respectful recognition for Bennie Mays's accomplishments and experiences. As his student the martyred King became more of a mythic presence and loomed larger in contrast with the pretenders to the mantle of leadership of the civil rights movement, Mays was sought out by people who wanted to hear what Dr. King was really like, what he did, and above all, what he would do if he were living. Mays taught a class for enthusiastic and idealistic students of all ethnic identities and from all backgrounds; and he was sought by local church and civil rights groups for his speeches and for his counsel. Bennie Mays came to admire President Hannah, a practical-minded scientist who had presided over the growth of Michigan State from an agricultural sciences college of some six thousand students to a full research university of nearly forty thousand students with its own medical studies program and other new programs all well regarded and highly rated by the Carnegie Foundation academic experts—and this in the same state as the much vaunted University of Michigan at Ann Arbor. Hannah established a basic school for incoming students often overwhelmed by university demands, and this innovation gained notice and was copied throughout the United States. More interesting still, Hannah established Spartan Roundtable, a forum for discussion groups at which students could approach him directly with any concerns. Despite his different academic discipline and despite the fact that Michigan State was a large public university, Hannah approached social issues much as did Bennie Mays. Hannah emphasized his personal relationship with students and also gave them personal guidance—an approach not unlike that of the schoolmaster of the House. In fact Hannah was more approachable on his campus than Bennie Mays had been at Morehouse for students and even for junior faculty if one wanted to lodge a complaint or make a suggestion. Sadie Gray Mays had always functioned as the person students and young faculty could approach if they had grown afraid of her husband or if they were ashamed of themselves. Bennie Mays did not see until later how his firm proclamations, iron will, and occasionally frosty distance could keep him from knowing what his younger charges were thinking and doing at Morehouse. By contrast Hannah, who obviously could never meet forty thousand folk in person and who was hardly an inspiration at the podium, did effectively use his Spartan Roundtable to hear the heartfelt concerns of his student body. Thus President Hannah was never surprised by his students' behavior, while President Emeritus Bennie Mays could indeed be stunned by student behavior at Morehouse.[24]

Like other academics with whom Bennie Mays worked and cooperated, Hannah was an old Eleanor Roosevelt liberal and always involved in socioeconomic affairs, especially on issues of liberal internationalism and economic development of the Third World. In April 1969 he left Michigan State to take charge of President Johnson's Agency for International Development (USAID). At the time USAID was regarded as a nonmilitary and "soft" program of economic assistance to Third World countries, rather than a "hard" part of the Cold War offensive. Later scholars have demonstrated that USAID was politically charged and even arrogant and dangerous in some of its operations, but in 1969 Bennie Mays failed to see those flaws. Thus he was proud to be associated with John Hannah, however briefly. The admiring visitor/adviser was troubled about what would happen to the university that had advanced only part of the way through President Hannah's ambitious reforms.[25]

Until a new president could be found through a nationwide search, Michigan State elevated Austrian-born, Yale-trained economist Walter Adams to be interim president. An immigrant who had grown up in Brooklyn and then interrupted his Yale studies to join U.S. ground forces in the European theater of World War II, Adams had earned a Bronze Star in combat and had seen plenty of challenges in his life. Even so he called his memoir about this period *The Test*—that is, a singular, emphatic challenge. Student protests about almost everything, especially curriculum and social governance, dominated the year. Like his admired predecessor, Adams also made himself available to student groups, actually frolicking on a recreation field with students at their leisure and practicing with the Spartan marching band. For these and other reasons, Adams was never surprised by the students' behavior or misbehavior—nor was he ever regarded by them as part of their problems. Indeed students considered him someone who could help find solutions. The interim president in fact acquitted himself quite well. Various faculty and student constituencies urged Adams to apply for the presidency, but he had made it quite clear that he would serve only until the right replacement could be found.[26]

Much as he admired John Hannah, Bennie Mays found to his delight that Walter Adams concerned himself with some of the broad trends that most concerned Mays as well: black studies, needs of black students on campus, race relations generally, socioeconomic needs of black residents in the city of East Lansing (and even more so in Detroit), the need for black doctors, and above all the need for expanded medical services to the poor of all ethnic identities in Michigan. An emerging issue was the tendency of football teams at major research universities, including the conference champion Michigan State Spartans, to focus more on the athletic prowess of their black players and less on their scholarly needs. Never a fan of big-time college football, the old small-college defensive end noted with disdain the poor academic performance of black Spartan football players, and he asked pointedly if the university had a policy of keeping African American players eligible to play rather than a policy aimed at the players earning their degrees. The old Pullman porter organizer also asked pointed questions about the future for black workers at the nearby Ford and General Motors and Chrysler plants, where the United Auto Workers sported a liberal rhetoric about civil rights but offered disproportionately small numbers of jobs for black youth and even smaller numbers of leadership positions for black people in the very black and very young Michigan of the day. These were radical questions, and moments of discomfort ensued for the left-leaning members of the faculty and staff on the East Lansing campus. Bennie Mays was sorry that he would have only two months as adviser to the thoughtful and effective Dr. Adams, but pleased that good things seemed to be in store for that state university under its interim president. It must be noted that Adams paid little heed to Bennie Mays, whom he respected but whose cool and distant—and rather hierarchical and even vertical style of management—Adams disapproved of and disowned in his own leadership.[27]

As for Mays and the issues of black athletes, Harry Edwards, a black sociologist and sports psychologist, was more loudly asking the same questions in that era, and labor historians and scholars of race relations were addressing themselves to the questions about Michigan's automobile and other heavy-industry enterprises. Many of these figures more famously antagonized white liberal audiences on the issues while meeting the backlash of Vice President Spiro Agnew and of Ronald Reagan, then governor of California. During these discussions and debates, Mays remained the man of *megalosukos,* unbending and dignified, asking his questions, seeking his answers, always inspiring with his fervor, always warmly encouraging, always in the Baptist tradition—as he understood it—of being tough on the sin but forgiving of the sinner. During his academic year at Michigan State, Bennie Mays could be pleased to see changes in attitudes on the campus as consciousness was raised in his old-fashioned University of Chicago and Baptist-preacher style, even as louder folk talked about their more self-conscious consciousness raising as a New Left technique. Mays could be pleased to see some material changes in habit too, as administrators and professors began to face the facts of the difficulties assailing young black people, whether aspiring athletes, aspiring automobile workers, or aspiring scholars.[28]

He was especially gratified when he learned that forces at Michigan State were developing momentum to find a qualified African American to take over the presidency. Bennie Mays was not consulted on the presidential search, and he was only indirectly involved in the eventual selection of Dr. Clifton Reginald Wharton, Jr., the first African American president at the Midwestern goliath of an institution. Wharton—an economist with research expertise in developmental economics and much experience in the field farming in Vietnam and other part of Asia—was known to the Mayses from working alongside them. Another Ph.D. from the University of Chicago, albeit considerably younger than the Mayses, Wharton was coworker on the Johnson team and had also worked with Bennie Mays on the Rockefeller Foundation and on behalf of the United Negro College Fund. The search committee did not use Bennie Mays to find such a talented scholar and administrator, nor did Dr. Wharton come to East Lansing in response to any personal appeal from Bennie Mays. Yet, the Morehouse man played his role in assuring the brilliant economist that Michigan State was serious about its intent to improve race relations.[29]

Yet there was pain for Mays too because large numbers of black Michigan State students stayed away from his class, his church sessions, and his presidential consultancy workshops. Instead many black students wore black armbands and practiced special handshakes and gestures and ways of speaking and even ways of walking that emphasized their celebrations of Eldridge Cleaver, Bobby Seale, Huey Newton, and Elijah Muhammad. These expressions of soul force and soul power dominated the campus language, but not in Dr. King's old usage and certainly not in Bennie Mays's usage of the same terms. In contrast with the exciting new phrases and new fashions and the fast-walking and frenetic-talking of the new black leaders on campus, Bennie Mays's old Piedmont drawl and his measured cadences were decidedly passé. Indeed, when an interview with Mays was recorded, staffers working with the tape asked themselves and visiting researchers if the slow speech and classical expressions were signs of a bygone era—if not senescence or even dementia. For all his successful connection to the left-leaning members of the faculty and administration and for all of his inspiration to eager, young white scholars, Bennie Mays failed to connect with a big percentage of the black-student community at East Lansing, and he rued this failure.[30]

In these final years both Bennie Mays and Sadie Mays were still exposing themselves to public scrutiny, still standing and seeking public assessment, she as candidate for school board, he as a classroom instructor and a presenter at church and civic workshops. For those who had walked behind them over the long years, Bennie and Sadie Mays remained magnificent; but for many of the young who knew nothing of them and nothing of their old struggles, Bennie and Sadie Mays were just two more old folks in a society where the civil rights movement was fractured and where radicalism was defined as armed resistance to oppression—and where liberalism was laughed at by the new radicals and resisted vigorously by the rapidly growing right-wing of the self-styled backlash. Above all, classical insights, social science logic, and reformist Baptism, the hallmarks of the men of the House and the legacies of teachers Case and Aubrey and student King—the stuff of Bennie and Sadie Mays—were becoming period pieces at best, stumbling blocks at worst. White liberals of all ages liked and respected Bennie Mays at Michigan State. Radicals white or black—and there were many—disdained the old pacifist warhorses.

With that mixed record of teaching and consulting at a great research university during a time of rapid change, Bennie Mays traveled to Atlanta for a planned session of Morehouse trustee discussions about strategies with the hard-driving new president, Hugh Gloster. These discussions, back at John Hope's much-refurbished Atlanta University system center in black Atlanta, involved all six campuses, but were focused in particular on grand new plans for Morehouse. Filled with excitement about prospects for black students and faculty at Michigan State, Bennie Mays returned to the scene of his own triumphs to meet with fund-raisers and consultants about new vistas for the House and indeed for black scholars of all ages at all institutions, public or private, large or small.

As he made his trip between campuses in April 1969, Bennie Mays knew that most universities and colleges were in some tumult, partly about the Vietnam War, partly because young students yearned for a curriculum that was more "relevant" (the most commonly occurring term concerning education that year), partly because the yeasty 1960s had built up hopes that really could not be fulfilled, partly because the young New Left had overestimated its power and influence, and partly because there will always be tensions between young aspirants and established elders, especially in the springtime on a college campus. It seems unlikely that any nationally coordinated efforts were developing, but there were related and parallel protests, all trending toward property damage and many with some threatened violence, not only on U.S. campuses but throughout the world. Mays knew about student demonstrations at Reserve Officer Training Corps (ROTC) headquarters at Brown, Columbia, and Harvard—and back at his own Howard. He knew of protests about treatment of black students at the predominantly white and privileged Colgate University. He did not disapprove of such demonstrations at all. However, he was sorry to learn that Yale students complaining about ROTC had knocked over a picket fence and set a small fire on the property; minimal as such damage was, it was the wrong symbol in a world where network television news could rapidly transmit an electronic image to far points of the globe. He prayed that no protestors would commit violence, and he prayed that all protestors—in the best spirit of Socrates and of *satyagraha*—would accept the full consequences of any punishment as an integral part of principled demonstration in pacifist traditions. Such protests were far more radical in nature and in execution than he imagined, and his prayers—while appropriate and even moving for a believer and his God—were spectacularly irrelevant in context of the campuses of that day.[31]

What he did not know on the eighteenth and nineteenth of April was the nature of protests at other campuses. At Tuskegee, the legacy of Booker T. Washington and Robert Moton, students locked their trustees in a room of a campus building and held them hostage there, demanding a more relevant curriculum and more student representation on trustee and administrative working committees. There were loud student demonstrations by black students about the need for black studies at Southern Illinois University, Carbondale. At Columbia University and San Francisco State University, voices were louder; crowds were larger; property damage was greater; and things generally seemed more ominous. Most prominently, students in Paris and Berlin made more radical demands about structural change in politics, and in their demonstrations there was actual fighting with university officials and police, resulting in destruction of some valued university properties and injuries to people on both sides; it became impossible to conduct classes for several weeks. These Paris and Berlin demonstrations in particular illustrated the principle of protest that, if the police could be drawn in, an overreaction by the "pigs" could gain allies for the protestors from previously neutral students. It was hard to tell how widespread Students for a Democratic Society (SDS) was on U.S. campuses, but at each American campus protest there were usually some SDS operatives, and there were usually some black students with black armbands who wore their hair in the Afro style popular among both races at that time. These widely photographed demonstrators gave credence to the idea that SDS and the Black Panthers were in some way cooperating and coordinating things—even though there is no evidence of such coordination—and considerable evidence that leaders of the white and black radical groups did not like each other. As some of these demonstrators disrupted classrooms, jostled professors, and above all "shouted down" their chosen opponents, their actions led the veteran left re-formist and civil rights activist C. Vann Woodward to conclude that danger-ous people had crept into campus discussions, people as dangerous as the brown shirts he had seen as a young traveler in Berlin during the late 1920s—activists presaging Adolf Hitler's rise to power. Although Woodward's response to such campus doings at his Yale and elsewhere was perhaps an immoderate overreaction, his view was that of Bennie and Sadie Mays as well.[32]

What Bennie Mays also did not know about student protest on April 18, 1969, involved Morehouse, the Atlanta University system, and his own meet-ing that day with some twenty-five trustees and university officials. In this case, what he did not know would hurt him.

April 17, 1969, was a Wednesday, and Bennie Mays was glad to be home with Sadie Gray Mays. The couple looked forward to some formal occasions on this long weekend, the kind of thing that the Mayses reveled in. There was a ban-quet that evening and other less-formal dinners with trustees and friends of the House. There was a series of Atlanta University system trustee meetings hosted at a student center by Atlanta University president Theodore D. Jarrett. In the way of the university system, there were also meetings involving Morehouse trustees, and thus Bennie Mays as president emeritus and Hugh Gloster as cur-rent president had roles to play in discussions about the system and about Morehouse plans. Also included were "Daddy King"—the Reverend Martin Luther King, Sr.—and white trustees such as stock-analyst Charles E. Merrill, benefactor Dorothy Danforth Compton, and Dr. Deland DeVinney and sev-eral other representatives from the Rockefeller Foundation. During the Wednes-day banquet, officials were interrupted briefly by students and professors who presented a short list of demands for discussion with trustees on Friday, April 19. Bennie Mays recalled the petitioners as rude "crashers," but the record seems to show that the small crowd led by history professor Alton Hornsby was peaceful and respectful and brief in its presentation. In any case Presidents Gloster and Jarrett and several of the trustees readily assented, and a time was apparently set for a short discussion with the petitioners on the morning of April

19. Neither Mays nor the current presidents among the college officials and none of the trustees recalled giving the matter a second thought, and the quiet group departed that evening unobtrusively. The official Thursday meetings went on as scheduled, although some officials and some protesters recall another brief encounter that day, April 18, 1969, after which presidents Jarrett and Gloster again agreed to an early Friday morning meeting with the petitioners.[33]

Nine o'clock Friday morning, April 19, 1969, was a different matter. Once some twenty-five trustees and officials had gathered in a meeting room on the third floor of the Atlanta University Student Center, a crowd that both Bennie Mays and newspaper accounts estimated as about one hundred people, hurried into the place, chaining the doors behind them. This time no one was respectful, and the members of the crowd shouted a great deal. Acting student Samuel L. Jackson—who eventually made quite a career playing tough, no-nonsense sports coaches, military officers, and other authority figures—loomed ominously. Jackson stood as tall and broad shouldered as young Bennie Mays had, but he was more muscular. And on this day he was as angry as Bennie Mays had been on the day he hoped to find Dr. Wallace Payne on his Pullman car. Mays later remembered Dr. Hornsby as being respectful in tone and manner, but the historian was certainly exercised about several issues. As Hornsby noted on a website he once established and consistently has said in his scholarly monographs, he considered segregation a fact and an intractable force, and he wanted college education to prepare young men for a life among black people and removed from white oppressors. The professor said that Euro-centered curriculum was bad for black men, who needed Afro-centered studies. Some students shouted that Morehouse had to do more than to train dentists, a complaint that thespian Jackson continued to repeat for decades. Demands were presented: the AU Center should be named for the slain Dr. King; there should be no white trustees at Morehouse or Atlanta University; there should be black history and black studies courses, and the curriculum should be relevant and centered on Africa and not on northwestern Europe. Dr. Jarrett was quick-thinking enough to send word to campus-security personnel to keep the white Atlanta police force out of this affair and also to warn the understaffed campus traffic officers and watchmen to keep a low profile and avoid confrontation with angry students. A sanguine feature of this episode was the way Dr. Jarrett avoided a face off between armed police officers, especially white ones, and protesting black students.[34]

But the confrontation between college officials and trustees on one side and demonstrating students on the other side was raucous and threatening enough. Quite early an angry and distressed Daddy King left the room, according to wire service reports, "declaring his family wanted no part of the tactics protesters were using in seeking to honor his slain son." Bennie Mays wrote in *Born to Rebel* that protesters became more offensive, shouting insults, including obscenities, and above all the painful "Tom!" As the hours wore on, it became apparent that whatever else, the protesters had succeeded in stopping any official trustee business for the long working weekend. The crowd turned mean. An elderly white trustee with an enlarged prostate was denied permission to use the toilet, and some of the protesters derided him in his obvious physical discomfort. Bennie Mays himself was prevented from calling Sadie Mays on the telephone even after he made it clear that he was concerned about her health and how she might respond to whatever the news media reported. As night came on, Dr. Gloster made a statement that caused trouble later: "This has been the most ignominious day in the history of Morehouse, and I will resign rather than give in to the protesters." The AP wire service picked up the two declarative phrases of his statement: (1) "This has been . . . ignominious day" and (2) "I will resign" without the qualifying condition ("rather than give in"), and some early versions of their story reported that President Hugh Gloster had resigned while locked up by one hundred student demonstrators. A more nuanced and longer version that showed Dr. Gloster's qualifying phrase and its conditional tense and mood made the rounds more slowly and with less impact than the bolder and splashier story of students compelling a college president to resign on the spot.[35]

Bennie Mays wrote in *Born to Rebel* that he lost patience and insisted that the elderly be allowed to use the toilet and that he be allowed to use the telephone to call his wife. Whether responding to Mays's presence, or to basic decency in themselves, or even to common sense, the protest organizers eventually permitted telephone calls and toilet breaks. They even allowed six trustees, all rather old and weak, to leave the scene altogether. Those permitted to leave included Clayton R. Yates, benefactor of the Poor People's March and other civil rights demonstrations and marches. By Saturday morning, April 20, there were eighteen officials and trustees still locked up with a considerably quieter group of protesters. During the midmorning of that Saturday, some thirty or forty protesters also left the scene. Meanwhile other students enrolled in the Atlanta University system began to speak up. Morris Brown College, a Methodist member institution whose student body was generally thought to be more conservative in all matters, sent students who issued a statement decrying the misbehavior of the protestors, supporting Dr. Gloster, Dr. Jarrett, and the officials and trustees in charge of the six member colleges. These students circulated a petition that rapidly gained hundreds of signatures. Daddy King's statement further discredited the protesters. Then the brilliant Japanese American linguist and scholar S. I. Hayakawa, speaking in Chicago, issued memorable declarations about such demonstrations in general. Some members of protesting ranks at Columbia University formally apologized for their own excessive actions.

Following these events and reports on them, much of the momentum once held by Professor Hornsby and acting student Jackson thereby dissipated. By 1:35 P.M. Saturday, the protesters had allowed the remaining eighteen detainees to have their freedom, and Bennie Mays went home to Sadie Mays as presidents Gloster and Jarrett and various trustees went home to their spouses and loved ones—and trustees who had traveled long and far went back to their hotels, probably wishing they were at home with loved ones as well. As was often the case with such demonstrations in this season, the emphasis then shifted away from the original protests—about relevant curriculum, black trustees, and black courses—and toward the issue of amnesty so that there would be no penalties such as suspension visited on the student protesters and no discipline visited on the professors who jointed them in the demonstration.[36]

Only a few newspapers circulating on April 20, 1969, carried an updated version of things. However, the following words went out over AP wire services and were carried in the *Cedar Rapids Gazette:* "Jubilant singing students indicated that they had won concessions on at least some of their demands." The AP also reported again that "Martin Luther King, Sr. said his family wanted no part of the strike." Finally it reported significantly that "no immediate statement was released by trustees. . . . They had called for removal of all white trustees and institution of a program of comprehensive black studies. . . . Gloster had announced his resignation. . . . Also imprisoned was Dr. Benjamin Mays, president emeritus and trustee of Morehouse. He delivered the eulogy at the slain King's funeral last year."[37]

Dr. Hugh Gloster faced the most pressing demands relating to his stewardship of Morehouse. Wire service reports had circulated throughout the United States indicating that he had resigned while being held hostage. A longer AP wire report had made it clear that he had only threatened to resign, but there was more than one version of the lockup and his response to it, so Gloster needed to get his version of the story out there for all to see. Above all, the president and the trustees at each of the six member institutions needed to make a clear response to the various demands of the "jubilant and singing" protesters. Was naming the center for Dr. King a "resignation" issue for each president? Was forming a committee to discuss courses on black history a resignation issue? Other questions needed addressing: were all students and Dr. Hornsby to be back in the classroom in the coming weeks? Were the white benefactors—with their relationships to the Rockefellers, the Danforths, the Merrills and to other Wall Street firms and philanthropic foundations—going to be forced off the boards of trustees? Perhaps more to the point for Bennie Mays, could Morehouse realistically recruit potential benefactors if toughs in the student body were going to lock them in a room and scream at them? And of course obscured beneath the histrionics of the shouting students was the more complex issue about the relationship between a strong academic school such as Spelman and a weaker academic school such as Morris Brown inside the Atlanta University system—not to mention the continuing efforts to combine and coordinate theological studies at the ITC and intricate negotiations to coordinate medical studies at the undergraduate institutions with the graduate programs at Howard, Meharry, and above all with the major research universities of the United States. All these things were dear to Bennie and Sadie Mays, and the chance to discuss some of their complexities had been lost thanks to the lost weekend of the lockup. At best the events were just lost opportunity. At worst the results could be the permanent loss of generous benefactors, the end of cooperation with major research universities, and the replacement of college governance grounded in wisdom and research by shouting thugs who knew a great deal about the theatrics of threatened violence and the slogans of a day but precious little about academic curriculum. In fact, at worst, Bennie and Sadie Mays could rightly wonder if their entire twenty-seven years at Morehouse had just been repudiated by soul power and black pride.

Once the Morris Brown students had presented their petition with its hundreds of signatures, Dr. Gloster issued a statement saying he had "reversed his decision to resign"—the implication being that, absent such a petition, he would have done so, a statement that Bennie Mays did not like, especially since the supporting initiative had come not from the men of Morehouse but from students at Morris Brown. Dr. Gloster also issued a statement in conjunction with Dr. Jarrett announcing that a committee "would study consolidation of" Morris Brown, Spelman, Clark and Morehouse colleges with Atlanta University and the ITC in a more thoroughly coordinated Atlanta University system involving all member schools; that more African American trustees would be added to the boards of the member institutions; that students would be given "greater voice" on all issues involving curriculum; and that the schools would consider adding black studies programs. Disposition of the status of protesters at their respective schools was left unaddressed for the nonce, largely for the reason that only a few students and one professor were clearly identified out of a group that obviously included many more members of the student bodies and surely a few other members of the member institution faculties.[38]

Despite Bennie and Sadie Mayses' fears and despite Dr. Hornsby's dreams, the affair was decidedly minor when contrasted with events on other colleges campuses. Samuel Jackson flexing his muscles and yelling and Professor Hornsby calmly articulating some proposals for curriculum revision were different from Mario Savio's actions at the Berkeley campus of the University of California.

The actions of one hundred demonstrators in Atlanta paled in comparison with those of the SDS at Columbia University or the genuinely destructive disputants in Berlin and Paris. Just as the student and faculty demonstrations at Atlanta University system were calmer and briefer and less dramatic than such demonstrations at larger universities, so too were the reforms and other changes that transpired in response to the demonstrations. Major research universities made significant changes in student involvement with curriculum, such as regular and anonymous student evaluations of their professors' teaching proficiencies and techniques. Various committees involved in campus governance at major research universities began to include some students, and boards of trustees at such institutions either included students as members of the board or arranged for regular reports by student representatives. Several prominent Ivy League schools, especially Harvard, Yale, Princeton, and Brown, dramatically banished ROTC from their campuses—as did Howard. The military became much discredited, even reviled, on many campuses. The committees that were formed at Morehouse mediated minor changes in curriculum and governance and never contemplated fundamental change. Indeed, when it was all over Morehouse fell into line with the regional universities and various small liberal arts colleges that followed many paces behind the research universities—and the impetus for such changes seems to have been the college campus demonstrations of late spring 1969, as well as those of spring 1968, which presaged the more active, vocal, and violent demonstrations of 1969. The still more violent and destructive demonstrations of spring 1970 seemed to mark not only the ending of the decade but also the ending of major protests and proclamations on campuses.[39]

A couple of long-term trends for the Atalanta University system and Morehouse may be noted. Professor Alton Hornsby was vindicated on curriculum change, as the course offerings were changed somewhat to provide some attention to Africa and Africana; yet it took years to bring the kind of African-centered curriculum that he called for in 1969. The historian was otherwise personally vindicated. Bennie Mays and Dr. Gloster both report that Dr. Hornsby was always respectful during the demonstrations, and eventually the Afrocentrist was awarded an endowed professorship, the Fuller E. Callaway chair, plus some time and space in the alumni publications to explain the curriculum emphasis that he wanted. In 1976 Dr. Hornsby took over as editor of the *Journal of Negro History,* retaining control for twenty-five years. This position allowed him to publish high quality Afrocentrist scholarly articles. He thus gained influence and prestige in the small and tightly focused world of black academics doing black scholarship. As for amnesty for students, it came, albeit tacitly, furtively, and with almost Machiavellian overtones. Of those one hundred students who locked the doors to the room and screamed at the elderly trustees, only Samuel L. Jackson was dismissed, and he under circumstances that suggest special arrangements. Leaving Morehouse, he joined the U.S. Marine Corps, and after completing his service, he was readmitted and attained his baccalaureate. The network of the House helped him because he made the acquaintance of cinema producer and Morehouse alumnus Spike Lee. Jackson starred in several of Lee's productions as a thuggish drug pusher but eventually hit his stride as a figure of black brotherly "tough love" in roles as an athletic director, military noncommissioned officer, or law enforcement officer.[40]

As far as Bennie and Sadie Mays were concerned, a couple of other things became clear for them, and they acted promptly on their understandings. They arranged that their personal papers, including personal copies and drafts of presidential correspondence, should be housed for scholarly examination at the archives of the Moorland-Spingarn Research Center at Howard University. Bennie Mays did not want faculty, staff, or students from Morehouse involved with his personal correspondence, memorabilia, or other papers. Only the official presidential records remained property of the archives at Morehouse, and Bennie Mays was content that those papers remain uncataloged and essentially inaccessible throughout the remaining decades of his life and deep into the twenty-first century. It was an important judgment that the place where he had worked only four years became the permanent repository for his personal and professional records rather than the place that he presided over for twenty-seven years. For a man of *megalosukos,* such a decision had to have been related to failures he saw not only in the student body on that April weekend of 1969 but also to failures he saw in Dr. Gloster and other leaders at the same time and place. Working on *Born to Rebel,* Bennie Mays used that forum to attack his demonstrating adversaries, none of whom he named and all of whom he lumped with the Cleavers, Sealeses, Newtons, and Carmichaels among the group that he judged to be failed pretenders to the mantle of Dr. King. Yet in that subjective and judgmental portion of his memoir, his narrative arrangement of the facts about the treatment of the Atlanta University system officials and the opaque aims and odd behaviors of the demonstrators seems more right than wrong—though again the protest was minor and he seems to have viewed the entire struggle as larger than it really was.[41]

Neither the Mayses nor the protestors sufficiently credited President Jarrett for the wisdom of his decisions not to bring in city police and to order campus police to avoid confrontation with protesters. Despite Bennie Mays's praise for Daddy King, the more relevant factor in maintaining the peace seems in retrospect to be President Jarrett, whose directive prevented any face-to-face confrontation between white police and black college students. Keeping policing authorities of all colors off the scene allowed cooler heads to prevail. Of all the characters involved in the hot, quick little affair, Dr. Jarrett emerges as the one with the real wisdom, a fact well-documented in the contemporaneous AP wire reports but not recollected by others who look back at the incidents.

Despite Dr. Hornsby's talk about preparing segregated African American students for a long future in segregation, the forward motion of integrationism at Morehouse is most obvious. More and more of the men of the House have pressed forward into leadership in integrated circumstances, not only Julian Bond and Daddy King, but also Spike Lee and Samuel Jackson. At least during the final quarter of the twentieth century, the fight over whether to prepare for separation or for integration seems to have been lost by the editor of the *Journal of Negro History* and won by the president emeritus. Indeed one of the things delayed in discussion by the student uprising was finally unveiled in 1970: yet another agreement by a major research university to work with graduates of Morehouse. The University of Pittsburgh announced in January 1970 that it would save nine places at its medical school for Morehouse men who had earned baccalaureate degrees in medical studies. As Bennie and Sadie Mays had willed it and worked to establish it, Morehouse remained *the* producer of African American medical doctors among historically black or integrated baccalaureate institutions. Long after the Mayses had passed on, Morehouse College retained its lead as the school that sent black medical students on to predominantly white and mainstream medical colleges in the North and the South. Morehouse also retained its lead in sending students of the law to predominantly white and mainstream colleges and universities in all regions. And in academic year 2008, the baccalaureate address at Morehouse commencement was delivered by a white student. All these things are pieces of the integrationist tradition set in motion long ago by John Hope and carried forward by Bennie Mays in defiance of white segregationists and black separatists.[42]

In a long life filled with epiphanies, Bennie Mays had come painfully but also joyfully to some understandings about people. At the end of the long weekend in April 1969, he came painfully but without joy to still another: the men of the House had failed at an important moment. According to the memoir writer, the protestors were really talking all about themselves and not about service or sacrifice in name of some principle. Bennie Mays's account, while chronologically accurate and fair enough from his starting point in logic, lacks the logician's principle of charity. Mays, who certainly knew the rules of debate and discourse, failed in his memoir to grant that his adversaries proceeded from honorable motives and failed to grant that they presented arguments worthy of consideration. Furthermore neither Bennie Mays nor Sadie Mays seems to have acknowledged that a vertical, or top-down, hierarchical arrangement for building curriculum and for managing instruction was no longer effective for faculty and students by the middle of the 1960s and certainly not in 1969. Both seem to have missed the situational irony that they themselves had instructed their charges, certainly including Hornsby and Jackson, in protest—albeit with different rules and responsibilities. Finally the couple, and especially Bennie Mays, seems to have missed the point that curriculum and modes of instruction evolve constantly, and no matter how effective they may be for one era, curriculum and modes of instruction cannot persist unchanged forever.[43]

Others would have to teach the Morehouse men of 1969, the men who would graduate in a few weeks and those who would graduate in 1970, 1971, 1972, and 1973, and on and on. Perhaps Dr. Gloster could find his moorings and lead the men of the House back to the prophetic touchstones of service and sacrifice. Perhaps Dr. Hornsby would emerge as another Carter Godwin Woodson, another E. Franklin Frazier, or another Rayford W. Logan. Perhaps over at the ITC some Morehouse man would emerge as another Mordecai Johnson, another Howard Thurman, or another Martin Luther King—father or son. Perhaps some student of politics and the law and communications would emerge as another James Madison Nabrit or another Julian Bond. But all of this was far to seek—and none of it was for Bennie and Sadie Mays to seek. They had handed over the helm, and Dr. Gloster would pilot the courses demanded by the Dr. Hornsbys and the Samuel Jacksons.

What Bennie Mays could do in the few weeks remaining of his appointment at Michigan State was to try to get across something of principled *satyagraha* and other principled classical protest to the handful of liberal students taking his class and to the little gaggle of liberal professors who came around to talk about what Dr. King was really like. And he could continue to preach it in his *Pittsburgh Courier* column. He could certainly get it across in *Born to Rebel* and in any public addresses that he made. But for the audience that most mattered to him, the folk that really counted, the men he had preached to in Sale Hall on Tuesdays—who included Dr. Hornsby (class of 1961), Samuel Jackson, and some one hundred of his classmates—Bennie Mays had flatly failed to get across the message of sacrifice, service, and accountability. And he had failed to hear their legitimate concerns, however rudely or crudely presented.

14

LEAVE ME A DOUBLE PORTION

1969–1984

The late springtime of 1969 was depressing indeed. Campuses were in tumult, and Nixon's southern strategy reinforced the power of senators such as Strom Thurmond, Richard Russell, and James Eastland while at the same time elevating to nationally respected status the old-time segregationist radio and television commentator Jesse Helms. The Eleanor Roosevelt liberals were ineffectual, and indeed the term largely disappeared. In fact—with New Left campus critiques from one side and the surprisingly powerful right-wing backlash from the other side—"liberal" had become a dirty word no matter how it was modified or however softly it was pronounced. To the backlash reactionists, "liberal" denoted softness and foolishness and connoted something in the way of apostasy to the white middle class. To the New Left and other self-styled radicals on the campuses, "liberal" denoted hypocrisy and connoted a Trojan horse for imperialism and racism. Such new terms and new usages made his writing projects quite challenging for Bennie Mays, despite the fact that in this same cruel springtime he had published a new collection of "single concept sermons," *Disturbed about Man*.[1]

At the end of April, Dick Rich, in his liberal and expansive mood, had arranged a reading and an autograph session for *Disturbed about Man* at his department store, Rich's, which was now fully integrated. A kind and appreciative crowd of friends and well-wishers had congregated there to celebrate the publication with the Mayses. The site was the same Magnolia Room, whose onetime segregation had occasioned some distancing between Rich and other business progressives from the integrationists, but whose eventual integration, when it came, had been dismissed as "too little and too late" by more thoroughgoing reformists who even called Daddy King "Tom" and sent the prophetic Martin Luther King, Jr., away in frustration and distress. Now things were different. Dick Rich and the self-styled progressives of the community were anxious to display their liberalism to a black downtown Atlanta. Given the new political realities in Georgia and the nation, Rich was acting with a certain amount of courage, and his gestures were appreciated. After all, the current governor of Georgia was none other than the virulent and bitter segregationist restaurateur Lester Maddox, who had defeated the champion of the progressive alliance, Ellis Arnall. The hatchet-wielding racist Maddox was emerging as a folk hero to the backlash, and the very symbol of the new racial realities in Richard Nixon's America. In such a new Georgia, it was a pleasure to stand and read about social justice and then to sit and sign books in Rich's integrated Magnolia Room.[2]

In his reading that day and in his published reflections, Bennie Mays still declared that there were white Christians who hoped for a better society and who would respond to the echoes of the old social gospel of Walter Rauschenbusch, Reinhold Niebuhr, William Stuart Nelson, and Howard Thurman— and of the elderly Bennie Mays. He had revised yet again his eulogy for Martin Luther King, Jr., had revised some other sermons and reflections, had added a concluding discussion of racial and ethnic tensions in the context of Christian responsibility, and then assembled the pieces into a modest collection whose title—*Disturbed about Man*—seemed to catch his mood and the mood in much of the country. He dedicated the book to the slain King—"who too was disturbed about man" in this day. Despite the title, the style was optimistic and encouraging, reflecting Mays's preaching and teaching style. He was still the social scientist in his detached analysis of data and his awareness of recent archaeological and manuscript findings among historicist theologians; yet at the same time he was quite folksy in casual and down-home references to everyday southern life. He did a superb job explaining the difficult and controversial theological concept that God and man are linked so that God suffers when man suffers—especially today, especially after the ascension of Jesus and the full development of the relationship between man and the Holy Spirit. Furthermore Mays explored the concept that "God is in need when Man is in need," that God and man are "inseparably tied together," and that this personal relationship is at its most poignant among the desperately poor, the sick, the disabled, the abandoned, "the least of these." Some critics even "got it" that this dark-complected man lately accused of being insufficiently "black" had arranged for a cover design that was black with silver letters on the narrow spine, offering "small rays of hope" in a time when there was more darkness in race pride than there was racial pride in darkness. Another sympathetic critic all but sang: "when reading ends, repairing can begin."[3]

Yet other critics said the collection was "weak in Christology" and not truly a part of current trends in theology. Generally *Disturbed about Man* received respectful notices in journals aimed at practicing ministers and lay readers. John

Knox Press experienced some difficulties in setting up readings, and the press may have missed some opportunities to showcase the book. It did not receive notices in scholarly publications read by divinity students, and within a few months it was also clear that few middle-brow citizens were going to hear about *Disturbed about Man*. Sales reached only a few thousand, most of those copies bought by younger associates and fellow reformists in the first weeks after its release. Only some university libraries bought the book—for instance it found its way to the shelves at the University of South Carolina, Emory, Howard, Columbia, and Yale, but not Harvard or New York University. Mays had aimed too low for the modern theologian but too high for the average college-educated casual reader, and he had spoken with too much "warmth of the author's personal piety" to reach an increasingly secular society. He had to wonder if he would ever find a reading audience among people of any color.[4]

Clearly there were new roles for the Mayses to play in their emeritus status, and complicating all such roles was the unavoidable, albeit unmentionable, fact of death. The time allotted to Sadie Mays to accomplish her final missions was indefinite, perhaps indeterminable, and short. For all that she brought her husband back to clear focus. She intended to serve on the Atlanta Board of Education on behalf of all colors and all political persuasions. One black academic, Dr. Rufus Clement of Morehouse, had once served on the board, but Sadie Mays wanted to make changes much more profound than Clement had attempted. To do so, she had to win election, and a political campaign took effort and energy. Her husband could support her in her campaign for the school board until he found his moorings and could begin anew with his writing campaigns. Even while Bennie Mays was counseling and observing at Michigan State University (and probably before that) Sadie Mays had fixed on public schools in Atlanta as her final and most important objective. It was past time that someone step forward to the school board who had some compassion for black children, some social science training in studying their childhood and adolescent problems, some social work experience in addressing those problems, and above all some common sense. She believed that a dangerous gap had opened between child rearing and training young men for leadership in college. Not only was the moment of need profound, but the opportunity was just right. Sadie Mays knew from personal work—block by city block, black church by black church, and session by session at the Butler Street YMCA—the workings of politics in the black communities of sprawling Atlanta. She among others had taken firm political action and sponsored some legal action, and black people in Atlanta voted—now in numbers large enough to liberalize racial politics in Atlanta.

She also had observed and learned the workings of the local "community power elite"—one of the labels applied to progressive white business and civic leaders, especially liberal Jewish men such as Ivan Allen, Sam Massell, Dick Rich, and Morris Abram. These men in particular expected black support for their campaigns and policies, and they gave back once in office—or, as with university administrator and educationist Morris Abram and retailer Dick Rich, they gave back once they gained access to officeholders. Sadie Gray Mays was a master at getting black voters to the polls; if she could bring in the little knot of liberal white professional voters, she could be on the Atlanta Board of Education and in position to do some good.[5]

She comprehended a problem that must be addressed on different levels. Years of segregation had made the schools a Jim Crow preserve with few desks in integrated schools available to black children and with few teaching jobs— and almost no administrative posts—available to black professionals. An integrated staff, heavy with white folk in supervisory and administrative offices, taught an almost exclusively black student body. Now that the law was finally changed, damnable effects of the law must be undone. The nature of school funding—property taxes laid on real estate—and the relatively new concept of the neighborhood school. During the lengthy reign of Jim Crow, children of either races routinely went well beyond their neighborhoods to attend schools for their color and class. Funding based on property values and districting by neighborhood combined to make great differences in the quality of black schools near black neighborhoods and white schools near white neighborhoods. White property was worth more, and the greater taxes made the local white schools high quality. With a new emphasis on neighborhood schools, white people moved away from black people, voted bond issues, and insisted that new schools be established in their neighborhoods. It was called "white flight," and it was an ironic and problematic result of ending the Jim Crow system.[6]

From the homes she and Bennie Mays had made on Pamplico Drive and then on Sewell Drive, Sadie Mays had been watching the patterns: a white-collar neighborhood of white professionals admitted some white-collar black professionals, who settled along the fringes of the existing neighborhood and got along reasonably well with their white neighbors. Then more white-collar black professionals gradually arrived, and white people began leaving, usually after some sporadic violence and some systematic property damage visited on the black newcomers. Somewhere past the magic 10 percent, the "tipping point" was reached, and after that point an integrated neighborhood quickly became a black neighborhood. The Mayses' home was now in a black neighborhood that had once been an integrated neighborhood. This pattern had

gone into motion in the late 1940s, and it advanced steadily throughout the
1950s. The city of Atlanta, once more than two-thirds white, was by the 1970
census more black than white—and its perimeter had expanded so that the city
was swollen to a size more than twice its original geographic area. Just beyond
the constantly moving perimeter lived the white people who had fled the city
in all directions to suburban developments that displaced old farming communities and small towns.[7]

Some of the great increase in black population was the result of black skilled
workers and black professionals moving into town, exactly the goal sought by
various progressive alliances and exactly the kind of occupation and housing
opportunities preached by the Urban League and celebrated in the *Pittsburgh
Courier* or the Johnson Company's *Ebony* magazine—and in the Mayses' parlor
and study. However, a much larger movement in this demographic revolution
came from white people moving out, more than sixty thousand moving beyond
the city limits between 1957 and 1970. Some black people moved in, but many
more white people moved out. Atlanta became a much blacker city than it had
been before; and many in the white city labor force—the petit bourgeoisie
who performed white-collar services—were now suburban residents who commuted into work downtown and then returned home each evening. As was
becoming painfully evident to Sadie Mays—and as would be chronicled decades later by professional scholars—the white suburbanites had not moved into
suburbs from the "rustic" rural countryside but rather they had run away from
the city. They did so largely in order to "rebuild" the segregated world that they
once lived in—or at least imagined that they had once lived in. The new segregationist suburbanites were not migrant "rural rustics" at all, but well-
educated and well-paid urbanites in flight from black people. A cynical scholar
rewrote Mayor Hartsfield's old one-liner, calling Atlanta: "the city too busy
moving to hate!"[8]

The neighborhood schools serving black children in their community were
now victim of poor funding and poor staffing, and the old white neighbors
were moving out to the suburban developments beyond the interstate highway
perimeter that redefined Atlanta's sprawling borders. The most protean of cities
in any case, Atlanta retained a black core from which businesses and schools
were removing themselves; cheap gasoline and the subsidized highway system
insured that white folk could move as far away as Chattanooga or Athens and
live among white people, sending their children to all-white schools while they
themselves commuted to jobs in the central business district of Atlanta—or in
some cases commuted to jobs in suburbs out on the perimeter far removed
from their own homes. The increasingly black student body of Atlanta was
taught by an overwhelmingly white group of educationists. Indeed barely 2
percent of teachers in Cobb County on perimeter of the city were black, and

the administrators were mostly male: white or black female administrators were barely 38 percent of the supervisory and managerial staff.[9]

Sadie Mays had mastered her facts and identified the problems for Atlanta schools. Part of the problem was also part of her solution: the overwhelmingly black population guaranteed some black representation on the school board, especially with a little help in the news media from the community power structure of progressive business leaders and educationists. She and Bennie Mays were already well-known to both communities, and they worked the crowds from the swanky Commerce Club to the humbler Butler Street YMCA to the modest basements of black Baptist churches.

Thus armed not only with social science data but also with a black community who could get out the vote and promises of help from white educators and businessmen, Sadie Mays began her campaign while Bennie Mays was yet in East Lansing and won election to the board in fall 1969. Given Bennie Mays's happy and unhappy distractions, Sadie Mays really did succeed without much help behind the scenes. It was a wonderful moment in women's history, in black history, and in Atlanta history. It also came at the end of her own magnificent life. On October 11, 1969, Sadie Mays succumbed to complications of cancer before she could actually take office. During the first eleven days of October, Bennie Mays was with her in the hospital ten and twelve hours per day. On the eleventh day, she drew her knees up, folded her legs beneath herself, closed her eyes, and quit breathing. The physicians signified her death with a certificate, and Sadie Gray Mays was gathered to her people in eternal rest beyond all the valleys.[10]

Unjustly relegated to Bennie Mays's shadow for decades during their married life, Sadie Gray Mays in death attracted attention, and not only in the black community. Her work on behalf of Happy Haven Nursing Center was rewarded when Morehouse men and liberals throughout the country contributed funds to have it named the Sadie Gray Mays Nursing Home. She rated a notice in the *New York Times,* albeit essentially as the wife of Bennie Mays, and the encomia flowed in to Sewell Drive and Morehouse. Brave and resilient, with a toughness belied by her unremitting smile and radiant warmth, the first lady emerita was remembered as a superb hostess, a generous supporter of aggrieved youth, a clever and adept fund-raiser, an insistent crusader, and a careful University of Chicago social scientist. Scattered through the happy memories of eulogizers were other, sharply etched ones: she had insisted even in the 1930s that white southerners address her as "Mrs. Mays" instead of "Sadie"; she had been an activist on behalf of her physically handicapped sister; she had worked hard on behalf of a young deaf boy whom she tutored through high school. That she lived a full and meaningful life was beyond dispute. Plenty of friends and associates wondered just what would happen to Bennie Mays after the autumn of 1969.[11]

Bennie Mays was effectively alone, for he essentially trusted no particular man or woman in that biblical sense of "taking sweet counsel." Everyone was proving to be most untrustworthy, or at least most ineffective. Among other things, he insisted on doing many things for himself and by himself. Continuing to live alone, he also continued his vigorous pace of fund-raising and travel, and he prided himself right up to the end on his ability to get himself through Atlanta traffic in his own automobile at the appointed time for his engagements, as he prided himself on making airplane departures by driving himself to the airport and parking his car by himself. In all these instances, some trivial and even humorous, some nothing less than noble, he remained true to his classical conceptions of *megalosukos* and *magnanimatatum* in the relationship with God. These Thomistic and yet Baptist conceptions remained his lodestar. They gave him direction, conviction, and courage when his living associates failed on those counts. Indeed his long and fervently held quest for that kind of classical magnificence helped to square the circle. Yet this man who confided little in others after 1969 still remained remarkably hopeful about people in general and remained signally optimistic about the passage of time and the course toward freedom, peace, and justice. The final phase of his long life and career was marked by his fascinating combination of distrust of associates yoked with great faith in the grand campaign that continued. Unhopeful about individual men and women, the lonely Bennie Mays still retained great hope in what a group of people could do if they had faith and they worked hard.

Looking back, it seems hard to believe that anyone was worried about Bennie Mays losing his way in the period after he buried his second wife—and his best friend. In fact for the period from 1969 to 1984, he is remembered as a man of dynamism, energy, determination, and above all optimism—by members of the school board, members of the Martin Luther King, Jr., Center for Nonviolent Social Change, reporters, educationists, ministers, historians, and other scholars with whom he worked in a full schedule. Yet he was without close associates of his own age, and there were moments of loneliness and discouragement. He fought off such emotions in such moments with long hours of scholarly work and professional travel. And he fought off such moments by drawing on his memories of Sadie Mays and by throwing himself into crowds of people with whom he was only casually—albeit professionally—acquainted and related. The correspondence shows a lonely man, but the record shows a man who was almost never alone and almost never inactive.[12]

Bennie Mays accepted three more big assignments. Largely to honor his departed Sadie Gray Mays, but also because there seemed no one else able to do the work, he agreed to run for the Atlanta Board of Education, eventually serving as board president during its most tumultuous years in the decade of the 1970s, when white racists and clever politicians made "busin'" an issue deployed against school desegregation. As if no children had ever traveled great distances to establish and maintain the Jim Crow schools that produced the original segregation! He also agreed to help Coretta Scott King and her children in maintaining and expanding the Martin Luther King, Jr., Center for Nonviolent Social Change, a facility that he insisted would be no mere memorial but a scholarly repository and a center for activism based on research and reason. He accepted a consultancy and advisory position with the Department of Health, Education, and Welfare (HEW), despite his extreme misgivings about the Nixon administration and its southern strategy.[13]

Election to the school board came easily enough, but the initial year of discussions about education was far from smooth, and Bennie Mays was soon too busy fighting real demons to dwell on his own depressed spirits, and certainly too engaged with city schools to spend much time thinking about himself. On the school board, Bennie Mays was doing what Sadie Mays wanted to do, and he never forgot his duty to the Atlanta schools. Soon after he was elected to the board, board members elected him their president, a post he held from January 2, 1970, to his retirement from the school board on January 1, 1981. For all but a portion of the 1973 sessions, he was the presiding member, and upon his leave taking from the board in 1981, he was elected president emeritus. He brought to the board his administrative acumen, his optimism, and his capacity for hard work. Indeed in 1977 he was still surprising board officials by his energy and "stamina," starting things off each morning at 7:00 A.M. and presiding over meetings into the late evening. He also traveled extensively for consultation and sometimes confrontation with state and federal officials on the issues affecting Atlanta's schools, its white and black schoolchildren, and its white and black teachers and administrators. At least in public statements, he was careful not to overstate the extent of white racism, and he took pains to avoid overgeneralization. Resolutely he maintained a public face of optimism and determination even though his private correspondence and occasional private remarks betrayed his sense of the intractable nature of resistance to an integrated education system of high quality. He was not offered, and he did not seek, an extension of his advisory consultancy in Nixon's HEW, and he did not judge his service for them fruitful. Indeed, in the privacy of personal correspondence, he confided to the elderly Dr. Mordecai Johnson that he longed to see "sanity on the question of busing and the right attitude toward the people on welfare on the part of those of us who are fortunate enough not to be there." But his public language was measured and precise and betrayed no such emotions.[14]

As Sadie Gray Mays had documented it over and over, Jim Crow, the insti-tution that Bennie Mays ruefully called "the cat with nine lives," continued to have its effects, and especially in "the city too busy *moving* to hate." When Mays took office in 1970, nearly one-half, 48 percent, of Atlanta's black youth, attended schools that were all-black, and when he left office at the end of the decade, that percentage had for practical purposes reached 90 percent. In fight-ing the "old cat" Jim Crow—now a set of practices and no longer a set of statu-tory laws—Bennie Mays as president of the board of public schools went back to the same place he had gone as president of Morehouse: to the liberals, espe-cially those in the NAACP and the Urban League and to the ministers, espe-cially in the Council of Churches in Christ. As he did so, he also found his opposition exactly where he had found it before, in none other than Senator Strom Thurmond of his native state, now given a place of authority in the Sen-ate as well as in the administration of Richard Nixon. Mays also found vicious opposition from Lester Maddox, whether the Atlanta restaurateur was in office as governor or out of office but still speaking loudly on behalf of backlash. President Mays was pleased to receive firm statements of support from the Georgia Council of Churches, whose membership resolved to "End Segrega-tion in Schools Now!" He was also pleased to receive funding for studies and other support from the Urban League, especially its director Vernon Jordan, but Mays soon realized that Governor Maddox with his toy weapons and his bold pronouncements had the rhetorical backing of the Nixon administration. Indeed on occasion the otherwise optimistic Mays announced that old Ben Tillman, the "Pitchfork" nemesis of his youth in the valley of the Saluda, was still abroad and still hurting black folk, although Mays knew perfectly well that Tillman had passed on back in 1918, and that Pitchfork's old political machin-ery and his operatives were long since gone. All the same Bennie Mays took pains to keep such notions away from white people and away from the official sessions of his school board.[15]

As had Sadie Mays, Bennie Mays knew that a sizeable concentration of black people actually scared many white people, whether in a neighborhood or a school. He tried to keep this fact in mind as he worked with principals and politicians and parents and other school officials to integrate a higher percent-age of black children into majority-white schools, always attempting to keep that integrating number of black children relatively small. Above all, he tried to prevent some all-white schools from suddenly becoming majority black. Sen-sitive to the fears of white parents, he tried to be reassuring, stating, "It is the responsibility of boards of education to provide ways and means whereby their fears will be dispelled." An obvious solution was to use public transit, to move the children by bus to schools in order to desegregate—as once such transit had been used to segregate schools regardless of where school-age children actually lived. As Sadie Mays had noted for him many times, in Jim Crow days there was little discussion about neighborhood schools, and it was in the normal course of things for black children to ride buses past as many as a dozen white schools in order to arrive at a black school some distance from their home. Also white children in the South of the Jim Crow era often lived close by black people and rode well past black schools to get to their white school.[16]

Nevertheless Sadie Mays had been wrong about white reaction to busing and white understandings of neighborhood schools, and Bennie Mays had to acknowledge that misreading and proceed accordingly. In the more prosperous South, especially Atlanta with its self-proclaimed Sunbelt status of new wealth, white people fully expected their children to attend schools in their neighborhood; they sometimes even moved relatively short distances from one house to another because the new house was zoned for a school that was reported to be of high quality. One of the measures of quality—it was quickly becoming apparent—was that the school had few black children. Nixon's people were particularly good at exploiting the fears of white middle class southerners, and since some of the busing had been ordered by federal judges, there were assaults on "activist" judges who "overstepped authority" in the effort to bring desegregation with "due deliberate speed"—some fifteen years or more after Chief Justice Earl Warren included that phrase in his response to legal work done by Bennie Mays's associate Thurgood Marshall and his former debate student James Madison Nabrit. Watching the Nixonians in fact, Bennie Mays announced that they intended nothing less than to undo the integration work accomplished by the Warren Supreme Court. What had once seemed a solid accomplishment and a respected entitlement—the right of black children to a decent education, a right hard to attain in public setting without racial integration—now seemed to be jeopardized.[17]

Almost at once it was made manifest that there were dangers that inhered when federal officials took no interest in defusing local white reactions to issues such as busing. Bennie Mays was horrified to learn that in the Pee Dee valley of his native South Carolina, a white mob in Lamar, none wearing robes and masks or otherwise trying to hide his identity, attacked a school bus of black children being transported to a formerly all-white school in an effort to bring integration. Lamar was no long drive from Ellen Harvin's Manning, certainly less than one hour. These many years after the Earl Warren Supreme Court had insisted on integration in this self-same region of South Carolina, the Lamar schools were still essentially segregated, and the mild and simple expedient of busing some black children to a previously all-white school had resulted in mob terrorism. Bennie Mays was infuriated. The attack should be a federal offense, he said. It should be recognized as an assault on the civil rights of children seeking an education. He knew Lamar officials would do nothing to the mob, and he was incensed that the Nixon people also seemed intent on doing nothing. In fact, Bennie Mays fumed, Nixon's "own rhetoric had helped cause" the attack, convincing Lamar's racists that the federal government with its southern strategy was on their side against black children. In his column for the *Pittsburgh Courier,* Bennie Mays recalled what it felt like to be bullied by a mob of white racists when one was a child, and he recalled what it felt like for black people of any age to be bullied by the law authorities in South Carolina and Georgia. He called the attack "The Lamar Incident," and he pushed NAACP and Urban League and liberal congressmen to take up the issue—as they did but to no avail. Uncharacteristically he spoke of the Lamar incident without much restraint to his school board audience—and found most of them, like a plurality of voting Atlantans, to be opposed to mob violence.[18]

Yet Bennie Mays could see that he was engaging a hopeless fight with regard to busing. Thus he told the school board, other Atlanta officials, and any citizens who would listen that "busing was not the issue." Rather "racism and [violent] resistance [to busing] is the issue, not busing." There was a desperate need for President Nixon to step forward, just as had Republican Dwight David Eisenhower with whom Nixon had served, and protect the lives and well-being of black citizens when white people attacked them because of some disagreement about school integration. Bennie Mays opined that any president should wish to have a legacy of maintaining order and stability and basic protection of life and limb of minorities, even if, like Ike, he had severe reservations about a Supreme Court ruling that set off white demonstrations. As Bennie Mays read his history and recalled the work of his students and associates in those legal cases, Eisenhower had responded the moral and the legal way, especially in Little Rock, Arkansas. Nixon's actual voting record in House and Senate and his behavior as vice president betrayed no racism and no tolerance of racist violence, and his southern strategy rhetoric and his inaction now completely befuddled Mays. Still there was little to gain from trying to understand Richard Nixon—and much to be lost by waiting for action from him and his people. The immediate issue was public schools in Atlanta, and what to do about those institutions. Bennie Mays announced as loudly as he could that there were no plans to bus children in Atlanta in order to achieve integration, no plans to disrupt neighborhood schools.[19]

This announcement begged the question of what Bennie Mays and the Atlanta Board of Education were planning to do. It took him a full thirty months, but Mays set himself and his hardworking board to search out a policy. If they could not find a solution bringing full justice, then at least there might be found an equable resolution with half a loaf and half a cup that could nourish the almost completely underfed and undernourished downtown schools.

His work with the King Center was good for Bennie Mays, and more important, he was good for the work. The widower had an excellent sense for organization; he spoke the language of scholars and counted among his friends and associates such noted historians as John Hope Franklin and C. Vann Woodward. He also attracted young scholars such as Orville Vernon Burton and could communicate with them about the right way to develop an archival collection. Burton, a white native of the same valley of the Saluda as Mays, became a particularly valued associate, who helped to organize Mays's *Pittsburgh Courier* opinion columns and some other writings for possible publication and otherwise put the retired academic in touch with currently practicing scholars. Perhaps most useful to the King Center were Mays's experiences and expertise as a fund-raiser. He still knew the right people to go to for individual philanthropic donations, and he was even better at writing grants addressed to private foundations and government agencies. Bennie Mays could still deliver a powerful eulogy, as he did on a triumphal return to East Lansing when Clifton Reginald Wharton asked him to introduce Coretta Scott King on an occasion in 1971, when the late prophet and his noble widow were honored at Michigan State University.[20]

As the 1960s wore on and then wore out, Mays had seen a long-term need involving the memory of his prized student. In Mays's considered opinion, the racially cool environment introduced in the 1970s was not a good time for black people, although some high-profile leaders of color attained office and prestige. As in the supercharged days of the 1960s, there continued to be real overall and absolute improvements in education, employment, and salary levels. Yet Mays was convinced that black people had begun to slip relative to white people in all material measures, that improvements in black material attainment reached a peak in 1970 and then slipped back, as white people—already ahead in living standards, progressed much more rapidly than did black people. Looking out ahead over the 1980s, the old math instructor's conviction was borne out years later by some social scientists, but Mays seems to have marked the inflection point too early. Considerable data show that when Mays thought black people were slipping in relative terms in the era of the 1970s, they were in fact still advancing, especially when compared to white improvement in material well-being. He was also convinced that the southern strategy was embraced with enthusiasm throughout the Deep South by the dominant white middle class and an impassioned white blue-collar class, especially by younger white males in both economic strata. Indeed in the 1966 contest for the gubernatorial nomination between Lester Maddox and the Mayses' old friend and ally Ellis Arnall, the "progressive candidate of the mainstream" (Arnall knew better than to call himself "liberal") had done no better among educated white-collar white folk than he had among the more obviously antagonistic blue-collar white folk. Meanwhile it seemed to Mays that the Democratic Party was becoming a black preserve in the South and that black people were losing the ear of mainstream Democrats outside the South, while the white southerners joining the Republican Party were gaining great influence in the GOP. As Mays noted to friends and as he wrote in his columns, Republicans deployed rhetoric about eliminating various federal programs that had been expanding from the time of Harry Truman through the early years of Richard Nixon. Mays saw a racist agenda in that rhetoric, for it was black people who benefited from such programs—and the social scientist knew that elimination of them could bring disproportionate hurt to black people.[21]

As things worsened materially for black people, strange things began to happen to Dr. King's reputation. Some people saw him as too nice, too mild, and too moderate, overlooking the deep radicalism in Dr. King's tactics, especially when he had broken with the political majority on the issue of the Vietnam War or when he had launched radical attacks on poverty and hunger. Ever the social scientist, Bennie Mays wanted to preserve the records as accurately as possible, so that people of a distant era would know the truth and perhaps be set free from the crazies on the right and the left who so misrepresented things. In Mays's opinion some figures on the right—including California governor and rising figure of Republican authority, Ronald Reagan—tried to fit Dr. King's historical persona into the moderate nice-guy mold. Then Mays decried a similar misrepresentation from those on the violent left, who celebrated Malcolm X, Eldridge Cleaver, and Huey Newton as the relevant radicals and treated Dr. King as some kind of irrelevance.[22]

Worse yet were the discussions and the speculations about extramarital sexual liaisons in which Dr. King had indulged during his short life. These revelations were deeply painful to Coretta Scott King of course, but they were corroborated by nothing less than the FBI, whose agents had been careful to make tape recordings of Dr. King's various indiscretions. Old-time associates such as the Reverend Ralph Abernathy, speaking language of another era when men of both races often boasted of their sexual activities, reminisced about Dr. King's "triumphs" in ways that angered women in a later era, when such womanizing was no "conquest" or "triumph" but rather an abuse. Locked in often unlovely struggle with Coretta Scott King over policy direction and other strategies for the SCLC, Abernathy published in 1989 what he had seen and what he knew about firsthand, but he and others were talking about King's infidelities quite early. More memorably the dogged investigator political scientist David Garrow sued the FBI to gain access to the tapes, and this otherwise respectful and even celebratory biographer thoroughly documented King's every act of sexual infidelity. Before Garrow or Abernathy published, however, the prophetic leader's after-hours actions had begun to attract more attention than his words or his courageous sacrifices. Mays did not live to see the seamiest of stories confirmed in publications; between 1969 and 1972 he had expressed his extreme resentment of idle talk that amounted to wounding gossip. There were indeed things completely fabricated, especially a screed titled *The King God Did Not Send* by John Williams, of which a frustrated Bennie Mays said in a review that the book "seems to be written purely to smear" King's reputation; and then he told his readers in his column, "whites did not accept Martin Luther King in life and do not accept him in death."[23]

This last cri de coeur was uncharacteristically pessimistic and also uncharacteristically judgmental of all white people, but it reflected the deep hurt Mays the mentor suffered, how hard the publicity and gossip were on the survivors. They were hard on Daddy King, who had not expected to bury his son—and certainly not before his son was forty. They were hard on Bennie Mays, who had not expected to bury his student before the student had reached middle age. They were extremely hard on Coretta Scott King, who had not expected to bury her husband before their children had attained much age at all and who had to hear the wounding stories while still deep in grief. Some enthusiasts tried to protect the pained survivors by denying that Martin Luther King, Jr., was a mortal with any flaws at all, and these misguided statements did their damage too, since the evidence of frailty was copiously documented. The Bennie Mays solution was to make all records professionally available, to cover all things thoroughly, and thereby let the intelligent person who wished to come to the King Center make up his or her own mind about "what manner of man" was this prophet. More to the point, he organized the King Center as a working and functioning agency for peaceful change, providing workshops and sending out experts to mediate and moderate disputes of all sorts.[24]

Although Bennie Mays did not live to see the full fruits of his labors, by the 1980s, the last decade for the old schoolmaster, the King Center was a well-run and well-respected institution featuring documents and exhibits and artifacts that were thoroughly researched and well organized and fully accessible. The center also offered staff counselors, who engaged the activist social involvements that Bennie Mays judged to be the real legacy of Martin Luther King, Jr. Long before it was apparent to visitors and consulting clients that the King Center was a fitting tribute—a useful and functioning research and action institution—to the prophet and his causes. Bennie Mays and the other trustees had set in motion processes to make it so. Coretta Scott King and other trustees insisted that Mays receive the 1972 Martin Luther King, Jr., Center Freedom Award, even though the honoree considered that the center's work and even his own had barely begun in that year.[25]

In the busy days of establishing the Martin Luther King, Jr., Center for Non-violent Social Change, continuing to raise money for causes, not least of which was Morehouse, and trying to do the school board work that Sadie Mays had set in motion, Bennie Mays also finished writing the memoir he had started two decades earlier. Having expended the three-year stipend from the Rockefeller Foundation gotten up by Deland DeVinney, Mays was pleased to receive an additional stipend in the late 1970s, this one covering expenses for approximately a year. It was arranged by black educator Samuel DuBois Cook and the Ford Foundation. The foundation money was well spent, for a badly kept secret was that Bennie Mays was better at raising money than at bargaining on his own behalf; he had never earned much, and he had assiduously given away most of the generous speaking fees whose total often came close to his presidential salary. He completed the memoir in 1971, and later that year Scribner's published *Born to Rebel* as a trade book, but one with an academic as well as a generalist audience.[26]

Mays still smarted from the insult "Tom" that had been thrown at him by the hostage takers in April 1969 and by other stray catcalls at certain speaking events, and he suspected that behind his back some students and junior faculty called him by their newest insult, "Dr. Thomas"—a witticism that pretended great respect for an "Uncle Tom" who had attained a Ph.D. Partly to answer such folk but for other reasons as well, he called his memoir *Born to Rebel.* This title was a piece of inspired genius. Often he was asked if he was related to baseball legend Willie Mays, who had also been nicknamed "Buck" in his own professional youth and who then worked with some journalists to produce *Born to Play Ball.* Always a little suspicious of professional athletes, especially if their exploits drew attention away from important issues of justice, Bennie Mays wanted to make quite clear that he had a real mission of rebellion, that the mission was significant, and that it was divinely ordained as well as classically joined. The title, like the book, is magnificent in a classical sense, for it combines an Augustinian sense of calling with Aristotelian habits of doing.[27]

   Born to Rebel was acclaimed by academics, being labeled in the *New York Review of Books* as a worthwhile work, but it was also picked up and read with appreciation by broad-minded citizens with a good general education in the liberal arts and a deep curiosity about the American dilemma of racism and resistance to racism that had come to the forefront in the 1960s. It was a good thing that publication and release were delayed until 1971, because the memoir writer had digested quite a good deal by that time and also because his potential audience had lost much of its appetite for angry black men. Also there was a realization that something significant had happened with regard to civil rights in the twentieth-century United States, that much of that revelation and accomplishment had been centered in the Deep South, that the real leadership had begun with black people in the Deep South, and that 1971 was a good time to hear from and pay attention to the few survivors left from those campaigns. By this year Bennie and Sadie Mays's sense that they had been marching in the vanguard of a long procession—rather than being "Toms" on the margins of the action—was largely accepted in the academy, and many people wanted to hear the testimony of those few survivors who, like the Mayses, had marched through it all, absorbed the punishments, and then—in Faulknerian phrase—had "endured and prevailed." Those who knew much could reflect that Bennie Mays had in fact held his own and was still here![28]

The writing in *Born to Rebel* is terse and lean, and it is paced just right. Despite his classical background, his academic experiences, and his career preaching, Mays employed a tone of voice that is easy to listen to and impossible for the generalist—and secular—lay reader to misunderstand. His tone is wise and determined, saddened by many wounds in lost battles and by the deaths of his most trusted associates and loves; yet the book is optimistic about black people, about the United States, and even about the South. Most striking is Mays's ability to develop some sense of drama in the events, even though most readers know at least the broadest patterns of the recent history. Also notable is the lack of bitterness. The book demonstrates his anger, but never any bitterness, not even in his brief and only partial account of the student lock-in at Atlanta University. He avoided the opportunity to settle scores with individuals, usually not even naming a nemesis with the important exceptions of Dr. Wallace Payne, Governor Lester Maddox, and Senators Benjamin Ryan Tillman, Strom Thurmond, and Richard Russell—and these villains he treated with respect if somewhat distantly. Mays was also careful to share credit, and he described his many accomplishments in the context of cooperative teamwork. Indeed one reason for a full biography is that his sense of fair play and modest understatement make it hard to know the actual extent of his own share in some of the major victories in the "long civil rights movement."

As theologian James W. Dawsey has noted, "It is a prayerful reflection on what could be, on the teleology of what a just God wants us to do."[29] One opens the book to a startling description from a child's point of view of Klan night riders ready to kill a four-year-old during the Phoenix Riot, and one closes the book convinced that many have fought a good fight and that it is the reader's duty now to take up that uncompleted fight. More than in any other venue, Mays in *Born to Rebel* read his audience aright and spoke to them in a way that readers have to respect and respond to. And for once there were readers in the multiple thousands—and discussion among those readers and others, even and especially at the University of South Carolina, where a professor made the memoir a centerpiece in a historical study of southern memoirs.

Born to Rebel has stayed in print, though now more to serve continuing academic interest among southern theologians, divinity students, and historians with interests in modern South Carolina and greater Atlanta. It was in keeping *Born to Rebel* in print and in attempting other writing and record gathering projects that Bennie Mays late in life made the acquaintance of Orville Vernon Burton, historian at the University of Illinois for some thirty years before coming back to South Carolina. Burton helped Mays to organize notes, especially the records of the "Mays" and "In My View" columns from the *Pittsburgh Courier,* which ran from 1942 to 1981. Burton had also recruited graduate students of all colors to study history with him at the University of Illinois, and he sent several of these students to Mays, most prominently Derek Rovaris, whose dissertation and subsequent published monograph on Mays's Morehouse made it unnecessary for Mays himself to write his planned institutional history. Burton was instrumental in gaining recognition for Mays in several places, including a historical marker at his birthplace in Greenwood County and an oil portrait hanging in the South Carolina State House.[30]

Other writing projects did not fare as well, but it seems fitting that the valedictory memoir is the best of Mays's late writing as well as the best writing of his career. The plan to print excerpts from speeches and perhaps the *Pittsburgh Courier* columns—sometimes seen as one large project and sometimes seen as two separate projects—was rather dimly realized in 1983 in *Quotable Quotes of Benjamin E. Mays,* a privately printed and distributed collection of things Mays often said, which he himself helped to subsidize in combination with ever-faithful associate Samuel DuBois Cook. The gathered aphorisms are fun to read, and when read aloud call to mind the schoolmaster marshaling the forces in Sale Hall; but as Ralph Luker notes, it is not always clear which quotes are from traditional sources and which from classical authors, and in any case such quotes need to be set into meaningful context. In her dissertation at Louisiana State University, Doris Levy Gavins accomplished what really needed to be done in *Quotable Quotes,* producing an excellent study of the rhetorical strategies used by Bennie Mays; that dissertation needs to be published and distributed widely. Mays's *Pittsburgh Courier* columns should also be collected in a book with introductions to explain their contexts, as Mays wanted to do himself, and that need is a striking one.[31]

There remained the uncompleted business of a providing decent public school education for all the children of the increasingly black downtown Atlanta.

Bennie Mays's study group and he himself had concluded that busing was not the answer. In the midst of all the backlash about "busin'," more and more white people ran away from the downtown schools faster than bus routes could be extended. In any case a 1970 change in federal policy had rewritten the rules in a way that busing could not address, and by 1973 Mays's school board had no choice but to make peace with the new reality. His resolution came to be called the Compromise of 1973, and some spoke the words sarcastically, with a clever reference to Booker T. Washington's own Compromise of 1895—"the races as separate as the fingers on a hand, but both races moving in the same direction." That comparison was painful for the veteran civil rights activist to contemplate, given the early-twentieth-century developments of full-blown Jim Crow and its accompanying "nadir of race relations" that followed Washington's Compromise. Bennie Mays hoped the comparison was irrelevant, and he vowed to make his compromise a moral and effective one by contrast. It had to work. After all Sadie Mays had not given her final months on behalf of a segregated school system.

The school board had to face this change in federal policy—not a change in enforcement, but an actual change in rules and practices in force. All over the South there were white private schools—"segregation academies," Mays called them—whose essential purpose appeared to be education for whites only. These schools were relatively expensive, and initially had a correspondingly small middle class enrollment. In 1970, however, a federal law allowed parents to take a tax exemption for the tuition expenses of such private schools, and that policy suddenly made the schools affordable for the broad middle class of white southerners. With this tax exemption, people did not need to move to some neighborhood with "quality"—that is, essentially white schools. Enrollment in the private schools dramatically increased, and white enrollment in Atlanta area public schools just as dramatically decreased. Another grave difficulty was that parents who were spending money, even with a tax exemption, on their children's education were in no mood to pay higher taxes to fund public schools—especially for black children. White flight to suburbia, segregation academies, changing tax base, and dramatically changing attitudes toward public schools damaged Atlanta's public school system. At one point Mays wrote a column called "The End of Public Schools," and he warned that it would be the poor white children who would suffer most when public schools became purely for the lower class of both races and when funding for those schools was decreased by voters whose own children were not involved.[32]

Still an integrationist in terms of graduate and professional training and in terms of the workforce, Bennie Mays faced the facts and declared, "I don't believe that racial integration in the schools is a must if we are to have first-class institutions. . . . It didn't take white students, for example, to qualify

Morehouse [to have a Phi Beta Kappa chapter, making it only the fourth Georgia school to qualify]." He went on to note that one in nine Morehouse graduates were admitted to graduate or professional programs, a ratio far superior to all but a few prestigious private colleges. What was needed was well-qualified teachers, adequate funding for equipment—especially expensive scientific laboratory equipment and then-new computer technology—and adequate funding for physical plants. If Atlantans paid for these resources, then black public schools would produce graduates able to go out and flourish in Morehouse or in largely white research universities. Perhaps at least a few of the "trapped" poor white children could take advantage of such resources, and someday, if the schools were eventually recognized for high quality, perhaps at least some of the white middle class would send their own children into city schools.[33]

Mays went before the public in meetings, and in such formal settings he was always superb. Now he also appeared on local television, and he did equally well in that venue. Using his height and sharp features to telegenic advantage, he stood or sat erect with chin held high if not thrust forward. He spoke slowly and with assurance, and he spoke precisely. Viewers might not know the classical concepts of *magnanimatatum* or *megalosukos,* but they came to recognize the dignity in his visage and in the honeyed nuance of his Piedmont dialect. He was a calming presence, even as he demanded that Atlantans spend money on downtown schools. He was in wonderful contrast with the continuing antics of Lester Maddox and the segregationist reactionaries. Atlantans, after all, as a group remained grateful for the busyness of their city—and for their forward and onward rushing prosperity. Atlantans remained grateful that Lester Maddox wielded only toy weapons and empty words and that he was not Bull Connor with attack dogs, fire hoses, and the full weight of metropolitan law and police on his side. For their city to lead the Deep South and to take a leadership role among East Coast cities, Atlantans could not comport themselves as unreasoning rednecks. Nor could they present themselves as elitists, reflecting but no longer acting on hundreds of years of fading wealth and prestige.

Instead, with Bennie Mays's encouragement of what they wanted anyway, Atlantans came to see themselves and came to behave much in the pattern set long ago by the diminished but not discredited progressive business elite. Atlantans proclaimed themselves to be modern, forward-thrusting and practical people, folk on the make to catch up with and surpass Chicago and San Francisco. In his television appearances, Bennie Mays at last found his middle-class audience, presenting them as they wished to see themselves. What he asked was for citizens in a rich city to dip into extremely deep coffers to support their city schools. He was not insisting that their children attend school in company of large numbers of black children, but rather with small numbers of black children. In those schools where no whites attended, it would cost

Atlantans, but the cost was fully manageable in material—and likely in spiritual terms too.

Samuel Odelle Piper, research physicist for Marietta Research Institute of Georgia Tech, spoke for many urban professionals when he recalled watching and listening to school board president Mays during the period 1970–74: "I remember being a student at Georgia Tech in the early 70s and seeing Benjamin Mays often on local news speaking for the Atlanta School Board. He had a reassuring presence on camera that guided Atlanta through difficult early days of desegregation that kept Atlanta from becoming another Birmingham."[34]

The specific Compromise of 1973 that Mays presented and presided over declared that the city of Atlanta was to spend money on these downtown schools. Another aspect of the compromise was that black people, especially black women, were to step into teaching jobs and take seats of power in administrative posts. Fortunately Georgia native Griffin Bell, then federal district judge, insisted in a series of rulings that the Atlanta school systems spend money on the largely black schools and that the city and the surrounding counties must address decades of discriminatory employment and aggressively hire black teachers and supervisors. On these rulings by Judge Bell, Stanley Palmetere, chief of the Nixon civil rights division of the U.S. Justice Department, was supportive and useful, much to the relief of the optimistic but anxious Mays. Important Justice Department officials responded to Palmetere, and federal judicial officials responded to Judge Bell; these agents—in tandem with liberals in municipal office—implemented the Compromise of 1973. Atlanta's schools gained significantly in funding, and more black people—most of them generally well-qualified—became teachers in those schools, while more black females—most of them also well-qualified—gained positions of authority. As expected, the schools' student bodies became overwhelmingly black. Of course there were still spokesmen for backlash, but such reactionists exercised little practical control over the city schools.[35]

Things did grow better, and when Bennie Mays took an honorable retirement at the end of 1980, his fellow school board members voted him president emeritus, and a handsome new school was built and named for him in a relatively affluent professional—and mostly black—part of Atlanta. Ironically his city's churches and schools were resegregated by the end of his integrationist career, but from those churches and schools emerged young leaders who could and did serve effectively and with honor in fully integrated forces, usually after training in historically white graduate and professional centers at major research universities. The result of the Compromise of 1973 was summed up in a way that summed up Bennie Mays's decade on the school board by none other than 1969 nemesis Alton Hornsby, Jr., who eventually did become a worthy historian in the tradition of Bennie Mays's associates Carter Woodson, Rayford Logan, and E. Franklin Frazier:

> Following his implementation of the "Compromise of 1973," Atlanta had a nearly all black school system, largely administered by blacks. These administrators, and their mostly black teaching staffs, launched often innovative programs to prepare poorer children for kindergarten. Other initiatives came from Atlanta's black middle class. One such venture, "Project Success," selected one class from an Atlanta school, tutored and otherwise supported the students and promised them college tuition upon graduation. . . . [T]here remained pockets of progress and success, particularly in affluent African American neighborhoods. In 1986, for example, nearly fifty black students were participants or alternates in the Atlanta PTA's Governor's Honors Programs. Almost one half of these were pupils at Douglass and Mays high schools in middle class black neighborhoods, but even Archer High School, located in the midst of one of Atlanta's poorest housing projects, had five students in the program. Also, during its 1987 and 1988 commencement programs, Mays High School listed one National Merit finalist, 15 National Achievement finalists, and over 150 college scholarship recipients, out of a graduating classes [*sic*] of 700 students. These scholarships were valued at more than $3 million. Scholarship institutions included Antioch College, Brown University, Emory University, The Georgia Institute of Technology, Duke University, Northwestern University, the University of California at Berkeley, Vanderbilt University, the Massachusetts Institute of Technology, Cornell University, Harvard University and Princeton University as well as Howard University, Morehouse College, and Spelman College—prestigious black schools. And, during this period, three black Atlanta public schools—Southwest Middle (1986), Frederick Douglass High (1984) and Benjamin E. Mays High (1987)—were named Georgia Schools of Excellence.[36]

Twilight honors came throughout Mays's final decade. Still more honorary degrees were bestowed—making a total of 251 according to the archivists at Howard University Library. One was from Emory University, the old center of a once distant and aloof New South Methodism, and the warm reception given him by the crosstown Atlantans said good things about his effect in a new and better day. In fact there were almost constantly arriving invitations to receive honorary degrees, and one from Columbia University had to be awarded posthumously because even Bennie Mays could not schedule enough travel in the few academic seasons (and few commencements) left him.[37]

Benjamin Mays (center) with President Jimmy Carter (right), a strong advocate for civil rights. Courtesy of the Moorland-Spingarn Research Center, Howard University.

The Martin Luther King, Jr., Center for Nonviolent Social Change in the nation's capital had given him recognition for service in the cause of peace with justice in 1980, and that same fall the Council of the District of Columbia had declared October 14 to be B. E. Mays Day. Meanwhile, the *Pittsburgh Courier,* no longer the periodical of choice for black professionals and academics, was revised and revamped under new ownership, and in 1981 the *New Pittsburgh Courier* awarded Mays its first Top Hat Award for service to the race in the year—but really for his lifetime. Still other honors in 1980 and 1981 were almost more appropriate were he already dead: The street where he and Sadie Mays had made their longtime home was renamed Benjamin E. Mays Drive Southwest; a crossroads in Greenwood County near current Epworth and where Hezekiah Mays's house once stood in the long-gone community of Rambo was named Benjamin E. Mays Crossroads. The General Assembly of South Carolina, often responding to newly enfranchised black voters but also responding to tireless efforts from historian Vernon Burton, placed an oil portrait of Mays in the State House; and at least one middle school in Spartanburg County was named the Benjamin E. Mays Middle School.[38]

One honor did not come his way, and that award was the Presidential Medal of Freedom. In retrospect it seemed fitting that in 1983 Ronald Reagan—so often seeming to be a charming and affable man who was above racism— refused to sign House Resolution 17 that the old rebel be awarded the medal. Illinois' Paul Simon and Georgia's Wyche Fowler had coordinated the effort, and the House of Representatives vote was overwhelming; but the southern strategy still needed to be served, and President Reagan and his people were in no mood to honor a principled leader of the civil rights movement who had so often and so effectively criticized them.[39] No man of *megalosukos* could spend much time crying over this slight. He had preached and taught since he gradu- ated from Bates College that one did not do the right thing in order to be recognized by other men. Indeed it could have been morally problematical to accept an insincerely proffered award from a man that Bennie Mays considered truly dangerous to black people, to the poor in general, and to the broader cause of peace with justice. In any case Bennie Mays in the last full year of his life was quite sufficiently honored by mortals, and he knew his energies were flagging and that is was time to prepare himself for the next journey, the one across all the valleys.

He spoke of "dying in harness," both to young Vernon Burton and to a former student, the journalist Jacob Wortham. Although he had retired from the school board and abandoned publishing projects, he kept up his correspon- dence and continued to travel, still driving himself to the airport and still mak- ing his flights on time. He still gave speeches, and he spoke well, albeit with weakened voice and slower pace. By the new year of 1984, he was clearly slow- ing down. Photographs show a still-erect man, but a man quite diminished in size, looking on some occasions almost emaciated—and definitely tired. There was also a story about a seriocomic episode that made the rounds back at More- house. Driving in the heavy traffic of rush hour, the aged schoolmaster had found himself unable to get into the lane for his exit ramp. He knew where it was, but he was not aggressive enough to force his way into the correct lane. He grew anxious and afraid as he continued driving, finally turning around far west of the city, not far from the Alabama boundary line. Those hearing the story responded according to their already formed attitudes: some with dis- belief, many with sorrow, and a few with mirth that the old tyrant had found something stronger than he. It did raise concerns, even in his own indomitable, if not stubborn, mind, about continuing to do everything for himself.[40]

It was not be an issue that came to conflict. On March 28, 1984, his body simply wore out, and he too drew up his knees, folded his legs underneath him- self, shut his eyes, and quit breathing.[41]

Benjamin Mays with his sister Susie Mays Glenn. Courtesy of the
Moorland-Spingarn Research Center, Howard University.

The reference to the Prophet Elijah leaving a double portion of his blessing for the Prophet Elisha is metaphorical for teaching and guiding purposes. It is how the magnificent one thought and spoke. As a University of Chicago scholar of biblical historicism, Bennie Mays knew that the ancients left a double portion to the eldest son, and that Prophet Elisha was asking to be treated like the eldest—and most favored son—in terms of a legacy with which to lead after the elder teaching prophet had departed.[42] Bennie Mays no longer declared belief in the more mystical aspects of the Bible, and he did not speak of the Prophet Elijah ascending in a special chariot into the sky and leaving no physical remains of himself but rather a magical cloak with which his successor, the Prophet Elisha could strike the waters to cause them to part. "Still a Baptist," as he always phrased it, he did not dwell in such imagery for narrative description. But he did speak of one prophet leaving clear direction for spiritual teaching and moral guidance to successor prophets. He did see his inspiring teachers as prophets in that Hebrew sense of being called by God to lead all people back to the right path of justice and peace. He did believe that he had benefited from at least a double portion of spirit from his guides. Refusing false modesty, he did believe he had found the right path and had left clear guidance for successor prophets to follow a path toward justice lit by the one true Lord, regardless of what earthly lords said or did. Also in refusing false modesty, he did believe that he left at least a double portion for those who followed him after he too had been gathered to his ancestors. He knew that he had found magnificence, *magnanimatatum* and *megalosukos.* He knew he was leaving a double portion for future generations.

Notes

Introduction

1. Mays, *Born to Rebel,* 45–47; Dallas Blanchard, interview with Mays, August 16, 1983, Southern Oral History Program, Southern Historical Collection, University of North Carolina Library, Chapel Hill (hereafter SHC).

2. Mays, *Born to Rebel,* 46.

Chapter 1. Seed of James, Branch of Prophets and Judges

1. For relationships between and among black and white families in Edgefield District, see Burton, *In My Father's House,* and Mays, *Born to Rebel,* chapter 1.

2. Edgar, *South Carolina,* chapters 1 and 2, talks about South Carolina as being a "colony of a colony," that is Barbados; Wood, *Black Majority;* Greene, *Imperatives, Behaviors, and Identities;* for quantitative and theoretical discussions of "colony of a colony," see Dunn, *Sugar and Slaves,* 111–16; 176, and Gray, *History of Agriculture in the Southern United States.*

3. Mays, *Born to Rebel,* 2. For Finnish names in the southern Piedmont, see Jordan and Kaups, *The American Backwoods,* 229, 238–39, 241–42. A. J. Rambo and Joseph Rambo are listed as slave owners in U.S. Census, 2nd ser., Slave Census, Edgefield District, 1850 (count of June 30, 1850).

4. For the white Mayses and their slaveholdings, see U.S. Census, 2nd ser., Slave Census, Edgefield District, 1850. Henry Hazel Mays is listed with a son, William H. Mays, and fourteen unnamed slaves, including one man of James's age and complexion and a child the age and complexion of Hezekiah (and the age of the white child, William H. Mays), U.S. Census, Population Census, Edgefield District, 1850 and 1860. After freedom, Hezekiah (also spelled Hesikah and Hezikah) is listed as a renting farmer with his wife, Vinia, born in Virginia, which squares with family memories ascribed to Julia and Louvenia, and with Vinia bearing eight children and losing one, U.S. Census, Population Census, Edgefield County, 1880 and 1890; Population Census, Brooks Township, Greenwood County, 1900. U.S. Census, Saluda Regiment, Edgefield District, 1860, lists Henry Hazel Mays, child William H., and the notoriously cruel overseer S. C. Deale with slaves the right ages for James, Julia, and Hezekiah. Ages for slave children owned by the other Mayses do not line up in this way, nor do ages for slaves owned by A. J. Rambo and Joseph Rambo. On September 25, 1880, William H. Mays married Nola Lou Barmore (who was remembered by the black Mayses as "Nora" instead of "Nola"); they appear in U.S. Census, Population Census, Edgefield County, 1880. More important, in U.S. Census, Agricultural Census, Edgefield County, 1880, William H. Mays's farm operation is detailed in the same line with his renters, including Hezekiah Mays for that year's agricultural census.

5. The exact statistic for illiteracy among nonwhites during the final five years of slavery and the first four years of freedom is 79.9 percent. That statistic would include some former slaves who had learned to read and write after slavery ended (U.S. Census, Historical Statistics, 1870). In the official statistics, Hezekiah Mays is listed among the 79.9 percent unable to read and write (U.S. Census, Population Census, Edgefield County, 1880 and 1890).

6. Mays heard and used the call/response of the Baptist minister; *call:* "How long / O, Lord / How Long?"; *response:* "Not long / Not long," or "Only a little while," or sometimes both blended as "Not long / Only a little while / Not long now / Only a little while now." The expected triumph of the just is on this earth, not in an otherworldly place. Here too Mays pronounced himself *Born to Rebel.* Sources include Psalms 94:3 and 6:3b, as well as references to the Hebrew prophets in Hebrews 10:37–38 and Romans 1:17, but mostly the Old Testament books of Isaiah (26:30) and Habakkuk (2:3–4); see notes on texts and sources in Jones, ed., *Jerusalem Bible* (hereafter JB).

7. Mays, *Born to Rebel,* 2.

8. Ibid.; see the discussion of this phrase in Stampp, *The Peculiar Institution,* chapter 2.

9. Mays, *Born to Rebel,* chapter 1; U.S. Census, Population Census, Edgefield County, 1880; on the marriage of Louvenia and Hezekiah Mays, see ibid., 1890.

10. On the Mayses' slaves see U.S. Census, Slave Census, Edgefield District, 1860. The phrase "he lived and moved and had his being" is attributed to the classic Greek philosopher-poet Epimanides. Mays used it in correspondence (Moorland-Spingarn Research Center, Howard University Library—hereafter MSRC) and also in his columns for the *Pittsburgh Courier,* 1942–1981. See the Reverend Craig R. Wylie to Roper, November 24, 2003, John Herbert Roper Papers, SHC.

11. Moore, *Social Origins of Dictatorship and Democracy;* Wright, *Old South, New South.*

12. No census of black landownership was taken in South Carolina. Joel Williamson used county property records for 1870 and 1880 to estimate 10 percent (Williamson, *After Slavery,* 155). Mays, *Born to Rebel,* mentions the mules in chapter 1. William H. Mays never reported ownerships of more than two mules to the census takers (U.S. Census, Agricultural Census, Edgefield County, 1880). At some time in the 1890s, William H. Mays sold his own farm but apparently continued to rent out some land to the black Mayses. The onetime lord of the land became a brick manufacturer in the city of Greenwood in the newly formed Greenwood County, U.S. Census, Population Census, Greenwood County, 1900.

13. Wortham, "Benjamin E. Mays at Eighty-One," 27–30.

14. Ibid.; Mays, *Born to Rebel,* 2.

15. Roper, "The Radical Mission"; the Reverend James F. Marshall is mentioned in the *Greenwood Index,* the *Edgefield Chronicle,* and the *Edgefield Advertiser,* 1898–1900; see "Rev. James F. Marshall, Widely Known Colored Minister Is Dead of Pneumonia at 84," *Greenwood Index-Journal,* February 9, 1936, 3.

Chapter 2. The Ravening Wolf

1. Mays, *Born to Rebel,* 1.

2. Tindall, *South Carolina Negroes, 1877–1900,* 233–59.

3. Kantrowitz, *Ben Tillman and the Reconstruction of White Supremacy;* Simkins, *Pitchfork Ben Tillman.* Simkins was known to Mays, who admired and often used Simkins's images of Tillman as rabble-rousing race baiter.

4. Preacher [Robert] Carroll, "Preacher Carroll Interviews Ben Tillman," *Edgefield Advertiser,* September 15, 1897.

5. Hoyt, "The Phoenix Riot, November 8, 1898," address, April 18, 1935, Kosmos Club, South Caroliniana Library, University of South Carolina, Columbia (hereafter SCL). See also articles in the *State* (Columbia), *Edgefield Chronicle,* and *Charleston Courier* during the summer and fall of 1898; including Kohn bylines in the *Charleston Courier* and other dailies and Norment bylines in the *State.* Ella Dargan of the Watson family kept notes and found some casualties missed by newspapermen, see correspondence, November 1898–March 1899, Watson Family Papers, SCL. Unless noted otherwise, all quotations in this chapter are from Hoyt, "The Phoenix Riot."

6. Simkins, *Pitchfork Ben Tillman;* Kantrowitz, *Ben Tillman;* Andrew, *Wade Hampton.*

7. Andrew, *Wade Hampton,* 463–87.

8. Hoyt, "The Phoenix Riot"; for Benjamin Randolph see Williamson, *After Slavery,* 182, 205–6, 260, 365–68.

9. "Ringing Appeal to the Faithful," *Greenwood Index,* October 13, 1898; Hoyt, "The Phoenix Riot"; Woodward, *Reunion and Reaction;* Simkins, *Pitchfork Ben Tillman;* Logan, *The Negro in American Life and Thought.*

10. [Johnson Sales Watson], Phoenix day book, 1900–1901, Harry LeGare Watson Papers, SCL.

11. Leland Smith, quoted in Hoyt, "The Phoenix Riot."

12. Ibid.

13. Williamson, *The Crucible of Race;* Brundage, *Lynching in the New South.* Both Brundage and Williamson note the kind of rituals remembered by Mays and Hezekiah and recounted in local press.

14. Kohn, *Charleston Courier,* November 1898; "Lynch Law," *Edgefield Advertiser,* November 6, 1898.

15. "The Trouble at Phoenix," *Greenwood Index,* November 10, 1898, names Will White and Joe Circuit and quotes unnamed members of the vigilance groups. I can find no other newspaper that carried this story in this way on November 10, 1898. Compare Hoyt, "The Phoenix Riot."

16. Ella Dargan to Harry LeGare Watson, November 15, 1898, Watson Family Papers, SCL.

17. "Closing Chapter," *Greenwood Index,* November 17, 1898.

18. Robert L. Henderson to Harry LeGare Watson, December 3, 1898, Watson Family Papers, SCL.

19. Ella Dargan to Harry LeGare Watson, November 10, 11, 12, and 15, December 20 and 30, 1898; Harry LeGare Watson to Ella Dargan, November 17, 1898, in which he correctly predicted the statement that Henderson issued on December 3, 1898, Watson Family Papers, SCL.

20. See "requisitions papers" filed by Governor William H. Ellerbe: to Governor Ellerbe by Henry W. Holloway and Robert F. McCaslin. See also "Negro Exodus," *Greenwood Index,* December 22, 1898; Kohn, quoted by Hoyt, "The Phoenix Riot"; "Negro Exodus," *State* (Columbia), December 20, 1898; Rice, editorial, "Negro Exodus," *State* (Columbia), December 21, 1898. The first census of newly formed Greenwood County (1900), was taken at the height of the "Negro exodus." The black population in Abbeville and Edgefield Counties in 1880 was recorded at 57,463, and in 1890 it was 63,623. The black population for the same area in 1900,

then including the new County of Greenwood, in 1900 was recorded at 59,097. "Sex, General Nativity, and Color," U.S. Census, Historical Statistics, 1900, table 19, p. 555.

21. "The Closing Chapter," *Greenwood Index,* November 17, 1898, describes the execution of James M. Collins. Collins is the only casualty not mentioned by Hoyt.

22. Ella Dargan to Harry LeGare Watson, November 15, 1898, Watson Family Papers, SCL.

23. General correspondence, November 8, 1898–May 30, 1899; telegrams received, November 8, 1898–May 30, 1899, especially marginal notations by private secretary Boyd Evans; telegrams sent, November 8, 1898–May 30, 1899, William H. Ellerbe Papers, South Carolina Department of Archives and History (hereafter SCDAH). See especially J. C. Boyd to Ellerbe, November 8, 1898; James W. Tolbert to Ellerbe, November 1, 1898; F. W. R. Nance to Ellerbe, November 15, 1898; note bills for services of security guards, Aug W. Smith to Ellerbe, especially November 19, 1898.

Chapter 3. A Rambo Boy after the Riot

1. *Charleston Courier,* November 9, 1898–February 1, 1899; *Greenwood Index,* November 9, 1898–February 1, 1899. See the reporting in the *State* (Columbia), especially Gonzalez editorials, January 1899. On the Mays family's reading habits, see Mays, *Born to Rebel,* 17. Telegrams received, November 1898–May 30, 1899, including O. G. Thompson to William H. Ellerbe, January 25, 1899, William H. Ellerbe Papers, SCDAH.

2. Ella Dargan to Harry LeGare Watson, November 9 and 15, December 4, 1898, and January 3, 1899, Watson Family Papers, SCL.

3. Mays, *Born to Rebel,* 25.

4. John 4:35.

5. Cotton prices noted in *Greenwood Index* and *Edgefield Advocate,* December 1898; "Negro Exodus," *Greenwood Index,* December 22, 1898; Rice, "Negro Exodus," *State* (Columbia), December 21, 1898; Kohn and Rice, quoted in Hoyt, "The Phoenix Riot"; "Sex, General Nativity, and Color," U.S. Census, Historical Statistics, 1900, table 19, p. 555. Ella Dargan to Harry LeGare Watson, December 4, 1898, Watson Family Papers, SCL.

6. Telegrams and letterbook, both with notes by private secretary Boyd Evans, 1898–99, William H. Ellerbe Papers, SCDAH.

7. "Colored Baptists Meet," *Greenwood Index,* May 5, 1898; column notice, *Greenwood Index,* June 23, 1898; S. H. McGhee, editorial note, *Greenwood Index,* September 15, 1898. See *Greenwood Index,* December 15, 1898–March 1899.

8. Gavins, interview with Mays, April 6, 1977, "The Ceremonial Speaking of Benjamin Elijah Mays"; Mays, *Born to Rebel,* 17.

9. Mays, *Born to Rebel,* 15.

10. Dallas Blanchard, interview with Mays, August 16, 1983, Southern Oral History Program, SHC.

11. Judges 1:14–15; Ecclesiastes 1:18.

12. Psalm 37:1–3, 7–11.

13. Aristotle, *The Nicomachean Ethics,* bk. 4:3; see H. H. Joachim, *Aristotle, the Nicomachean Ethics: A Commentary,* and for Mays's use of Aristotle, see Gavins, "The Ceremonial Speaking of Benjamin Elijah Mays"; Philippians 4:5.

Chapter 4. The Student

1. Harlan, *Separate but Unequal,* 205 and 205n.

2. U.S. Census, Historical Statistics, ser. D, p. 91. In 1911 a farm laborer averaged $338 per year, or approximately $7.04 per week for a forty-eight-week year; Bennie and H.H. reported earning $7.50 per week but only of course in good times.

3. U.S. Census, Historical Statistics, ser. D, p. 93. There is no data for 1911, but in 1919 the average weekly earnings for railroad workers, including Pullman porters, was $25.87 for an average work week of 43.8 hours. Mays's railroad work in 1919 earned him $310.

4. Roper, "The Radical Mission."

5. Ibid.; Cornelius C. Scott, "When Negroes Attended the State University," *State* (Columbia), May 8, 1911, 10; folders for Scott, George W. Clinton, William Henry Heard, and Isaac L. Purcell, Whitefield McKinlay Papers, Carter Godwin Woodson Collection, Manuscript Division, Library of Congress.

6. 1 Kings 3:15.

7. Gravestone markings for Theodosia Richardson, Ellen E. Harvin, and Rufus Richardson in the Richardson family plot, Memorial Cemetery, Manning, South Carolina; gravestone rubbings, John Herbert Roper Papers, SHC. U.S. Census, Clarendon County, 1890 and 1900. Lauretta Hilton to Jane Caldwell, April 16 and 17, 2003, John Herbert Roper Papers, SHC.

8. Ibid. Also DC #6554, March 30, 1920, Sumter County, South Carolina Department of Health and Environmental Control, Division of Biostatistics, SCDAH (hereafter DC #6554, SCDAH). U.S. Census, Slave Census, Clarendon District, 1860.

9. Lauretta Hilton to Jane Caldwell, April 16 and 17, 2003; Hilton to Roper, April 20 and May 19, 2003, John Herbert Roper Papers, SHC. Mays, *Born to Rebel,* 153; Smith, *Notable Black American Men,* 782. See DC #6554, SCDAH.

10. Mays, *Born to Rebel;* "Benjamin E. Mays," *American National Biography,* edited by Garraty and Carnes, 795. Song of Songs 6:1, Wansbrough, ed., New Jerusalem Bible (1990 trans., hereafter NJB), 1037n. Mays was probably using the Goodspeed translation and his own student translations.

11. Song of Songs 6:2, NJB, 1037n.

12. Gavins, "The Ceremonial Speaking of Benjamin Elijah Mays," 6, 30–35.

13. Lorin Webster to Mays, July 31, 1916, quoted in *Born to Rebel.*

14. Amos 7:9.

15. Amos 7:7–8.

16. Psalm 85:10.

17. Rufus Richardson gravestone rubbing and notes, John Herbert Roper Papers, SHC. Bennett, *Before the Mayflower* (6th ed.), 346–48; Franklin and Moss, *From Slavery to Freedom* (7th ed.), 332; 371st Infantry; National Guard units; American Battle Monuments Commission, *93d Division;* U.S. Army Center of Military History.

18. Job 19: 27, verse as revised for "Order of the Burial of the Dead," Book of Common Prayer (1928).

Chapter 5. Wisdom in Northern Light

1. Mays, *Born to Rebel,* 50.

2. U.S. Census, Historical Statistics, A 95–123; Black Exodus, 1898–99, correspondence, William H. Ellerbe Papers, SCDAH.

3. Scrapbook of Montrose Jonas Moses, 1930, 1931, 1932, and passim, Montrose Jonas Moses Papers, Manuscript Division, Duke University.

4. Aristotle, *Nicomachean Ethics,* bk. 4:1123–25.

5. Webster, "The Supposed Speech of John Adams," 350 (also published as "Daniel Webster Puts a Speech in the Mouth of John Adams").

6. Ibid.

7. J. B. Felton to L. B. McCord, July 19, 1951, Jeanes schoolteachers folders, Clarendon County School Board Papers, SCDAH. Felton described all Jeanes teachers for 1922–51 in Clarendon County. See also the pamphlet titled *Jeanes Teachers* (1926), Clarendon County High School Records, Clarendon County Courthouse, Manning, S.C.

8. Aristotle, *Nicomachean Ethics,* bk. 4:1123–25.

9. Ibid. Mays, *Born to Rebel;* Aristotelian notes in Gavins, "The Ceremonial Speaking of Benjamin Elijah Mays."

10. Correspondence with A. Craig Baird, especially Mays to Baird, November 10, 1945, Mays Papers, MSRC; Gavins, interview with Mays, April 6, 1977, "The Ceremonial Speaking of Benjamin Elijah Mays."

11. Thonssen and Baird, *Speech Criticism* (1948 ed.), 21; Aristotle, *Rhetoric,* bk. 1, 13–17.

12. "The Greatest Man in America," *Greenwood Index,* March 12, 1898, 1. The *Index* claimed that five thousand people attended Bryan's speech.

13. Gavins, interview with Mays, April 6, 1977, "The Ceremonial Speaking of Benjamin Elijah Mays."

14. Baird correspondence, Mays Papers, MSRC.

15. Joel Williamson, "Tom Dixon," *St. Andrews Review,* no. 23 (Spring–Summer 1982): 42–83.

16. Goybet, quoted in Franklin and Moss, *From Slavery to Freedom,* 335; Bennett, *Before the Mayflower,* 347; American Battle Monuments Commission, *93d Division* (Washington, D.C.: U.S. Government Printing Office, 1944); for trench warfare see Fussell, *The Great War and Modern Memory,* and Leed, *No Man's Land.*

17. Theodore Roosevelt, quoted in Scott, *Scott's Official History of the American Negro in the World War,* 19.

18. Gravestone rubbing, Rufus Richardson headstone.

19. Correspondence with Baird and others, including Frank B. Adair to Mays, March 1, 1946, and Trevor Arnett to Mays, July 14, 1945, Mays Papers, MSRC; on Augustine see Gavins, "The Ceremonial Speaking of Benjamin Elijah Mays," 19–30. Mays, "After Fifty Years" (Bates College reunion), Mays Papers, MSRC; *Pittsburgh Courier,* July 4, 1970, 10.

20. Mays, *Born to Rebel,* 60.

21. "Benjamin E. Mays," *American National Biography,* edited by Garraty and Carnes, 795.

Chapter 6. For Every Time There Is a Season

1. On "bread from heaven," see John 6:31–35.

2. Gavins, "The Ceremonial Speaking of Benjamin Elijah Mays"; Mays columns in *Pittsburgh Courier,* 1942–81.

3. Mays, *Born to Rebel,* 59; Lauretta Hilton to Roper, April 16 and May 19, 2003, John Herbert Roper Papers, SHC. On Sallie Conley and Gilbert DuBose, see DC #6554, SCDAH. Mays, *Born to Rebel,* 59, 67, 66, 153.

4. Brotherhood of Sleeping Car Porters, Records of Sleeping Car Porters [1921] 1925 ser. A, Chicago Historical Society.

5. Ibid.; compare Mays, *Born to Rebel,* 63–65.

6. Brotherhood of Sleeping Car Porters, Records of Sleeping Car Porters [1921] 1925, ser. A, Chicago Historical Society.

7. Ibid.

8. Measuring line and plumb line, Zechariah 1 and 2, Amos 7.

9. Burton and Goodspeed, *A Harmony of the Synoptic Gospels for Historical and Critical Study;* Mays used it at the University of Chicago both in 1921 and in 1933–37. Goodspeed also worked on *The New Testament: An American Translation* (1923), which eventually went through some twenty-five editions, and on *How Came the Bible?*

10. Isaiah 60:22.

11. Drake and Cayton, *Black Metropolis,* 6, 11, 186, and 194.

12. Abbeville, Greenwood, and Edgefield newspapers show acceptance of Wade Hampton III dining with black officials in 1880s, but the same papers expressed anger over Theodore Roosevelt and Booker T. Washington's dining together in 1901. See *Abbeville Press and Banner, Edgefield Advertiser, Edgefield Chronicle,* and *Greenwood Index,* SCL. Clark, *The Southern Country Editor,* 304–37; Tindall, *South Carolina Negroes, 1877–1900,* 306–8.

13. Aristotle, *Nicomachean Ethics,* bk. 4: i, ii; images from Mark 2:15–17, Matthew 9:10–17, and Luke 5:29–32.

14. Goodspeed, *The New Testament: An American Translation;* Jelks, "Mays's Academic Formation, 1917–1936," 111–19; Arnold, *Near the Edge of Battle;* Peden, *The Chicago School;* Storr, *Harper's University;* catalog of courses, 1920–21, Registrar, Special Collections, University of Chicago.

15. Hynes, *Shirley Jackson Case and the Chicago School;* Jelks, "Mays's Academic Formation, 1917–1936"; catalog of courses. Purinton, "Some Recent Books," *Bates Alumni Magazine,* clipping in Mays Papers, MSRC.

16. Case, *The Social Triumph of the Ancient Church,* "Gentile Forms of Millennial Hope," and *Social Origins of Christianity.*

17. Ibid.

18. Case, *Experience with the Supernatural in Early Christian Times,* "Christianity and the Mystery Religions," "Gentile Forms of Millennial Hope," and "Gentile Religions of the Ancient Mediterranean World."

19. Mays, "Pagan Survivals in Christianity."

20. Ibid.; Rauschenbusch, *A Gospel for the Social Awakening,* edited by Mays; Luker, *The Social Gospel in Black and White,* 311–12.

21. Rauschenbusch, *The Belated Races and the Social Problem,* quoted in Luker, *The Social Gospel in Black and White,* 320.

22. Rauschenbusch, *A Gospel for the Social Awakening;* Luker, *The Social Gospel in Black and White,* 311–22.

23. Jeanes Fund Fellows, Clarendon County, n.d. (1933?), Clarendon County Historical Society, Manning, S.C.; Lauretta Hilton to Roper, April 16 and May 19, 2003, John Herbert Roper Papers, SHC.

24. Logan, "John Hope," *Dictionary of Negro Biography;* John Brown Watson, correspondence with John Hope, John Brown Watson Papers, John Hay Library and Archives, Brown University (hereafter JHLA). Jones, *A Candle in the Dark.*

25. U.S. Census, Population Census, Fulton County, Ga., 1930, vol. 1, 251.

26. Mays, *Born to Rebel;* see also correspondence between John Hope and John Brown Watson, John Brown Watson Papers, JHLA.

27. John Hope, quoted by John Brown Watson at the dedication of Morehouse Library in honor of Hope, April 30, 1932, John Brown Watson Papers, JHLA; Hope's phrase about lightning, quoted in ibid.; Hope's phrase about leadership, quoted by Hattie Rutherford Watson, Hattie Rutherford Watson Papers, JHLA.

28. Hope to John Brown Watson, February 4, 1924, John Brown Watson Papers, JHLA.

29. Mays, *Born to Rebel;* correspondence between Hope and John Brown Watson, John Brown Watson Papers, JHLA.

30. Mays, *Born to Rebel,* 66.

31. Brotherhood of Sleeping Car Porters Papers, Records of Sleeping Car Porters [1921] 1925, ser. A, Chicago Historical Society.

32. John Brown Watson and Hattie Rutherford Watson Papers, JHLA, especially Mays to Hattie Rutherford Watson, October 31, 1940.

33. Matthew 13:45–46. Mays, *Born to Rebel,* and columns for *Pittsburgh Courier,* 1942–81; John Brown Watson correspondence, 1925, John Brown Watson Papers, JHLA.

34. Psalm 31:11, 14–16, 24.

35. Fishes and loaves, or "multiplication of the loaves," or "miracle of the loaves": Matthew 14 and 15; and Mark 6 and 8; Luke 9, and John 6. Thomas Aquinas, *Summa Theologica,* 3: Q. 1, art. 5, pt. 2-2; see Gavins, "The Ceremonial Speaking of Benjamin Elijah Mays"; for "whooping the benches," see Luker, "Plagiarism and Perspective: Questions about Martin Luther King, Jr.," and Mays's columns, *Pittsburgh Courier,* 1942–81.

36. Mosca, *The Ruling Class.*

37. Frazier, *Black Bourgeoisie;* see also *The Negro in the United States.*

38. Mays accepted Frazier's interpretation of the Ku Klux Klan, Blanchard, interview with Mays, August 16, 1983, Southern Oral History Program, SHC. See also Maclean, *Behind the Mask of Chivalry.*

39. Mays, *Born to Rebel,* 87.

40. Green, *Ely: Too Black, Too White,* 1–139, especially 110; John Brown Watson to Samuel Howard Archer, September 13, 1937, John Brown Watson Papers, JHLA.

41. Mays, *Born to Rebel,* 91; Thomas Aquinas, *Summa Theologica,* 3: Q. 1, art. 1–4, pt. 2-11, and 3: Q 47, art. 4, pt. 2-11; Jones, *A Candle in the Dark.*

42. Mays, *Born to Rebel,* 93.

43. DC#6554, SCDAH. On placenta previa, embolism, sepsis, nursing diagrams, and prescribed nursing procedures, see Taber and Thomas, *Taber's Cyclopedic Medical Dictionary.*

44. Taber and Thomas, *Taber's Cyclopedic Medical Dictionary.*

45. DC#6554, and Sumter County, DC, 1920–1923, SCDAH.

46. Gravestone rubbing from Richardson plot, and correspondence of Lauretta Hilton and Roper, John Herbert Roper Papers, SHC; correspondence of John Hope and John Brown Watson and Hattie Rutherford Watson, 1921–25, John Brown Watson and Hattie Rutherford Watson Papers, JHLA.

47. Harlan, *Booker T. Washington: The Wizard of Tuskegee,* 140–42, 260–61; Mills, *The Power Elite;* on Rockefeller, see George Rice Hovey to Samuel Howard Archer, January 23, 1923, correspondence of John Hope and John Brown Watson and Hattie Rutherford Watson, 1921–1925, John Brown Watson Papers, JHLA.

48. Hovey to Samuel Howard Archer, January 23, 1923; correspondence of John Hope and John Brown Watson and Hattie Rutherford Watson, 1921–1925, John Brown Watson Papers, JHLA.

49. Ibid. Woodward, *The Strange Career of Jim Crow;* interviews with C. Vann Woodward and Glenn Weddington Rainey, John Herbert Roper Papers, SHC. Mays included *The Strange Career of Jim Crow* on a list of "must read" books, n.d. (1960?), Mays Papers, MSRC.

50. Mays, *Born to Rebel,* 86–90.

51. Ibid. See also Dykeman and Stokely, *Seeds of Southern Change.*

52. Gavins, "The Ceremonial Speaking of Benjamin Elijah Mays," 236.

53. Harlan, *Booker T. Washington: The Wizard of Tuskegee,* 139.

54. John Brown Watson to John Hope, September 7, 1923, and November 11, 1924; Watson to tax receiver, Fulton County, Ga., June 26, 1925, John Brown Watson Papers, JHLA.

55. John Brown Watson to Samuel Howard Archer, September 13, 1937; obituary notices and correspondence, John Brown Watson Papers, JHLA. Mays, *Born to Rebel,* 93, 97–98, 101; Rauschenbusch, *The Belated Races.*

56. Mays, *Born to Rebel,* 93, 97–98, 101. Rauschenbusch, *The Belated Races and the Social Problems;* Case, *The Social Origins of Christianity;* "Shiloh," *Harper's Bible Dictionary;* Mays, "The Goal," address at the Older Boys Conference, February 26, 1926, Benedict College, Columbia, S.C.; published in Gordon, ed., *Sketches of Negro Life and History in South Carolina,* 203.

57. Mays, *Born to Rebel,* 93, 97–98, 101; Mays, "The Goal."

58. Mays, occasional addresses, 1926–81, private collection; Gavins, "The Ceremonial Speaking of Benjamin Elijah Mays," and "Mays's Commencement Addresses," *Walking Integrity,* edited by Carter, 298; Boyer, introduction to *Lift Every Voice and Sing II.*

59. Widow's mite, Mark 12:41–44; Mays, *Born to Rebel,* 97–98, 101.

60. Mays, *Born to Rebel,* 97–98, 101; James W. Dawsey to Roper, July 22, 2005, John Herbert Roper Papers, SHC.

61. Bennett, *Before the Mayflower,* 378, and "The Last of the Great Schoolmasters," *Walking Integrity,* edited by Carter, 333–40; Shaw, quoted in Mays, *Born to Rebel,* 93.

62. Secrest, "James Madison Nabrit, Jr."; "Howard Thurman" in *The African American Almanac,* 29; Farmer, *Lay Bare the Heart,* 135–36.

63. Gavins, "The Ceremonial Speaking of Benjamin Elijah Mays" and Mays's columns in the *Pittsburgh Courier,* 1942–81; Green, *Ely: Too Black, Too White,* 110.

64. Mays, *Quotable Quotes,* 10.

65. Mays, *Born to Rebel* and *Quotable Quotes,* 11.

66. Mays, *Quotable Quotes,* 7.

67. Ibid., 7.

68. Burton, *In My Father's House,* 116, 117, 223, 224, 238; Scarbrough, *Masters of the Big House;* and Faulkner, *Absalom, Absalom!,* 229–35; Henry Hazel Mays, U.S. Census, Population Census, Edgefield District, 1860, Edgefield County, 1870, and Edgefield District, Slave Census, 1850 and 1860.

69. Mays, *Born to Rebel,* 93, 95, 174.

70. Ibid., 95–101.

71. Ibid.

72. Mays, *Quotable Quotes,* 6.

73. Dykeman and Stokely, *Seeds of Southern Change,* 75; Rovaris, "Mays and Morehouse" and "Mays's Leadership and Morehouse College," in *Walking Integrity,* edited by Carter, 353–75.

74. Mays, quoted in Carter, "The Life of Benjamin Elijah Mays," *Walking Integrity,* edited by Carter, 3; Acts 6:15.

75. Mordecai Wyatt Johnson, "Modern Racial Issues," address to the Carolina Public Forum, May 8, 1931, Forum Papers, YMCA Papers, University Archives, University of North Carolina.

Chapter 7. My Times Are in Thy Hands

1. Mays, *Born to Rebel,* 99.

2. Mays, "Pagan Survivals in Christianity"; McNeill, Spinka, and Willoughby, eds. *Environmental Factors in Christian History,* especially introduction.

3. McNeill, Spinka, and Willoughby, eds. *Environmental Factors in Christian History,* especially introduction; Mays, "Pagan Survivals"; see also Jelks, "Mays's Academic Formation, 1917–1936," 122–23.

4. Mays, "Pagan Survivals," 5, 40–41, 43–45; stoicism, 63–88.

5. Ibid., 1–2, 41, 29.

6. Ibid., 66–68.

7. Ibid.

8. Exodus 3:14 (KJV); John 8:58 (KJV).

9. Mays, "Pagan Survivals," 29.

10. Ibid., 89.

11. Ibid., 61.

12. Ibid., 66.

13. Mays, *Born to Rebel,* 99–100, and "Pagan Survivals."

14. Mays, *Born to Rebel,* 100; William O. Brown, African Studies Papers, Boston University; Hill, foreword to the William O. Brown issue of *African Studies Bulletin,* 241–42; Cowan, "To William O. Brown" and "Ten Years of African Studies."

15. Mays, *Born to Rebel,* 100.

16. McCall, "William Oscar Brown, 1899–1969"; African Studies Papers, Boston University; Brown, "Race Prejudice."

17. Psalm 31:15, 24.

18. Mays, *Born to Rebel,* 101–2.

19. Ibid., 29–30.

20. Ibid.

21. Ibid., 30–31.

22. Ibid., 28–32; Williamson, *New People* and *The Crucible of Race;* correspondence with James L. Hunt, with enclosures, Georgia statutes, John Herbert Roper Papers, SHC; Morris, *Southern Slavery and the Law;* Smith, *Strange Fruit.*

23. Williamson, *New People;* Mays, *Born to Rebel,* 32–33.

24. Sadie Gray Mays, quoted in Mays, *Born to Rebel,* 33.

25. Maclean, *Behind the Mask of Chivalry.* Sadie Gray Mays, quoted in Mays, *Born to Rebel,* 33.

26. Mays, *Born to Rebel,* 33.

27. Gordon, ed. *Sketches of Negro Life and History in South Carolina,* passim, but especially Ransom, "The New Negro"; Haven, "Asa H. Gordon."

28. Mays, *Born to Rebel,* 101

29. Ibid., 102; statistics, *Official Report to South Carolina General Assembly,* 1926.

30. Mays, *Born to Rebel,* 103; see also Hall, *Revolt against Chivalry.*

31. Mays, *Born to Rebel,* 103.

32. Ibid.

33. Ibid., 104.

34. Gordon, ed., *Sketches;* Haven, "Asa H. Gordon."

35. Gordon, ed., *Sketches;* Haven, "Asa H. Gordon"; Frazier, *Black Bourgeoisie,* 153–73; Edward Franklin Frazier Papers, MSRC.

36. Mays, *Born to Rebel,* 103; Wortham, "Benjamin E. Mays at Eighty-One," 27; Luker, *The Social Gospel in Black and White;* Rauschenbusch, *A Gospel for the Social Awakening* and *The Belated Race and the Social Problems;* Haselden, *The Racial Problem in Christian Perspective;* McDonough, "Men and Women of Good Will," 475–77; Chappell, *A Stone of Hope.*

37. Carter, "The Life of Benjamin Elijah Mays," *Walking Integrity,* edited by Carter, 5; Mays, *Born to Rebel,* 98.

38. Mays, *Born to Rebel,* 98–105.

39. Ibid., 100–105, 120.

40. "Call" of lament, Psalm 13; "response" of hope, Hebrews 10:37, 38; Isaiah 26:20; Habakkuk 2:3–4; Romans 1:17.

Chapter 8. New Negroes on Detour

1. Mays called the period 1924–35 his "detour," *Born to Rebel,* 100–34. On southern agricultural recession, see U.S. Census, Historical Statistics, 301, col. K-302, K-303; Tindall, *The Emergence of the New South,* 138–42; Hawk, *Economic History of the South,* 503–20, with a chart on p. 517 showing dependence on the export of cotton; Vance, *Human Geography of the South,* especially tables 13–15 on income and farm values. On South Carolina rural difficulties and the onset of the Great Depression, see Lewis Pinckney Jones to Roper, July 26, 1998, John Herbert Roper Papers, SHC.

2. Van Dyke, "The Story of the Other Wise Man," quoted in Mays, *Quotable Quotes,* 15–16.

3. Mays, *Born to Rebel,* 106.

4. Franklin, *From Slavery to Freedom* (rev. ed., 1969), 448–49; Parris and Brooks, *Blacks in the City.* The parable of Martha and Mary is in Luke 11:38–42.

5. For example "Back Stabber"—first recorded by the O'Jays in 1972 and later covered by Tina Turner in 1979 and by many others in the 1980s—reprised the old theme.

6. Mays, *Born to Rebel,* 107; the term "miseducation" was apparently first used by Carter G. Woodson in *The Mis-Education of the Negro* (1933), but Frazier also used it often especially in *Black Bourgeoisie.*

7. Thomas, *My Story in Black and White,* 96–97.

8. Psalm 55:11, 13, 21 (KJV).

9. Mays, *Born to Rebel,* 110–13; Parris and Brooks, *Blacks in the City,* 165–66; Thomas, *My Story in Black and White,* 103. Mays often cited Romans 1:15.

10. Parris and Brooks, *Blacks in the City,* 165.

11. Thomas, *My Story in Black and White,* 103 and passim.

12. Ibid.; Mays, *Born to Rebel,* 110–13.

13. Mays, "It Cost Too Much." Mays, *Born to Rebel,* 117–18; typescript for *Born to Rebel,* Mays Papers, MSRC.

14. Mays, *Born to Rebel,* 118–19; compare Thomas, *My Story in Black and White,* 104–6.

15. Thomas, *My Story in Black and White,* 104–6.

16. Ibid.

17. Ibid.; compare Mays, *Born to Rebel,* 119–20, which makes no mention of this conference.

18. Thomas, *My Story in Black and White,* 104–6; compare Mays, *Born to Rebel.*

19. The image of "first lightning" is in John Brown Watson, "Dedication of Morehouse College Library in Honor of John Hope" (unpublished typescript), April 30, 1932, John Brown Watson Papers, JHLA. Raper, *The Tragedy of Lynching.*

20. Raper, *Preface to Peasantry.*

21. Mays and Raper, "A Study of Negro Life in Tampa" (1926), unpublished working paper in Arthur Franklin Raper Papers, SHC.

22. Mays, *Born to Rebel,* 107–8.

23. Ibid.

24. Ibid.

25. Ibid., 120, 125.

26. Ibid., 121.

27. Ibid., 125.

28. See Mays, "The Development of the Idea of God in Contemporary Negro Literature" (hereafter cited as "The Idea of God") and Gavins, "The Ceremonial Speaking of Benjamin Elijah Mays."

29. Mays, "The Idea of God," 120–25; Psalm 121:1 (KJV). The psalmist asks "Whence cometh my help?" and the response is from the Lord.

30. Mays, "The Idea of God," 124–26; the parable of table scraps is in Matthew 40:21–28 and Mark 7:24–30.

31. Mays, "The Idea of God," 124–26.

32. Ibid., 130.

33. Ibid.; the image of rope and fagot is used in White, *Rope and Faggot.*

34. Mays, "The Idea of God," 129–30. Statistics on lynching are from White, *Rope and Faggot,* and Raper, *The Tragedy of Lynching;* for black attitudes toward lynching, see Frazier, *The Black Bourgeoisie,* 130–49; compare Williamson, *New People* and *The Crucible of Race.*

35. Philippeans 4:3–4a (JB).

36. Mays, "The Idea of God," 129–30; see Frazier, *Black Bourgeoisie,* especially 130–49; notes (1927), Edward Franklin Frazier Papers, MSRC.

37. Psalm 150 (JB).

38. Psalm 150n (JB); Mays, "The Idea of God," 130.

39. Dryden, "The Secular Masque," 282–85.

40. Mays, "The Idea of God," 131; Mays and Nicholson, *The Negro's Church;* Nicholson, "An Occupational Study of the Christian Ministry among Negroes"; "The Rev. Dr. J. W. Nicholson Was Episcopal Clergyman," *St. Louis Post-Dispatch,* January 1, 1991, C4.

41. Mays, *Born to Rebel,* 131; Johnson, *A Preface to Racial Understanding,* 155, cites data gathered by Daniel; U.S. Census, Historical Statistics, 1930, lists 39,245 African American churches serving 5,203,487 members who spent more than $43,024,258, primarily on church buildings; Mays and Nicholson used the term "overchurched" in *The Negro's Church.*

42. The plumb line image is in Amos 7:7–9 and Zechariah 1 and 2; Mays and Nicholson, *The Negro's Church;* Mays, "The Idea of God," 132–33; Johnson, *A Preface to Racial Understanding,* 155–57.

43. Statistics compiled by Nicholson in *What Is Happening to the Negro in the Protestant Episcopal Church?;* Nicholson, *The Contemporary Opportunities of the Protestant Episcopal Church;* Mays, "The Idea of God," 132.

44. Mays, *Born to Rebel,* 135.

45. Dennis C. Dickerson discovered the information about this conference. See Dickerson, "African American Religious Intellectuals and the Theological Foundations of the Civil Rights Movement, 1930–1955," 217–29. See also "Whither the Negro Church?" (conference seminar), April 13–15, 1931, Yale Divinity School Archives (hereafter cited as "Whither the Negro Church?").

46. Dickerson, "African American Religious Intellectuals and the Theological Foundations of the Civil Rights Movement, 1930–1955," 217–29. See also "Whither the Negro Church?"

47. "Whither the Negro Church?," 5, 7; quoted in Dickerson, "African American Religious Intellectuals," 218.

48. "Whither the Negro Church?," 5, 7; quoted in Dickerson, "African American Religious Intellectuals," 218.

49. Ibid.

50. "Whither the Negro Church?," 48; quoted in Dickerson, "African American Religious Intellectuals," 218–19.

51. Mays, "The Idea of God," 132; Mays quoted the King James version of John 10:16.

52. Proper 28, also Collect for Advent, Book of Common Prayer (1928).

53. Psalm 34: 8; NJB, 845n. Book of Common Prayer (1928), 348. "Taste and See," *Lift Every Voice and Sing II,* 154.

54. Dunbar, quoted by Mays in "Every Man, Every Woman [Life is a Series of Gethsemanes]," address, April 1946, Detroit, Speeches and Addresses of Mays, Mays Papers, MSRC.

55. Ibid.

Chapter 9. The Great Commission and Its Filling

1. Matthew 28:16–20, (JB).

2. Mays, "The Idea of God," 8n. See the data collection in Works, correspondence, 1936, Mays Papers, MSRC.

3. Mays, "The Idea of God," ii–iv, 1–2.

4. Ibid.; see Dickerson, "African-American Religious Intellectuals and the Theological Foundations of the Civil Rights Movement, 1930–1945," on Aubrey and Wieman; Jelks, "Mays's Academic Formation, 1917–1936," 111–29. Compare Wieman, "Confessions of a Religious Seeker" (ca. 1970), Henry Nelson Wieman Papers, Southern Illinois University Library and Archives, Carbondale (hereafter SIU).

5. A. Alvarez, "The Noble Poet," *New York Review of Books,* July 18, 1985, 7–10; Warren, "William Faulkner," 1:467–79.

6. On "whooping the benches," see Mays and Nicholson, *The Negro Church.*

7. Kaiyi Chen, "Guide to the Aubrey Papers, 1915–1956," Edwin Ewart Aubrey Papers, University of Pennsylvania Archives and Research Center Library, Philadelphia. Federal Council of Churches: Ralph W. Bullock to Mays, August 6, 1945, and other correspondence with Bullock about Aubrey and FCC, Mays Papers, MSRC.

8. Chen, "Guide to the Aubrey Papers, 1915–1956," and book reviews, 1926–1936, Edwin Ewart Aubrey Papers, University of Pennsylvania.

9. Conference on Church Workers in Colleges and Universities, University of Chicago, 1931, Edwin Ewart Aubrey Papers, University of Pennsylvania. Aubrey, "Church Workers," *Religion and Higher Education,* introduction by Matthews and Kelly; for information on Communist Party USA (CPUSA) aid to poor, see interviews with Glenn Weddington Rainey, John Herbert Roper Papers, SHC.

10. Healing images are in Matthew 9:13, Mark 2:17, and Luke 5:11 (JB); for living water and bread of life, see John 4 and 7:37–39 (JB). Aubrey, *Present Theological Tendencies.*

11. Ibid., and Aubrey, *Religion and the Next Generation.*

12. Aubrey, *Present Theological Tendencies.* See also W. E. Garrison's review of this book in *Christian Century* (clipping) and "Doctrines of Change," Edwin Ewart Aubrey Papers, University of Pennsylvania.

13. Wieman, "Confessions of a Religious Seeker."

14. Ibid.

15. Ibid. Wieman described himself as "lonely" and without influence at the University of Chicago.

16. Wieman, *The Source of Human Good, Religious Experience and Scientific Method;* "Whither the Negro Church?"; Dickerson, "African-American Religious Intellectuals and the Theological Foundations of the Civil Rights Movement, 1930–1945," and Jelks, "Mays's Academic Formation, 1917–1936."

17. Wieman, "Confessions of a Religious Seeker" and other writings, Henry Nelson Wieman Papers, SIU; see "Whither the Negro Church?"; Dickerson, "African-American Religious Intellectuals and the Theological Foundations of the Civil Rights Movement, 1930–1945"; Jelks, "Mays's Academic Formation, 1917–1936."

18. Wieman, "Confessions of a Religious Seeker" and other writings, Henry Nelson Wieman Papers, SIU; see "Whither the Negro Church?"; Dickerson, "African-American Religious Intellectuals and the Theological Foundations of the Civil Rights Movement, 1930–1945"; Jelks, "Mays's Academic Formation, 1917–1936." Quotations are from Wieman, "Confessions of a Religious Seeker."

19. Mays adopted the phrase "praise and thanksgiving" from the version of Psalm 100 in the Book of Common Prayer (1928); Mays, "The Idea of God," iii, iv.

20. Mays, "The Idea of God," iv.

21. Ibid., 1–12.

22. Ibid., 14–15.

23. Ibid., 1–15, 16, 26, 63.

24. Dunbar, quoted in Mays, "The Idea of God," 63–65.

25. Mays, "The Idea of God," 64.

26. Ibid., 65–68.

27. Ibid. Lewis, *W. E. B. Du Bois,* vol. 1: *Biography of a Race, 1868–1919.* Du Bois, *The Souls of Black Folk,* especially chapter 12, "Of Alexander Crummell"; Du Bois, *The Philadelphia Negro;* Du Bois's *Crisis* editorials, especially 1931, republished as "The Negro and Communism," *The Oxford W. E. B. Du Bois Reader,* 344; 400–409; Williamson, *A Rage for Order,* 65–69, 206; Williamson, "W. E. B. Du Bois" and "G. W. F. Hegel," *The Crucible of Race,* 399–413; Kellogg, *NAACP.*

28. Mays and Nicholson, *The Negro Church;* Mark 9:24.

29. Mark 9:24.

30. Mays, "The Idea of God."

31. Isaiah 58:5–12.

32. On Kelly's racism, see Roper, *Paul Green,* 172–3; Mays, *Born to Rebel,* 136. Wright, "Worshippers from Afar."

33. Mays, *Born to Rebel,* 135.

34. Ibid.

35. Ibid.

36. Ibid.

37. Ibid., 135–38; Logan, *Howard University.*

Chapter 10. In the Nation's Capital

1. John Brown Watson, correspondence with Brown alumni, John Brown Watson Papers, JHLA.

2. Mays, *Born to Rebel,* 139–48; Mays correspondence with Mordecai Wyatt Johnson, Mays Papers, MSRC; FBI interview with Johnson and response, Mays files, FBI, copies in possession of the author; Logan, *Howard University,* 247–321.

3. Logan, *Howard University,* 582 and passim; Locke, ed., *The New Negro.*

4. See Mays, *Born to Rebel* and his columns in the *Pittsburgh Courier,* 1942–81.

5. Matthew 23:37.

6. Mays, *Born to Rebel,* 139–48; Mays correspondence with Mordecai Wyatt Johnson, Mays Papers, MSRC; FBI interview with Johnson and response; Logan, *Howard University,* 247–321.

7. Correspondence, Edwin Ewart Aubrey Papers, University of Pennsylvania. Mays and Nicholson, *The Negro Church;* Mays to Stewart A. Newman, December 31, 1945, Mays Papers, MSRC. Mays, "The Religious Life and Needs of Negro Students," 333–34, 347.

8. Psalm 17:2.

9. Mays, *Born to Rebel,* 139–48; correspondence of Mays and Mordecai Wyatt Johnson, Mays papers, MSRC; Johnson notes, Mays FBI files; Logan, *Howard University,* 247–321; correspondence, Edwin Ewart Aubrey Papers, University of Pennsylvania; Mays and Nicholson, *The Negro Church;* Senator Coleman Livingston Blease, *Congressional Record,* Sen. Bills & Res., 70th Congress, 2nd session, vol. 69, pt. 8, May 8, 1928, 8080–81. Minority report, Congressmen B. G. Lowrey, Malcolm C. Tarver, and René Louis De Rouen.

10. Representative Louis C. Cramton, *Congressional Record,* HR Bills & Res., 70th Congress, 2nd session, vol. 69, pt. 1, December 14, 1927, 648–49: Cramton, HR 15089. Mays, *Born to Rebel,* 139–48. For maneuvers by Congressmen Tarver, John Rankin, Lowrey, John Philip

Hill, and Carl Vinson; see Rankin's attack on black people in *Congressional Record,* HR Bills and Res., 69th Congress, 2nd session, December 20, 1926, 779. For maneuvers twelve years later see *Congressional Record,* HR Bills and Res., 75th Congress, vol. 83, pt. 1, February 21, 1938, 2249.

11. Psalm 17:7–8 (JB). For Mays's use of songs of David and psalmody, see Gavins, "The Ceremonial Speaking of Benjamin Elijah Mays."

12. Correspondence of Mordecai Wyatt Johnson and Mays, 1936–40, Mays Papers, MSRC; see data in Mays, *Born to Rebel,* 139–48; see tables and appendix in Logan, *Howard University;* for appropriation data see *Congressional Record,* HR Bills and Res., 70th Congress, 2nd session, vol. 70, pt. 1, December 13 and 14, 1928, 632, 648.

13. Mary McLeod Bethune, Kelly Miller, Sadie Gray Mays, and Mays, 1936–40, Mays Papers, MSRC. Society notices in the "Purely Personal" column of the *Pittsburgh Courier,* such as January 18, 1936, 14. Bethune, "From Day to Day," *Pittsburgh Courier,* February 12, 1938, 14; Miller, "Race Faces 1936 with Hope and Fear," *Pittsburgh Courier,* January 4, 1936, A2. District of Columbia integration of NYA, *Pittsburgh Courier,*1936–40 and correspondence of Sadie Gray Mays, Mays, and Bethune; for Roosevelt's "alphabet agencies," see Tindall and Shi, *America,* vol. 2, chapter 28.

14. "Howard Law School Back in New Home," *Pittsburgh Courier,* January 11, 1936, 6; McNeil, *Groundwork;* Kellogg, *NAACP.*

15. Mays, *Born to Rebel,* 139–48, see tables and appendix in Logan, *Howard University;* for appropriation data see *Congressional Record,* HR Bills and Res., 70th Congress, 2nd session, vol. 70, pt. 1, December 13 and 14, 1928, 632, 648. Logan, *Howard University;* 258–65.

16. Mays did not name names in *Born to Rebel,* 139–48; compare Logan, *Howard University;* 247–321.

17. Carter, *Scottsboro;* Rankin's remarks, *Congressional Record,* HR Bills and Res., 75th Congress, vol. 81, pt. 3, April 15, 1937, 3546–49. Senators Theodore Bilbo and Richard Russell on Communist efforts to "amalgamate" races and create a "Negro" republic: Russell's remarks, *Congressional Record,* Sen. Bills and Res., 75th Congress, vol. 83, pt. 1, January 26, 1938, 1102; Bilbo's remarks, *Congressional Record,* Sen. Bills and Res., 75th Congress, vol. 83, pt. 1, February 7, 1938, 1549–63.

18. Rovaris quote the phrase in "Mays's Leadership and Morehouse College," and Mays used it throughout correspondence, 1940–71, Mays Papers, MSRC. On Louis, see Chester Washington, "Sez Ches" column, *Pittsburgh Courier,* January 12, 1935, A5; "Lewis [*sic*] Has Won Ten in a Row," *Pittsburgh Courier,* December, 8, 1934, A4; and "New 'Black Hope' Looms in Heavyweight Horizon," *Pittsburgh Courier,* December 22, 1934, A5.

19. Logan, *Howard University;* 247–321; Mays, *Born to Rebel,* 139–48.

20. Mays, *Born to Rebel,* 149, on Ickes; correspondence, Mays Papers, MSRC. Parable of the banquet, Matthew 22:1–14, 14n (NJB).

21. Cramton's remarks on HR 15089, *Congressional Record,* HR Bills and Res., 70th Congress, 2nd. session, vol. 69, pt. 1, December 14, 1927, 648–49; narrative and quoted phrase from Mays, *Born to Rebel,* 147.

22. Mays, *Born to Rebel,* 147.

23. Ibid., 146. Aubrey, notes for Cole Lectures in Religion, Vanderbilt University, 1941, and Aubrey, memorandum, "Ethical Reality and Functions of the Church . . . ," n.d. (1933–34), Edwin Ewart Aubrey Papers, University of Pennsylvania.

24. Mays, *Born to Rebel,* 146. Aubrey, notes for Cole Lectures in Religion, Vanderbilt University, 1941, and Aubrey, memorandum, "Ethical Reality and Functions of the Church . . . ," n.d. (1933–34), Edwin Ewart Aubrey Papers, University of Pennsylvania.

25. Mays, *Born to Rebel,* 146. Aubrey, notes for Cole Lectures in Religion, Vanderbilt University, 1941, and Aubrey, memorandum, "Ethical Reality and Functions of the Church . . . ," n.d. (1933–34), Edwin Ewart Aubrey Papers, University of Pennsylvania.

26. Mays's optimism, 1937–39, Mays Papers, MSRC. Compare Mays, *Born to Rebel,* 146–50. Proper scholarship, Edwin Ewart Aubrey Papers, University of Pennsylvania: "Do We Need Conviction?" n.d. (December 1932), 55; Aubrey's address, Cole Lectures, Vanderbilt University, 1940, and Shailer Mathews's response: Mathews to Aubrey, October 26, 1940; "Purpose," *New Humanist* (clipping).

27. Aubrey, "Do We Need Conviction?" (clipping); Aubrey to C. T. Holmes, July 27, 1936; Aubrey, "The Minister as a Creative Theologian," "The Reconstructive Forces of the Christian Religion," and "The Role of Theology in Contemporary Culture," 435—all in Edwin Ewart Aubrey Papers, University of Pennsylvania.

28. Burton, *In My Father's House;* Mays, *Born to Rebel,* 156–57; 196–98. Notes on Gandhi and "waging peace," Mays diary, 1937, Mays Papers, MSRC; "Whither the Negro Church?"; Zachary Dresser to Roper, October 6, 2006, with enclosed copy of "Whither the Negro Church?"; for Mays's "top down" leadership, see Rovaris, "Mays's Leadership and Morehouse College"; for Mays on meritocracy, see "We Must Become Competent," typescript, 1949, Mays Papers, MSRC. "Sees US Culture," interview with Aubrey, *Chicago Tribune* clipping, 1936; Aubrey to C. T. Holmes, July 27, 1936; C. T. Holmes to Aubrey, March 10, 1936—all in Edwin Ewart Aubrey Papers, University of Pennsylvania.

29. Mays, "If I'm Hard on the South" (column), *Pittsburgh Courier,* January 29, 1949, 15. For Booker T. Washington and the "talented tenth," see Harlan, *Booker T. Washington,* vol. 2: *The Wizard of Tuskegee, 1901–1915;* For Du Bois and the "talented tenth," see chapter 12, "Of Alexander Crummell," in *The Souls of Black Folk,* 62–73, 152–60, especially 72. For correspondence about *The Souls of Black Folk,* see *Correspondence of William Edward Burghardt Du Bois,* 1:35, 47–49.

30. "Prejudiced Washington Now Asks for 'Lily White' Trolley Express," *Pittsburgh Courier,* January 4, 1936, 4; Kelly Miller, "Race Suggestions for 1936," *Pittsburgh Courier,* January 11, 1936, A2; Charles Hamilton Houston, "Position of NAACP in Fight for Professional Schools in Va. Cited," *Pittsburgh Courier,* January 11, 1936, A2.

31. Jesse O. Thomas to Mays, January 21, 1946, and Mays to Thomas, January 23, 1946; Thomas to Mays, January 23, 1946; and Mays to Thomas, January 23, 1946 [separate posting], Mays Papers, MSRC.

32. Jesse O. Thomas to Mays, January 21, 1946, and Mays to Thomas, January 23, 1946; Thomas to Mays, January 23, 1946; and Mays to Thomas, January 23, 1946 [separate posting], Mays Papers, MSRC.

33. John J. O'Connor's remarks, *Congressional Record,* HR Res. & Bills, Congress, vol. 81, April 12, 1937, 3383; Tarver's remarks, ibid., 3437.

34. For Bilbo's misrepresentations on miscegenation and rape, see Williamson, *A Rage for Order,* 188–89; for "changeover" see Williamson, *New People,* 50–53, 109; for Lena Horne, see ibid., 162, 234. Gettleman, "Thurmond Family Struggles with Difficult Truth," A1; see also Middleton, *Knowing Who I Am,* 68.

35. Russell's remarks, *Congressional Record,* Sen. Bills and Res., 75th Congress, vol. 83, pt. 1, January 26, 1938, 1102 *Baptist Guidelines for Calling Ministers,* copy in High Point Baptist Church, Meadowview, Virginia; Bunie, *Robert L. Vann of the Pittsburgh Courier;* Brewer, "Robert L. Vann and *Pittsburgh Courier*"; Dyer, "Power in Black and White"; Mays column, *Pittsburgh Courier,* 1942–81.

36. "Whither the Negro Church?"; Mays, *Born to Rebel,* 155–58.

37. For Gandhi see Mays, *Born to Rebel,* 155–58; for Hobbes and "peaceableness," see Strauss, *Natural Right and History,* 161. Aubrey got there earlier and taught it to Mays, see correspondence, 1926–36, especially chart and syllabus, 1934, Edwin Ewart Aubrey Papers, University of Pennsylvania. For Ruby Bates see Carter, *Scottsboro;* McCoy bylines, *Pittsburgh Courier,* 1937–77.

38. Martin Luther King, Jr., used the phrases "soul force" and "marvelous militancy of pacifism" in his March on Washington, or "I Have a Dream," speech, August 28, 1963. E. W. Kensworthy, "200,000 March for Civil Rights," *New York Times,* August 28, 1968, 1. King quotes: "I Have a Dream . . . Peroration," ibid. King went off text but still covered his themes. "Martin Luther King, Jr., Papers Project," *Journal of American History* 78 (June 1991): 23–25. Mays used "soul force" in chapel at Howard and at Morehouse when King was a student there; Mays apparently learned "marvelous militancy of pacifism" from King. See *The Papers of Martin Luther King, Jr.,* 1:121–57.

39. "Dean Mays to Attend World YMCA Meet in India in '37," *Pittsburgh Courier,* November 7, 1936, 10, "All Colors and Sects at Oxford," *Pittsburgh Courier,* August 7, 1937, 4. Mays, *Born to Rebel,* 155–57; Mays diary (1936), Mays Papers, MSRC.

40. Mays, *Born to Rebel,* 156. Aubrey chart and syllabus, 1934, Edwin Ewart Aubrey Papers, University of Pennsylvania. Mays diary (1936), Mays Papers, MSRC.

41. Mays, *Born to Rebel,* 157; Mays diary (1936), Mays Papers, MSRC.

42. *Pittsburgh Courier,* 1936–84, on "Negrophobic" violence, especially on trains.

43. For the concept "heart to fight," see Pettigrew, *A Profile of the Negro American,* 10 and passim. Mays diary (1936), Mays Papers, MSRC.

44. Mays labor activism, Brotherhood of Sleeping Car Porters, Records of Sleeping Car Porters, Chicago Historical Society.

45. Huggins, *Harlem Renaissance; Chicago Defender* Archives, Chicago; Ottley, *The Lonely Warrior;* Wolseley, *The Black Press;* Poston, *A First Draft of History;* Frank A. Young correspondence, John Brown Watson Papers, JHLA.

46. Bunie, *Robert L. Vann of the Pittsburgh Courier;* Brewer, "Robert Lee Vann and the *Pittsburgh Courier*"; for usage of "Race" and "Negro," see *Pittsburgh Courier,* 1936–84, especially "Race Faces 1936 with Hope and Fear," January 4, 1936, A2. For Abbott, race, and the *Chicago Defender,* see Ottley, *The Lonely Warrior,* and Wolseley, *The Black Press.*

47. "Head of National Bar Assoc. Endorses Vann for Supreme Court," *Pittsburgh Courier,* January 22, 1938, 2. "Lynch Demon's Grim Toll Reaches Twenty in 1935," *Pittsburgh Courier,* January 4, 1936, 4. Du Bois became increasingly leftist in 1936–38; see news feature, "Forum of Fact and Opinion: Valedictory," *Pittsburgh Courier,* January 22, 1938, 11. Miller, "Race Faces 1936 with Hope and Fear," *Pittsburgh Courier,* January 4, 1936, A2. For J. R. McCoy's coverage of the Scottsboro case, see *Pittsburgh Courier,* 1937–72. See also coverage by J. A. Rogers, Samuel Daniels, George Schuyler, and Vernon Jordan, *Pittsburgh Courier,* op-ed section, 1932–81.

48. "Purely Personal" columns, *Pittsburgh Courier,* 1936–84. Mays, "The Church YMCA Relationship," *Pittsburgh Courier,* April 23, 1938, 19. "Five American Races Study," *Pittsburgh Courier,* July 23, 1938, 19, and "Dean Mays Steams to Sweden," *Pittsburgh Courier,* May 14, 1938, 19. Mays columns, *Pittsburgh Courier,* 1942–81.

49. Aubrey used the phrases "reaching forward" and "reaching back" with regard to proper scholarship, especially in "Do We Need Conviction?" December 1932, 55; Aubrey's address, Cole Lectures, Vanderbilt University, 1940, and Shailer Mathews's response: Mathews to Aubrey, October 26, 1940; Aubrey, "Purpose," 16–19—all in Edwin Ewart Aubrey Papers, University of Pennsylvania.

50. See Rovaris, "Mays and Morehouse," and Gavins, "The Ceremonial Speaking of Benjamin Elijah Mays," for Mays's different styles and ability to change style rapidly; Gavins, "Mays's Commencement Addresses," *Walking Integrity,* edited by Carter, 289–329.

51. "Mother of Dean Mays Is Dead," *Pittsburgh Courier,* April 9, 1938, 6; death certificate, "Louvenia Carter Mays," April 9, 1938, SCDAH; Mays, *Born to Rebel,* especially chapter 1.

52. On Hezekiah Mays see Mays, *Born to Rebel,* especially 38–39, 48–49; and "Hezekiah Mays," U.S. Census, Population Census, Greenwood County, 1900, 1910, and 1920.

53. "Father of Howard Dean Passes," *Pittsburgh Courier,* June 25, 1938, 19. "Hezekiah Mays," June 25, 1938, SCDAH.

54. Mays, *Born to Rebel,* 148 and chapter 10. Correspondence 1939 and 1940, Mays Papers, MSRC.

55. Mays, *Born to Rebel,* especially 170. Notes by Hattie Rutherford Watson, Spelman trustee, on Howard University and Morehouse College discussions as she remembered them, Hattie Rutherford Watson, 1940, and John Brown Watson, 1940, Hattie Rutherford Watson and John Brown Watson Papers, JHLA.

56. Mays, *Born to Rebel,* 170–73. Correspondence with Trevor Arnett, 1935–40, copies of Kendall Weisiger to Mays, [May 30?] 1940, and Mays to Kendall Weisiger, May 31, 1940, Mays Paper, MSRC. Original copies of Weisiger and Mays correspondence and trustees' minutes, Trustees Records, Morehouse College Archives.

57. Mays, *Born to Rebel,* 170–73. Correspondence with Trevor Arnett, 1935–40, copies of Kendall Weisiger to Mays, [May 30?] 1940, and Mays to Kendall Weisiger, May 31, 1940, Mays Paper, MSRC. Original copies of Weisiger and Mays correspondence and trustees' minutes, Trustees Records, Morehouse College Archives. Notes by Hattie Rutherford Watson, 1940, Hattie Rutherford Watson Papers, JHLA.

58. "HU Dean Becomes Morehouse Prexy," *Pittsburgh Courier,* June 29, 1940, 5. Correspondence, Trevor Arnett, John Hervey Wheeler, W. W. Alexander, and Kendall Weisiger, May 10–July 1, 1940, Mays Papers, MSRC.

Chapter 11. In My Father's House

1. Rovaris, "Mays and Morehouse"; Mrs. John Hope to Hattie Rutherford Watson, April 25, 1939; for Hubert see correspondence of Hattie Rutherford Watson and Mays, 1940, Hattie Rutherford Watson, JHLA; Mays, *Born to Rebel,* chapter 13.

2. John Brown Watson to the president of the senior class, April 21, 1936; John Brown Watson to Mays, January 26, 1938, with enclosure, a typescript letter to the *Arkansas Democrat;* Mays to John Brown Watson, February 2, 1938, and John Brown Watson to Mays, January 3, 1939—all John Brown Watson Papers, JHLA.

3. Aubrey, memorandum of the Chicago Ecumenical Discussion Group, n.d. (1933–34); "A Theology Relevant to Religious Education," *Religious Education* 34 (October–December 1939): 195–201; lecture, March 14, 1934, Edwin Ewart Aubrey Papers, University of Pennsylvania. Mays, "I Cannot Sing Dixie" (clipping), n.d. (196-?), Mays Papers, MSRC.

4. Mays, *Born to Rebel,* chapter 13; Rovaris, "Mays and Morehouse"; Mays, "The Most Neglected Area of Negro Education," reprint pamphlet for trustees and for John Brown Watson, John Brown Watson to Mays, January 3, 1939, John Brown Watson Papers, JHLA. John Brown Watson and Hattie Rutherford Watson comments, correspondence, John Hope, John Brown Watson Papers, Hattie Rutherford Watson, JHLA, especially Hattie Rutherford Watson to Hope, June 27, 1935. Mays to Ralph H. Edwards, March 26, 1946, Mays Papers, MSRC.

5. Johnson and Pickens, *Benjamin E. Mays and Margaret Mitchell;* "Margaret Mitchell's Renewed Role as Benefactor of Morehouse College."

6. Johnson and Pickens, *Benjamin E. Mays and Margaret Mitchell;* "Margaret Mitchell's Renewed Role as Benefactor of Morehouse College"; Pyron, *Southern Daughter.*

7. For "schoolmaster" imagery, see Bennett, *Before the Mayflower* and "Benjamin Elijah Mays: The Last of the Great Schoolmasters." Obituary for Margaret Mitchell, *New York Times,* August 17, 1949; Kirkpatrick, "Mitchell Estate Settles 'Gone with the Wind' Suit"; and "Margaret Mitchell's Renewed Role as Benefactor of Morehouse College," 58. See Mays's calculations and tabulations in correspondence with Hattie Rutherford Watson, especially October 15, 1954, and January 19, 1956, Hattie Rutherford Watson, JHLA; Reitzes, *Negroes and Medicine.*

8. Current, *Phi Beta Kappa in American Life;* data from Morehouse College collected by Mays and shared and discussed with Hattie Rutherford Watson, Mays to Hattie Rutherford Watson, January 19, 1956, Hattie Rutherford Watson, JHLA.

9. Current, *Phi Beta Kappa in American Life;* see also Tickton and Ruml, *Teaching Salaries Then and Now.*

10. Mays to Hattie Rutherford Watson, January 19, 1956, Hattie Rutherford Watson, JHLA; copy of memorandum, Mays to TIAA, October 5, 1945, Mays Papers, MSRC. Mays brought the institutional contribution up to 5 percent; calculations on pay scale adjusted for inflation from the pre-1975 Consumer Price Index, U.S. Census, Historical Statistics, 1965–75; since 1975 U.S. Census, Statistical Abstracts; Mays's chart for Hattie Rutherford Watson compared Morehouse salaries and benefits to those at average white institutions and to those listed in the *Chronicle of Higher Education.*

11. Kelsey, "Social Thought of Contemporary Southern Baptists," and *Social Ethics among Southern Baptists, 1917–1969;* biography and correspondence of Martin Luther King, Jr., and Mays, Kelsey Papers, Drew University Archives. Mays, Eulogy for Dr. Charles Hubert, Morehouse Chapel, January 26, 1944; published as "Tribute to Dr. Charles Hubert."

12. Mays, *Born to Rebel,* 180–86; for evolution of thoughts see correspondence with W. W. Sikes (American Friends Service Committee), especially Sikes to Mays, September 13, 1945, and Mays to Sikes, September 25, 1945, Mays Papers, MSRC.

13. Kelsey to Mays, March 13, 1946, and Mays to Ernest Tolbert, October 3, 1945, Mays Papers, MSRC. Correspondence of Kelsey and Mays, 1945, Mays Papers, MSRC. Introduction to *The Papers of Martin Luther King, Jr.,* 1:1–79, especially 37. Recollections of Graves Hall: interview with Harvey E. Beech (September 25, 1996), by Anita Foye, Southern Oral History Program, SHC. Correspondence with Johnson on publishing Bennett's *What Manner of Man,*

Mays Papers, MSRC; Mays on Johnson, Ford Foundation money, and money from Charles E. Merrill, Jr., Mays, *Born to Rebel,* 188–89.

14. Carnegie Foundation for the Advancement of Teaching, *A Classification of Institutions of Higher Education;* Rovaris, "Mays and Morehouse."

15. Mays, *Born to Rebel,* 117; on the Stoics and Marcus Aurelius, see Gavins, "The Ceremonial Speaking of Benjamin Elijah Mays." On Fred Gassett see interview Harvey E. Beech by Anita Foye (September 25, 1996), Southern Oral History Program, SHC.

16. Mays to Ernest Tolbert, October 3, 1945, and Calvin L. Singleton [January?] 1946, Mays Papers, MSRC; Breneman, *Liberal Arts Colleges,* and "Are We Losing Our Liberal Arts Colleges?," 16–21, 29; Carnegie Foundation for the Advancement of Teaching, *A Classification of Institutions of Higher Education.*

17. Mays to Samuel L. Spears, April 2, 1946, and F. A. Toomer, December 14, 1945, and September 22, 1945; Toomer to Mays, September 18, 1945; Mays to Ornan A. Pratt, May 22, 1946; income statement drafts for IRS, 1946, 1947, and 1957, Mays Papers, MSRC. College finances, 1940–56, Mays Papers, MSRC. Mays to F. A. Toomer, September 22, 1945, Mays to H. Council Trenholm, October 8, 1945, and Mays to Jesse O. Thomas, 21 January 21, 1946—all in W. W. Alexander files, North Carolina Council on Interracial Cooperation Papers, SHC; see also Frank Porter Graham Papers, 1937–47, SHC.

18. Rovaris, "Mays and Morehouse." Between 1940, when the market value of the endowment was $1,114,000 and Mays's retirement in 1967, when it had risen to $6,000,000 dollars, Mays's development team beat the rate of inflation and the normal return on investment in high-grade bonds or in average stock-market yields. Mays's team went 43 percent better than the average return *after taking account of inflation.*

19. Correspondence between Mays and Hattie Rutherford Watson, Hattie Rutherford Watson Papers, JHLA; see Mays to Ornan A. Pratt, May 22, 1946, Eunice V. Baker, June 3, 1946, and William K. Russell, June 21, 1946, Mays Papers, MSRC.

20. Clipping, March 12, 1937, and "Dedication of Atlanta University Library," April 30, 1932, Hattie Rutherford Watson Papers, JHLA.

21. For "creative pessimism," see correspondence of John Hope and John Watson Brown; obituary notices clipped by Brown and Hattie Rutherford Brown, John Hope Papers and John Brown Watson and Hattie Rutherford Watson Papers, JHLA. W. W. Alexander, quoted in Dykeman and Stokely, *Seeds of Southern Change,* and also in North Carolina Council on Interracial Cooperation Papers, 1925–55, SHC.

22. Correspondence of John Hope and John Watson Brown; obituary notices clipped by Brown and Hattie Rutherford Brown, John Hope Papers and John Brown Watson and Hattie Rutherford Watson Papers, JHLA. W. W. Alexander, quoted in Dykeman and Stokely, *Seeds of Southern Change,* and also in North Carolina Council on Interracial Cooperation Papers, 1925–55, SHC; Rovaris, "Mays and Morehouse."

23. Jesse O. Thomas to Mays, May 14, 1946, Mays Papers, MSRC; Tyson, *Blood Done Sign My Name;* on United Front, Popular Front, antiwar, civil rights, and Interracial Councils, see Roper, *Paul Green,* and compare Mays's columns in the *Pittsburgh Courier,* 1942–45.

24. Wines, *Ethics, Law, and Business,* 147. A. Phillip Randolph, in Bennett, *Before the Mayflower,* 354–55, 366, 525. On Mays, Randolph, and labor, see "Mays" entries, Brotherhood of Sleeping Car Porters Papers.

25. Mays to James M. Burton, July 1, 1945, Mays Papers, MSRC; commencement program, 1945, Robert W. Woodruff Library and Archives, Morehouse College.

26. King, quoted in introduction to *The Papers of Martin Luther King, Jr.,* 1:37. Roper, *Paul Green,* 198–99.

27. King, quoted in ibid. Mays to W. W. Thomas, November 10, 1945, Mays Papers, MSRC.

28. Correspondence of Mays and Bullock, especially Mays to Bullock, August 6, 1945; on invitations and follow-up correspondence, 1945–47, Mays Papers, MSRC. Mays, *Born to Rebel,* 370. Compare typescript list with corrections, 1971, Mays Papers, MSRC.

Chapter 12. "To your tents"

1. 1 Kings 12:16 (NIV 1973, RSV, and New Oxford Annotated Bible 1973). In a note to 2 Samuel 20:1–2 in the New Oxford Annotated Bible, editors May and Metzger say that the Benjaminite tribe was "most disaffected" of tribes in the last days of David's rule; see also ibid., chronological table and essay, 1548. Mays, *Quotable Quotes,* 20. 1 Kings 23 (KJV). On Sadie Mays as speechmaker, see Mays to Ralph E. Edwards, March 26, 1946, Mays Papers, MSRC.

2. Mays diary, 1936–37, Mays Papers, MSRC; Marcus Aurelius, Gavins, "The Ceremonial Speaking of Benjamin Elijah Mays." See Du Bois, *Against Racism,* for Du Bois and Stalin. For Aubrey's anti-Communism see Edwin Ewart Aubrey Papers, University of Pennsylvania. For Mays's anti-Communism see his *Disturbed About Man;* for his views on World War II, see his "My View" columns in the *Pittsburgh Courier,* 1942–45; and for his views on the UN, see his "My View" columns in the *Pittsburgh Courier,* 1950. For his inconsistent pacifism, see his essays "The Obligations of the Individual Christian" and "I Have Been a Baptist All My Life"; "Dr. Mays Remembers Heartbreak of King," *Pittsburgh Courier,* April 18, 1970, campus section, 7; and his "My View" column "Viet, anti-People Policy to Blame for Turmoil," *Pittsburgh Courier,* June 20, 1970.

3. Mays and Aubrey notes on Charles Wesley and Geneva Bible; Aubrey, "New Humanism"; Aubrey's address, Cole Lectures, Vanderbilt University, 1940; Shailer Mathews to Aubrey, October 26, 1940; Aubrey, "The Oxford Conference, 1937"; see Samuel J. Cavert clipping, 1937, Edwin Ewart Aubrey Papers, University of Pennsylvania. for Samuel DuBois Cook on Mays and consequences, see Cook's introduction to Mays, *Quotable Quotes,* xvii and xix.

4. Mays, *Quotable Quotes,* 4–5. Mays *Pittsburgh Courier* columns: "Statesman Bunche," July 2, 1949, and "Mays and Wells Off to Europe [World Council of Churches]," July 2, 1949, 10.

5. Cook, introduction to Mays, *Quotable Quotes,* xviii–xix. "Mays and Wells Off to Europe" *Pittsburgh Courier,* July 2, 1949; "Few Negro Leaders Take High Places [Ralph Bunche]," *Pittsburgh Courier,* June 18, 1949, 10; Mays, "Statesman Bunche," *Pittsburgh Courier,* July 2, 1949, 10. Typescript notes, n.d. (1950s), for chapter 11 of *Born to Rebel;* notes, address, WCC Northwestern University, August 14–31, 1954; Mays to Eunice V. Baker, June 3, 1946; Mays, "Every Man and Every Woman" (undated typescript), April 1946, Detroit, Mich., Mays Papers, MSRC. Quotation, Isaiah 1:18 (NIV and most other translations. Mays, "Perhaps Georgians Could Wait," *Pittsburgh Courier,* February 5, 1949, 15.

6. Mays's column endorsed Truman early in fall 1948 and continued to support him; see, for example, "Terrible Prophecy," *Pittsburgh Courier,* March 5, 1949.

7. Mays, "We Must Become More Competent," *Pittsburgh Courier,* June 5, 1949.

8. "Regional Plan [Meharry]," *Pittsburgh Courier,* January 1, 1949, 2. See entries on Edith Irby Jones, George W. Haley, Christopher Columbus Mercer, Jr., Silas Hunt, Wiley Austin

Branton, and Jackie Shropshire in *Encyclopedia of Arkansas History and Culture,* http://encyclo
pediaofarkansas.net/ (accessed October 31, 2011); "Before Little Rock: Successful Arkansas
Integration at the University of Arkansas in 1948," University of Arkansas Libraries Sympo-
sium, September 15, 2007, Fayetteville, Ark.

9. Mays, quoted in "Regional Plan [Meharry]"; Reitzes, *Negroes and Medicine.*

10. "Regional Plan [Meharry]"; Reitzes, *Negroes and Medicine.*

11. United Negro College Fund (UNCF) correspondence, 1949–50, Mays Papers, MSRC.
"College Fund Drive Will be Sparked by Big Meet in Atlanta," *Pittsburgh Courier,* February
12, 1949, 2. F. D. Patterson, Phelps-Stokes Fund, and Hazen Foundation, correspondence, especially Mays to Eugene Smathers, February 23, 1959, Mays to F. D. Patterson, August 16, 1960,
and Christmas card message of reformism, Mays and Sadie Gray Mays, December 25, 1958—
all Mays Papers, MSRC.

12. Images of Jesus, especially John 4:1–41 and 6:41–51; for Mays's images of Jesus, see Gavins,
"The Ceremonial Speaking of Benjamin Elijah Mays."

13. Correspondence with Edmund O. Cerf, 1958; Mays to Blake Clark [*Reader's Digest*],
November 25, 1958; Mays to Edward O. Cerf [*Life*], October 4, 1958; Mays to Huston Smith
["Search for America"], May 8, 1959; McGill and *Atlanta Constitution* correspondence, espe-
cially Mays to Fields, September 17, 1958; Mays to Richard B. Stolley [*Life*], n.d. (1958)—all
Mays Papers, MSRC.

14. Rovaris, "Mays and Morehouse," on *Born to Rebel* typescripts; Burton, foreword to *Born
to Rebel* (1987 ed.); Burton, "Born to Rebel," in *Walking Integrity,* edited by Carter, 33–80;
Rauschenbusch, "The Social Meaning of the Lord's Prayer" (typescript), 1950, Mays Papers,
MSRC, published as "Prayers of the Social Awakening" in Rauschenbusch's *A Gospel for the
Social Awakening,* 167–68.

15. Rauschenbusch, *A Gospel for the Social Awakening;* Mays correspondence with the Edward Hazen Foundation, Mays Papers, MSRC.

16. Mays correspondence with Thurgood Marshall, especially October 26, 1960, and December 14, 1960, Mays Papers, MRSC.

17. F. D. Patterson to Mays, August 16, 1960; Mays to Samuel Hoskins, December 11, 1958;
Aimee Isgrig to Mays, October 31, 1958; Mays to Laurin Edmondson, May 9, 1961; Mays to
Marjorie Green, March 1, 1961; Thurgood Marshall to Mays, October 26, 1960, and December 14, 1960; Mays to John O. Boone [NAACP], February 13, 1959; Roy Wilkens to Mays, June
20, 1961; Harold C. Fleming (SRC) to Mays, April 6, 1961; Mays memorandum to Constance
Curry (SCLC) on sit-ins, n.d. (October 1960)—all Mays Papers, MSRC. In all cases Mays not
only addressed a demonstration for a specific date but also reflected on activities throughout
the 1950s.

18. Butler T. Meaders to Thurgood Marshall, October 3, 1960; Mays to Constance Baker
Motley, January 3, 1961; Mays to J. T. Brooks, July 13, 1960; "O Folder, 1960–61," for organi-
zational activities; Mays to Donald M. Mauck, February 28, 1961, on being called a Communist; Mays to Mauck, February 22, 1961, on plans for demonstration in Columbus, Georgia;
Mays to Harold C. Fleming, April 6, 1960; SRC news release, August 7, 1960, about sit-ins;
folders on Homer Brown [Virginia Union College] and Mary Bethune Cookman, n.d.
(1950s)—all Mays Papers, MSRC. Mays columns: "As I See It," relating to false charges of
Communism in civil rights activism, and "Air Force Integration," *Pittsburgh Courier,* October
29, 1949, 10; "It Is as Clear as Day That Governor Talmadge Will Do His Best to Keep Negroes

Down," November 26, 1949, *Pittsburgh Courier,* 15. Joseph D. Bibb, "Calling All Ghosts [Talmadge and Communist charges]," *Pittsburgh Courier,* March 18, 1950, 18.

19. Glenn Adams, "Commentary on Brown v. Board of Education," American Psychological Association, 2008; Clark, "Effects of Prejudice and Discrimination on Personality Development," Midcentury White House Conference on Children and Youth, 1950, revised and published as *Prejudice and Your Child;* Richard Severo, obituary for Kenneth Clark," *New York Times,* May 2, 2005; typescripts for *Born to Rebel,* n.d. (1950s),and folder labeled "Kenneth Clark," 1949–55, Mays Papers, MSRC.

20. Kluger, *Simple Justice* (revised edition, 2004); Tushnet, *The NAACP's Legal Strategy; Brown v. Board of Education* documents; University of Michigan Library; Obituary for James Madison Nabrit, *Journal of Black Higher Education,* no. 18 (Winter 1997/1998): 23.

21. Kluger, *Simple Justice* (revised edition, 2004); Tushnet, *The NAACP's Legal Strategy; Brown v. Board of Education* documents; University of Michigan Library; Obituary for James Madison Nabrit, *Journal of Black Higher Education,* no. 18 (Winter 1997/1998): 23. Roper, *C. Vann Woodward, Southerner,* chapter 7. Roper interviews with Woodward, John Herbert Roper Papers. SHC. Mays's list of "must read" books, n.d. (1960?); Mays to Danforth Foundation/Camp Miniwanca conference [featuring Sadie Gray Mays], August 29–September 4, 1960; and folders for Waties Waring and James Madison Nabrit—all Mays Papers, MSRC. "Heart to fight," quoted in Pettigrew, *A Profile of the Negro American,* 10.

22. "National Leaders Laud Ban on School Desegregation," *Pittsburgh Courier,* May 29, 1954, 31; Mays, "As I See It: The Future Is With Judge Waring," *Pittsburgh Courier,* March 22, 1952, 9. Job and Psalm 31, both cited by Mays in op-ed pieces; quotation from Mays to Samuel Hoskins, December 11, 1958, Mays Papers, MSRC.

23. Roper, *C. Vann Woodward,* chapter 6. Interviews with Woodward, John Hope Franklin, Leroy Graf, Bennett Harrison Wall, and August Meier; Bell Irvin Wiley to Roper, November 27, 1978, John Herbert Roper Papers, SHC.

24. *Segregation Decisions.* Bailey, "The Southern Historical Association and the Quest for Racial Justice." The quotation about white women is from an interview with Bennett Harrison Wall, April 12, 1979, John Herbert Roper Papers, SHC.

25. Bailey, "The Southern Historical Association."

26. Harold Habein to Mays, October 3, 1958, and other correspondence with Habein; Mays to Mattie Adams, July 14, 1958, and n.d. (summer 1958); Mays, "The Federal Courts and the Ballot," typescript apparently written for the *Pittsburgh Courier,* n.d. (1958); Mays to Roy Wilkens, July 12, 1960—all Mays Papers, MSRC. For Sadie Gray Mays 1958 and 1959 campaigns for voting rights, see J. A. Rogers, "History Shows," *Pittsburgh Courier,* January 3, 1959, 5; Kelly Anderson, "Kelly Anderson Leads Negroes' Push for Voting Rights," *Pittsburgh Courier,* March 21, 1959, 18.

27. See Rovaris, "Mays and Morehouse." In *Pittsburgh Courier:* full-page display advertisement, May 24, 1958, 8; "Morehouse Proud of Her Brand New Physical Plant," May 24, 1958, 6. Mays, "My View: The Total Is 32," December 20, 1958, 14; "My View: Reward for Excellence," May 16, 1959, 5; "Morehouse Teachers Leaders of Future," May 30, 1959, 8; and "Dr. Mays to Speak Twice Here Sun. [Pittsburgh's Heinz Center]," August 22, 1959, 1–2.

28. Rovaris, "Mays and Morehouse"; Mays, *Born to Rebel,* 237–39; folders for Sealantic/John D. Rockefeller, 1956–61, Interdenominational Center for Religious Studies, Morehouse

School of Religion; American Association of Theological Schools, 1956–61, Mays Papers, MSRC; adjusted value of money calculated using the S. Morgan Friedman Inflation Calculator, based on consumer price index for 1958–75, U.S. Census, *Historical Statistics* (1975) and 1976–2007, U.S. Census, *Statistical Abstracts* (2010).

29. "Before Little Rock"; Mays to Laura Edmondson, May 9, 1961, Mays Papers, MSRC. In *Pittsburgh Courier:* Frank C. Bolden, "Sen. Kennedy Raps Ike," October 17, 1959, 2; George E. Barbour, "Kennedy Didn't Ask Ala. Governor Support," December 19, 1959, 6; Mays columns "In My View": "Kasper and Faubus," August 15, 1959, 5; "Looks Like a New Day," November 21, 1959, 5; and "A Great Address," February 11, 1961, 9; Mays feature, "The Democrats Are In Power," August 15, 1959, 5.

30. Mays to Edmondson, May 9, 1961; Mays, *Born to Rebel,* 227; David M. Hardy to John H. Roper, August 17, 2005, file 161-HQ365, Mays FBI files, 1961–79, copies in possession of author and filed in John Herbert Roper Papers, SHC; summary statement clearing Mays "as to his character, loyalty, general standing and ability," filed with P. Kenneth O'Donnell on March 6, 1961.

31. Mays, "My View: Senator Russell," *Pittsburgh Courier,* April 11, 1959, 9; Mays, *Born to Rebel,* 224. Mays to Edmondson, May 9, 1961; and Mays to Marjorie Green, March 1, 1961, Roy Wilkens to Mays, January 20, 1961; Harold C. Fleming to Mays, April 6, 1961; Mays to Constance Baker Motley (Curry), January 3, 1961—all in Mays Papers, MSRC; Mays, "My View: At Long Last! [Horace Ward and University of Georgia]," *Pittsburgh Courier,* January 21, 1961, 5.

32. Caro, "Johnson's Dream, Obama's Speech"; Caro, *The Years of Lyndon Johnson,* vol. 2: *Means of Ascent,* especially 170. and vol. 3: *Master of the Senate,* 886–90, 941, 996, 1003–4; Mays,"My View: I Talked with the Vice President," *Pittsburgh Courier,* February 1, 1964, 10.

33. Caro, *The Years of Lyndon Johnson,* vol. 3: *Master of the Senate,* 886–90, 998; statement, unattributed testimony, October 10, 1969, FBI files, 161-HQ365. David M. Hardy to Roper, copies in John Herbert Roper Papers, SHC. Farmer, quoted in Caro, "Johnson's Dream, Obama's Speech."

34. Caro, *The Years of Lyndon Johnson,* vol. 3: *Master of the Senate,* 886–90, 998; statement, unattributed testimony, October 10, 1969, FBI files, 161-HQ365. David M. Hardy to Roper, copies in John Herbert Roper Papers, SHC. Farmer, quoted in Caro, "Johnson's Dream, Obama's Speech." Mays columns in the *Pittsburgh Courier:* "My View: I Talked with the Vice President," February 1, 1964, 10; "My View: Now the Debate and Passage," February 22, 1964, 10; "My View: The President's Inaugural Address," February 6, 1965, 10; "My View: As Selma Goes, So Goes the Nation," February 15, 1965, 10; "My View: Let's Face It," March 20, 1965, 10; "My View: What Is the Solution?," May 6, 1965, 10; *Pittsburgh Courier* byline writers: "House Approves Strongest Civil Rights Bill in History of U.S.," February 15, 1964, 2; "Civil Rights Bill Has Teeth," June 27, 1964, 1. Caro, "Johnson's Dream, Obama's Speech." Ralph E. Kogee, "Precious Gems from LBJ Speech Will Roar Across the Centuries," *Pittsburgh Courier,* March 20, 1965, 1. Mays, "My View: Why We Can't Wait," August 22, 1964, 10.

35. Mays, "Why I Am Hard on the South" typescript, n.d. [1968?], Mays Papers, MSRC.

36. "Notices," *Journal of Negro History* (1968). Compton's gift would be $944,025.65 in 2007 dollars, according to calculations of the Morgan Friedman Inflation Calculator, using the consumer price index from 1967 to 2007, as compiled by the U.S. Department of Commerce in

U.S. Bureau of the Census, *Historical Statistics of the United States* (Washington, D.C.: U.S. Government Printing Office, 1974) and *Statistical Abstracts of the United States* (Washington, D.C.: U.S. Government Printing Office, 2007).

37. The dismissive phrase was employed to describe the able black scholars at South Carolina University during the Reconstruction era, apparently first by bitter antebellum professor Maximilian LaBorde and later in print by university historian Edwin Luther Green, in *A History of the University of South Carolina* (Columbia: R. L. Bryan, 1909). Despite—or because of—everything, the state of South Carolina and the University of South Carolina remained the place of honor and personal dishonor for Mays. See especially Mays, "Why I Am Hard on the South."

Chapter 13. "Myne owne familiar friend"

1. Psalm 55:14–15, 26b, Coverdale translation in Book of Common Prayer (1928). On Sadie Gray Mays's cancer, see correspondence, 1968–69, especially Mays to Lloyd O. Lewis, n.d. (1965) and correspondence with Harold Habein, 1965, Mays Papers, MSRC.

2. Appendix H, Mays, *Born to Rebel;* commencement program, 1967, Morehouse College, and letters of congratulation, 1967, Mays Papers, MSRC.

3. Correspondence with DeLand DeVinney, 1967; commencement programs, 1967, Morgan College, Harvard University, and Grinnell College; On Martin Luther King, Jr., at Grinnell, see Mays, *Born to Rebel,* 269–70; Mays, "My View" columns, *Pittsburgh Courier,* 1967–68, especially "A Hope for Peace [Humphrey]," *Pittsburgh Courier* clipping, fall 1968. Mays *Pittsburgh Courier* columns: "Are We Equally Concerned?" May 9, 1970; "President and Minorities [Nixon and Strom Thurmond]," May 16, 1970; "Is It Happening Again [end of Johnson's Second Reconstruction]," May 23, 1970; and "Gov't Bias Against Negroes," August 29, 1970.

4. Mays, "A Hope for Peace." On King see *Born to Rebel,* and Mays's *Pittsburgh Courier* columns: "Prophecy Come True," July 18, 1970; "Viet, Anti-People Policy to Blame for Turmoil," June 20, 1970; "Dr. Mays Remembers Heartbreak of King," *Pittsburgh Courier,* April 18, 1970, campus section 7; Mays, "Montgomery to Memphis," April 18, 1970, and "Segregation: Cat with 9 Lives," February 28, 1970.

5. M. J. Milner, "Abingdon Minister Recalls Fight Led by Classmate King," *Bristol Herald Courier,* January 17, 1993, B1.

6. Mays *Pittsburgh Courier* columns: "Killing Black Colleges," June 13, 1970; "Viet, Anti-People Policy to Blame for Turmoil," June 20, 1970; "Worthy of Evaluation," July 11, 1970. "After Fifty Years," July 4, 1970. On Marcus Garvey see Mays, *Born to Rebel,* 303–8; on Black Muslims, see ibid., 309–10; and on Stokely Carmichael and Black Panthers, see ibid., 314.

7. Mays to Samuel Hoskins, December 11, 1958, Mays Papers, MSRC, and E. W. Kensworthy, "2,000 March for Civil Rights," *New York Times,* August 28, 1968, 1. Mays, introduction to Bennett, *What Manner of Man,* 1–11.

8. Mays, "Eulogy at the Funeral Services of Martin Luther King, Jr.," April 9, 1968, Morehouse College, reprinted as appendix C in *Born to Rebel,* 358–60; Mays,"Heartbreak," *Pittsburgh Courier,* April 18, 1970.

9. R. W. Apple, Jr., "Kennedy Appeals for Nonviolence," *New York Times,* April 5, 1968, 33; Apple, "Damage in Riots Cost $45 Million," *New York Times,* April 13, 1968, 13.

10. Du Bois, *Against Racism;* Williamson, *Crucible of Race;* interview with Herbert Aptheker (March 23, 1985) and correspondence with Malcolm Call and Herbert Aptheker, especially Call

to Roper, with enclosures, September 24, 1984, and Aptheker to Roper, July 1, 1985, and July 16, 1985, John Herbert Roper Papers, SHC. On Stokely Carmichael see Mays, *Born to Rebel,* 314.

11. Carson, *In Struggle;* on Julian Bond and SNCC, see "Julian Bond," http://www.2souls2 .com/calendar/January/julian_bond2.htm (accessed November 1, 2011). Brown (later Jamil Al-Amin), *Die, Nigger, Die!;* Thelwell, introduction to 2002 edition of *Die, Nigger, Die!.*

12. Cleaver, *Soul on Ice;* "Black Panther Figure Supports Reagan Drive," *New York Times,* September 17, 1980, 24A; Gates and Wallace, "A Revolutionary Turns Right"; Macklin, "Activist Eldridge Cleaver, 62, Dies."

13. On Malcolm X and Elijah Muhammad, see Mays, *Born to Rebel,* 307–8; compare Malcolm X, *The Autobiography of Malcolm X.*

14. Jane Caldwell to Roper, November 20, 2008, and Whitney Mullins to Roper, December 9, 2009, John Herbert Roper papers, SHC; guide to John Hannah Papers, commencement program, June 9, 1968, University Archives Historical Collections, Michigan State University (hereafter UAHC, MSU).

15. Guide to John Hannah Papers, UAHC, MSU; "Commencement Remarks," *State News* (Michigan State University), June 9, 1968; Mays, "Commencement Address" (audio version), June 9, 1968, Vincent Video Library, Michigan State University; and "Commencement Remarks, MSU," Mays Papers, MSRC. Mays, "Eulogy," *Negro History Bulletin* 31 (May 1968).

16. "Martin Luther King, Jr.," box, installation 3, 1968–69, Mays Papers, MSRC: Ralph L. Yarbrough to Mays, June 6, 1968, with copy of eulogy Yarbrough inserted in *Congressional Record:* "Yarbrough Remarks," *Congressional Record,* May 27, 1968, E4653; and "Thurmond Remarks," *Congressional Record,* May 27, 1968, E4653.

17. On Coretta Scott King and SCLC officers, see "Martin Luther King, Jr.," box, installation 3, 1968–69, Mays Papers, MSRC.

18. Ibid. Correspondence with C. R. Yates and notes for address, June 19, 1968, "Martin Luther King, Jr.," box, installation 3, Mays Papers, MSRC.

19. Correspondence with C. R. Yates and notes for address, June 19, 1968, "Martin Luther King, Jr.," box, installation 3, Mays Papers, MSRC.

20. "Martin Luther King" box, installation 3, Mays Papers, MSRC.

21. Certificate of Death 32583, Georgia Division of Human Resources, Office of Vital Records, October 11, 1969. "Mrs. Benjamin Mays" (obituary), *New York Times,* October 13, 1969, 43; see also Mays, *Born to Rebel,* 270; correspondence with James B. Gilbert and Harold Habein, 1954–55 and "Happy Haven" folder, 1966–69, Mays Papers, MSRC.

22. For Mays's 1941 heart problems (?) in Cuba, see *Born to Rebel,* 167–68. Wortham, "Benjamin E. Mays at Eighty-One"; correspondence, 1965–81, especially physician's notes and appointments, Mays Papers, MSRC.

23. See correspondence with Jane Caldwell and Whitney Mullins, John Herbert Roper Papers, SHC. Papers of John A. Hannah, 1968–69, Office of the President, UAHC, MSU.

24. Hannah, archival field directory, Office of the President, 1941–69, UAHC, MSU.

25. Ibid. Mays, *Born to Rebel,* 315; Mays Papers, MSRC.

26. Adams, *The Test;* Papers of John A. Hannah; 1969; Walter Adams, 1969–70; and Clifton Reginald Wharton, 1970–71—all Office of President, UAHC, MSU. Correspondence between Walter Adams and Don Stevens, especially Adams to Stevens, October 16, 1969, Office of the President, UAHC, MSU.

27. Adams, *The Test* and correspondence, Walter Adams, Office of the President, UAHC, MSU,

28. Edwards, *The Revolt of the Black Athlete;* "Mexico: 1968; The Problem Olympics," entire issue, *Sports Illustrated,* September 30, 1968.

29. Grace-Kobas, "Wharton Criticizes Lack of Vision in U.S. Foreign Policy."

30. Blanchard, interview with Mays, August 16, 1983, Southern Oral History Program, SHC.

31. AP wire-service reports carried on April 19, 1969, in the *Clearfield (Pa.) Progress, Iowa City Press Citizen,* and *Fresno Argo;* longer versions appeared in the *Appleton (Wis.) Post Crescent, Ironwood (Mich.) Daily Globe, Newark (Ohio) Advocate, Benton Harbor (Mich.) News-Palladium, Charleston (W.Va.) Gazette,* and *San Mateo Times.* See also Suri, *Power and Protest.*

32. AP wire-service reports, *Appleton (Wis.) Post Crescent, Warren (Pa.) Times Mirror Observer,* and *Newark (Ohio) Advocate.* Roper, interview with C. Vann Woodward, October 12, 1980, John Herbert Roper Papers, SHC. Woodward to Glenn Weddington Rainey, October 4, 1966, Rainey Papers, Special Collections, Robert W. Woodruff Library, Emory University; Woodward to William Carleton and Manning J. Dauer, July 16, 1972, private collection; and Roper, *C. Vann Woodward, Southerner,* chapter 9.

33. AP wire-service reports, April 19, 1969, in the *Syracuse Herald-Journal* and other papers.

34. AP wire-service report about Theodore D. Jarrett in the *Syracuse Herald-Journal,* April 19, 1969, 1, and other papers. Mays, *Born to Rebel,* 311–15.

35. "Resignation statement," *Benton Harbor (Mich.) News-Paladium* and *Charleston (W.Va.) Gazette,* April 19, 1969. Compare the longer version of the AP wire-service report in the *Syracuse Herald-Journal, Appleton (Wis.) Post Crescent, Holland (Mich.) Evening Standard, Fremont (Calif.) Argos,* and *Newark (Ohio) Independent.*

36. "Resignation statement," Columbia SDS leader apology, and Hayakawa, *Benton Harbor (Mich.) News-Paladium* and *Charleston (W.Va.) Gazette,* April 19, 1969.

37. "Lock-up Ends," *Cedar Rapids Gazette,* April 21, 1969, 1–2.

38. AP wire stories: "60 Militants Release Trustees," *Elyria (Ohio) Chronicle Telegram* April 21, 1969; long version in *Weirton (W.Va.) Daily Times, Amarillo Globe Times, San Antonio Light, Fremont (Calif.) Argus, Charleston (W.Va.) Gazette, Lebanon (Pa.) Daily News,* and *San Mateo Times,* April 21, 1969. Gloster and Jarrett, full statements, *Carbondale Southern Illinoian,* April 21, 1969; see Bass and Nelson, *The Orangeburg Massacre.*

39. Suri, *Power and Protest;* Bell and Kristol, eds., *Confrontation;* special issue on student dissent, *Daedalus* 103, no. 1 (1974).

40. Mays, Born to Rebel, 312–14; Alton Hornsby, Jr., "The Historically Black Colleges of Atlanta," Atlanta and Historians, supplement to American Historical Association, Perspectives December 2006, http://www.historians.org/perspectives/issues (accessed January 15, 2012); Lena Williams, "Samuel L. Jackson: Out of Lee's 'Jungle' into Limelight," *New York Times,* June 9, 1991, 20; Dils, *Samuel L. Jackson.*

41. Guide to Mays Papers, MSRC; Mays, *Born to Rebel,* 311–15.

42. "Morehouse Will Send 9 Blacks to Pitt-Med," *Pittsburgh Courier,* January 24, 1970, 3. *Morehouse Alumni News,* June 2008.

43. Damer, *Attacking Faulty Reasoning; Daedalus,* 103 (1974).

Chapter 14. Leave Me a Double Portion

1. Mays, *Disturbed about Man; Disturbed about Man* folder; and "Martin Luther King, Jr.," folder, installation 2—all in Mays Papers, MSRC.

2. Correspondence with Richard H. Rich, April 28, 1969, installation 2, Mays Papers, MSRC.

3. *Disturbed about Man* folder, Mays Papers, MSRC; *Disturbed about Man,* 55; Jarmen, review of *Disturbed about Man, Reformed Journal,* December 1969, 4; notice for *Disturbed about Man, Atlanta Constitution,* April 27, 1969; Bonise, review of *Disturbed about Man, St. Anthony Messenger,* 1969.

4. Sales figures are from publisher's correspondence and clippings in *Disturbed about Man* folder, Mays Papers, MSRC.

5. Hunter, *Community Power Structure;* Mills, *The Power Elite;* Key, "Georgia: Rule of the Rustics," in *Southern Politics in State and Nation,* 106–29. On backlash and the modern southern Republican Party, see Black and Black, *Politics and Society in the South,* and Black, *Southern Governors and Civil Rights;* Bartley, *The Creation of Modern Georgia;* Kruse, *White Flight: Atlanta and the Making of Modern Conservatism.*

6. Kruse, *White Flight,* 270–83n.

7. Ibid.; Gladwell, *The Tipping Point.*

8. Key, *Southern Politics in State and Nation;* compare Kruse, *White Flight,* 2–5.

9. "Cobb Must Have More Black Teachers," *Pittsburgh Courier,* January 10, 1981, 1; Mays, "Wait and See," *Pittsburgh Courier,* January 17, 1981; Mays, "The End of Public Schools," *Pittsburgh Courier,* March 5, 1981. Mays, quoted in Kruse, "The Fight for Freedom of Association," in Webb, ed. *Massive Resistance,* 109–10; Hornsby, *A Short History of Black Atlanta,* especially chapters 3 and 4.

10. Certificate of Death 32583, Georgia Division of Human Resources, October 11, 1969. "Mrs. Benjamin Mays" (obituary), *New York Times,* October 13, 1969, 43; Mays to Lewis, October 1, 1969, Mays Papers, MSRC.

11. Sadie Gray Mays, see Mays, *Born to Rebel,* 11, 43, 106–35, 140–65, 168–69; "Happy Haven" folder, Mays Papers, MSRC, especially 1969 entries on her death and the renaming of the nursing center. The deaf student was James Singleton; see Sadie Gray Mays to Mordecai Wyatt Johnson, November 17, 1961, and Johnson to Sadie Gray Mays, December 1, 1961. "Happy Haven" contributions, 1969, Mordecai Wyatt Johnson Papers, MSRC.

12. Correspondence, 1969–84, Mays Papers, MSRC: "Martin Luther King, Jr., Center for Nonviolent Social Change" folder, installation 2. See remarks about *Pittsburgh Courier* columns in Burton, "Born to Rebel," in *Walking Integrity,* edited by Carter, 74–80; Burton to Roper, February 2, 2009, John Herbert Roper Papers, SHC.

13. Chronology in Mays, *Born to Rebel.* Burton, "Born to Rebel," 33–80; guide to Mays collection, Michael Winston and staff: "biographical sketch," "chronology," and "accession history and notes," Mays Papers, MSRC.

14. Wortham quotes school officials in "Benjamin E. Mays at Eighty-One." "Man in a New Job," *Pittsburgh Courier,* January 24, 1970, 1; and Kruse, *White Flight.* Statement Mays to Mordecai Wyatt Johnson, December [25?], 1973, Mordecai Wyatt Johnson Papers, MSRC.

15. Mays, "Ga. Council of Churches Spoke Out," *Pittsburgh Courier,* January 31, 1970, 10; Mays, "We Fear Most What Never Happens," *Pittsburgh Courier,* February 7, 1970, 10; "Cat

with Nine Lives," Mays, "Four Southern Governors," *Pittsburgh Courier,* February 28, 1970, 10; Mays, "President Supports South," *Pittsburgh Courier,* March 14, 1970, 10; in Mays, "President and Minorities," *Pittsburgh Courier,* May 16, 1970, 10.; and Mays, "They Are Still with Me," *Pittsburgh Courier,* August 15, 1970, 10.

16. Mays, "We Fear Most What Never Happens," *Pittsburgh Courier,* February 7, 1970, p. 6. For "tipping point" see Mays, "President Supports South," *Pittsburgh Courier,* March 14, 1970, 10; Gladwell, *The Tipping Point.*

17. Mays, "President Made History," *Pittsburgh Courier,* May 2, 1970, 10.

18. Mays, "The Lamar, S.C., Incident," *Pittsburgh Courier,* March 28, 1970, 10. Betha Louise Roper Piper to Roper, July 11, 2010, John Herbert Roper Papers, SHC.

19. Mays, "Busing Not the Issue," *Pittsburgh Courier,* March 21, 1970, 10.

20. "Martin Luther King, Jr., Center for Nonviolent Social Change" folder, installation 2, Mays Papers, MSRC; Burton, "Born to Rebel"; *Pittsburgh Courier,* Burton to Roper, February 2, 2009, John Herbert Roper Papers, SHC.

21. Mays columns throughout 1970 and 1971: "Almost Unbelieveable," *Pittsburgh Courier,* February 14, 1970, 10; "Government Bias against Negroes," *Pittsburgh Courier,* August 29, 1970, 10. Carter, *The Politics of Rage;* Black, *Southern Governors and Civil Rights;* Kruse, *White Flight,* 230–33; data showing the serious relative material decline and some absolute material decline—especially in educational levels, employment levels, and compensation level with those declines traced specifically to the Reagan era—may be found in Phillips, *The Politics of Rich and Poor.*

22. Mays, *Disturbed about Man;* folders "Martin Luther King" folder, "Martin Luther King, Jr., Center for Nonviolent Social Change" folder, installation 2, Mays Papers, MSRC. *Born to Rebel;* typescript for *Born to Rebel,* Mays Papers, MSRC.

23. Garrow, *Bearing the Cross;* Abernathy, *And the Walls Came Tumbling Down;* Mays, "Montgomery to Memphis," *Pittsburgh Courier,* April 18, 1970, 10; Mays, "Dr. Mays Remembers Heartbreak of King," *Pittsburgh Courier,* April 18, 1970, 7; "Martin Luther King, Jr., Center for Nonviolent Social Change" folder, installation 2, Mays Papers, MSRC. See also Mays correspondence, 1972–84, Martin Luther King, Jr., Center for Nonviolent Social Change, Atlanta.

24. "Martin Luther King, Jr., Center for Nonviolent Social Change" folder, installation 2, Mays Papers, MSRC.

25. Notices, photographs, and correspondence, "Martin Luther King, Jr., Center for Nonviolent Social Change" folder, installation 2, Mays Papers, MSRC.

26. Mays, *Born to Rebel;* Carter, "The Life of Benjamin Elijah Mays," *Walking Integrity,* edited by Carter; Burton, foreword to *Born to Rebel* (1987).

27. Mays, *Born to Rebel,* 314–18; on Willie Mays and House men, see *Born to Rebel,* 289. See also Willie Mays, *Born to Play Ball.*

28. Faulkner phrase from *The Sound and the Fury.*

29. James W. Dawsey to Roper, December 25, 2011, John Herbert Roper Papers, SHC.

30. Chronology of honors in guide to Mays Papers, MSRC.

31. Mays, *Quotable Quotes;* Gavins, "The Ceremonial Speaking of Benjamin Elijah Mays."

32. Mays, "White Private Schools," *Pittsburgh Courier,* August 1, 1970, 10; Mays, "The End of Public Schools," *Pittsburgh Courier,* March 5, 1981, 10.

33. Wortham, "Benjamin E. Mays at Eighty-One."

34. Samuel Oelle Piper to Roper, June 22, 2010, John Herbert Roper Papers, SHC.

35. Ibid. Hornsby, *A Short History of Black Atlanta,* chapter 3; "Griffith Bell" (obituary), *New York Times,* January 5, 2009; on Palmetere and Nixon, see Roper, "The Voting Rights Extension of 1982."

36. Hornsby, *A Short History of Black Atlanta,* 40–41.

37. Guide to collection, Mays Papers, MSRC.

38. Ibid. "John H. Sengstecke" (obituary), *New Pittsburgh Courier,* May 28, 1997; Brewer, "Robert Lee Vann and the *Pittsburgh Courier.*"

39. HR Resolutions 17, 1983, *Congressional Record;* Carter, "Life of Benjamin E. Mays," *Walking Integrity,* edited by Carter, 29.

40. Interview with Ronald McGinnis, July 5, 2010, John Herbert Roper Papers, SHC; Wortham, "Benjamin E. Mays at Eighty-One."

41. "Bennie Mays, Renowned Black Educator, Dies," *Washington Post,* March 29, 1984, C6.

42. 2 Kings 2.

BIBLIOGRAPHY

Works by Benjamin Elijah Mays

Books

"Pagan Survivals in Christianity." A.M. thesis, University of Chicago, 1925.

The Negro's Church, by Mays and Joseph W. Nicholson. New York: Institute of Social and Religious Research, 1933. Reprint, New York: Ayers, 1973.

"The Development of the Idea of God in Contemporary Negro Literature." Ph.D. diss., University of Chicago, 1937. Published as *The Negro's God as Reflected in His Literature.* New York: Chapman & Grimes, 1938.

Seeking to Be Christian in Race Relations. New York: Friendship Press, 1946.

The Moral Aspects of Segregation [1965]. Atlanta: Southern Regional Council, 1968.

Disturbed about Man. Richmond: John Knox Press, 1969.

Born to Rebel: An Autobiography. New York: Scribners, 1971. Revised with a foreword by Orville Vernon Burton. Brown Thrush Reprints. Athens: University of Georgia Press, 1987. Republished with a revised foreword by Burton, 1996; reprinted, 2002.

Lord, the People Have Driven Me On. New York: Vantage, 1981.

Quotable Quotes of Benjamin E. Mays. New York: Vantage, 1983.

Edited Books and Contributions to Books

"The New Negro Challenge to the Old Order." In *Sketches of Negro Life and History in South Carolina,* edited by A. H. Gordon, 192–212. New York, 1929.

"Race." In *Christus Victor,* edited by Denzil G. M. Patrick. Geneva: World Conference of Christian Youth, 1939.

"Race." In *Encyclopedia of Religion,* edited by Vergilius Ferm. New York: Philosophical Library, 1945.

"The Inescapable Christ." In *Representative American Speeches,* edited by A. Craig Baird. New York: H. W. Wilson, 1946; and *Best Sermons,* edited by G. Paul Butler. New York: Crowell, 1946.

"The Obligations of the Individual Christian." In *The Christian Way in Race Relations,* edited by William Stuart Nelson, 209–28. New York: Harper, 1948.

"Christian Light on Human Relationships." In *The Eighth Congress of the Baptist World Alliance.* Philadelphia: Judson Press, 1950.

Rauschenbusch, Walter. *A Gospel for the Social Awakening.* Edited by Mays. New York: Association Press for the Hazen Foundation, 1950.

"Our Greatest Fears Are Fears of Things That Never Happen." In *Sunday Evening Sermons: Fifteen Selected Addresses Delivered before the Noted Chicago Sunday Evening Club,* edited by Alton M. Motter. New York: Harper, 1952.

"The Case for Integration." In *Contemporary Civilization.* Chicago: Scott, Foresman, 1959.

"Race: The Negro Perspective." In *The Search for America,* edited by Huston Smith. Englewood Cliffs, N.J.: Prentice-Hall, 1959.

"Materialism and Secularism." In *Christian Mission Today.* New York: Abingdon Press, 1960.

"The Challenge to Religion as It Ponders Science." In *Religion Ponders Science,* edited by Edwin Prince Booth. New York: Appleton-Century, 1964.

"The Christian in Race Relations." *Rhetoric of Racial Revolt,* edited by Roy L. Hill. Denver: Gordon Bell Press, 1964.

"I Have Been a Baptist All My Life." In *A Way Home: The Baptists Tell Their Story,* edited by James Saxon Childers. Atlanta: Tupper & Love / New York: Holt, Rinehart & Winston, 1964.

"Why I Believe There Is a God." In *Why I Believe There Is a God: Sixteen Essays by Negro Clergymen.* Chicago: Johnson, 1966.

Introduction to *What Manner of Man: A Biography of Martin Luther King, Jr.,* by Lerone Bennett, Jr. Chicago: Johnson, 1968.

Selected Periodical Publications

"It Cost Too Much." *Tampa Bulletin,* April 7, 1928.

"The Religious Life and Needs of Negro Students." *Journal of Negro Education* 9 (July 1940): 337, 341, 342.

Op-ed columns. *Pittsburgh Courier,* 1942–81.

Eulogy for Dr. Charles Hubert, Morehouse Chapel, January 26, 1944. Published as "Tribute to Dr. Charles Hubert," *Morehouse Alumnus,* July 1944.

"When Do I Believe in Man." *International Journal of Religious Education* 21 (September 1944).

"The Time is Always Ripe." *Women's Press* 39 (March 1945).

"Democratizing and Christianizing America in This Generation." *Journal of Negro Education* 14 (Fall 1945): 527–34.

"No Justice for Negroes in the South!" *Pittsburgh Courier,* January 29, 1949, 1.

"Have You Forgotten God?" *Our World,* November 1952.

Eulogy for Dr. Martin Luther King, Jr. *Negro History Bulletin* 31 (May 1968). Republished in *Born to Rebel,* 357–60.

"Why I Went to Bates." *Bates College Bulletin,* alumni issue, 63 (January 1966), n. pag.

Manuscript Collections and Archives

Atlanta History Center, Atlanta, Ga.
    Collected photographs, 1965
Special Collections, Boston University
    African Studies Papers
Brotherhood of Sleeping Car Porters Papers, Chicago, Ill.
Clarendon County Archives, Clarendon County Courthouse, Manning, S.C.
    "Education for Negroes in Clarendon County," n.d.

Clarendon County Board of Education
David M. Rubenstein Rare Book and Manuscript Library, Duke University, Durham, N.C.
  Montrose Jonas Moses Papers
Drew University Archives, Madison, N.J.
  George Dennis Sale Kelsey Papers
John Hay Library and Archives, Brown University Libraries, Providence, R.I.
  John Brown Watson Papers
  Hattie Rutherford Watson Papers
Library of Congress, Manuscript Division, Washington, D.C.
  Whitefield McKinlay Papers, Carter Godwin Woodson Collection
University Archives Historical Collections, Michigan State University, East Lansing, Mich.
  Commencement program, June 9, 1968
  Walter Adams Papers
  John Hannah Papers
  State News
  Vincent Video Library
Moorland-Spingarn Research Center, Howard University Library, Washington, D.C.
  Edward Franklin Frazier Papers
  Mordecai Wyatt Johnson Papers
  Benjamin Elijah Mays Papers
Robert W. Woodruff Library and Archives, Morehouse College, Atlanta, Ga.
  Pamphlets, bulletins, commencement programs
Special Collections, Robert W. Woodruff Library, Emory University, Atlanta, Ga.
  Glenn Weddington Rainey Papers
University of Michigan Library, Ann Arbor, Mich.
  NAACP legal strategy; *Brown v. Board of Education* documents
University of Pennsylvania Archives and Research Center Library, Philadelphia
  Edwin Ewart Aubrey Papers
South Carolina Department of Archives and History, Columbia
  Clarendon County Board of Education Records
  Governor William H. Ellerbe Papers
South Caroliniana Library, University of South Carolina, Columbia
  James Allen Hoyt, "The Phoenix Riot," Kosmos Club
  Watson Family Papers
  Harry LeGare Watson Papers
Southern Historical Collection, University of North Carolina Library, Chapel Hill
  Frank Porter Graham Papers
  Morris Randolph Mitchell Papers
  National Association for the Advancement of Colored People Board of Directors,
    1950–55.
  North Carolina Council on Interracial Cooperation
  North Carolina Council on Human Relations Records
  Penn School Papers
  Arthur Franklin Raper Papers

John Herbert Roper Papers
Southern Oral History Program: interviews with Harvey E. Beech and Dallas Blanchard
Southern Illinois University Library and Archives, Carbondale
  Henry Nelson Wieman Papers
University of Michigan Library, Ann Arbor
  Brown v. Board of Education Archive. On-line at http://www.lib.umich.edu/brown
    -versus-board-education/ (accessed November 1, 2011)
Yale University Divinity School, New Haven, Conn.
  Jerome Davis Papers

Secondary Sources

Abernathy, Ralph. *And the Walls Came Tumbling Down: An Autobiography.* New York: Harper & Row, 1989.

Adams, Walter. *The Test.* New York: Macmillan, 1971.

The African American Almanac. 8th rev. ed. Detroit: Gale Group, 2000.

American Battle Monuments Commission, *93d Division: Summary of Operations in the World War.* Washington, D.C.: U.S. Government Printing Office, 1944.

American National Biography. Edited by John A. Garraty, and Mark C. Carnes. 24 vols. New York: Oxford University Press, 1999.

Andrew, Rod, Jr. *Wade Hampton: Confederate Warrior to Southern Redeemer.* Chapel Hill: University of North Carolina Press, 2008.

Apple, R. W., Jr. "Kennedy Appeals for Nonviolence." *New York Times,* April 5, 1968, 33.

Aristotle. *The Art of Rhetoric.* Translated by John Henry Freese. London: Heinemann, 1926.

———. *The Nicomachean Ethics.* Translated by Drummond Percy Chase. Everyman's Library. London: Dent, 1911.

Arnold, Charles H. *Near the Edge of Battle: A Short History of the Divinity School and the Chicago School of Theology, 1866–1966.* Chicago: Divinity School Association, University of Chicago, 1966.

Aubrey, Edwin Ewart. "Critical Comments on Historical and Superhistorical Elements in Christianity by John A. Mackay." *Journal of Religion* 17 (Winter 1937): 1–11.

———. *From Skepticism to Christian Action.* Address to the Student-Faculty Conference of the YMCA-YWCA. Antonio, California, December 27, 1939–January 2, 1940. Los Angeles: Student Charter Associate Office, 1940.

———. "The Holy Spirit in Relation to the Religious Community." *Journal of Theological Studies* 41 (Winter 1940): 61.

———. "Is Knowledge Power?" *Bushnell Journal of Education* 19 (Winter 1944): 1–5.

———. *Man's Search for Himself.* Cole Lectures in Religion, Vanderbilt University. Nashville: Cokesbury Press, 1941.

———. "The Minister as a Creative Theologian." *Baptist Times,* November 1937, 835.

———. "New Humanism," *New Humanist* 7 (1934): 16–19.

———. "Our Liberal Heritage." *Chronicle* (American Baptist Historical Society), October 1944.

———. "The Oxford Conference, 1937," *Journal of Religion* 17 4 (October 1937): 379–96.

———. *Present Theological Tendencies.* New York: Harper, 1936.

———. "The Prospect of a Social Theology." *Journal of Religion* 21 (Winter 1941): 354–63.

———. "The Reconstructive Forces of the Christian Religion." *Christianity and the Evolving Social Order* 18 (January 1934).

———. "The Role of Theology in Contemporary Culture." *Journal of Religion* 14 (October 1934): 428–35.

———. "Sancta Sophia: Wisdom of God" (book review), *Christian Century,* February 23, 1938, 291.

———. "Sees U.S. Culture Doomed Unless Christianity Acts" [interview]. *Chicago Daily Tribune,* January 28, 1936.

———. "Theological Education in the Postwar World." *Crozer Quarterly* 22 (Winter 1945): 3–18.

———. "A Theology Relevant to Religious Education." *Religious Education* 34 (October–December 1939): 195–201.

———. "What is Modernism?" *Journal of Religion* 15 (Fall 1935): 426–47.

Bailey, Fred A. "The Southern Historical Association and the Quest for Racial Justice." *Journal of Southern History* 71 (November 2005): 833–69.

Baker, Ray Stannard. *Following the Color Line: An Account of Negro Citizenship in the American Democracy.* 1908. Williamstown, Mass.: Corner House, 1973.

Bartley, Numan V. *The Creation of Modern Georgia.* 2nd ed. Athens: University of Georgia Press, 1990.

Bass, Jack, and Jack Nelson, *The Orangeburg Massacre.* New York: World, 1970.

Beckner, Chrisanne. *100 African Americans Who Shaped American History.* Milwaukee: World Almanac Library, 1995.

Bell, Daniel, and Irving Kristol, eds. *Confrontation: The Student Rebellion and the Universities.* New York: Basic Books, 1969.

Bennett, Lerone, Jr. *Before the Mayflower: A History of the Negro in America 1619–1962.* Chicago: Johnson, 1962. Revised as *Before the Mayflower: A History of the Negro in America 1619–1964.* Chicago: Johnson, 1964. Revised as *Before the Mayflower: A History of Black America.* 6th ed. New York: Penguin, 1993.

———. "Benjamin Elijah Mays: The Last of the Great Schoolmasters." *Ebony* 59 (September 2004): 172, 174.

———. *What Manner of Man: A Biography of Martin Luther King, Jr.* Introduction by Benjamin Elijah Mays. 1964. 3rd ed., rev. Chicago: Johnson, 1968.

Berry, Mary Frances. "Brown Out?" Review of Risa Goluboff's *The Lost Promise of Civil Rights. Democracy,* no. 6 (Fall 2007): 85–92.

Black, Earl. *Southern Governors and Civil Rights: Racial Segregation as a Campaign Issue in the Second Reconstruction.* Cambridge, Mass.: Harvard University Press, 1976.

Black, Earl, and Merle Black, *Politics and Society in the South.* Cambridge, Mass.: Harvard University Press, 1987.

Blum, Edward J. *W. E. B. Du Bois, American Prophet.* Philadelphia: University of Pennsylvania Press, 2007.

Botkin, Benjamin A. *Lay My Burden Down: A Folk History of Slavery.* 1945. Reprinted, Brown Thrasher Books. Athens: University of Georgia Press, 1989.

Boulware, Marcus H. *The Oratory of Negro Leaders: 1900–1968.* Westport, Conn.: Negro Universities Press, 1969.

Boyer, Horace Clarence, ed. *Lift Every Voice and Sing II: An African American Hymnal.* New York: Church Publishing, 1993.

Breneman, David W. "Are We Losing Our Liberal Arts Colleges?" *College Board Review,* no. 156 (Summer 1990): 16–21, 29.

———. *Liberal Arts Colleges: Thriving, Surviving or Endangered?* Chicago: University of Chicago Press, 1994.

Bretall, Robert W. ed. *The Empirical Theology of Henry Nelson Wieman.* New York: Macmillan, 1963.

Brewer, James Howard. "Robert Lee Vann and the *Pittsburgh Courier,*" M.A. thesis, University of Pittsburgh, 1941.

Brown, H. Rap (later Jamil Al-Amin). *Die, Nigger, Die.* 1967. Reprinted with an introduction by Ekwuene Michael Thelwell. Chicago: Lawrence Hill Books, 2002.

Brown, Richard Maxwell. *Strain of Violence: Historical Studies of American Violence and Vigilantism.* New York: Oxford University Press, 1975.

Brown, William Oscar, "Race Prejudice: A Sociological Study." Ph.D. diss., University of Chicago, 1930.

Browning, James B. Review of *The Georgia Negro. Journal of Negro History* 23 (April 1938): 234–35.

Brundage, W. Fitzhugh. *Lynching in the New South: Georgia and Virginia, 1880–1930.* Urbana: University of Illinois Press, 1993.

Buchanan, Annabel Morris, ed. *Folk Hymns of America.* New York: Fischer, 1938.

Bunie, Andrew. *Robert L. Vann of the Pittsburgh Courier: Politics and Black Journalism.* Pittsburgh: University of Pittsburgh Press, 1974.

Burhoe, Ralph. "Henry Nelson Wieman: Philosopher of Natural Religion, 1889–1974." *Unitarian Universalist Directory.* Boston, 1976.

Burton, Ernest De Witt, and Edgar Johnson Goodspeed. *A Harmony of the Synoptic Gospels for Historical and Critical Study.* New York: Scribners, 1917.

Burton, Orville Vernon. *In My Father's House Are Many Mansions: Family and Community in Edgefield, South Carolina.* Chapel Hill: University of North Carolina Press, 1986.

Carnegie Foundation for the Advancement of Teaching. *A Classification of Institutions of Higher Education.* Princeton: Princeton University Press, 1987.

Caro, Robert A. "Johnson's Dream; Obama's Speech," *New York Times,* August 27. 2008.

———. *The Years of Lyndon Johnson.* Vol. 1: *The Path to Power.* New York: Knopf, 1982. Vol. 2: *Means of Ascent.* New York: Knopf, 1990. Vol. 3: *Master of the Senate.* New York: Knopf, 2002.

Carson, Clayborne. *In Struggle: SNCC and the Black Awakening of the 1960s.* Cambridge, Mass.: Harvard University Press, 1981.

Carter, Dan T. *The Politics of Rage: George Wallace, The Origins of the New Conservatism, and the Transformation of American Politics.* New York : Simon & Schuster, 1995.

———. *Scottsboro: A Tragedy of the American South.* London: Oxford University Press, 1971.

Carter, Lawrence Edward, Sr., ed. *Walking Integrity: Benjamin Elijah Mays, Mentor to Martin Luther King, Jr.* Macon, Ga.: Mercer University Press, 1998.

Case, Shirley Jackson. "Christianity and the Mystery Religions." *Biblical World* 43 (Winter 1914): 3–16.

———. *The Evolution of Early Christianity: A Genetic Study of First-Century Christianity in Relation to Its Religious Environment.* Chicago: University of Chicago Press, 1914.

———. *Experience with the Supernatural in Early Christian Times.* New York: Century, 1929.

———. "Gentile Forms of Millennial Hope." *Biblical World* 50 (Spring 1917): 67–68.

———. "Gentile Religions of the Ancient Mediterranean World." *World of Religion* 3 (1923): 64–68.

———. *The Millennial Hope: A Phase of War-Time Thinking.* Chicago: University of Chicago Press, 1918.

———. *The Social Origins of Christianity.* Chicago: University of Chicago Press, 1923.

———. *The Social Triumph of the Ancient Church.* New York: Harper, 1933.

———. "A Valuation of *Hastings' Encyclopedia:* Gentile Religions of the Ancient Mediterranean World." *Journal of Religion* 3 (Winter 1923): 64–68.

Chappell, David L. *A Stone of Hope: Prophetic Religion and the Death of Jim Crow.* Chapel Hill: University of North Carolina Press, 2003.

Clark, Kenneth Bancroft. *Prejudice and Your Child.* Boston: Beacon Press, 1955.

Clark, Thomas Dionysius. *The Rural Press and the New South,* Walter Lynwood Fleming Lectures. 1947. Reprint, Westport, Conn.: Greenwood Press, 1970.

———. *The Southern Country Editor.* 1948. Reprinted with an introduction by Gilbert C. Fite. Southern Classics Series, edited by John G. Sproat. Columbia: University of South Carolina Press, 1991.

Cleaver, Eldridge. *Soul on Ice,* New York: McGraw-Hill, 1968.

Cowan, L. Gray. "Ten Years of African Studies," *African Studies Bulletin* 12 (April 1969): 1–8

———. "To William O. Brown, Jr." *African Studies Bulletin* 12 (December 1969): 243–47.

Current, Richard N. *Phi Beta Kappa in American Life: The First Two Hundred Years.* New York: Oxford University Press, 1990.

Dalmoth, Diggs. "A Hope for Peace." *Pittsburgh Courier,* January 1, 1969, 10.

"Damaging Riots Cost $45 Million." *New York Times,* April 13, 1968, 13.

Damer, T. Edward. *Attacking Faulty Reasoning.* Belmont, Calif.: Wadsworth, 1980.

De Gree, Melvin. *Brickhouse Dreams: The True Story of Young Benjamin E. Mays.* Reston, Va.: Trail of Success, 1992.

Dils, Tracey E. *Samuel L. Jackson.* Philadelphia: Chelsea House, 2000.

"Dr. William Brown of African Center." *New York Times,* February 4, 1969, 39.

Donald, David Herbert. *Charles Sumner and the Coming of the Civil War.* New York: Knopf, 1960.

D'Orso, Michael. *Like Judgment Day: The Ruin and Redemption of a Town Called Rosewood.* New York: Putnam, 1996.

Drake, St. Clair, and Horace R. Cayton. *Black Metropolis: A Study of Negro Life in a Northern City.* 2 vols. 1945. Revised and enlarged ed. 2 vols. New York: Harper & Row, 1962.

Dryden, John. "The Secular Masque." *Poems by John Dryden,* 282–85. London: Dent, 1949.

Du Bois, William Edward Burghardt. *Against Racism: Unpublished Essays, Papers, Addresses, 1887–1961.* Edited by Herbert Aptheker. Amherst: University of Massachusetts Press, 1985.

———. *Correspondence of William Edward Burghardt DuBois.* Vol. 1.: 1877–1934. Edited by Herbert Aptheker. Amherst: University of Massachusetts Press, 1973.

———. *The Oxford W. E. B. Du Bois Reader.* Edited by Eric J. Sundquist. New York: Oxford University Press, 1996.

———. *The Philadelphia Negro: A Social Study.* Philadelphia : Published for the University of Pennsylvania, 1899.

———. *The Souls of Black Folk.* Chicago: McClurg, 1903.

Dunbar, Paul Lawrence. *Lyrics of Lowly Life.* 1896. Reprint, New York: Citadel Press, 1984.

Dunn, Richard S. *Sugar and Slaves: The Rise of the Planter Class in the English West Indies, 1624–1713.* 1972. Reprinted with a foreword by Gary B. Nash. Chapel Hill: University of North Carolina Press for the Omohundro Institute of Early American History and Culture, 2000.

Dyer, Ervin. "Power in Black and White." *Pitt Magazine,* Winter 2010, 18–23.

Dykeman, Wilma, and James Stokely. *Seeds of Southern Change: The Life of Will Alexander.* Chicago: University of Chicago Press, 1962.

Edgar, Walter B. *South Carolina: A History.* Columbia: University of South Carolina Press, 1998.

Edwards, Harry. *The Revolt of the Black Athlete.* New York: Free Press, 1969.

Farmer, James. *Lay Bare the Heart: An Autobiography of the Civil Rights Movement.* New York: Arbor House, 1985.

Foner, Eric. *Free Soil, Free Labor, Free Men: The Ideology of the Republican Party before the Civil War.* New York: Oxford University Press, 1970.

———. *Freedom's Lawmakers: A Directory of Black Officeholders during Reconstruction.* Rev. ed. Baton Rouge : Louisiana State University Press, 1996.

Franklin, John Hope. *From Slavery to Freedom: A History of Negro Americans.* 1947. 3rd ed., revised and enlarged. New York: Random House, 1969. Revised and enlarged by Franklin and Alfred B. Moss, Jr., as *From Slavery to Freedom: A History of African Americans.* 7th ed. New York: McGraw-Hill, 1994.

Frazier, E. Franklin. *Black Bourgeoisie: The Rise of a New Middle Class.* 1956. Reprint, New York: Free Press, 1965.

———. *The Negro in the United States.* New York: Macmillan, 1949.

Frederickson, George Milton. "A Man but Not a Brother: Abraham Lincoln and Racial Equality." *Journal of Southern History* 41 (Winter 1975): 39–58.

Fussell, Paul. *The Great War and Modern Memory.* New York: Oxford University Press, 1975.

Garrow, David J. *Bearing the Cross: Martin Luther King, Jr., and the Southern Christian Leadership Conference.* New York: Morrow, 1986.

Gates, David, with Amy Wallace. "A Revolutionary Turns Right." *Newsweek,* September 17, 1984, 13.

Gavins, Doris Levy. "The Ceremonial Speaking of Benjamin Elijah Mays: Spokesman for Social Change 1954–1795." Ph.D. diss., Louisiana State University, 1978.

George, Henry. *Progress and Poverty: An Inquiry into the Cause of Industrial Depression and of Increase of Want with Increase of Wealth, The Remedy.* 1890. Reprint, New York: Robert Schalkenbach Foundation, 1942.

Gettleman, Jeffrey. "Thurmond Family Struggles with Difficult Truth," *New York Times,* December 20, 2003, A1.

Gladwell, Malcolm. *The Tipping Point: How Little Things Can Make a Big Difference.* Boston: Little, Brown, 2000.

Goluboff, Risa. *The Lost Promise of Civil Rights.* Cambridge, Mass.: Harvard University Press, 2007.

Goodspeed, Edgar John. *How Came the Bible?* New York: Abingdon/Cokesbury Press, 1940.

Gordon, Asa H. *The Georgia Negro: A History.* Ann Arbor, Mich.: Edwards Brothers, 1932.

———, ed. *Sketches of Negro Life and History in South Carolina.* New York, 1929.

Gordon, Ralph C. "Charles R. Drew: Surgeon, Scientist, and Educator." *Journal of Investigative Surgery* 18 (September/October 2005): 223–25.

Grace-Kobas, Linda. "Wharton Criticizes Lack of Vision in U.S. Foreign Policy." *Cornell Chronicle* 27 (April 25, 1996): 10–12.

Gray, L. C. *History of Agriculture in the Southern United States to 1860.* 2 vols. Washington, D.C.: Carnegie Institution of Washington, 1933.

Green, Ely. *Ely: Too Black, Too White.* Edited by Elizabeth N. and Arthur Ben Chitty. Amherst: University of Massachusetts Press, 1970.

Greene, Jack P. *Imperatives, Behaviors, and Identities: Essays in Early American Cultural History.* Charlottesville: University Press of Virginia, 1992.

Hall, Jacquelyn Dowd. *Revolt against Chivalry: Jessie Daniel Ames and the Women's Campaign Against Lynching.* 1979. Revised, New York: Columbia University Press, 1993.

Harlan, Louis R. *Booker T. Washington.* Vol. 1: *The Making of a Black Leader, 1856–1901.* New York: Oxford University Press, 1972. Vol. 2: *The Wizard of Tuskegee, 1901–1915.* New York: Oxford University Press, 1983.

———. *Separate but Unequal.* Chapel Hill: University of North Carolina Press, 1959.

Harper's Bible Dictionary. Edited by Paul J. Achtemeier and others. San Francisco: Harper & Row, 1985.

Haselden, Kyle. *The Racial Problem in Christian Perspective.* Walter Rauschenbusch Lectures of Colgate Divinity School. New York: Harper, 1959.

Haven, Lee. "Asa H. Gordon." *Savannah State Archives* 1 (Spring 1994): n.pag.

Hawk, Emory Q. *Economic History of the South.* New York: Prentice-Hall, 1934.

Henderson, Butler T. "Bennie Mays and Morehouse." *Bates Alumnus,* January 1969: 3.

Hill, Adelaide Cromwell. Foreword to the William O. Brown issue. *African Studies Bulletin* 12 (December 1969): 241–43.

Holt, Thomas. *Black over White: Negro Political Leadership in South Carolina during Reconstruction.* Urbana: University of Illinois Press, 1977.

Hornsby, Alton, Jr. *A Short History of Black Atlanta, 1847–1990.* North Richland Hills, Tex.: Ivy Halls Academic Press, 2006.

Hudson, Charles. *The Southeastern Indians.* Knoxville: University of Tennessee Press, 1976.

Huggins, Nathan Irving. *Harlem Renaissance.* 1972. Updated, with a foreword by Arnold Rampersad. New York: Oxford University Press, 2007.

Hunter, Floyd. *Community Power Structure: A Study of Decision Makers.* Chapel Hill: University of North Carolina Press, 1953.

Hynes, William J. *Shirley Jackson Case and the Chicago School: The Socio-Historical Method.* Chico, Calif.: Scholars Press, 1981.

Ignatius of Loyola. *The Spiritual Exercises.* Translated Elder Mullen. Grand Rapids, Mich.: Christian Classics Ethereal, 1999.

Jelks, Randal M. "Mays's Academic Formation, 1917–1936." In *Walking Integrity: Benjamin Elijah Mays, Mentor to Martin Luther King, Jr.,* edited by Lawrence Edward Carter, Sr., 111–29. Macon, Ga.: Mercer University Press, 1998.

Joachim, H. H. *Aristotle, the Nicomachean Ethics: A Commentary.* Edited by D. A. Rees. Oxford: Clarendon Press / New York: Oxford University Press, 1951.

Johnson, Charles Spurgeon. *A Preface to Racial Understanding.* New York: Friendship Press, 1936.

Johnson, Ira Joe, and William G. Pickens. *Benjamin E. Mays and Margaret Mitchell: A Unique Legacy in Medicine.* Winter Park, Florida: Four-G, 1996.

Jones, Edward Allen. *A Candle in the Dark: A History of Morehouse College.* Valley Forge, Pa.: Judson Press of American Baptist Churches, 1967.

Jordan, Terry G., and Matti Kaups. *The American Backwoods Frontier: An Ethnic and Ecological Interpretation.* Baltimore: Johns Hopkins University Press, 1989.

Kantrowitz, Stephen. *Ben Tillman and the Reconstruction of White Supremacy.* Chapel Hill: University of North Carolina Press, 2000.

Kellogg, Charles Flint. *NAACP: A History of the National Association for the Advancement of Colored People.* Baltimore: Johns Hopkins University Press, 1962.

Kelsey, George Dennis Sale. *Social Ethics among Southern Baptists, 1917–1969.* Lanham, Md.: Scarecrow Press, 1977.

———. "Social Thought of Contemporary Southern Baptists." Ph.D. diss., Yale University, 1946.

Key, V. O., Jr., with the assistance of Alexander Heard. *Southern Politics in State and Nation.* 1949; Knoxville: University of Tennessee Press, 1984.

Kifner, John. Obituary for Eldridge Cleaver. *New York Times,* May 2, 1998, B8.

Kindred, Dave. "A Gust of 'Wind' That Left a Legacy." *Atlanta Constitution,* May 19, 1997, C3.

King, Martin Luther, Jr. *The Papers of Martin Luther King, Jr.* Edited by Clayborne Carson, Ralph E. Luker, Penny A. Russell, and Louis R. Harlan. 6 vols. Berkeley: University of California Press, 1992–2007.

Kirkpatrick, David D. "Mitchell Estate Settles 'Gone With the Wind' Suit." *New York Times,* May 10, 2002.

Kluger, Richard. *Simple Justice: The History of Brown v. Board of Education and Black America's Struggle for Equality.* 1977. Revised, New York: Random House, 2004.

Kraditor, Aileen S. *Means and Ends in American Abolitionism: Garrison and His Critics on Strategy and Tactics, 1834–1850.* New York: Pantheon, 1969.

Kruse, Kevin Michael. *White Flight: Atlanta and the Making of Modern Conservatism.* Princeton: Princeton University Press, 2005.

Leed, Eric J. *No Man's Land: Combat and Identity in World War I.* New York: Cambridge University Press, 1979.

Levine, Lawrence W. *Black Culture and Black Consciousness: Afro-American Folk Thought from Slavery to Freedom.* New York: Oxford University Press, 1977.

Lewis, David Levering. *W. E. B. Du Bois.* Vol. 1: *Biography of a Race, 1868–1919.* New York: Holt, 1993. Vol. 2: *The Fight for Equality and the American Gentry, 1919–1963.* New York: Holt, 2000.

Lewis, John, with Michael D'Orso. *Walking with the Wind: A Memoir of the Movement.* New York: Simon & Schuster, 1998.

Litwack, Leon F. *Been in the Storm so Long: The Aftermath of Slavery.* New York: Knopf, 1980.

Locke, Alain, ed. *The New Negro: An Interpretation.* New York: A. & C. Boni, 1925.

Logan, Rayford Whittingham. *The Betrayal of the Negro from Rutherford B. Hayes to Woodrow Wilson.* New York: Collier, 1965.

———. *Howard University: The First Hundred Years, 1867–1967.* New York: New York University Press, 1969.

———. *The Negro in American Life and Thought: The Nadir 1877–1901.* New York: Dial Press, 1954.

———. *The Negro in the United States: A Brief History.* Princeton, N.J.: D. Van Nostrand, 1957.

Logan, Rayford W., and Michael R. Winston, eds. *Dictionary of American Negro Biography.* New York: Norton, 1982.

Luker, Ralph E. "Plagiarism and Perspective: Questions about Martin Luther King, Jr." *International Social Science Review* 68 (Fall 1993): 152–60

———. "Quoting, Merging, and Sampling the Dream: Martin Luther King and Vernon Johns." *Southern Cultures* 9 (Summer 2003): 28–48.

———. *The Social Gospel in Black and White: American Racial Reform, 1885–1912.* Chapel Hill: University of North Carolina Press, 1991.

MacLean, Nancy. *Behind the Mask of Chivalry: The Making of the Second Ku Klux Klan.* New York: Oxford University Press, 1994.

Macklin, William R. "Activist Eldridge Cleaver, 62, Dies." *Philadelphia Inquirer,* May 2, 1998, D1.

"Margaret Mitchell's Renewed Role as Benefactor of Morehouse College." *Journal of Blacks in Higher Education,* no. 36 (Summer 2002): 58.

Matthews, Verner R. "The Concept of Racial Justice of Benjamin Elijah Mays (1895–1984) and Its Relevance to Christian Education in the Black Church." Ph.D. diss., New York University, 1991.

Mays, Willie. *Born to Play Ball.* New York: Putnam, 1955.

McCall, David F. "William Oscar Brown, 1899–1969." *African Studies Bulletin* 12 (April 1969): i–vi.

McDonald, Pam. "Martin Luther King, Jr., in Simsburg." M.L.S. thesis, Syracuse University, 2000.

McDonough, Julie Anne. "Men and Women of Good Will: A History of the Commission on Interracial Cooperation and Southern Regional Council, 1919–1954." Ph.D. diss., University of Virginia, 1993.

McNeil, Genna Rae. *Groundwork: Charles Hamilton Houston and the Struggle for Civil Rights.* Philadelphia: University of Pennsylvania Press, 1983.

McNeill, John Thomas, Matthew Spinka, and Harold R. Willoughby, eds. *Environmental Factors in Christian History.* Essays in Honor of Shirley Jackson Case. Chicago: University of Chicago Press, 1939.

Mills, C. Wright. *The Power Elite.* New York: Oxford University Press, 1956.

Milner, Martha J. "Abingdon Minster Recalls Fight Led by Classmate King." *Bristol Herald Courier,* January 17, 1993, B1.

Moore, Barrington. *Social Origins of Dictatorship and Democracy: Lord and Peasant in the Making of the Modern World.* Boston: Beacon Press, 1966.

Moore, John Hammond. *South Carolina Newspapers.* Columbia: University of South Carolina Press, 1988.

Morris, Aldon M. *The Origins of the Civil Rights Movement: Black Communities Organizing for Change.* New York: Free Press, 1984.

Morris, Thomas D. *Southern Slavery and the Law, 1619–1860.* Chapel Hill: University of North Carolina Press, 1995.

Mosca, Gaetano. *The Ruling Class.* Edited by Arthur Livingston. Translated by Hannah D. Kahn. 1896. Reprint, New York: McGraw-Hill, 1939.

Mynders, Alfred. "Next to the News." *Chattanooga Times,* November 13, 1955. Republished as "Notice," *Journal of Negro History* 2 (Spring 1967): 166.

Nicholson, Joseph William. *The Contemporary Opportunities of the Protestant Episcopal Church: A Proposal for a Confidential Clinical Counseling Service to Small and Subsidized Churches.* N.p.: Published by the author, 1973.

———. "An Occupational Study of the Christian Ministry among Negroes." Ph.D. diss., Northwestern University, 1932.

———. *What Is Happening to the Negro in the Protestant Episcopal Church?* N.p.: Ad Hoc Clergy Committee, 1968.

Odum, Howard Washington. *Rainbow Round My Shoulder: The Blue Trail of Black Ulysses.* Indianapolis: Bobbs-Merrill, 1928.

Ottley, Roi. *The Lonely Warrior: The Life and Times of Robert S. Abbott.* Chicago: Regnery, 1955.

Parris, Guichard, and Lester Brooks. *Blacks in the City: A History of the National Urban League.* Boston: Little, Brown, 1971.

Peden, Creighton. *The Chicago School: The Voices of Liberal Religious Thought.* Bristol, Ind.: Wyndham Hall Press, 1987.

Pettigrew, Thomas F. *A Profile of the Negro American.* Princeton: Princeton University Press, 1964.

Phillips, Kevin. *The Politics of Rich and Poor: Wealth and the American Electorate in the Reagan Aftermath.* New York: Random House, 1990.

Pocock, J. G. A. "Machiavelli, Herrington, and English Political Ideologies in the Eighteenth Century." *William and Mary Quarterly,* 3rd ser., 22 (Fall 1965): 549–83.

Poston, Ted. *A First Draft of History.* Edited by Kathleen A. Hauke. Athens: University of Georgia Press, 2000.

Prather, H. Leon, Sr. *We Have Taken a City: The Wilmington Racial Massacre and Coup of 1898.* Cranbury, N.J.: Fairleigh Dickinson University Press, 1984.

Pyron, Darden Asbury. *Southern Daughter: The Life of Margaret Mitchell.* New York: Oxford University Press, 1991.

Randall, James Garfield. *Mr. Lincoln—A Personal Portrait on the Human Side of Lincoln from J. G. Randall's Writings.* Edited by Richard N. Current. New York: Dodd, Mead, 1957.

Randall, James Garfield, and David Herbert Donald. *The Civil War and Reconstruction.* 1961. Rev. ed. Lexington, Mass.: Heath, 1969.

Ransom, Reverdy. "The New Negro." *Negro Year Book.* Tuskegee, Ala., 1926.

Raper, Arthur F. *Preface to Peasantry: A Tale of Two Black Belt Counties.* Chapel Hill: University of North Carolina Press, 1936.

———. *The Tragedy of Lynching.* Chapel Hill: University of North Carolina Press, 1933.

Rauschenbusch, Walter. *The Belated Races and the Social Problems.* New York: American Missionary Association, 1914.

———. *A Gospel for the Social Awakening: Selections from the Writing.* Edited by Mays. New York: Association Press for the Hazen Foundation, 1950.

———. "The Negro and the Church." *Crisis* 7 (February 1914): 232–33.

Reitzes, Dietrich C. *Negroes and Medicine.* Cambridge, Mass.: Harvard University Press, 1955.

"Remembering the Martyrs of the Movement," *Ebony,* 45 (February 1990): 58.

Roper, John H. *C. Vann Woodward, Southerner.* Athens: University of Georgia Press, 1987.

———. *Paul Green: Playwright of the Real South.* Athens: University of Georgia Press, 2003.

———. "The Radical Mission: The University of South Carolina in Reconstruction." M.A. thesis, University of North Carolina at Chapel Hill, 1973.

———. "The Voting Rights Extension Act of 1982." *Phylon* 45, no. 3 (1984), 188–96.

Rovaris, Dereck Joseph. "Mays and Morehouse: How Benjamin E. Mays Developed Morehouse College, 1940–1976." Ph.D. diss., University of Illinois: 1995.

Scott, Emmett Jay. *Scott's Official History of the American Negro in the World War.* Chicago: Homewood Press, 1919.

The Scribner Encyclopedia of American Lives. Edited by Kenneth Jackson. Vol. 1. New York: Scribners, 1998.

Secrest, Rose. "James Madison Nabrit, Jr." In *Encyclopedia of Civil Rights in America,* edited by David Bradley and Shelley Fisher Fishkin, 2:625. Armonk, N.Y. Sharpe Reference, 1998.

The Segregation Decisions: Papers Read at a Session of the Twenty-first Annual Meeting of the Southern Historical Association, Memphis, Tennessee, November 10, 1955. Atlanta: Southern Regional Council, 1956.

Simkins, Frances Butler. *Pitchfork Ben Tillman, South Carolinian.* Southern Biography Series, edited by Fred C. Cole and Wendell Holmes Stephenson. Baton Rouge: Louisiana State University Press, 1946.

Smith, Jessie Carney. *Notable Black American Men.* Detroit: Gale, 1999.

Smith, Lillian Eugenia. *Strange Fruit.* New York: Reynal & Hitchcock, 1944.

Spear, Allan H. *Black Chicago: The Making of a Negro Ghetto, 1890–1920.* Chicago: University of Chicago Press, 1967.

Stampp, Kenneth Milton. *The Peculiar Institution: Slavery in the Ante-bellum South.* New York: Knopf, 1956. Reprint, 1982.

Storr, Richard J. *Harper's University: The Beginning: a History of the University of Chicago.* Chicago: University of Chicago Press, 1966.

Strauss, Leo. *Natural Right and History.* Charles R. Walgreen Foundation Lectures, Autumn 1949. 5th ed., revised. Chicago: University of Chicago Press, 1965.

Suri, Jeremi. *Power and Protest: Global Revolution and the Rise of Detente.* Cambridge, Mass.: Harvard University Press, 2003.

Taber, Clarence Wilbur, and Clayton L. Thomas. *Taber's Cyclopedic Medical Dictionary,* 16th ed., revised. Philadelphia: F. A. Davis, 1989.

Thomas, Jesse O. *My Story in Black and White.* New York: Exposition Press, 1967.

Thomas Aquinas. *Summa Theologica.* Translated by the fathers of the English Dominican Province, 3 vols. New York: Benziger Brothers, 1947–48.

Thonssen, Lester, and A. Craig Baird. *Speech Criticism: The Development of Standards for Rhetorical Appraisal.* New York: Ronald Press, 1948. Enlarged by Waldo W. Braden, 1970.

Tickton, Sidney, and Beardsley Ruml. *Teaching Salaries Then and Now.* New York: Ford Foundation, 1972.

Tindall, George Brown. *The Emergence of the New South, 1913–1945.* History of the South Series, edited by Ellis Merton Coulter and Wendell Holmes Stephenson. Baton Rouge: Louisiana State University Press, 1969.

————. *South Carolina Negroes, 1877–1900.* Columbia: University of South Carolina Press, 1952.

Tindall, George Brown, and David E. Shi, *America: A Narrative History.* 2 vols. New York: Norton, 1992.

Tushnet, Mark V. *The NAACP's Legal Strategy against Segregated Education, 1925–1950.* Chapel Hill: University of North Carolina Press, 1987.

Tyson, Timothy B. *Blood Done Sign My Name: A True Story.* New York: Crown, 2004.

Vance, Rupert B. *Human Geography of the South: A Study in Regional Resources and Human Adequacy.* Chapel Hill, University of North Carolina Press, 1932.

Washington, Joseph R., Jr. *Black Religion, the Negro, and Christianity in the United States.* Boston: Beacon Press, 1964.

Warren, Robert Penn. "William Faulkner." *New Republic,* 1946. Republished in *Literary Opinion in America,* edited by Morton Dauwen Zabel. 2 vols. 3rd. ed, revised. New York: Harper & Row, 1962. 1:467–70

Watson, A. C., "The Logic of Religion." *American Journal of Theology,* 20 (Winter 1916): 81–101.

Webb, Clive, ed. *Massive Resistance: Southern Opposition to the Second Reconstruction.* New York : Oxford University Press, 2005.

Webster, Daniel. "The Supposed Speech of John Adams, 26 July 1826," *Selected Orations: A Collection of Over One Hundred Choice Speeches and Selections,* edited by Albert Mason Harris, 348–52. Nashville, Tenn.: Cokesbury Press, 1924. Republished as "Daniel Webster Puts a Speech in the Mouth of John Adams." In *Lend Me Your Ears: Great Speeches in History.* edited by William Safire, 171–76. 2nd ed., revised. New York: Norton, 1997.

White, Walter Francis. *Rope and Faggot: A Biography of Judge Lynch.* 1929. Reprinted with an introduction by Kenneth Robert Janken. South Bend: University of Notre Dame Press, 2001.

Wieman, Henry Nelson. *Religious Experience and Scientific Method.* New York: Macmillan, 1926. Reprint, 1971.

————. *The Source of Human Good.* Atlanta: Scholars Press, 1995.

Williams, Rowan. *Lost Icons: Reflections on Cultural Bereavement.* London: Morehouse Continuum Paper, 2000.

Williamson, Joel. *After Slavery: The Negro in South Carolina during Reconstruction, 1861–1877.* Chapel Hill: University of North Carolina Press, 1965.

————. *The Crucible of Race: Black-White Relations in the American South since Emancipation.* New York: Oxford University Press, 1984. Abridged as *A Rage for Order: Black/White Relations in the American South since Emancipation.* New York: Oxford University Press, 1986.

————. *New People: Miscegenation and Mulattoes in the United States.* 1980. Rev. ed., Baton Rouge: Louisiana State University Press. 1995.

Wines, William A. *Ethics, Law, and Business.* Mahwah, N.J.: Lawrence Erlbaum Associates, 2006.

Wolseley, Roland Edgar. *The Black Press, U.S.A.* Ames: Iowa State University Press, 1971.

Wood, Gordon S. *The Creation of the American Republic, 1776–1787.* Chapel Hill: University of North Carolina Press for the Institute of Early American History and Culture, 1969.

Wood, Peter H. *Black Majority: Negroes in Colonial South Carolina from 1670 through the Stono Rebellion.* New York: Knopf, 1974.

Woodson, Carter Godwin. *The Mis-Education of the Negro.* 1933. Reprint, Lexington, Ky.: SoHo, 2011.

Woodward, C. Vann. *Reunion and Reaction: The Compromise of 1877 and the End of Reconstruction.* Boston, Little, Brown, 1951.

———, *The Strange Career of Jim Crow.* 3rd rev. ed. New York, Oxford University Press, 1974.

Wortham, Jacob J. "Benjamin E. Mays at Eighty-one." *Black Enterprise* 7 (May 1977): 27–30.

Wright, Gavin. *Old South, New South: Revolutions in the Southern Economy since the Civil War.* New York: Basic Books, 1986.

Wright Richard. "Worshippers from Afar." In *The God That Failed,* edited by Richard Crossman, 115–62. New York: Harper, 1950.

Wyatt-Brown, Bertram. *Honor and Violence in the Old South.* New York: Oxford University Press, 1986.

———. *Southern Honor: Ethics and Behavior in the Old South.* New York: Oxford University Press, 1982.

X, Malcolm, with assistance of Alex Hailey. *The Autobiography of Malcolm X.* New York: Grove Press, 1965.

INDEX